STAFF
RECRUITMENT,
RETENTION,
&TRAINING
STRATEGIES

FOR COMMUNITY HUMAN SERVICES ORGANIZATIONS

STAFF
RECRUITMENT,
RETENTION,
&TRAINING
STRATEGIES

FOR COMMUNITY HUMAN SERVICES ORGANIZATIONS

by

Sheryl A. Larson, Ph.D.
Research Associate
Research Director

and

Amy S. Hewitt, M.S.W., Ph.D.
Research Associate
Director of Interdisciplinary Training

Research and Training Center on Community Living
Institute on Community Integration
University of Minnesota
Minneapolis

with invited contributors

·P A U L·H·
BROOKES
PUBLISHING Co.®

Baltimore • London • Sydney

Paul H. Brookes Publishing Co.
Post Office Box 10624
Baltimore, Maryland 21285-0624

www.brookespublishing.com

Typeset by Integrated Publishing Solutions, Grand Rapids, Michigan.
Manufactured in the United States of America by
Sheridan Books, Ann Arbor, Michigan.

Preparation of this book was supported by Grant No. H133B031116 from the U.S. Department of Education, Office of Special Education and Rehabilitative Services, National Institute on Disability and Rehabilitation Research (NIDRR), to the University of Minnesota, Institute on Community Integration, Research and Training Center on Community Living. The contents of this book do not necessarily reflect the official position of NIDRR or the U.S. Department of Education.

With the exception of the "In the Spotlight" segment on pages 332–335, the "In the Spotlight" segments that appear throughout this book describe actual community human services organizations. Other, unlabeled case studies, however, are composite or fictionalized accounts that do not represent the lives of specific individuals, and no implications should be inferred.

The photograph on the cover was taken by Jerry Smith.

Library of Congress Cataloging-in-Publication Data

Staff recruitment, retention, and training strategies for community human services
  organizations / by Sheryl A. Larson and Amy S. Hewitt.
    p.   cm.
  Includes bibliographical references and index.
  ISBN 1-55766-708-X (pbk.)
    1. Human services personnel—Supervision of.   2. Human services
  personnel—Recruiting.   3. Human services personnel—Selection and
  appointment.   4. Human services personnel—In-service training   5. People
  with disabilities—Services for—Administration.   6. Personnel management.
  I. Larson, Sheryl A. (Sheryl Ann), 1963–   II. Hewitt, Amy S.

  HV40.54.S73   2005
  361'.0068'3—dc22
                                                            2004062295

British Library Cataloguing in Publication data are available from the British Library.

CONTENTS

ABOUT THE AUTHORS

Sheryl A. Larson, Ph.D., Research Associate and Research Director, University of Minnesota, Institute on Community Integration, Research and Training Center on Community Living, 214B Pattee Hall, 150 Pillsbury Drive SE, Minneapolis, MN 55455

Sheryl A. Larson has 23 years of experience in providing services to individuals with intellectual or developmental disabilities as a residential counselor, behavior analyst, program evaluator, consultant, personal advocate and researcher. She earned a B.A. in psychology and elementary education from Bethel College in St. Paul, Minnesota, and an M.A. and Ph.D. in educational psychology from the University of Minnesota, College of Education and Human Development. Her dissertation examined factors associated with turnover in small group home settings. She is Research Director and a principal investigator at the Research and Training Center on Community Living, where she has worked since 1987, directing projects involving survey and intervention research, secondary analysis of large data sets, and research synthesis on residential services, personnel issues, disability statistics, and community integration for individuals with intellectual or developmental disabilities. Dr. Larson has authored or co-authored more than 100 publications on those topics. Recent books include *Using Survey Data to Study Disability: Results from the National Health Survey on Disability*, co-edited with B.M. Altman, S.N. Barnartt, and G.E. Hendershot (Elsevier JAI, 2003), and *Staff Recruitment and Retention: Study Results and Intervention Strategies*, co-authored with K.C. Lakin and R.H. Bruininks (American Association on Mental Retardation [AAMR], 1998).

Dr. Larson currently directs two National Institute on Disability and Rehabilitation Research (NIDRR) field-initiated projects, including one to create a national technical assistance model to support front-line supervisors and another to conduct analyses using the National Health Interview Survey to describe characteristics of and outcomes for people with disabilities living in their own or family homes. She has worked with her colleagues at the University of Minnesota to develop statewide workforce plans and to provide technical assistance on workforce issues to providers and families in several states. She has made more than 150 presentations at national, state, regional, and local conferences and workshops, including workshops on staff recruitment and retention for more than 3,000 managers and supervisors. She is an AAMR Fellow, President of the AAMR Community Services Division, a consulting editor of *Mental Retardation* and *Journal of Intellectual and Developmental Disability* and has participated in NIDRR and Centers for Disease Control and Prevention grant review panels. She received a Presidential Award from AAMR for workforce research. She serves on the Minnesota Governor's Council on Developmental Disabilities as the higher education representative and is on the Board of Directors of No Place Like Home, a program providing supportive housing to adults with disabilities.

Amy S. Hewitt, M.S.W., Ph.D., Research Associate and Director of Interdisciplinary Training, University of Minnesota, Institute on Community Integration, Research and Training Center on Community Living, 214D Pattee Hall, 150 Pillsbury Drive SE, Minneapolis, MN 55455

Amy S. Hewitt has an extensive background and work history in the field of developmental disabilities and has worked in various positions over the past 23 years, including as a residential Program Director and Director of Training. She is currently Research Associate and Director of Interdisciplinary Training at the University of Minnesota, Institute on Community Integration, where she directs several federal and state research, evaluation, and demonstration projects in the areas of direct support professional (DSP) workforce development and community human services for people with disabilities. Dr. Hewitt is a national leader in the area of workforce development and community supports for individuals with developmental disabilities.

Dr. Hewitt's current projects include the College of Direct Support, a national training curriculum development project that currently offers training to more than 100,000 DSPs throughout the United States; Mobilizing for Change, an Administration on Developmental Disabilities field-initiated project to develop an on-line training curriculum for frontline supervisors (College of Frontline Supervision); Removing the Revolving Door, a national project to develop and implement a train-the-trainer technical assistance model in five states to teach others how to effectively work with organizations to reduce DSP turnover and vacancy rates; Kansans Mobilizing for Workforce Change, a systems change project to improve retention and recruitment of DSPs in community human services organizations; and The Illinois Comprehensive Workforce Development Initiative to Achieve Improved Individual Outcomes for Citizens with Intellectual and Developmental Disabilities, a statewide systems change project to reduce direct support professional turnover.

Dr. Hewitt has authored and co-authored many curricula, journal articles, and manuscripts. She is a managing editor of *Frontline Initiative*, a national newsletter for DSPs; a contributing editor for *LINKS*, a newsletter of ANCOR; and guest editor of *Mental Retardation*, a journal of the American Association on Mental Retardation (AAMR). She is currently a board member for Arc Hennepin-Carver and for Friendship Ventures. She is a founding member and past Co-chair of the National Alliance for Direct Support Professionals and a past board member of the AAMR.

About the Contributors

Lynda Anderson, M.A., M.P.H., is a doctoral candidate at the University of Minnesota. She has more than 20 years of experience in the field of developmental disabilities. She has worked as a program director, service coordinator, advocate, and policy planner and in other related capacities in the field of developmental disabilities. She was a graduate student at the Institute on Community Integration.

Beth A. Knoblauch, M.A., lives in Minneapolis, Minnesota, with her family. She was a graduate student at the Institute on Community Integration. She co-authored the College of Direct Support curriculum and supported work in the area of direct support professional workforce development.

Jody Kougl-Lindstrom, M.S.W., Adult Developmental Disabilities Unit Supervisor, Ramsey County Human Services Department, 160 E. Kellogg Boulevard, 7th Floor, St. Paul, MN 55101

Jody has worked in the field of helping with people with disabilities in various capacities for more than 11 years, including as a direct support professional, job coach/counselor, and service coordinator. She is a supervisor of service coordinators for people with developmental disabilities in Ramsey County, Minnesota. Ms. Kougl-Lindstrom was a graduate student at the Institute on Community Integration.

Traci L. LaLiberte, M.S.W., B.S., Doctoral Candidate, University of Minnesota School of Social Work, 1404 Gortner Avenue, St. Paul, MN 55108

Traci L. LaLiberte is a doctoral candidate at the University of Minnesota, where she specializes in child welfare and disability studies. She has been an active professional in the fields of child welfare and developmental disabilities since the early 1990s. Ms. LaLiberte is the 2003 recipient of the Mary A. McEvoy Award for Public Engagement and Leadership. Ms. LaLiberte facilitates training seminars for front-line supervisors in the field of developmental disabilities nationwide and has also developed curricula for the College of Direct Support.

Elizabeth Lightfoot, Ph.D., M.S.W., Assistant Professor of Social Work, University of Minnesota, 105 Peters Hall, 1404 Gortner Ave, St. Paul, MN 55108

Elizabeth Lightfoot is Assistant Professor of Social Work at the University of Minnesota, and she is also affiliated with the University of Minnesota's Institute on Community Integration. Dr. Lightfoot received her Ph.D. in public policy from Indiana University and M.S.W. from the University of Minnesota. Her research has focused on the politics and implementation of disability antidiscrimination policy, and she is exploring the intersection between aging and disability policy issues.

Susan N. O'Nell, Project Coordinator, University of Minnesota, Institute on Community Integration (ICI), Research and Training Center on Community Living, 210B Pattee Hall, 150 Pillsbury Drive SE, Minneapolis, MN 55455

Susan N. O'Nell has worked at the ICI since 1995, with a focus on workforce development and training of direct support professionals and front-line supervisors. Ms. O'Nell has developed several training curricula in both traditional and multimedia formats. She coordinates the instructional design and development of the on-line curriculum for the College of Direct Support and the College of Frontline Supervision. Prior to working at the ICI, Ms. O'Nell worked for 12 years as a direct support professional supporting people with developmental disabilities.

Patricia Salmi, M.S., Doctoral Candidate and Design Specialist, Department of Design, Housing, & Apparel, University of Minnesota, 240 McNeal Hall, 1985 Buford Avenue, St. Paul, MN 55108

Patricia Salmi is a physical environments design professional who specializes in accessibility issues for persons with intellectual disabilities (ID). Pat has taught special education and has worked as a design professional for more than 20 years. She is currently enrolled in a doctoral program with an emphasis in accessibility in the built environment for individuals with ID. Pat is the 2003 winner of the ASID (American Society of Interior Designers) Education Foundation/Joel Polsky Academic Achievement Award for her master's thesis, *An Exploration of Critical Factors for Accessibility and Wayfinding for Adults with Mental Retardation.*

John K. Sauer, M.S.W., M.Ed., Program Coordinator, University of Minnesota, Institute on Community Integration (ICI), 150 Pillsbury Drive SE, Minneapolis, MN 55455

John K. Sauer is Program Coordinator at the ICI and is intensely involved in the life of his sister, who has mental retardation. His experience in supporting his sister to move from an institution, where she had lived for most of her life, to a community supported living program and his efforts to ensure that she receives person-centered supports have given him critical insight into the need for a competent and stable direct support professional workforce. He has 35 years of experience working in human services as a social worker, policy and program developer, administrator, educator, human resources development manager, trainer, and organizational change consultant at the local, state, and national levels and for nonprofit, corporate, educational, and governmental agencies.

Lori Sedlezky, M.S.W., is an independent consultant offering services in program design and evaluation, curriculum development, and staff training to human services organizations. Previously, she worked as director of programs and services at Arc Hennepin-Carver; project coordinator at the Institute on Community Integration, University of Minnesota; and program manager for community-based vocational and residential services. She received her master's degree in social work and bachelor's degree in psychology from the University of Minnesota.

Foreword

In 1980 my colleagues and I at the University of Minnesota completed the first national study of turnover among people providing direct support to individuals with developmental disabilities. In that study we examined rates of job staying and job leaving and associated individual and organizational factors in community and institutional settings. Thinking back on that research, it is in some ways difficult to comprehend how substantially the system of support for individuals with developmental disabilities has changed. Today the number of individuals with developmental disabilities living in state institutions is about one quarter of the number of 25 years ago. Eight times as many people with developmental disabilities receive residential support in community settings as 25 years ago. Then there was an average of 20 people per residential setting; today there is an average of 3. The idea of supporting people with developmental disabilities within their family home was then little more than an idealistic dream; today it is a key component of almost all state service systems, now assisting more than 400,000 families (Prouty, Smith, & Lakin, 2003). These changes have been evident in varying degrees in all state systems of long-term services and supports (LTSS), and in important ways these changes have transformed the lives and opportunities of hundreds of thousands of individuals with developmental disabilities. Yet, important aspects of LTSS remain as they were 25 years ago. One of the most constant and important of these aspects remains, to use the words of Secretary of Labor Elaine Chao (2002), that direct support professionals (DSPs) are "the cornerstone of America's long-term care system" and that the nation's "fundamental, long-term challenge [in supporting people with developmental disabilities] is to develop a committed, stable pool of workers who are willing and able to provide quality care."

There are other ways in which the circumstances of DSPs today are much as they were a quarter of a century ago. We wrote then, as we still believe, "That the starting wage paid for this [direct support] work is often comparable to what high school students make wrapping hamburgers is a national disgrace" (Lakin & Bruininks, 1981b, p. 168). Sadly, the same is true today. Recently, we noted that the average wage of DSPs in 2000 was 55% of the average for all workers covered by unemployment insurance and that the average beginning wage for DSPs in community human services settings ($15,247 annually) was essentially equal to the poverty level for a family of three ($14,630) (Lakin, Polister, & Prouty, 2003).

There are other similarities between what we observed 25 years ago and what we see today. In our studies 25 years ago, we estimated a national turnover rate of 54% among DSPs employed in private residential settings. Today turnover rates among DSPs in private community residential settings are consistently within the 40%–70% range (see Chapter 1 for a review of these studies). Twenty-five years ago we estimated a turnover rate of 33% among DSPs employed in state institutions, essentially equal to the 28% national average for all state institutions in 2002 (Larson, Coucouvanis, &

Prouty, 2003). The primary factors we reported to be associated with people staying in (as opposed to quitting) direct support jobs 25 years ago were pretty much the same as those identified in research today: having relatively higher amounts of and/or satisfaction with compensation (pay and benefits), sensing that one's job fits within a career path, having satisfying relationships with co-workers and supervisors, having good communication within the organization, sensing that one's judgment and expertise are recognized and trusted, feeling that one's skills are being developed and used, considering one's job interesting and rewarding, feeling that one's job fulfills one's initial expectations for it, feeling that one's work is valued, and so forth (Lakin & Bruininks, 1981a, 1981b; Lakin, Bruininks, Hill, & Hauber, 1982; Lakin, Hill, Bruininks, Hauber, & Krantz, 1983).

Certain important changes have occurred with regard to understanding and responding to the challenge of providing the "committed, stable pool of workers" that Secretary Chao rightfully recognized is the most essential component of our national system of LTSS. Today, much more than 25 years ago, the struggle to provide this pool of workers is viewed as significant within the national policy agenda. For example, in the Developmental Disabilities Assistance and Bill of Rights Act of 2000 (PL 106-402), Congress observed that "as increasing numbers of individuals with developmental disabilities are living, learning, working and participating in all aspects of community life, there is an increasing need for a well-trained workforce that is able to provide the services, supports, and other forms of direct assistance required to enable the individuals to carry out those activities" (42 U.S.C. § 150001 [a][14]).

One primary cause of increased attention to the DSP workforce within the national policy arena has been the elevation of community LTSS to the level of national commitment. A substantial body of successful experience and documented benefits, a growing appreciation of basic human rights, and other factors have provided important foundations for a national commitment to ensuring people with developmental disabilities a place in the communities of their birth or choice. These foundations were greatly solidified in the passage of the Americans with Disabilities Act (ADA) of 1990 (PL 101-336), its interpretation by the U.S. Supreme Court in *Olmstead v. L.C.*, and the subsequent commitment of the Bush Administration to fully accept, enforce, and contribute to the commitments of the ADA and *Olmstead* through an interdepartmental campaign known as the New Freedom Initiative.

In *Olmstead* the U.S. Supreme Court ruled that Title II of the ADA clearly, legally, and enforceably requires states to provide the services, programs, and activities developed for individuals with disabilities in the "most integrated setting appropriate." The Supreme Court concluded specifically that states were obligated to place qualified individuals with disabilities in community settings, rather than in institutions, when treatment professionals determined that a community placement was appropriate; when the individuals themselves did not oppose an appropriate community placement; and when the state in which the person lived could reasonably accommodate the community placement, taking into account the resources available and the needs of others with disabilities. Two years after the *Olmstead* decision, President Bush signed an Executive Order in June 2001, referred to as the New Freedom Initiative, that stipulated that "the United States is committed to community-based alternatives for individuals with disabilities and recognizes that such services advance the best interests of Americans" and that requested assistance from federal agencies in the fulfillment of that commitment.

So, one principal reason that the DSP workforce is an object of national attention is that it is national policy that people with disabilities be provided with appropriate community supports. While the government can promise appropriate community supports, it cannot provide them without the "committed, stable pool of workers" referred to by Secretary Chao. A primary challenge in fulfilling the national commitment to providing people with community supports is recruiting, training, and retaining sufficient numbers of DSPs to do so. The growing difficulties and frequent failures in meeting this challenge have reached the stage of national crisis. In 2003 this crisis was recognized in concurrent resolutions of the U.S. Senate and U.S. House of Representatives. Referred to as the Direct Support Professional Recognition Resolution, each resolution expressed the findings of the Congress that "private providers and the individuals for whom they provide supports and services are in jeopardy as a result of the growing crisis in recruiting and retaining a direct support workforce" (H. Con. Res. 94, 2003; S. Con. Res. 21, 2003). The resolutions found that "this workforce shortage is the most significant barrier to implementing the Olmstead decision and undermines the expansion of community integration as called for by President Bush's New Freedom Initiative, placing the community support infrastructure at risk." The resolutions concluded,

> It is the sense of the Congress that the Federal Government and States should make it a priority to ensure a stable, quality direct support workforce for individuals with mental retardation or other developmental disabilities that advances our Nation's commitment to community integration for such individuals and to personal security for them and their families.

To be sure, we have a national crisis in providing sufficient numbers of qualified DSPs to meet the needs of individuals with developmental disabilities. Considering residential services alone, including data on service recipients in 2003, average staffing ratios from national and state studies, statistics on ratios of full-time to part-time employees, and DSP turnover rates that average about 50% per year, it is estimated that about 350,000 new DSPs were hired to provide residential supports for individuals with developmental disabilities in 2003. What is most notable about that number, in addition to its size, is that an estimated 94% of that total was made up of people hired to replace DSPs who left existing positions, while only about 6% were people hired for newly developed community supports positions. The ability to meet the current LTSS system's appetite for new employees has in many areas reached the point of non-sustainability. This is increasingly evident in the substantial and growing numbers of position vacancies reported by individual service providers and in state studies. Efforts to recruit more and more people into work situations in which most will leave in their first year is increasingly debilitating to organizations and, furthermore, devastating to the people with disabilities who experience nonstop withdrawal of people upon whom they depend to know, understand and help them.

Present circumstances promise little in the way of notable improvement in the national crisis in the DSP supply in the foreseeable future. Although a generally poor job market can play a significant role in increasing recruitment and tenure of DSPs during the short term, demographic factors continue to suggest long-term difficulties in providing a sufficient DSP workforce if past practices are relied on. The relatively low birth rates of the 1960s and the 1970s have led to tighter labor supplies in low-paying, high-demand jobs, especially those that typically draw their labor pool from among young adults, as has been the case with direct support. Such problems are substantially exacerbated in caregiving industries that have been traditionally staffed by women, as has been the case with direct support. Women today are much less likely to assume a secondary income role within a family for work roles that permit flexibility and are much more likely to seek career-related opportunities. Competition for people interested in DSP roles is also growing across LTSS systems, especially competition for people to support the growing population of aging Americans receiving nursing, assisted living, and home health services. The Bureau of Labor Statistics (2001) has projected that the number of personal care and home health positions in the United States will increase by 62% between 2000 and 2010.

These conditions pose major challenges to the recruitment of DSPs. More DSPs will need to be drawn from nontraditional employment pools (see Chapter 2). Pay and benefits need to grow, but given substantial budget crises in most states, compensation increases without increases in productivity will be difficult to obtain. Productivity through reduced per-person use of paid direct support is a concept seldom attended to in community human services systems. Flexible and creative alternatives in compensation need to be developed and need to derive not only from the employing agencies, but also from the local, state, and national partners who have shared in the commitment to support individuals with developmental disabilities in the community and therefore in the responsibility to ensure sufficient DSPs to do so (see Chapter 15). The gaps between employee skills and job demands need to be narrowed through competency-based training (see Chapters 6 and 7). We know what the DSP job entails (Taylor, Bradley, & Warren, 1996); we have simply lacked the commitment to ensure that people are trained in the specific skills needed to be successful in the DSP role and to recognize and reward those who demonstrate those skills.

All of us, above all else, must recognize the incredible resource that trained and experienced DSPs are for the individuals and families they support, for the organizations to which they belong, and for the achievement of national policy commitments to individuals with developmental disabilities. Commitments to conserving this valuable national resource must be made. If DSP turnover were to be reduced by 2% per year over the next 10 years (i.e., from 50% to 30% in 2% per year increments), the total number of DSPs who would need to be recruited to fill both vacated and new DSP positions 10 years from now would be more than 200,000 fewer than at current rates of DSP turnover. This would be a substantial undertaking, but it is not impossible. Organizations that have committed to integrating packages of demonstrably effective human resources interventions into their day-to-day practices have accomplished such outcomes in substantially shorter periods of time. Organizations that have carefully reviewed research on factors associated with effective recruitment and retention and have reformed their organization's culture to accommodate such factors have achieved such outcomes. There is a substantial and valuable knowledge base for improving human resources operations within community human services and support organizations. That knowledge base offers specific guidance in areas of needed effective performance, such as 1) recruitment, staff selection, and informed understanding of job content (see Chapters 2–4); 2) orientation, training, and new employee support (see Chapter 5); 3) supervision, team building, and human resources management (see Chapters 11 and 12); and 4) employee recognition and career advancement (see Chapter 9). Structured attention to the accumulated knowledge in these areas brings results. For example, when the authors of this book undertook a project with 13 agencies in Minnesota to integrate a basic package of recruitment, retention, and training strategies, the effort yielded an average 33% reduction in DSP turnover in 24 months (Hewitt, Larson, Sauer, Anderson, & O'Nell, 2001).

More than ever before, we need these kinds of results in every organization supporting individuals with developmental disabilities. Attaining such results is about more than ensuring sufficient numbers of DSPs to fulfill obligations to individuals with developmental disabilities and their families, although to be sure this alone is enormously difficult. We have asked DSPs in community settings to do far more than we can expect without substantial experience, good training, and positive regard for their work and its importance. We have asked them to work with high levels of autonomy and responsibility in supporting people with a wide range of substantial functional, behavioral, health, and other impairments. They simply cannot be effective in meeting such expectations if they are employed by organizations that accept the constant withdrawal and replacement of their most important staff members and all of the concomitant disruption, loss of knowledge, and decrements in performance.

This book does not for a second accept the status quo with regard to the DSP workforce and the effects of its general instability on individuals with developmental disabilities. This book provides a comprehensive review of the research and experiential knowledge base that offers us good hope that we can fulfill our national commitments to individuals with developmental disabilities. Within this book is a wealth of information about the causes and remedies of staff turnover and of the organizational practices that reduce its likelihood and mitigate its effects. Researched interventions are described to assist in recruitment and orientation of new staff and to ensure that those considering a DSP role understand fully the nature and expectations of that role. Comprehensive attention is given to structured analysis of the skills required of DSPs and to the training content, organization practices, and new employee supports that lead to successful beginnings to new roles. This book provides organization leaders with concrete ideas and examples of how to improve organizational culture and better recognize and respond to individual and collective employee needs. It addresses the important role of the front-line supervisor and the essential skills demanded of people who most typically find themselves promoted from the ranks of DSP with little if any preparation for a very different new role in supervising other DSPs. In short, this book is rich in information, ideas, and resources of substantial potential benefit to organizations that study and apply its contents.

On a personal level I can attest to the passion and commitment that the authors bring to this book. These are people with years and years of highly relevant experience in the real world of human services. They are people experienced in direct support. They are people who have worked as trainers and supervisors of DSPs. They are people who have been on the receiving end of direct support as parents, guardians, and siblings of individuals with developmental disabilities. They are people whose years of combined work experience in human services outside the university far exceed the number of years within. They are people who have trained others to use the concepts and practices described in this book and they have studied the effects. These experiences all contribute to a book that is very practical and well grounded in the reality of community human services and supports. While all of this experience outside of academia contributes greatly to the quality and usefulness of this book, I am particularly pleased that all involved in its development have found their way to the University of Minnesota and to the opportunities it has afforded them to compile this very useful resource. I am certain as you begin to explore the richness of this book, you will be as well.

K. Charlie Lakin, Ph.D.
Director, Research and Training Center on Community Living
Institute on Community Integration
University of Minnesota

REFERENCES

Americans with Disabilities Act (ADA) of 1990, PL 101-336, 42 U.S.C. §§ 12101 *et seq.*

Bureau of Labor Statistics. (2001). *BLS releases 2000–2010 employment projections* (USDL 01-443). Washington, DC: Author. Also available on-line: http://www.bls.gov/news.release/ecopro.nr0.htm

Chao, E. (2002, September 24). *The direct support workforce crisis.* Presentation at the annual government affairs conference of the American Network of Community Options and Resources, Washington, DC. Also available on-line: http://www.dol.gov/_sec/media/speeches/20020924_ANCOR.htm

Developmental Disabilities Assistance and Bill of Rights Act Amendments of 2000, PL 106-402, 42 U.S.C. §§ 6000 *et seq.*

H. Con. Res. 94, 108th Cong., 150 Cong. Rec. 10301 (2003) (enacted).

Hewitt, A., Larson, S., Sauer, J., Anderson, L., & O'Nell, S. (2001). *Partnerships for success: Retaining incumbent community support human service workers by upgrading their skills and strengthening partnerships among workforce centers, educational programs, and private businesses. University of Minnesota subcontract final report.* Minneapolis: University of Minnesota, Institute on Community Integration, Research and Training Center on Community Living.

Lakin, K.C., & Bruininks, R.H. (1981a). *Occupational stability of direct-care staff of residential facilities for mentally retarded people.* Minneapolis: University of Minnesota, Center on Residential Services and Community Living.

Lakin, K.C., & Bruininks, R.H. (1981b). Personnel management and quality of residential services for developmentally disabled people. In T.C. Muzzio, J.J. Koshel, & V. Bradley (Eds.), *Alternative community living arrangements and social services for developmentally disabled people.* Washington, DC: The Urban Institute.

Lakin, K.C., Bruininks, R.H., Hill, B.K., & Hauber, F.A. (1982). Turnover of direct care staff in a national sample of residential facilities for mentally retarded people. *American Journal on Mental Deficiency, 87,* 67–42.

Lakin, K.C., Hill, B.K., Bruininks, R.H., Hauber, F.A., & Krantz, G.C. (1983). Factors related to job stability of direct-care staff of residential facilities for mentally retarded people. *Journal of Community Psychology, 11*(3), 228–235.

Lakin, K.C., Polister, B., & Prouty, R. (2003). Wages of non-state direct support professionals lag behind those of public direct support professionals and the general public. *Mental Retardation, 41*(2), 178–182.

Larson, S.A., Coucouvanis, K., & Prouty, R.W. (2003). Staffing patterns, characteristics and outcomes in large state residential facilities in 2002. In R.W. Prouty, G. Smith & K.C. Lakin (Eds.), *Residential services for persons with developmental disabilities: Status and trends through 2002* (pp. 47–59). Minneapolis: University of Minnesota, Institute on Community Integration, Research and Training Center on Community Living.

Olmstead v. L.C., 527 U.S. 581 (1999).

Prouty, R.W., Smith, G., & Lakin, K.C. (Eds.). (2003). *Residential services for persons with developmental disabilities: Status and trends through 2002.* Minneapolis: University of Minnesota, Institute on Community Integration, Research and Training Center on Community Living.

S. Con. Res. 21, 108th Cong., 150 Cong. Rec. 3751 (2003) (enacted).

Taylor, M., Bradley, V., & Warren, R., Jr. (1996). *Community support skill standards: Tools for managing change and achieving outcomes.* Cambridge, MA: Human Services Research Institute. (Available from the publisher, 2336 Massachusetts Avenue, Cambridge, MA 02140; 617-876-0426; fax: 617-492-7401; http://www.hsri.org)

ACKNOWLEDGMENTS

There are so many people to acknowledge and thank for their many contributions to this book and the body of research and knowledge that supports it.

We have had the extraordinary opportunity to work with Charlie Lakin for the past 15 years. A mentor, colleague, generous boss, and true humanitarian, he has pioneered the research related to direct support workforce issues and champions our continued interests and dedication. Without question he has been the most influential person in the guidance of our work.

We say often that we have the greatest jobs in the world. This is only because we have the opportunity to work every day with extremely intelligent, multitalented, dedicated, and passionate people who come to work each day with the sole mission of working to make the world more inclusive for all citizens. Without your support and contributions, this book would not have been possible. We are certain that a more effective, collegial, and supportive work team could not exist and we are privileged to be a part of it.

We have both worked as direct support professionals (DSPs) during our careers. These experiences certainly have shaped our understanding of the important roles these professionals play in supporting individuals with disabilities and their families. Even more influential are the many stories shared by the DSPs with whom we have worked over the past 15 years—these stories reflect their realities. These realities combine a love for the work, a profound commitment to the people they serve, and a shared experience of sometimes being disrespected and oppressed on the job. We know and advocate through our work that quality community human services are only possible with a competent, well-qualified, and stable DSP workforce. We are committed to continuing our advocacy until policy makers throughout the country understand this reality and implement effective solutions that include better wages, access to affordable benefits, adequate and relevant training, and appropriate career pathways.

Over the years we have been fortunate to work with many colleagues throughout the country who share our passion and commitment to finding systemic solutions to workforce challenges such as high rates of turnover, increased vacancies, and poor training. Notably, our friends and colleagues at the Human Services Research Institute have been research pioneers on this important topic. It is ever true that the collective is far more powerful and beneficial than any one entity, and our work together validates this point.

We both have been touched by the lives and experiences of many people with disabilities and their family members. Yet, our personal experiences with Nathan (Amy's brother-in-law) and Jerry (Sherri's friend) have proved to us daily the importance of finding solutions to the workforce challenges in community human services. Experiencing personally the effects of no-shows, employees who come and go, poorly trained staff, and difficulty in finding new staff has significantly influenced our research agenda and passion for finding solutions to the challenges that negatively affect our family and friends and the thousands of people who receive support services each and every day.

It is impossible to understand direct support issues, explore solutions, and evaluate their effectiveness without the support and commitment of organizations and individuals who employ direct support professionals. We have had the opportunity to learn from and work with so many organizations and their committed employees. The time and resources devoted by these many organizations is remarkable, and we are so thankful to them for allowing us to conduct our work in partnership with them.

To the editorial staff at Paul H. Brookes Publishing Co., thank you for your patience with our many delays. Thank you also for your gifted editing, which has greatly enhanced the quality of this book.

To my mother, who would have been so proud.

In me, I see her commitment to education and the power of knowledge,
the love of cooking, compassion for others who are less privileged,
and, as my friends and colleagues would tell you, the tendency
to "tell it like it is," sometimes inappropriately.

You are so missed.

—ASH

To my parents.

Thank you for your loving support and faithful model.
This book was made possible by your sacrificial giving to support
my education and career pursuits.

—SAL

INTRODUCTION

Recruitment, retention, and training of direct support professionals (DSPs) are among the most challenging issues facing community human services organizations in the United States. Supervisors, managers, and human resources personnel in community human services organizations are always looking for solutions to the challenges of recruitment, retention, and training of their employees. Turnover, high vacancy rates, and poor staff training are costly to organizations, but, more important, these conditions have detrimental outcomes for the people receiving support services from the organization's employees (Larson, Hewitt, & Lakin, 2004). It is imperative to find and utilize effective solutions to these workforce challenges. This book, although not all inclusive of effective strategies, describes intervention strategies that will make a difference if designed and implemented within your organization.

This book describes research-based strategies that community human services organizations can use to assess and address workforce challenges they face. In addition, the book includes examples that show how existing organizations have successfully used the strategies and provides illustrative worksheets, forms, and flowcharts that organizations can use. The book also describes strategies that can be used to get buy-in from affected stakeholders so that the strategies will work when implemented. This introduction provides an overview of the book and how the book can be used by organizations.

STRUCTURE OF THE BOOK

The strategies discussed in this book represent an interrelated set of interventions. To effectively address recruitment, retention, and training challenges, organizations will probably need to use more than one strategy. Opening with a comprehensive literature review of recruitment, retention, and training challenges (Chapter 1), this book includes five sections. The first four sections focus on specific strategies, and the fifth section focuses on the bigger picture and describes the problems and solutions at a policy level. Section I reviews the recruitment, selection, and hiring process and suggests strategies to improve performance and outcomes in those areas. Section II focuses on interventions that introduce a newly hired employee to an organization and on interventions that assist all employees to develop and apply new skills. Section III covers supervisory and management interventions for motivation and support. Section IV describes the need for organizational change and strategies to assess your organization and plan for change. Section V discusses interventions that go beyond the walls of a single organization to make policy-level changes.

A NOTE ON TERMINOLOGY

In this book we use the term *direct support professional (DSP)* to refer to a person whose primary job responsibility is to provide support, training, supervision, and personal assistance to people with disabilities. A DSP may have other duties, but at least 50% of his or her hours are spent directly supporting individuals with disabilities or their families. We use the term *front-line supervisor (FLS)* or *supervisor* to refer to a person whose primary job responsibility is to supervise individuals in DSP roles. FLSs may provide some direct support, but at least 50% of their work hours are devoted to their supervisory role. We use the term *managers* to refer to people who supervise FLSs and other organization staff members. When the term *staff* is used in this book, it is a general reference to the people who work for the organization, not just DSPs or people with a particular job function.

HOW TO USE THIS BOOK

This book was developed to meet the needs of FLSs and managers in community human services organizations who support individuals with various disabilities. Other audiences include human resources personnel and administrators, as well as students and educators who train students to become supervisors and managers in human services organizations.

Although some people will read this book from cover to cover, others may focus on chapters that address interventions in areas that present the most pressing challenges for them. No matter the order in which the chapters are read, we hope that readers will eventually read and learn about all of the interventions. Our experience as consultants and managers has taught us that the development, implementation, and use of more than one of the many strategies described in this book are needed to adequately address the challenges faced by most organizations. Readers who are unsure about which interventions to focus on first may wish to read Chapter 13 on assessing challenges and Chapter 14 on selecting and implementing intervention strategies that are a good match to the problems their organization actually has. In addition, regardless of the intervention selected, readers should review Chapters 12–14 before implementing the intervention so that the organization is prepared to successfully change practices and to assess the effectiveness of those changes.

CHAPTER STRUCTURE

Each chapter follows the same basic structure. Chapters begin with a basic introduction to the content covered. This is followed by a list of the FLS competencies related to that topic. For each intervention strategy, the problem addressed by the strategy or intervention is described, a basic summary of research findings related to the problem is discussed, and information about how to use the strategy is provided. Chapters include information about how to develop, implement, and evaluate each strategy. Stories and illustrations about how the strategy has been used are provided to help readers understand how they might use the strategy or intervention. Because organizational change is difficult, each chapter identifies typical barriers experienced when implementing the intervention covered and identifies strategies to overcome those barriers. Chapters end with a list of questions to be considered as the strategies are implemented and lists of resources and cited references that supplement the information covered. Many of the chapters also contain tools that organizations can use during strategy implementation.

Overview

Each chapter begins with a brief overview of the content of that chapter.

Targeted Front-Line Supervisor Competencies

This book is based on and builds on the competencies needed by FLSs as described in *The Minnesota Frontline Supervisor Competencies and Performance Indicators* (Hewitt, Larson, O'Nell, Sauer, & Sedlezky, 1998). These competencies are based on a comprehensive job analysis conducted to identify the specific knowledge, skills, and attitudes (KSAs) required of FLSs. Although the competencies were originally developed in Minnesota, a research project tested their applicability nationally. Preliminary, not-yet-published analyses of those data show that all of the competency areas and the vast majority of specific competencies are relevant to most or all FLSs (Doljanac, Larson, Hewitt, & Salmi, 2004). Broad competency areas in the FLS competencies are summarized in Figure 1. Each chapter identifies and comprehensively addresses primary FLS competencies within these broad areas; most chapters also list related competencies, which are covered in part but are not the main focus of the text. Chapter 6, which addresses competency-based training, provides more information about how these competencies can be used to design and evaluate training.

Understanding the Problem

The premise of this book is that most human services organizations face challenges with recruitment, retention, and training of their direct support workforce. Each chapter tackles a different problem, such as turnover that occurs within the first 6 months of employment (Chapter 3), poor orientation and training practices (Chapter 5), and lack of support and training for supervisors (Chapter 11). The Understanding the Problem sections are designed to describe the specific problem to be addressed by the interventions and strategies outlined within the chapter.

Research Support for Solutions

The Research Support for Solutions section provides an overview of research support for the interventions described in each chapter. It provides a quick foundation of why the interventions discussed in a chapter are worthy of further pursuit and use. For a comprehensive overview of the literature related to the challenges of recruitment, retention, and training in community human services, refer to the literature review chapter (Chapter 1).

Strategies for Responding to the Problem

Each chapter summarizes one or more interventions and strategies designed to improve workforce challenges. Most chapters describe just one intervention, but some chapters include multiple interventions to address a certain type of problem. For ex-

Broad Competency Areas for Front-Line Supervisors

1 *Staff Relations:* Front-line supervisors (FLSs) enhance staff relations by using effective communication skills, encouraging growth and self-development, facilitating teamwork, employing conflict resolution skills, and providing adequate supports to staff.

2 *Direct Support:* FLSs provide direct supports to individuals with disabilities and model such supports to direct support professionals (DSPs) by assisting with living skills, communicating and interacting with individuals supported, facilitating community inclusion, maintaining an appropriate physical environment, providing transportation, maintaining finances, developing behavioral supports, and demonstrating the importance of supported individuals becoming active citizens in their neighborhoods and local communities.

3 *Facilitation and Support of Individual Support Networks:* FLSs facilitate and support the development and maintenance of support networks for individuals served through outreach to family members, community members, and professionals and through coordination of personal planning sessions in collaboration with each individual supported.

4 *Program Planning and Monitoring:* FLSs oversee program planning and monitoring by planning and developing individual goals and outcomes with supported individuals; coordinating and participating in support network meetings; monitoring, documenting, and reporting progress toward meeting outcomes; and communicating with other service organizations.

5 *Personnel Management:* FLSs coordinate personnel management by hiring new staff, conducting performance reviews, facilitating teamwork and staff meetings, creating job descriptions, delegating tasks and responsibilities, encouraging effective communication, defusing crises and conflicts between staff, and implementing grievance and formal contract procedures.

6 *Training and Staff Development Activities:* FLSs coordinate and participate in DSP orientation and in-service training by orienting new staff, arranging for staff to attend training sessions, maintaining training records, and supporting ongoing staff development.

Figure 1. Broad competency areas for front-line supervisors (FLSs). (From Hewitt, A., Larson, S.A., O'Nell, S., Sauer, J., & Sedlezky, L. [1998]. *The Minnesota frontline supervisor competencies and performance indicators: A tool for agencies providing community services.* Minneapolis: University of Minnesota, Institute on Community Integration, Research and Training Center on Community Living; adapted by permission.)

7   *Public Relations:* FLSs promote public relations by educating community members about individuals with disabilities, advocating for the rights and responsibilities of individuals with disabilities, developing media presentations, and recruiting volunteers and contributions.

8   *Maintenance:* FLSs coordinate and participate in home, vehicle, and personal property maintenance.

9   *Health and Safety Issues:* FLSs ensure that individuals supported are safe and living healthy lives by monitoring safety issues; coordinating, monitoring, and documenting medical supports; practicing appropriate emergency procedures; responding to emergencies; and promoting supported individuals' rights regarding health and safety issues.

10   *Financial Activities:* FLSs ensure fiscal responsibility and management by supporting individuals with banking and other financial maintenance agreements; developing, managing, and implementing household budgets; developing contracts for services with outside vendors; and completing audits of household and consumer finances.

11   *Scheduling and Payroll:* FLSs ensure staff are scheduled, are paid, and receive time off when staff request it.

12   *Vocational Supports:* FLSs coordinate vocational training and opportunities for supported individuals through advocacy, supporting people in completing daily job tasks, assisting individuals in meeting quality standards, finding and developing community jobs for people, and communicating as needed with other support organizations regarding vocational issues.

13   *Policies, Procedures, and Rule Compliance:* FLSs understand and implement current federal, state, and local licensing rules and regulations, organization policies and practices, and protection of the rights of supported individuals.

14   *Office Work:* FLSs communicate effectively in writing and over the telephone; complete various office tasks; and utilize the computer effectively for word processing, developing spreadsheets, managing databases, and using e-mail.

ample, the chapter on realistic job previews (RJPs; Chapter 3) identifies only that one intervention, whereas the chapter on supporting supervisors (Chapter 11) identifies nearly a dozen distinct intervention options. These strategies and interventions are described in enough detail to provide readers with the necessary how-to information so that they can develop and implement the intervention strategy.

Overcoming Implementation Barriers

It is difficult for any organization to change its practices and even harder at times for a single supervisor or manager to effect change within his or her organization. For each intervention, numerous barriers can be anticipated when implementation is being initiated. These challenges are difficult and many and the solutions to them are multifaceted and difficult, so we use the Overcoming Implementation Barriers section of each chapter to identify some of the potential barriers and to provide tips and suggestions to the reader for how to overcome each barrier. The chapter on selecting intervention strategies (Chapter 14) explains a process that organizations can use to identify the barriers that they think they will face and suggests strategies for addressing those barriers as interventions are developed, implemented, and evaluated.

Questions to Ponder

It is easy to fall into the trap of thinking, "We already do all of this stuff." The reality is that although you may in fact use any given intervention, you may not fully implement it or you may have overlooked issues and items in your thought processes and implementation processes. Each chapter presents a list of questions to help you think about the extent to which a problem exists within your organization and the extent to which the interventions that have been described are being used or could be used within your organization. We hope that the answers to these various questions will assist you in determining your intervention needs and the priority that should be given to each of these needs.

It is also easy to think, "We've been there and done that." Unfortunately, that is often just an excuse for not wanting to change. Perhaps you have tried a version of a particular intervention and it did not work. If that is the case, before you close the door on that intervention, review whether the intervention you tried is really the same as the one described. What you tried may have had a similar name but not a similar design. If after reviewing what you did and what is recommended, you find that you did try the intervention, the next question is whether the intervention was actually implemented the way you intended for it to be implemented. Many times a good idea falls short because the implementation plan is ineffective. Another point to consider is whether changes in the organization (in the employees or in the people supported) have been so extensive that it might be good to see if the intervention will work in the new circumstances. Finally, whatever intervention you select, we strongly encourage you to use a good evaluation process so that you have real data on whether the intervention actually was implemented as designed and whether it resulted in the desired outcomes.

Conclusion

Each chapter includes a brief synopsis of the information that was covered. This is intended to serve as a final wrap-up for the reader.

In the Spotlight

The In the Spotlight passages placed throughout the chapters provide the reader with real-life examples of organizations and individuals who have put into practice the interventions and strategies described in each chapter. A brief description of the organization or individual is provided along with a description of the interventions they have used to address their workforce challenges. Anticipated or actual outcomes related to the use of various interventions are also provided. Most chapters contain at least one spotlight. In some cases, the spotlights were written by the targeted organizations; in other cases, the chapter authors summarized information about an organization based on the results of technical assistance provided to that organization. Some of the spotlights highlight organizations that have been recognized nationally as Moving Mountains award winners by the Research and Training Center on Community Living at the University of Minnesota and the National Alliance for Direct Support Professionals.

Resources

The content in this book is only the tip of the iceberg in terms of available information on recruitment, retention, and training of staff in community human services. We identify other related materials and resources that will provide you with additional information, more detail, or related content. These resources are often books, web sites, research articles, or organizations that have copious information regarding the topic at hand.

Tools

One of the goals of this book is to provide readers with hands-on practical tools that they can use while developing and implementing many of the strategies we have suggested. The tools at the ends of the chapters include comprehensive assessment materials, checklists, and forms that can be easily adapted to a specific organization. We encourage readers to try these tools and tell others about them.

References

Each chapter contains reference citations to literature in the field. It was critical to us that the interventions we describe and recommend in this book be research based. These cited references are compiled at the end of the book. This comprehensive list of the research articles, book chapters, monographs, and other materials provides the reader with an indication that the literature supports the strategies and interventions in each chapter. Students who are using this book as a textbook may find it useful to locate and read the cited articles and other resources to get a better understanding of the research.

CONCLUSION

We hope that this book will be a living document with updates as new interventions are uncovered through research, training, and technical assistance activities. As we move forward we would love to hear from you about how you have used this book, what worked for you, and what did not work so well. If you have a success story that could be shared in future editions of this volume, we would love to hear about it. If you are using an intervention that is working particularly well, but the intervention is not mentioned in this book, let us know. We want to spread the word about strategies that work.

REFERENCES

Doljanac, R., Larson, S.A., Hewitt, A.H., & Salmi, P. (2004). *National validation study of competencies and training for frontline supervisors and direct support professionals.* Unpublished manuscript, University of Minnesota, Institute on Community Integration, Research and Training Center on Community Living, Minneapolis.

Hewitt, A., Larson, S.A., O'Nell, S., Sauer, J., & Sedlezky, L. (1998). *The Minnesota frontline supervisor competencies and performance indicators: A tool for agencies providing community services.* Minneapolis: University of Minnesota, Institute on Community Integration, Research and Training Center on Community Living.

Larson, S.A., Hewitt, A.S., & Lakin, K.C. (2004). Multiperspective analysis of workforce challenges and their effects on consumer and family quality of life. *American Journal on Mental Retardation, 109,* 481–500.

1

RECRUITMENT, RETENTION, AND TRAINING CHALLENGES IN COMMUNITY HUMAN SERVICES

A Review of the Literature

SHERYL A. LARSON,
AMY S. HEWITT, AND BETH A. KNOBLAUCH

Direct support professional (DSP) recruitment, retention, and training challenges are a serious threat to the quality of supports for people with disabilities. The struggle to solve these problems has become inseparable from the commitment to improve the quality of life of individuals receiving supports. These problems clearly thwart the ability of states to continue developing and sustaining community supports as the primary service model for people with disabilities.

This chapter reviews factors that contribute to recruitment, retention, and training challenges and describes the current situation that organizations supporting individuals with disabilities face in addressing these challenges. The messages of this chapter are three. First, if you are a supervisor, administrator, or human resources professional who is struggling with recruitment, retention, and training challenges, you are not alone. The research findings described in this chapter show that these are widespread and growing challenges. Second, this chapter can help you to evaluate how your current situation compares with the situation in similar organizations around the country. It provides baseline information at the national level for the challenges discussed in this book. The studies cited in this chapter measure many of the same variables that an organization needs to evaluate in developing a plan for change (as discussed in Chapters 13 and 14). The research findings in this chapter will provide help in understanding how to interpret the assessment information. Finally, this chapter introduces the concept expanded on throughout the rest of this book: Although recruitment, retention, and training challenges are growing, many things can and should be done to address them. This book provides concrete information about how to select and use interventions that have been proven in research to be helpful in addressing recruitment, retention, and training challenges.

This chapter builds on two previous reviews of the literature on staff recruitment, retention, and training, which provide the historical background for the book. The first review (Lakin, 1981) examined hundreds of studies and other reports that documented the history of recruitment and retention from 1900 to 1978. The second review examined more than 1,000 studies and other reports conducted between approximately 1975 and 1995 (Larson, Lakin, & Bruininks, 1998). For this chapter, 43 of the state, regional, and national studies conducted between 1990 and 2001 that focused on recruitment, retention, and training of DSPs supporting individuals with intellectual or developmental disabilities in the United States are reviewed. In most cases only the most recent study conducted in each state is cited. In a few instances, two studies from the same state are included because they provide different information.

TARGETED FRONT-LINE SUPERVISOR COMPETENCIES

Supervisors and managers of community human services organizations for individuals with disabilities are responsible for many different tasks. This chapter focuses on providing background information needed by FLSs and managers to put the recruitment, retention, and training challenges they face into a national perspective.

Primary Skills

FLSs monitor turnover, recruitment success, and employee job satisfaction, and use the results to improve personnel practices.

UNDERSTANDING THE PROBLEM

The dawn of the 21st century finds supports to people with intellectual disabilities (previously called mental retardation) and to people with developmental disabilities at a crossroads. There is great energy around concepts of full citizenship, inclusion, and self-determination. At the same time, there is great frustration as families, consumers, and service providers struggle to find, train, and keep DSPs to meet people's basic needs. Numerous studies detail the thousands of dollars in recruitment and training lost every time a DSP leaves a position (U.S. Department of Labor, as cited in Mercer, 1999; Employment Management Association, 2001; George & Baumeister, 1981; Zaharia & Baumeister, 1978). But the most significant cost of DSP turnover, vacancies, and inadequate training is the loss in quality of life for the people who need stable and skilled support from people with whom they share understanding, trust, and respect.

Community supports for individuals with disabilities have grown and changed substantially in the last 30 years. The shift from institutional to community human services has many dimensions of significance to the DSP workforce. As service settings shifted from rural to primarily urban service settings, DSPs were drawn increasingly from communities with higher costs of living, where people were more transient, and where there was more competition for employees. The shift toward community supports brought to direct support work much smaller working environments. In 1977, the average size of all settings in which people with intellectual disabilities lived (excluding individuals living with family members) was 22.5 people; in 2003 it was 2.8 (Prouty, Smith, & Lakin, 2004). The number of different places (other than family homes) in which people with intellectual disabilities received residential services increased from 11,006 to 145,581 during that period. Similar changes were observed in day and vocational services. For example, the number of adults with intellectual disabilities working in integrated community employment with ongoing job supports (supported employment) rather than in sheltered workshops increased from 9,882 in 1986 to more than 140,000 in 1996 (Wehman, Revell, & Kregel, 1998).

Along with the changing size and location of services and supports for people with intellectual disabilities, expectations of DSPs have changed dramatically from primarily caregiving to providing active support and training for community and social inclusion. Whereas in the 1970s most DSPs supporting individuals with intellectual disabilities worked in state or private institutions with on-site co-workers, supervisors, administrators, and medical and therapy professionals, today many DSPs work without an on-site supervisor. Often, they work alone. In community settings, DSPs have greater responsibility for decisions affecting people's health and safety and are responsible for providing opportunities for significant social and community involvement. They support people living in the community who have serious physical, health, and developmental limitations; who often do not communicate verbally; and who may exhibit behaviors hurtful to others or to themselves.

Many DSPs are taking these increased responsibilities in stride and are providing excellent supports. Others lack the skills, however, to succeed in their expanded roles without additional support and training. Newspapers and television programs provide exposés on the failures of DSPs to make the right decisions, fulfill their basic commitments, and/or demonstrate the necessary skills to meet the needs of the vulnerable people they are hired to assist (e.g., Boo, 1999; Corcoran & Fahy, 2000). These stories raise concern about success in hiring people with the essential capabilities to do what the DSP role demands. These stories also raise questions about whether systems exist to adequately train and measure the performance of DSPs in the essential tasks of their work roles. The stories suggest that the basic administrative and technical assistance needed by DSPs often are not available and that substantially greater realism, attention, and expectations are needed in assuring that DSPs are adequately prepared for the roles and responsibilities of continually decentralizing community human services. In response to the realities of direct support work, the expectations and responsibilities of those who perform it and the means to allow them to do so successfully should receive the highest and most serious attention from professional, service provider, advocacy, and government organizations.

Who Are Direct Support Professionals?

Understanding the characteristics and responsibilities of DSPs is important because many of the recruitment, retention, and training challenges faced by organizations are influenced by those characteristics. Organizations need to understand the characteristics and responsibilities of DSPs in their own organizations so that they can consider those characteristics when developing interventions.

The exact number of DSPs supporting individuals with intellectual disabilities is not known because the way the U.S. Department of Labor gathers and reports this information does not adequately capture the group of people who provide direct support in nonmedical settings. In 2002, however, an estimated 57,856 full-time equivalent (FTE) DSPs worked in state-operated residential institutions, which works out to 1.34 FTE DSPs per resident (Larson, Coucouvanis, & Prouty, 2003). Community residential settings supporting individuals with intellectual or developmental disabilities (ID/DD) employ an average of 1.43 FTE DPSs per person supported (Larson, Hewitt, & Anderson, 1999). Since there were 359,446 individuals with ID/DD receiving residential supports in 2003 (Prouty et al., 2004), we can estimate that 514,008 FTE DSPs worked in community residential settings in that year. An estimated 90,500–125,000 DSPs support approximately 312,000 individuals in vocational settings (Larson et al.,

1999). In addition to DSPs in residential and vocational programs specifically for individuals with ID/DD, other DSPs support people with disabilities in their own or family homes. Home health aides held about 561,000 jobs in 2000 (Bureau of Labor Statistics [BLS], 2001b). The proportion of home health aides supporting individuals with ID/DD is unknown. Although these numbers provide a glimpse of the magnitude of the direct support profession, the actual size of this workforce is probably much larger than these estimates indicate.

Roles and Responsibilities

The roles and responsibilities of DSPs have shifted dramatically as the context of their work has shifted from large congregate care settings to community settings such as individuals' own homes, small group homes, and community jobs. When supports for individuals with developmental disabilities were based on the medical model of care, DSPs in large institutions had duties similar to the role of nursing aides in congregate care settings as described by the BLS today:

> Nursing aides help care for...individuals confined to hospitals, nursing care facilities and mental health settings.... [They] perform routine tasks under the supervision of nursing and medical staff. They answer patients' call lights, deliver messages, serve meals, make beds and help patients eat, dress, and bathe. Aides may also provide skin care to patients... help patients get in and out of bed and walk.... keep patients' rooms neat, set up equipment, [or] store and move supplies.... Aides observe patients' physical, mental, and emotional conditions and report any change to the nursing or medical staff. (BLS, 2004a, p. 29)

Today, particularly in community settings, the role and responsibilities of DSPs have expanded considerably beyond the duties just described for nursing aides. DSP roles today are much less prescribed by specific standards, expectations, or supervisory control. Today, DSPs are responsible for tasks revolving around providing opportunities for inclusion in the community. They teach self-advocacy and empowerment skills, assist individuals in selecting and coordinating recreational activities, and help consumers learn how to gain access to community resources (California State Auditor, 1999; Taylor, Bradley, & Warren, 1996). DSPs also may support individuals in creating and maintaining personal relationships with friends and family and assist supported individuals to develop and attain their own personal life goals. In addition to these new roles, DSPs are still expected to perform all of the tasks that were previously required (e.g., self-care, home care). A Minnesota study found that nearly every small community group home surveyed expected DSPs to prepare meals (100%), provide transportation (99%), do laundry (98%), and clean (97%). Gardening, shoveling or mowing, and building maintenance or repairs were also included in the job responsibilities in some of these homes (Larson, Lakin, & Bruininks, 1998). Although DSPs may still teach new skills to the individuals they support and provide these basic caregiving and home maintenance tasks, the focus of the DSP role has shifted from staff control to self-determination and consumer control.

In recognition of these shifting roles and responsibilities, several efforts to codify those roles have been undertaken in recent years. In 1993, the U.S. Department of Education funded a project to develop national voluntary skill standards for 23 industries, one of which was community human services (*Community Support Skill Standards* [CSSS]; Taylor et al., 1996). The project conducted a job analysis that included a national

Table 1.1. Competency areas in the *Community Supports Skill Standards* (CSSS)

1. Participant empowerment
2. Communication
3. Assessment
4. Community and service networking
5. Facilitation of services
6. Community living skills and supports
7. Education training and self-development
8. Advocacy
9. Vocational, educational, and career support
10. Crisis intervention
11. Organizational participation
12. Documentation

Source: Taylor, Bradley, & Warren, 1996.

validation process to define the role of DSPs serving a wide range of individuals with disabilities in this new context of partnership, productivity, empowerment, consumer direction, and community interdependence. The following definition of the role of DSPs was one of the outcomes of this effort: "The Community Based Human Service Practitioner assists the participant to lead a self-directed life and contribute to his or her community, and encourages attitudes and behaviors that enhance inclusion in his or her community" (Taylor et al., 1996).

The CSSS (Taylor et al., 1996) identify benchmarks describing the skills required of master employees (see Table 1.1). Those benchmarks describe excellent, experienced employees recognized by peers and supervisors as skilled and competent. Whether by this analysis or by others (e.g., Hewitt, 1998a), it is clear that the knowledge, skills, and attitudes (KSAs) required of DSPs have expanded dramatically. Unfortunately, specific training and education to foster these KSAs, respect for the people that display them, or compensation in proportion to these people's increasingly demanding jobs have not followed.

Demographic Characteristics

In a 1977 national study of DSP turnover, 78% of 1,001 DSPs were female, 40% had some post–high school education, and 56% were younger than 30 years old at hire (Lakin, 1981). In studies conducted since the early 1990s, the percentage of DSPs who were female ranged from 66% to 96%, with the median being 81.5% (see Table 1.2). More than 50% of all DSPs have some college education, and as many as 35% have college degrees. The average age of DSPs ranged from 32 to 39 years old, with the median being 35 years old. The racial and ethnic characteristics of DSPs varied dramatically depending on the state. In Minnesota, 95% of DSPs who were surveyed were European American, whereas in New York City only 39% were European American. The percentage of non–European Americans varied widely from organization to organization.

A Changing Employment Context

Several external forces have exerted significant pressures on people and organizations providing supports to individuals with intellectual disabilities since the early 1990s. Among the most prominent of these factors is the changing context. Some of these factors have worked to diminish the pool of potential employees at the very time when the demands of the work would have best been served by the increased selectivity offered by a larger pool of potential employees. Nevertheless, as efforts are made to address the development of a sufficient workforce to meet growing expectations, those efforts must attend to the changing marketplace.

An Aging American Workforce

The most pervasive and far-reaching force affecting the supply of DSPs has been the aging of the baby boom generation (those born between 1946 and 1964). Between 1976 and 1986 the number of people in the United States 20–44 years old grew by 20 million (Fullerton, 1997). Since the majority of DSPs are in this age group, these increases helped provide new employees to provide supports to an expanding number of people with disabilities. However, between 1986 and 1999 the number of people 20–44 years old grew by only 4.75 million people (U.S. Census Bureau, 2001a), while the number of DSP positions grew far more substantially. Moreover, the number of people in this age group is actually projected to decline by 1.33 million between 1999 and 2010, further reducing the pool of recruits for DSP positions. Figure 1.1 shows the actual and projected change in the percentage of the U.S. population ages 20–44 between 1970 and 2010. Clearly, new employees to meet the growing demand for direct support services will have to come from beyond the group of people ages 20–44 years.

Growing Demand for Support

Although the number of people in the traditional ages for DSPs is projected to decrease, the demand for community social services is expected to skyrocket in the next several years. The number of people in the United States ages 85 and older grew from 3.02 million in 1990 to 4.12 million in 1999. This group will continue to grow to an estimated 5.79 million by 2010 (U.S. Census Bureau, 2001a). The BLS (2001b) projected that the number of personal and home care aides will increase 62% between

Table 1.2. Gender, age, race, and education of direct support professionals (DSPs)

Study	State or area	% female	Average age (in years)	% white	Some post–high school[a]	College degree
Cunningham (1999)	AK	96%	—	—	83%	29%
Wheeler (2001)	CA	66%	39.0	40%	—	—
Rubin, Park, and Braddock (1998)	IL	79%	—	60%	—	—
Fullagar et al. (1998)	KS	81%	34.7	—	—	—
Coelho (1990)	MI	82%	—	—	74%	23%
Hewitt, Larson, Lakin (2000)	MN	83%	—	95%	58%	
Test, Solow, and Flowers (1999)	NC	82%	37.3	54%	82%	32%
Askvig and Vassiliou (1991)	ND	92%	31.8	94%	71%	0%
Ebenstein and Gooler (1993)	New York City	79%	—	39%	—	—
Legislative Budget and Finance Committee (1999)	PA	—	—	—	22%	18%
Larson and Lakin (1992)	USA	74%	32.9	—	81%	35%

[a]The some post–high school group includes those who have a college degree.

Key: —, data not reported.

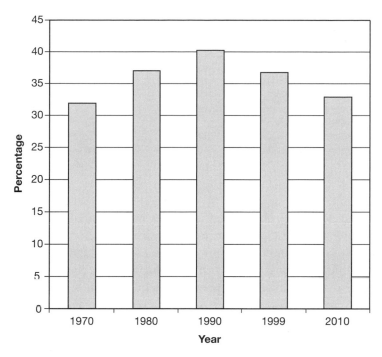

Figure 1.1. Actual and projected change in the U.S. population ages 20–44 years old, 1970–2010. (*Sources:* U.S. Census Bureau, 1990, 2001b.)

2000 and 2010. This means that the demand for DSPs will increase dramatically while the supply of new employees (at least those ages 20–44 years) will decline.

Recruitment Difficulties

The impact of the changing employment context is evident in research regarding the most challenging issues facing providers of supports to individuals with disabilities. Several studies have identified staff recruitment as the biggest issue facing providers today. Studies such as those conducted in Massachusetts (Cohen, 2000), Minnesota (Hewitt, Larson, & Lakin, 2000), North Carolina (Test, Solow, & Flowers, 1999), Ohio (Barry Associates, 1999), and Oklahoma (Oklahoma Department of Human Services, Developmental Disabilities Services Division, 2000), as well as national studies (e.g., Irwin Siegel Agency, 2001; Larson et al., 2001), found that the majority of organization administrators are experiencing significant difficulty in finding DSPs to fill vacant positions (and keeping them once they have been hired). Studies have reported vacancy rates for DSPs ranging from 6% in Oklahoma to 17% in Alaska (see Table 1.3).

The extent and impact of recruitment challenges can be illustrated by findings from a 2000 evaluation of Minnesota's Home and Community Based Services Waiver system (Hewitt, Larson, & Lakin, 2000). In that study, 75% of administrators reported problems with finding qualified applicants. More important, service coordinators reported that the number of people in the lives of supported individuals (e.g., turnover) and recruiting staff were serious or extremely serious problems. Similarly, 50% of people with a family member who received supported living services reported

Table 1.3. Direct support professional (DSP) vacancy rates

Study	State or area	Vacancy rate
Johnston (1998)	AK	17%
Effective Compensation, Inc. (2001)	CO	11%
Hewitt, Larson, and Lakin (2000)	MN	8%
Oklahoma Department of Human Services, Developmental Disabilities Services Division (2000)	OK	6%
Legislative Budget and Finance Committee (1999)	PA	13%
Division of Developmental Disabilities (2001)	WA	7%
ANCOR (2001a)	USA	11%

that staff turnover was a problem. Staffing issues were particularly troublesome for families receiving in-home supports or respite services. Only 46% of families reported they received the total number of hours of respite services they were allocated, and 56% said in-home supports were not available when needed (primarily because DSPs were not available to provide those supports; Hewitt, Larson, & Lakin, 2000).

Other Challenges

Wages

Wages for DSPs in community human services settings have been considered problematic since at least the mid-1970s. The BLS releases wage statistics each year for several human services occupations. Table 1.4 summarizes the number of people and average wages for nursing aides, orderlies, and attendants; home health aides; personal and home care aides; and psychiatric aides. Hourly wages in 2000 for those positions ranged from an average of $7.67 for personal and home care aides to an average of $10.79 for psychiatric aides. Unfortunately, similar federal wage data are not available for community DSPs.

Of particular concern is the wage gap between DSPs in public (mostly institutional) versus private community settings. In 1979, starting wages for DSPs in public institutions averaged $4.01 nationally compared with $3.49 for DSPs in private facilities, meaning that public DSP wages were 14% higher than private DSP wages (Lakin, 1981). A 1990 national study reported average wages in institutions were $8.72 per hour compared with $5.97 in private community settings, meaning that public DSP wages were 46.1% higher than private DSP wages (Braddock & Mitchell, 1992).

The most recent national study of DSP wages examined only public institutional settings. In that study, wages of DSPs in 2002 averaged $9.62 to start (ranging from $6.55 per hour in Louisiana to $16.48 per hour in California) and $12.33 overall (ranging from $7.52 per hour in Wyoming to $24.15 per hour in California) (Larson et al., 2003).

No national studies of wages in community settings have been conducted since 1990. A policy research review completed in 2002, however, summarized wage studies conducted between 1998 and 2002 from 42 states (Polister, Lakin, & Prouty, 2002). That study reported average starting wages for DSPs in private community residential settings of $7.33 and average wages in those settings of $8.68. In contrast, wages

• **Table 1.4.** National wage and employment statistics, 2000

Position: Job description[a]	N employed	Mean hourly wage
Nursing aides, orderlies, and attendants: Provide basic patient care under direction of nursing staff. Perform duties such as feeding, bathing, dressing, grooming, moving patients, or changing linens. Excludes home health aides and psychiatric aides.	1,273,460	$9.18
Home health aides: Provide routine, personal health care, such as bathing, dressing, or grooming, to older adults and individuals who have disabilities or who are convalescing in the home or in a residential care facility.	561,120	$8.71
Personal and home care aides: Assist older adults or adults who have disabilities with daily living activities at the individuals' homes or in daytime nonresidential facilities. Duties performed at residences may include keeping house (making beds, doing laundry, washing dishes) and preparing meals. May provide meals and supervised activities at nonresidential facilities. May advise supported individuals on nutrition, cleanliness, household utilities, and other matters.	271,280	$7.67
Psychiatric aides: Assist patients with intellectual disabilities or emotional disturbance, under direction of nursing and medical staff.	57,680	$10.79

[a]Job descriptions adapted from Bureau of Labor Statistics (BLS). (n.d.). *Standard occupational classification (SOC) system.* Retrieved from http://www.bls.gov/soc/. Wage and employment statistics source: BLS (2001b).

for DSPs in state-operated residential settings in 2000 were an average of $9.49 to start, and $11.67 overall. The Polister et al. (2002) study focused only on wages in residential settings. A similar summary of wage data compiled since 1997 can be seen in Table 1.5. The primary difference is that some of the studies reported in Table 1.5 include DSPs in vocational settings as well as in residential settings.

Wages in private settings ranged from $7.30 for residential and vocational settings in Kansas in 1997 to $15.18 in residential and vocational settings in Alaska in 1999. In every state where both public and private wage information was available, DSPs in public settings earned more than those in private settings. Public DSPs earned anywhere from 43% more than private DSPs (Minnesota vocational) to an astonishing 122% more (California). Clearly wages for DSPs continue to be low overall, with DSPs working for private providers earning considerably less than those working in the public sector. It seems fairly certain that the cost savings of community human services have come at the expense of the DSPs working in settings who are paid significantly less than DSPs in institutional settings.

There are several reasons to be concerned about low wages for community DSPs. In many cases, DSPs, especially those who work part time, earn less than the poverty rate for a family of four (see Table 1.6). This is problematic for several reasons, not the least of which is that people who do not earn enough to support their families often have to work multiple jobs to make ends meet. This in turn increases the chances that they will come to work tired or distracted by their other duties. The greatest risk of maltreatment comes from caregivers who are overly tired or stressed (Hewitt, unpublished research, 2004).

Lower wages have also been found to be associated with higher turnover rates in many studies (Larson, Lakin, & Bruininks, 1998). Clearly, wages do matter. They do

Table 1.5. Average hourly wages for direct support professionals (DSPs) in public and private residential and vocational settings

Study	Year data collected	State or area	Organization type	Private	Public[a]	Public and private
Cunningham	1999	AK	Both	$15.18	—	—
Johnston	1998	AK	Both	$9.14	—	—
Wheeler	2001	CA	Residential	$8.55	*$18.99*	—
Colorado Department of Human Services, Office of Health and Rehabilitation Services, Developmental Disabilities Services	2000	CO	Both	—	*$9.15*	$8.95
Rubin, Park, and Braddock	1998	IL	Residential	$7.36	$10.65	—
Fullagar et al.	1998	KS	Both	$7.30	*$11.20*	—
The Marketing Solutions Co.	2001	MI	Residential	—	*$15.57*	$8.44
The Marketing Solutions Co.	2001	MI	Vocational	—	—	$8.65
Hewitt, Larson, and Lakin	2000	MN	Residential	$8.81	*$15.51*	—
Hewitt, Larson, and Lakin	2000	MN	Vocational	$9.80	$14.06	—
Test, Solow, and Flowers	1999	NC	Both	—	*$9.30*	$9.24
Scioto Group	2001	OH	Both	—	*$13.41*	$9.60
Legislative Budget and Finance Committee	1999	PA	Both	$8.13	*$14.11*	—
Utah Association of Community Services	2001	UT	Both	$8.44	*$8.54*	—
Division of Developmental Disabilities	2001	WA	Residential	$9.76	$13.25	—
M. Mulliken Consulting	2003	WI	Residential	$8.81	*$14.32*	—
M. Mulliken Consulting	2003	WI	Vocational	$9.93	—	—
Heinlein	2001	WY	Residential	$7.38	*$10.00*	—
Larson, Coucouvanis, and Prouty	2003	USA	Residential	—	$12.33	—

[a]Numbers in italics are public residential institution averages taken from Larson, Coucouvanis, and Prouty (2003), with data from 1998 or 2000 reported, depending on which is closer to the study date.

Key: —, data not reported.

have an impact on the outcomes of interest in this book (e.g., turnover, vacancy rates). However, although changing public policy to increase wages for DSPs can help, many other things can help as well. The remaining chapters in this book describe strategies such as improved recognition (see Chapter 9), realistic job previews (see Chapter 3), and selection (see Chapter 4), and interventions that have research support to suggest that they can help reduce turnover and vacancy rates.

Inadequate Benefits

The type of benefits available to DSPs is also a problem. Most but not all organizations offer health care benefits to some DSPs. The percentage of employers offering health care

Table 1.6. Poverty level and hourly wages for full-time employees in a family of four with two children

Year	Poverty level	Hourly wage
2004	$18,850	$9.06
2003	$18,400	$8.85
2002	$18,100	$8.70
2001	$17,650	$8.49
2000	$17,050	$8.20
1999	$16,700	$8.03
1998	$16,450	$7.91
1997	$16,050	$7.72

Source: U.S. Department of Health and Human Services, 2004.

benefits ranged from a low of 30% in California to a high of 98% in Minnesota (see Table 1.7). Often, only the benefits required by statute are offered to part-time DSPs. There is, however, an important caveat in interpreting these numbers. In the Minnesota study, although 98% of employers offered health care to some employees, only 58% of DSPs were eligible to receive those benefits (Larson, Lakin, & Bruininks, 1998). That is because in many organizations only full-time DSPs are eligible for benefits, whereas many DSPs work part-time (e.g., 43.9% in Minnesota, according to Hewitt, Larson, & Lakin, 2000).

High Turnover Rates

The primary reason for concern about wages for DSPs is that, as mentioned previously, lower wages have consistently been shown to be associated with higher staff turnover (Braddock & Mitchell, 1992; Hewitt, Larson, & Lakin, 2000; Lakin, 1981; Larson, Lakin, & Bruininks, 1998). Staff turnover rates have consistently averaged between 45% and 70% since the mid-1970s in community residential settings for individuals with intellectual disabilities (Braddock & Mitchell, 1992; George & Baumeister, 1981; Lakin, Bruininks, Hill, & Hauber, 1982; Larson & Lakin, 1992; Larson, Lakin, & Bruininks, 1998). Studies since 1998 have estimated that turnover in community vocational settings averaged between 33% and 86%; in residential settings averaged between 43% and 84%; and in studies of both residential and vocational set-

Table 1.7. Percentage of organizations offering benefits to at least some direct support professionals (DSPs)

Study	Year data collected	State or area	Health	Dental	Retirement	Education	Life	Vision	PTO
Johnston	1998	AK	83%	70%	61%	43%	65%	39%	78%
California State Auditor	1999	CA	30%	26%	21%	—	18%	14%	30%v
Rubin, Park, and Braddock	1998	IL	92%	68%	81%	44%	—	—	—
Fullagar et al.	1998	KS	93%	—	68%	12%	—	—	68%v
The Marketing Solutions Co.	2001	MI	96%	—	—	—	—	—	—
Larson, Lakin, and Bruininks	1998	MN	98%	82%	78%	32%	89%	—	72%
Test, Solow, and Flowers	1999	NC	77%	63%	64%	2%	9%	2%	73%
Scioto Group	2001	OH	96%	80%	—	54%	92%	49%	—
Oklahoma Department of Human Services, Developmental Disabilities Services Division	2000	OK	53%	28%	37%	—	80%	28%	87%
M. Mulliken Consulting	2003	WI	87%	—	79%	70%	—	—	—
Braddock and Mitchell	1992	USA	97%	64%	57%	58%	—	—	—

Key: PTO, paid time off (includes sick, vacation, and holiday, except v connotes vacation only); —, data not reported.

tings, averaged between 30% and 66% (see Table 1.8). It is important to recognize that a national turnover study has not been conducted in community settings since 1990. The average turnover rate in the studies reported in Table 1.8 was 52.7%. The data may have been calculated using a variety of formulas, however, making direct comparisons somewhat risky.

In addition to the problems associated with recruitment challenges, turnover is problematic because it reduces continuity in the lives of individuals supported and because of the high cost associated with replacing a leaving employee. Although turnover rates have remained fairly steady over time, recruitment and retention challenges have reached a crisis level because recruiting replacement employees has become so difficult.

Training Challenges

There never seems to be adequate time or money to train DSPs. For the most part, training has not been driven by the individual needs of DSPs and the people they support. Instead, training has been driven by regulations that were developed to identify

Table 1.8. Direct support professional (DSP) turnover in residential and vocational organizations

Study	Year data Collected	State	Organization type	Management	Turnover
Johnston	1998	AK	Both	Private	66%
California State Auditor	1999	CA	Both	Private	50%
Effective Compensation, Inc.	2001	CO	Residential	Private	52%
Effective Compensation, Inc.	2001	CO	Vocational	Both	51%
Rubin, Park, and Braddock	1998	IL	Residential	Private	43%
Fullagar et al.	1998	KS	Both	Private	61%
The Marketing Solutions Co.	2001	MI	Residential	Both	65%
Hewitt, Larson, and Lakin	2000	MN	Residential	Both	44%
Hewitt, Larson, and Lakin	2000	MN	Vocational	Both	33%
Test, Solow, and Flowers	1999	NC	Both	Both	41%
NYSARC	2000	NY	Both	—	30%
Barry Associates	1999	OH	Both	Private	47%
Heneman and Schutt	2001	OH	Both	Private	38%
Oklahoma Department of Human Services, Developmental Disabilities Services Division	2000	OK	Residential	—	66%
Legislative Budget and Finance Committee	1999	PA	Both	Private	42%
Utah Association of Community Services	2001	UT	Both	Private	58%
Division of Developmental Disabilities	2001	WA	Residential	Private	54%
M. Mulliken Consulting	2003	WI	Residential	Private	84%
M. Mulliken Consulting	2003	WI	Vocational	Private	86%
Heinlein	2001	WY	Residential	Private	52%
ANCOR	2001	USA	Residential	Private	43%
Average					**52.7%**

Key: —, data not reported.

the minimal level of training required of a DSP. To be effective in their work, DSPs need far more training than prescribed by regulations. Yet, provider organizations consistently identify training as a challenge. Without providing adequate training, it is unrealistic to expect DSPs to be competent or to expect them to consider the job a career.

Although there are clear advantages to training DSPs, there are many barriers to providing effective training. Training is costly. Adequate resources for training are rarely built into budgets for community support services. Training requires people to leave their daily responsibilities long enough to attend training. In the context of decentralized 24-hour supports, bringing DSPs together for training has become more difficult. Given the continually changing roles and responsibilities of DSPs, locating or developing high-quality training materials presents an ongoing challenge that has not always been successfully addressed.

Training for DSPs is often not competency based and is not transportable from one employer to another. Furthermore, most training is based on seat time (the amount of time a DSP is physically present in a training session) rather than on demonstration of competence in actual work settings. A 1990 national study reported that private community residential service providers required an average of 36.6 hours of classroom training and 36.9 hours of on-the-job training for new DSPs (Braddock & Mitchell, 1992). Included in that training are topics such as CPR, medication administration, and review of policies and procedures. However, because training is not typically competency based and typically does not yield a recognized credential, if a DSP takes a job with a new company or in a new state, he or she has to repeat the same basic training that he or she may have already mastered.

Unfortunately, unlike recruitment and retention, data on training challenges are much more limited. One study in Minnesota examined the extent to which DSPs felt they were proficient in various skills (Hewitt, Larson, & Lakin, 2000). In that study 135 DSPs reported they felt most proficient in respecting people with disabilities, understanding rights of people with disabilities, preventing abuse and neglect, and ensuring consumer safety. They reported feeling least proficient in organizational participation (quality assurance, budgets, committees); vocational, educational, and career supports; education training and self-development for staff; advocating for people with disabilities and community human services; and networking (community access, facilitating friendships). Overall, 92% agreed or strongly agreed that the orientation and training they had received prepared them to complete most of their job duties and 59% agreed or strongly agreed that the orientation and training program used by their employer was excellent. A study in North Carolina (Test, Flowers, Hewitt, & Solow, 2004) found that administrators thought that DSPs needed training in documentation, communication, and crises intervention. DSPs, however, reported that they wanted training on crisis intervention, education, self-development, and advocacy.

While the characteristics of and challenges faced by DSPs are very important for organizations that are struggling with recruitment, retention, and training, DSPs are not the only important group. Understanding the characteristics and needs of FLSs is also important in addressing recruitment, retention, and training challenges.

In the Spotlight: University of Wyoming, Wyoming Institute for Disabilities

Only a few states, including Wyoming, have a formal system for collecting and publishing updated statistics on DSP wages, turnover, vacancy rates, and related topics. In 2000, the Wyoming State Legislature asked for a study of wages and salaries of nonprofessional direct care personnel to analyze the qualifications needed by those individuals, and to examine the cost of increasing wages to a competitive level. The Wyoming Department of Health contracted with the University of Wyoming, Wyoming Institute for Disabilities, to conduct this study. The study included four components: an investigation of the context, a survey of former certified nursing assistants, a survey of direct support staff who left their positions between January and June 2001, and a survey of agencies providing health care surveys (Heinlein, 2001). The study's final report, published in 2001, noted that there were 673 DSP vacancies daily for all Wyoming Department of Health providers. The study found that turnover averaged 52% for DSPs serving adults receiving supports funded by the Medicaid Home and Community-Based Services Waiver program.

In the 2002 legislative session, the executive summary of this report (http://ddd.state .wy.us/; scroll down in the main window and click "Direct Care Staff Wage Survey Executive Summary") was used successfully by the Wyoming Department of Health, individuals with disabilities, parents, professionals, advocates, and others to support the need for a substantial wage increase for DSPs. The 2002 legislature passed a bill authorizing expenditure of an additional $19.8 million over 2 years for wages and benefits for DSPs who support adults receiving supports under the Medicaid Home and Community-Based Services Waiver program. The money was distributed through individual budgets for adults receiving services. The requirement for organizations that receive the money is that the starting hourly wage for DSPs will be no lower than $8.00 and that the average wage for all DSPs will be $10.23. This compares with a $6.79 average starting wage and a $7.38 average wage for these same providers before the increase.

The state is committed to an ongoing program of data collection to learn how the wage increase was implemented. The next round of data collection will be 6 months after the increase is instituted. This data collection is just one of several efforts in Wyoming to improve recruitment, retention, and training for DSPs. A preliminary summary of the effect of this initiative showed that as the average wage for DSPs increased from $7.38 in 2001 to $10.32 in 2002, the turnover rate decreased from 52% to 37%. The state is also implementing a statewide training program based on the College of Direct Support (see Chapter 7) and a statewide recruitment campaign similar to the one Massachusetts implemented (see Chapter 2).

Who Are Front-Line Supervisors?

FLSs are people whose primary responsibility is the supervision and support of DSPs. These supervisors may perform some direct support tasks, but they spend less than 50% of their hours working in direct support roles. This book focuses on helping organizations address the challenge of finding, keeping, and training DSPs, and supervisors play a key role to that end.

Front-Line Supervisor Roles and Responsibilities

The competencies needed by FLSs have been described in *The Minnesota Frontline Supervisor Competencies and Performance Indicators* (Hewitt et al., 1998; see Figure 1 in the Introduction), which are based on a comprehensive job analysis that identified the specific knowledge, skills, and attitudes (KSAs) required of FLSs. These competencies and performance indicators were initially developed to reflect the roles of supervisors in Minnesota. Data collection for a national validation of these competencies was completed in 2003. Preliminary, not-yet-published analyses confirm that all of the competency areas and the vast majority of the competency statements are relevant to FLSs throughout the country, whereas a handful are relevant only in some organizations (Doljanac, Larson, Hewitt, & Salmi, 2004).

The number of FLSs working in community support organizations for individuals with disabilities is unknown. One Minnesota study, however, found that in community residential settings, there was one FLS for every 6.8 DSPs, and in vocational settings there was one FLS for every 7.3 DSPs (Hewitt, Larson, & Lakin, 2000). If these numbers were applied to the estimates of the number of DSPs reported earlier in this chapter, there would be an estimated 75,589 FLSs in community residential settings and 12,400–17,000 FLSs in community vocational settings in the United States. These figures are extremely tentative because they are estimates based on estimates. Still, until a better data source becomes available, they are the best we have.

Demographic Characteristics

Very little has been published describing the demographic characteristics of FLSs in community human services settings. One study conducted in 1994 found that in Minnesota, 84% of residential FLSs were women (Larson, Lakin, & Bruininks, 1998). Their average age was 33.6 years. They had provided supports to individuals with disabilities for an average of 9.3 years and had been in their current assignment for an average of 28.8 months. Supervisors had an average of 15.7 years of education.

Challenges in Supporting Front-Line Supervisors

While there is not as much information about FLSs as there is about DSPs, a few studies have provided information about wages and turnover rates for FLSs. Studies in five states have reported wage information for supervisors in community programs. Studies reported average starting wages ranging from $10.64 to $11.80 per hour, with average wages ranging from $11.21 to $15.48 per hour (see Table 1.9). In a national study of large state institutions supporting individuals with intellectual or developmental

Table 1.9. Hourly wages for front-line supervisors (FLSs)

Study	State	Wage year	Setting	Average starting wage	Average wage
Hewitt, Larson, and Lakin	MN	2000	Residential	$10.83	$12.17
Hewitt, Larson, and Lakin	MN	2000	Vocational	$11.80	$13.08
The Marketing Solutions Co.	MI	2001	Both	$10.64	$12.01
Scioto Group	OH	2000	Both	$11.61	$14.16
Legislative Budget and Finance Committee	PA	1999	Both	$10.90	$11.21
Division of Developmental Disabilities	WA	2001	Residential	—	$11.77
M. Mulliken Consulting	WI	2003	Residential	—	$11.24
M. Mulliken Consulting	WI	2003	Vocational	—	$15.48

Key: —, data not reported.

disabilities, average hourly starting wages for FLSs were $13.60 and average hourly wages were $16.07 in 2002 (Larson et al., 2003).

Studies in five states have reported turnover and/or vacancy rates for FLSs. Turnover for supervisors in vocational settings ranged from 8% to 16%, with turnover in residential settings or in a combination of residential and vocational settings ranging from 14% to 34% per year (see Table 1.10). Vacancy rates for FLSs ranged from 3% in Washington State to 8% in Pennsylvania. Although these rates are substantially lower than the turnover and vacancy rates reported for DSPs, they are still high enough to cause alarm. One study found that DSP turnover was significantly higher in homes that had newer FLSs (Larson, Lakin, & Bruininks, 1998).

FLSs play a critical role in addressing recruitment, retention, and training challenges. Not only do they often implement the interventions designed to address these workforce challenges, but also what they do has a direct impact on recruitment, retention, and training outcomes. A study by the Gallup organization found that in 2,500 business units with 105,000 employees, five factors were related to retention:

- Do I know what is expected of me at work?
- Do I have the materials and equipment I need to do my work right?
- Do I have the opportunity to do what I do best every day?
- Does my supervisor, or someone at work, seem to care about me as a person?
- At work, do my opinions count? (Buckingham & Coffman, 1999, p. 33)

These are all factors that can be influenced by the behavior of the FLS. Another study found that problems with supervisors, along with conflicts with co-workers and wages, were one of the three top reasons people wanted to leave their direct support positions (Larson, Lakin, & Bruininks, 1998). That same study found that supervisors who reported that treating their employees fairly was important had significantly lower turnover than those who did not choose that as a top priority. Clearly what supervisors say and do makes a difference. The good news is that this is a challenge that can be addressed. This book is designed to assist supervisors and managers to improve the way they do their jobs so that recruitment, retention, and training challenges can be overcome.

Table 1.10. Turnover and vacancy rates for front-line supervisors (FLSs)

Authors	Year data collected	State	Organization type	Turnover	Vacancy rate
California State Auditor	1999	CA	Residential	14%	—
Effective Compensation, Inc.	2001	CO	Both	34%	6%
Ernst & Young	1991	CT	Residential	22%	—
Ernst & Young	1991	CT	Vocational	8%	—
The Marketing Solutions Co.	2001	MI	Both	22%	—
Larson, Hewitt, and Anderson	1999	MN	Both	—	4%
Hewitt, Larson, and Lakin	2000	MN	Residential	28%	—
Hewitt, Larson, and Lakin	2000	MN	Vocational	16%	—
Legislative Budget and Finance Committee	1999	PA	Both	24%	8%
Division of Developmental Disabilities	2001	WA	Residential	25%	3%

Key: —, data not reported.

QUESTIONS TO PONDER

1. How can you use the facts presented in this chapter regarding the changing demographics of the U.S. population to support the need to change the recruitment, selection, hiring, training, and retention strategies used in your organization?
2. How do DSP and FLS wages in your organization compare with average wages for those positions in your state? If average wage data for your state were not reported in this chapter, how could you get this information?
3. Does your organization offer paid leave (vacation, sick days, holidays) to all employees regardless of whether they are full or part time?
4. What workforce facts and figures do you want to learn more about for your state or organization? (Chapter 13 explains how to compute turnover and vacancy rates for your organization.)
5. What surprised you most in this chapter? What will you do to learn more?

CONCLUSION

This chapter provides an overview of research on the characteristics and current challenges for both DSPs and FLSs. A substantial amount of research has been conducted describing the characteristics and workforce outcomes for DSPs and FLSs, but much more is needed. One key need is to update research showing wage, turnover, and vacancy rates and the relationships among these factors in community support settings as they evolve and change to monitor progress and identify emerging needs. Federal and state policy makers not only need to commit the resources to address the challenges of recruitment, retention, and training but also need to routinely gather information about the status and impact of efforts to improve outcomes in those areas.

Recruitment, retention, and training challenges are common to most organizations that provide supports and services to individuals with disabilities. We hope that this chapter helps put these challenges into perspective. The data can be used as a reference point against which the challenges of individual organizations can be compared. This might show that an organization's experience is rather typical. Or, perhaps it might show that in certain areas the organization had substantially more difficulty than did the organizations described in this chapter. Whatever challenges an organization faces, the remainder of this book focuses on specific research-based strategies that can be used to address those challenges.

RESOURCES

Bureau of Labor Statistics (BLS) (http://www.bls.gov/)

The BLS web site provides up-to-date national and state data and some local data on wages, employment levels, unemployment rates, and background information for more than 700 occupations.

U.S. Census Bureau (http://www.census.gov/)

The U.S. Census Bureau web site provides population estimates and projections, income and poverty statistics, and housing information for the United States, individual states, and local communities. Best known for the decennial census, the U.S. Census Bureau also uses a systematic program of annual and periodic surveys to collect and disseminate information describing the U.S. population.

Larson, S.A., Lakin, K.C., & Bruininks, R.H. (1998). *Staff recruitment and retention: Study results and intervention strategies.* Washington, DC: American Association on Mental Retardation.

This monograph describes the results of a 3-year longitudinal study of newly hired DSPs in Minnesota. It also contains a comprehensive literature review of previous research on the problems of turnover and the interventions that can ameliorate those problems.

Prouty, R.W., Smith, G., & Lakin, K.C. (2004). *Residential services for persons with developmental disabilities: Status and trends through 2003.* Minneapolis: University of Minnesota, Institute on Community Integration, Research and Training Center on Community Living. (Also available on-line [click under RISP 2003]: http://rtc.umn.edu/risp/index.html)

This report is part of a series of annual reports that describe residential services for people with developmental disabilities. Every year, state developmental disabilities directors are surveyed regarding how many people are receiving various services. Every other year, a special survey is sent to all state institutions serving individuals with intellectual or developmental disabilities. That survey gathers wage and turnover information for each state for DSPs and FLSs. Other research findings from the University of Minnesota related to DSP and FLS characteristics and needs can be found at http://rtc.umn.edu/wddsp.

I

FINDING AND
HIRING EMPLOYEES

2

Recruiting Direct Support Professionals

Sheryl A. Larson and Amy S. Hewitt

Recruitment is the process that an organization uses to let people know that a position is available and to describe that position in a way that leads the potential employees to apply for and accept a job if it is offered (Wanous, 1992). In the 1970s and 1980s, when members of the baby boom generation were in their 20s and 30s, most organizations that provided direct human services could easily recruit employees to fill vacancies created by growth or by staff turnover. Increases in the demand for supports and changes in demographic trends, however, have made it far more difficult for organizations to find new employees. This chapter reviews strategies that improve the likelihood that the people the organization wants to hire will be attracted to the organization by increasing the number of potential recruits who learn about job opportunities (marketing the organization and expanding the recruitment pool). It also reviews strategies to improve the match between potential recruits and the organization through the use of inside sources.

Recruitment is one component of an organizational entry process that also includes realistic job previews (helping applicants learn about the organization so they can make an informed decision about whether to accept an offered job), selection (assessing candidates to choose those that are most likely to perform the job competently and who will stay in that job), orientation (helping newcomers through the process of initial adjustment), and socialization (the process through which new employees adjust to their work group and the culture of the larger organization) (Wanous, 1992). Chapters 3, 4, and 5, respectively, are devoted to these other components of the organizational entry process and should be considered together with this chapter during the development of a comprehensive organizational entry process.

TARGETED FRONT-LINE SUPERVISOR COMPETENCIES

Competent front-line supervisors (FLSs) who are effective recruiters will exhibit an array of skills. The primary competencies for effective recruitment are from the Personnel Management competency area. Effective recruitment also involves several related skills from the Staff Relations and Promoting Public Relations competency areas (see Figure 1 in the Introduction for a description of these competency areas).

Primary Skills

FLSs recruit new direct support professionals (DSPs) by posting open positions both within the organization and externally in newspapers and on job boards, by encouraging existing staff to recruit potential new hires, and by networking with high schools, technical schools, 2- and 4-year colleges, job centers, welfare-to-work programs, and other sources of potential hires.

FLSs articulate the difference between recruitment and selection and the importance of both.

Related Skills

FLSs seek staff opinions and input regarding various issues (e.g., program plans, budgets, procedures) and empower staff to make decisions.

FLSs provide education to community members regarding people with developmental disabilities (e.g., rights, responsibilities, dispelling of myths).

FLSs recruit and mentor community volunteers, interns, and students.

FLSs assist in the development of promotional materials, including newsletters, newspaper articles, brochures, videotapes, and contacts with media.

UNDERSTANDING THE PROBLEM

Organizations providing community supports to individuals with disabilities have reported challenges with workforce issues since such supports were first introduced. A national study of community residential settings in 1978 found that 84% of administrators had problems recruiting, retaining, or training staff (Bruininks, Kudla, Wieck, & Hauber, 1980). Today, those struggles have not only continued, but have also intensified. In North Carolina, 70% of administrators reported having problems finding new DSPs (Test, Solow, & Flowers, 1999). In Alaska, 82% of administrators reported major problems finding qualified direct support professionals (Johnston, 1998). In Minnesota, the proportion of administrators reporting problems finding qualified employees increased from 57% in 1995 to 75% in 1999 (Hewitt, Larson, & Lakin, 2000; Larson, Lakin, & Bruininks, 1998). More than 50% of administrators in Minnesota reported moderate to severe barriers to effective recruitment in the following areas (Larson, 1997):

- Lack of qualified applicants (reported by 69% of administrators)
- Inadequate pay or compensation (67%)
- Challenging hours (evenings, nights, weekends, holidays; 55%)
- Applicants who do not demonstrate adequate work ethic (52%)

Service coordinators in Minnesota noted that recruiting foster families and residential and in-home staff were serious problems for Minnesota's Home and Community-Based Services Waiver program (Hewitt, Larson, & Lakin, 2000).

Recruitment problems are costly. For example, in Alaska, organizations reported spending $353.33 per DSP position per year on overtime (Johnston, 1998). In Minnesota, the average in 2000 was $300.80 per DSP position per year (Hewitt, Larson, & Lakin, 2000). In Kansas in 2003 the average overtime cost per DSP position per year was $476 (Kansans Mobilizing for Workforce Change Stakeholder Advisory Group, 2004). That money could be spent on upgrading services or on increasing wages, but because of unfilled hours due to vacant positions or employee absences, it is being used for overtime. Another cost of recruitment is advertising expenses. Advertising costs range from \$68.64 per DSP per year in Alaska to \$496.83 per DSP per year in Minnesota (Hewitt, Larson, & Lakin, 2000; Johnston, 1998; Larson, Hewitt, & Anderson, 1999).

Recruitment challenges are substantial. Vacancy rates in recent reports ranged from 0% for full-time positions in Hawaii to 33% for part-time positions in Pennsylvania (see Table 2.1), with a median of 8% for all positions and 16% for part-time positions. DSP positions were vacant for an average of 2.8 weeks in Minnesota residential and vocational settings (Larson et al., 1999), 4.0 weeks in Alaska residential settings (Johnston, 1998), 4.3 weeks in Minnesota Home and Community-Based Services Waiver settings (Hewitt, Larson, & Lakin, 2000), and 10.5 weeks in New York residential settings (NYSARC, 2000). FLSs in residential settings reported that they offered positions to 53% of all applicants (an indication of having little choice regarding whom to hire; Larson, Lakin, & Bruininks, 1998). In Kansas in 2003, 43% of administrators reported curtailing services to newcomers due to workforce challenges (Kansans Mobilizing for Workforce Change Stakeholder Advisory Group, 2004). These challenges are severe and require intervention. Given the changing labor market described in Chapter 1, new approaches may be needed to find an adequate supply of DSPs.

Labor market issues affect recruitment of qualified DSPs. For example, the unemployment rate in the United States declined from 8.5% in 1975 to 6.0% in 2003 (Bureau of Labor Statistics [BLS], 2004b). In addition, the number of women in the U.S. ages 20–44 years (the group most likely to work as DSPs) increased in the early 1990s but is projected to decline from 50.57 million in 2000 to 50.01 million in 2005 and 49.93 million in 2010 (U.S. Census Bureau, 2000a, 2000b, 2000c).

At the same time, the demand for support services is increasing. Between 2002 and 2012 the number of personal and home care aides needed is projected to increase

Table 2.1. Vacancy rates in community settings supporting individuals with intellectual disabilities

Study	State or area	Vacancy rate
Johnston (1998)	AK	17%
Kansans Mobilizing for Workforce Change Stakeholder Advisory Group (2004)	KS	8%
Hewitt, Larson, and Lakin (2000)	MN	8%
Oklahoma Department of Human Services, Developmental Disabilities Services Division (2000)	OK	6%–7%
ANCOR (2001a)	USA (community)	11%
Larson, Coucouvanis, and Prouty (2003)	USA (institution)	6%
National Association of State Directors of Developmental Disabilities Services and Human Services Research Institute	Residential (1999–2001)	
	CT	6%, 16%[a]
	DE	9%, 20%[a]
	HI	0%, 10%[a]
	IN	7%, 11%[a]
	MA	11%, 17%[a]
	NE	5%, 12%[a]
	PA	12%, 33%[a]
	WA	6%, 16%[a]

[a]The first number is for full-time positions, the second for part-time positions.

by 246,000 (40%), the number of home health aides needed is projected to increase by 279,000 (48%), and the number of nursing aides, orderlies, and attendants needed is projected to grow by 343,000 (BLS, 2003–2004). These demographic realities suggest that recruitment problems may get worse before they get better.

Finally, the demographic composition of the workforce is changing. Success in the future may require substantial changes in who is recruited and how they are contacted. Between 1995 and 2050, the proportion of the U.S. population that is European American is projected to decline from 73.6% to 52.8%, with the greatest change accounted for by an increase in the proportion of Americans of Hispanic origin (projected to increase from 10.2% to 24.5%; U.S. Department of Labor, 1999). During this period, immigration will account for almost two thirds of the nation's population growth.

RESEARCH SUPPORT FOR SOLUTIONS

Researchers examined recruitment practices and the effectiveness of various recruitment approaches. Three studies in organizations supporting people with disabilities documented the most common recruitment strategies used in those settings (Larson, Lakin, & Bruininks, 1998; NYSARC, 2000; Test et al., 1999). In all three studies, the most commonly used recruitment strategy was newspaper advertisements. Recruitment by or among current or former employees was the next most commonly used strategy. Fewer than half of the organizations used job fairs, employment or referral agencies, or television or radio advertisements.

Two studies examined the use of various recruitment incentives (Johnston, 1998; Larson et al., 1999). More than two thirds of organizations supporting individuals with disabilities reported trying to attract new employees by offering competitive benefits, time off without pay, and paid leave time. More than half reported using competitive wages and flexible hours. Just over 40% reported offering hiring bonuses to new recruits. Fewer than one quarter reported using targeted recruitment practices such as offering recruitment bonuses to current employees who find new employees, and almost none offered transportation or child care.

Effective recruitment practices ensure that potential recruits receive adequate information during the hiring process so that they have realistic expectations about the job. If such information is not provided, there may be a mismatch between what employees want from the job and the organization's climate (the way things are done). This mismatch can reduce satisfaction and organizational commitment and can lead to voluntary turnover (Wanous, 1992). For example, a prospective employee may want daily access to his or her supervisor. In reality, however, it may turn out that the employee only sees the supervisor once every 2–3 weeks. This mismatch between what the person wants and what the organization offers may eventually reduce the employee's job satisfaction and lead the person to quit his or her job. Several recruitment strategies take this principle into account by finding ways to provide information to potential recruits to help them make an informed decision about the match between them and the potential employer. One such strategy is using inside recruitment sources. Another such strategy, realistic job previews, is highlighted in Chapter 3.

Job applicants can hear about openings either through inside sources or outside sources. Inside sources provide information not typically available to people outside the company (Wanous, 1992). Inside sources include people who have worked for the organization before, current employees, volunteers, board members, and others who have direct connections to the organization and who can provide the inside scoop about what the job is about. Outside sources provide less specific information about the organization as a place to work (Wanous, 1992). Examples of outside sources include advertisements; job fairs; employment agencies; and high school, technical college, and college placement offices.

The research support for using inside recruitment sources is fairly direct. In a summary of 12 studies, job survival (the number of months a new hire stays in the organization) was 24% higher for employees recruited using inside sources than for employees using outside sources (Wanous, 1992). The benefit was greater among organizations that had high turnover rates. Another study found that employees who heard about the job through multiple informal sources, those who were rehired, and those who learned about the company through a clinical rotation had the most prehire knowledge, whereas those recruited through walking in or through advertisements had the least prehire knowledge. Increased prehire knowledge was associated with lower turnover among 234 nursing applicants (Williams, Labig, & Stone, 1993). Other studies have confirmed the benefits of using inside recruitment sources in increasing information about and commitment to the job, improving the extent to which prehire expectations are met, and improving job survival (Saks, 1994; Taylor, 1994; Zottoli & Wanous, 2000). The Saks study showed that both recruitment source and information provided by the organization were significant contributors to job survival. A study conducted in 1995 of newly hired DSPs in residential settings also supported the effectiveness of inside sources in human services settings (Larson, Lakin, & Bruininks, 1998). The study found that 57% of new hires who stayed 12 months had heard about the job from an inside source, compared with only 36% of new hires who left during the first 12 months (a statistically significant difference). Finally, whether through internships or work experience, previous experience is associated with lower turnover rates (e.g., Balfour & Neff, 1993; Lakin & Bruininks, 1981). Clearly, using inside sources as a primary means for finding new recruits is effective.

STRATEGIES FOR RESPONDING TO THE PROBLEM

Market the Organization to Potential New Employees

To compete successfully for a dwindling supply of employees, community human services organizations must consider what sets them apart from other human services organizations and from other service industries. They must then develop, implement, and evaluate comprehensive marketing plans designed to let prospective and new employees know what the organization is about—its mission, vision, and values; its history; and its commitment to DSPs. The marketing plan should identify the important characteristics of the culture of the organization so that they can be shared with potential and new recruits. The plan should answer these questions: What is unique about the organization? Why would a prospective employee choose it over the organization down the street?

An effective marketing plan should do the following (Caudron, 1999):
1. Identify the needs and perceptions of current employees and potential new hires.
2. Craft an organizational identity.
3. Create or update the organization's mission and vision statements.
4. Identify and remove barriers to attracting high-quality recruits.
5. Package the organization's image.
6. Spread the word to potential employees.
7. Enhance the organization's visibility.
8. Monitor and update the plan as needed.

Questions to ask when implementing these steps can be found at the end of this chapter. Caudron's model illustrates activities that can be used by community human services organizations to recruit DSPs. The steps in this process are described next.

1. Identify the Needs and Perceptions of Current Employees and Potential New Hires

The first step includes clarifying who current and potential employees are, what they need, and how they view the organization. Identifying the needs and perceptions of current employees and potential new hires involves conducting staff satisfaction surveys (for new hires, current employees, and exiting employees). Benchmark information for staff satisfaction surveys and new hire surveys can be found in studies such as Larson, Lakin, and Bruininks (1998). In that study, 36% of new hires accepted their job because they needed the income or benefits, 35% accepted because they had an interest in the organization or the people served by the organization, 17% accepted because they needed the training or experience provided by the job, and 11% accepted their position for other reasons (the percentages do not add up to 100% due to rounding). A study of DSPs from 70 Ohio organizations found that 67.2% heard about their jobs from an inside source, 20.7% heard only from an outside source, and 12.1% heard from both inside and outside sources (Doljanac, Larson, & Salmi, 2003). A marketing plan for DSPs should include a variety of information to reach those who are looking for jobs for different reasons.

2. Craft an Organizational Identity

The next step in the marketing process is to decide how the organization wants to be perceived by potential new employees and the general public. What does the organization want to be known for? Does this organization want to be known as the organization that bends over backwards to be flexible in supporting employees? As the organization that provides leading-edge supports to consumers by offering a highly trained staff? As the organization that offers competitive compensation packages by involving employees in extensive fund-raising activities?

Crafting an identity may involve making difficult choices about the most essential components to communicate to potential employees. In developing this marketing identity, the organization must be certain to involve people at all levels and in all aspects of the organization. Potential employees will be able to describe the relative benefits the organization has to offer because many of them have worked for more than one organization. Individuals who receive supports from the organization and their family members along with case managers can provide frank insight into the quality of the organization's services. For nonprofit organizations, members of the board of directors may be able to share the community's perspective of the organization. Listening to these voices will improve the accuracy of the organization's marketing approaches.

3. Create or Update the Organization's Mission and Vision Statements

Mission and vision statements are discussed briefly in Chapter 12 of this book. In developing the organization's mission and vision, it is important to address both the vision of how the organization will support individuals with disabilities and the vision of the organization as an employer. The marketing plan will rely on the mission statement to guide activities to make improvements needed to successfully convey the organization's identity to current and future employees. The organization's mission and vision should match or align closely with the marketing message. For example, if the vision statement emphasizes competent, well-trained staff members but the marketing message is that anyone can do this work, the inconsistency could be misleading or confusing to potential recruits.

4. Identify and Remove Barriers to Attracting High-Quality Recruits

Once the organization has identified its target image and has mission and vision statements to guide the change process, the next step is to identify components of the organization that do not support this image, mission, and vision and to make changes needed to bring the organization into compliance with the image and mission. This may include ensuring that all administrators, managers, and supervisors in the organization have the skills needed to accomplish the mission and uphold the image as well as the attitude needed to convey this mission and image to those they work with. These skills include administrators', managers', and supervisors' being competent in their jobs, understanding the mission and image, performing their jobs in a way that upholds the image, effectively communicating the mission and image to employees, and ensuring that employees in turn have the skills and attitudes needed to accomplish the mission and uphold the organization's image. Conducting focus groups, interviews, or employee satisfaction surveys (see the end of Chapter 13) can help to identify areas that may need to change. This information will help the organization to consistently deliver the identified image (Caudron, 1999).

5. Package the Organization's Image

Packaging the organization's image involves developing distinctive names, logos, colors, and slogans for the organization (Caudron, 1999). The packaging of human services organizations should focus, at least in part, on describing how people interact with one another to achieve the organization's mission and vision. Marketing materials and strategies should use the names, logos, colors, slogans, and descriptions of how people interact with one another to clearly convey the organization's desired image to potential employees. It is important to ensure that these images, logos, colors, and slogans are updated regularly so that they do not become outdated. Although updating these elements can be expensive, this is necessary because each generation of recruits has a different set of life experiences. The baby boom generation grew up going to schools that excluded people with disabilities or that segregated them. Their firsthand knowledge of people with disabilities may have been limited to people within their family or to the pitying language used by telethons to raise funds. By contrast, later generations have been exposed to television shows and movies that depicted people with disabilities in a more positive way (e.g., *Life Goes On, ER, Joan of Arcadia, Radio*) and have gone to schools that, in many states, included students with a wide range of abilities and disabilities. The organization's image should be updated to convey the current culture of the organization and society at large. Sometimes simple changes such as a new catch phrase or updated photos can make a world of difference.

6. Spread the Word to Potential Employees

Once an organization has packaged its new image, it is time to spread the word to potential employees about why they should consider working for the organization instead of some other community human services organization. Many such organizations focus on spreading the word about specific current openings, but that is not sufficient. Spreading the word also includes communicating a consistent message about the organization as a potential employer on an ongoing basis. Using public relations techniques such as identifying how the organization wants to be perceived and identifying three to five key messages to support that perception is important in the organization's advertising (Caudron, 1999). However, before an advertising campaign is initiated, the core messages for that campaign should be identified and shared with the full range of people associated with the organization to confirm that the messages are meaningful and accurate and to solicit their involvement in sharing the messages with people they know. Once the core messages have been finalized, current employees, individuals receiving supports, board members, volunteers, and others associated with the organization can be asked to share printed and other types of materials with people they know to encourage those people to consider working for the organization.

7. Enhance the Organization's Visibility

Now that the organization has crafted an image and has developed marketing messages or slogans to communicate, that information needs to be shared both within the organization and in the community at large. Enhancing the organization's visibility means communicating both about current job openings and about potential careers in human services. There are many ways to communicate the organization's image to current and potential employees. Paid advertising in newspapers or magazines and on the radio or television is only one strategy. Other strategies include but are not limited to having current employees spread the word about job openings to their friends and family members; using public service radio or television to share stories about community human services to enhance the visibility of the industry; developing a web site to communicate the organization's image, mission, and vision to potential employees; issuing press releases with positive stories about the organization's structure and the outcomes it helps achieve; making recruitment videos; and posting job openings on free web sites or with agencies that connect people with jobs.

Organizations have used many innovative strategies to spread the word. These innovative marketing and recruitment practices share an approach that is becoming more common in human services: consortia or groups of employers working together to address common recruitment challenges. For example, the Colorado Association of Community Centered Boards developed a statewide recruitment campaign that developed a brand image for the industry and then used recruitment videos, print ads, and radio spots to look for people who wanted to "make a difference in the lives of others" (Collins, 2000). In the first year, the campaign brought 332 responses to print ads, 30 responses to radio spots, 26 responses to postings on the web site (http://www.caccb.org), and almost 100 confirmed hires.

A similar campaign was developed in Ohio. The Ohio campaign included developing marketing materials such as brochures, posters, flyers, press releases, and a customizable videotape for marketing and recruitment (Thomas, 1999). Before embarking on this campaign, data were collected demonstrating the extent of recruitment challenges. Having a baseline was helpful in assessing the effectiveness of the campaign as it was implemented.

Provider associations and informal consortia addressing recruitment challenges have emerged in other states such as Minnesota and Oregon and have developed materials or resources to assist in recruitment efforts (Association of Residential Resources in Minnesota, 1998; Craven, 1999). These efforts reflect a growing awareness of the need for human services organizations to work collaboratively to address recruitment challenges.

More traditional forms of advertising may also be important in getting the word out. Those sources include print advertisements in the help-wanted section of local newspapers and web site advertisements. The most effective places for print ads may vary depending on the size of the community and on the educational requirements for new hires. Many supervisors report higher success with print ads placed in local community papers than with those placed in large metropolitan area newspapers, especially when recruiting individuals who are not required to have college degrees. Increasing the diversity of the organization's workforce may require advertising in culturally specific newspapers. In some cases this may even include advertisements in non–English language papers. Some organizations have found success in targeting certain types of potential recruits, such as women who work in manufacturing jobs who might be interested in a career change. Those organizations found that advertising in the manufacturing section of the newspaper yielded a new group of recruits because their ads really stood out. In addition to newspaper ads, print ads that are posted at libraries, supermarkets, local colleges and universities, and workforce centers can also enhance an organization's visibility. Such ads can usually be larger to more completely market the organization's image.

Not all print ads are the same. Some are much more likely to effectively market the organization's image than others. Consider the example in Figure 2.1. This ad reflects a typical ad found in a large metropolitan newspaper. Unfortunately, an ad like this one may draw few new applications, especially when placed in a metropolitan newspaper with a large circulation. Often organizations find newspaper ads to be costly, so they use acronyms and abbreviations to reduce their cost. This is a mistake. The ads need to be written so that they can be understood by potential applicants who

---

SOCIAL SERVICES   RESIDENTIAL SERVICES

XYZ agency has the following positions available working with persons with DD and/or TBI: FT coordinator, PT mornings, eves, wkends & sleep night. Great pay & benefits. Call 555-555-5555. EOE/AA

Figure 2.1.   Traditional newspaper advertisement.

may not have experience in the industry (who make up about half of all new hires; Larson, Lakin, & Bruininks, 1998). Advertisements containing acronyms and abbreviations are not inviting to applicants, especially if applicants are unfamiliar with these terms.

Compare the ad in Figure 2.1 with the revised ad in Figure 2.2. These two ads for the same position are very different. The first ad uses words and acronyms that may be unfamiliar to potential recruits. It also advertises great pay and benefits. Unless the organization has unusual sources of funds, however, this statement is misleading at best. The first ad also fails to indicate why a person should want to apply.

The revised ad is easier to understand because it does not use abbreviations or acronyms. It points out that the job offers challenging opportunities that allow an applicant to make a difference in someone's life. It also provides a specific name to contact for more information. It is only eight words longer, so it would not be significantly more expensive. Finally, it emphasizes the organization's values to provide supports using reliable, caring, and trained staff members.

8. Monitor and Update the Plan as Needed

Work on a marketing plan does not end when it has been implemented. It requires ongoing attention to be sure that the plan attends to the everchanging needs and desires of current and potential employees. Each generation of employees has a unique set of interests and needs. An effective marketing plan will thus have to be reviewed regularly.

SOCIAL SERVICES

Challenging and Personally Rewarding Jobs Available

XYZ Organization is looking for enthusiastic, reliable, and caring people to help people with intellectual disabilities. Make a difference in someone's life. Full and part time available. We'll train. Equal Opportunity Employer. Call Amanda 666-555-4444.

Figure 2.2.   Well-written newspaper advertisement.

In the Spotlight: Massachusetts Department of Mental Retardation

The Massachusetts Department of Mental Retardation has developed a comprehensive recruitment program that targets DSPs. The Rewarding Work campaign began in 1998 with a collaboration of 25 provider organizations in the Boston area, the state government, and a marketing communications company (Parker & James Communications, Inc.). The project began by assessing the existing recruitment situation, asking provider organizations questions such as the following:

- Where did your organization recruit its workers?
- How many people did your organization need?
- What pay and benefits were offered?
- What was your organization's turnover rate?
- What recruiting tactics has your organization tried? What worked? What didn't?
- What hasn't your organization tried?

In the next phase of the project, the marketing communications company held six directed group discussions, involving approximately 40 DSPs. The meetings were held at work sites without managers or supervisors present. Although the participants came from a variety of backgrounds, a consistent story emerged. Those who kept working in direct support positions did so because they could make a difference and their efforts were deeply and sincerely appreciated by people with disabilities. The campaign's theme—"Some people are lucky enough to love their work"—emerged directly from these discussions.

Once the research had been compiled, an initial marketing plan was developed. The recruitment campaign was kicked off in May 1999 with a well-publicized event at the State House. A well-known local radio personality was master of ceremonies, and the Commissioner of Human Services and legislative leaders spoke. Organizations honored outstanding staff members, who told their stories. Marketing materials, including a poster and an informational brochure, were handed out at the launch.

The marketing strategies used in the campaign included direct mail campaigns (to retired military, retired teachers, and other groups), bus billboard ads, stories profiling DSPs in community and college newspapers, and a job fair. A web site (http://www.rewardingwork.org/) was also created. A toll-free telephone hotline was also set up. The web site describes available jobs in general terms, has a search engine to locate provider organizations in the local community, contains profiles of DSPs, provides resources for people looking for a job (including an on-line application used to schedule job interviews), and describes Massachusetts for prospective employees from out of state. All leads generated by the site are forwarded to participating organizations in the community where the applicant is interested in working. Participating providers have access to a password-protected web site where they can screen applications by location and other key variables. All inquirers receive an initial screening telephone call from a project recruiter. The state of Massachusetts provided the funding for the marketing agency, whereas providers contributed a fee on a sliding scale basis to purchase marketing materials for the project.

The project proved very successful, with 2,000 inquiries in the first year. It expanded from just the Boston area to statewide in 2001. Information about this project has been shared at many conferences on direct support. Several other states have begun their own marketing campaigns as a result.

Expand the Pool of Potential New Recruits

Given the demographic trends in the United States and the increased need for additional employees within community human services settings, organizations will have to work hard to expand the pool of people from whom they select employees. Short-term recruitment strategies such as posting help-wanted advertisements or even recruitment campaigns are the most common strategies used by community human services organizations. Such strategies, however, are typically designed to find people who are already interested in a job or career in the industry to work for a particular organization. Long-term recruitment success will require strategies that actually expand the pool of potential employees. Strategies such as cultivating relationships with career and placement resources through networking with area high school guidance counselors, college and university career counselors, and postsecondary training program staff are important to recruiting high-quality candidates over the long term (Levy, Levy, Freeman, Feiman, & Samowitz, 1988).

Draw on Varied Sources of Recruits

One potential source of new recruits is recent immigrants to the United States. Many human services organizations have had great success in recruiting immigrants into direct support positions. Immigrants bring with them new experiences and insights into the roles and work of direct support. Many immigrants are highly educated and have had years of experience in health or human services careers in their home countries. Effective marketing to immigrants requires identifying ethnically and culturally diverse publications, community centers, and organizations.

Organizations that actively recruit immigrants will need to make organizational practices culturally competent. Orientation, training, and communication practices may need to be adapted to accommodate people who speak or who are learning English as a second language. In addition, company benefits for holidays and scheduled time off may need to be modified and existing staff may need training to encourage effective teamwork in diverse teams. Supporting families and individuals who receive services to develop effective communication strategies will be important as well. Resources such as *The Power of Diversity* curriculum (Sedlezky et al., 2001) can help organizations become more culturally competent.

Finding adequate supplies of employees also depends on tapping other sources of potential recruits, including older or displaced employees and people from groups that have traditionally experienced high unemployment rates (e.g., unskilled employees, high school dropouts). Another source of potential recruits is from occupations in which employment is declining. Between 2002 and 2012 the biggest declines in employment are projected to be for farmers and ranchers (declining by 238,000 jobs), sewing machine operators (91,000), and word processors and typists (93,000) (BLS, 2003–2004). To recruit and train these individuals as DSPs, organizations will need to work with community education and training programs such as school-to-work initiatives, welfare-to-work initiatives, postsecondary education programs, lifelong learning programs, community centers, and vocational/technical programs. State- and federally funded workforce centers or one-stop shops provide valuable information for employers and can be an excellent resource for those who want to expand their recruitment sources. The value of these types of recruitment strategies, especially if they include an internship (whether paid or not), is that they provide good information about what to expect in the job.

Use Innovative Training Programs

Several different programs have attempted to expand the pool through innovative training programs. For example, Minnesota developed a comprehensive pre- and in-service training program for DSPs called Community Supports for People with Disabilities (see Chapter 15). In one part of the state, the technical college coordinator for the program recruited high school students into the program to provide them with a good introduction to the work of a DSP, with the goal of helping students who might not otherwise have considered careers in direct support to decide for themselves whether such a career is interesting to them while they earn college credits.

A pilot project in the city of Minneapolis used the Community Supports Program as a platform for training and recruiting individuals who were previously welfare recipients into careers in direct support. Of the 27 students who began the training, 20 completed the program. Of those 20 completers, at least 13 found jobs in human services organizations. Approximately 63% of the training participants were of non–European American ethnicity, 52% were receiving public assistance when they entered the program, 44% were single parents, 30% were male, and 22% identified themselves as having a disability (O'Nell & Westerman, 1998).

Initiate Long-Term Recruitment Strategies

Individual provider organizations also have initiated long-term recruitment strategies. For example, one provider in a community with particularly low unemployment rates developed a paid internship program for high school students. The program was created through a partnership between the provider and a local high school. A few high school juniors or seniors were selected to participate in the program each year. These students worked with current DSPs in residential settings. Although the interns did not work unsupervised, they did provide extra support to enable individuals in those settings to expand their leisure and community activity options. At the end of the school year, interns were recognized by the organization at the high school's all-school awards program. The awards presentation raised awareness of the program among other students at the school and increased interest among the students regarding participating in future years.

Several tools have been developed to assist schools, workforce centers, and employers communicate about possible careers in human services. One of the best tools, Career Pathmaker (Taylor, Silver, Hewitt, VanGelder, & Hoff, 1997), was developed by the Human Services Research Institute. Career Pathmaker provides an excellent introduction to the human services industry for individuals who are unfamiliar with it. Career Pathmaker guides potential employees through a series of structured exercises and questions to help them identify and document their skills, attitudes, and life experiences that are related to entry-level positions in human services or health care.

The activities can be self-paced or can be completed with an employment counselor or as part of a career exploration class. Other resources are listed in the Resources section of this chapter.

Use Inside Recruitment Sources

Although the emphasis of this chapter is on long-term recruitment and strategic planning, organizations can also take action in the short term to improve their recruitment success. The source of potential new hires can make an important difference in whether those recruits will stay with the organization. Staff members who are recruited using inside recruitment strategies stay longer. Inside sources are individuals who know what the job is really like and who can provide a potential new employee with reliable information about the job so that the potential recruit can truly make an informed decision.

Use Internal Postings

Many strategies can be used to increase the number of applicants who hear about a job opening from an inside source. The most obvious of these is to make sure that current employees are notified when openings exist so that those who are looking for a change can learn of opportunities within their current organization rather than looking for a job with another organization. Internal postings are important both for positions that would be lateral moves and for positions that are potential advancements. Components of a good internal posting include geographic location, hours; characteristics, preferences, and needs of people supported; minimal job requirements (e.g., having a car); and supervisor information. Organizations that provide supports in many different communities or states can use internal postings to keep employees who move for whatever reason working in the company.

Promote from Within

Promoting from within can be a powerful tool for recognition and for retention of current employees. Some organizations worry that posting positions internally will result in people hopping from one program to another, which can be disruptive. Another way to look at this shifting is that the DSP may be trying to find his or her niche or to recover from burnout in his or her current position. Helping the employee find a place where he or she feels comfortable and connected to the individuals supported, co-workers, and supervisors can improve job satisfaction and increase the likelihood that the person will stay.

Offer Recruitment Bonuses

Providing recruitment bonuses to current employees who are listed as the source of job information for new hires can encourage inside recruitment. A survey by the Society for Human Resource Management (2001a) reported that 49% of organizations across industries offer a formal recruitment referral bonus program for nonexempt employees and that another 17% offer an informal program. Recruitment referral bonuses have been used for DSPs supporting individuals with disabilities in Ohio (where 41% of employers used bonuses; Barry Associates, 1999), Alaska (where 9% of employers used bonuses; Johnston, 1998), and Minnesota (where 22% of employers used bonuses; Larson et al., 1999). Several factors should be considered when establishing a recruitment bonus program. Probably the most important consideration is that current employees need to be active participants in planning and implementing any incentive program that affects them. They need to be part of the team that develops the marketing plan (described earlier in this chapter) so that they understand the message the organization is trying to convey to potential recruits. They also need to understand that the goal is not to simply find people to apply for a job but rather to identify people whose interests and skills are a good match with the organization and who will want to work for the organization for an extended period.

Recruitment bonus programs vary widely. Table 2.2 shows an array of options for recruitment bonus programs. For example, the type and size of the incentive offered may vary. Some organizations offer gift certificates to restaurants or hotels or tickets to sporting events, while others offer cash bonuses ranging from $25 to more than $750. Some companies add a second-level incentive in which all employees who earn a recruitment bonus during the year become eligible for a drawing for a super bonus such as a laptop computer or a vacation (Solomon, 1998). The amount and type of incentive offered should be determined by the organization in consultation with current employees to ensure that it is meaningful, within the context of other recognition programs, and sufficient to change the behavior of those employees.

Table 2.2.   Recruitment bonus program options

Participants	Current employees
	Supported individuals and their family members
	Board members
	Other stakeholders
Type of award	Cash ($50–$1,000)
	Grossed up (the person gets the stated amount after taxes)
	Not grossed up (taxes reduce the amount of the reward)
	Gift certificates
	Dining
	Specialty stores
	Sporting event tickets
	Company products (e.g., T-shirts, mugs, briefcases)
	Entry into a quarterly cash drawing
	Paid time off
	Use of a company car
	Trips
	Gifts (e.g., television, compact disc or MP3 player)
Timing options	At hire
	After 30 days
	After 90 days
	After 6 months
	After 1 year

Several strategies can be used to increase the effectiveness of a recruitment bonus program. Effective bonus programs do the following (Brounstein & Visconti, 1992; Martinez, 2001):

- Define who is eligible for the incentive
- Keep the rules simple
- Market the program
  - Publicize the criteria for participation in the incentive program
  - Share information about the program during orientation for new hires
  - Use paycheck stuffers and the company newsletter or computer network to publicize the program
  - Kick off the program each year
- Maintain an internal job posting system
- Maintain clear records
- Provide feedback to employees about the status of their referrals
- Give the referral award in time increments rather than all at once (e.g., at 6 and 12 months after the person is hired)
- Are patient and give the program time to work

The timing of the incentive is important. Since most DSPs who leave their positions leave during the first 6 months after they are hired, a recruitment bonus program should provide an incentive for employees to refer individuals who will surpass that 6-month tenure mark. Therefore, although it is important to provide some incentive soon after the hiring of a new employee (e.g., after the person completes orientation), it is also important that part of the incentive be offered at a later time (e.g., 6 or 12 months after hire). Criteria for the initial bonus might include that the new hire has to actually work for 30 days before the bonus is paid. The behavior that is important to reinforce is not just finding a person to fill the position, but finding a qualified, interested individual who will remain in the position for at least 6–12 months. The advantage to a tiered approach is that the initial bonus can reinforce an employee for bringing a new recruit to the organization and the long-term bonus reinforces the employee for helping that new recruit survive the initial employment period.

Market the Inside Recruitment Campaign

Think creatively about who can act as inside recruiters for the organization. For example, individuals who receive supports, family members, and board members of the organization may know of people who would be interested in working for the organization. Offering gift certificates or cash bonuses to those individuals when they find recruits can expand the pool of applicants while also empowering those individuals to become active participants in addressing recruitment challenges.

Hand Out Recruitment Cards

Recruitment cards are another tool that might be useful for organizations considering implementing a recruitment bonus program. Recruitment cards are the same size as typical business cards, but instead of identifying particular employees, they identify the organization's hiring authority. Current employees and others can distribute the cards to potential recruits to provide specific information about whom to call to pursue a job opportunity. These cards list the short version of the organization's mission statement with an invitation to apply for a position. One advantage of using recruitment cards is that an employee can write his or her name on the back of the card as the referring person so that he or she can get credit for the recruit.

Offer Incentives to Attract New Employees to the Organization

Human services organizations are increasingly using hiring bonuses to attract new employees. As employment in service occupations such as hotels, restaurants, entertainment, and telemarketing grows, some individuals who may have been attracted to jobs in human services are being lured away by hiring bonuses ranging from a few hundred to a few thousand dollars. *The Wall Street Journal* cited a Society for Human Resource Management study noting that 39% of all employers, as diverse as White Castle and Burger King and AT&T and Microsoft, are providing hiring bonuses (Lubin, 1997). To remain competitive, human services organizations have had to introduce either one-time hiring bonuses or rapid increases in wages during the first year of employment. Hiring bonuses should be developed using the same principles as recruitment bonuses. That is, some of the hiring bonus should be paid shortly after hire, but since the goal is not just to get people to start the job but also to find people who will stay, part of the hiring bonus should be paid 6–12 months after hire.

Considerations for Developing and Using Recruitment Strategies

Recruitment can be viewed as both an ongoing process (every year, *x* number of new employees in *y* job class will need to be hired) and as an event (a specific job opening exists now). Before implementing a recruitment plan for a particular opening, the organization should evaluate how the opening corresponds with current overall staffing needs. The organization should ask at least the following questions:

- Could current employees increase their hours to fill the position?
- Could other open positions be combined with this one to make it a more attractive position?
- Can an internal candidate fill the job, thereby creating an opening for a more entry-level position?
- Can the vacancy be filled on a temporary basis and then be eliminated?
- Can the position be eliminated altogether? (Brounstein & Visconti, 1992, p. 75)

Developing an effective recruitment plan requires a systemic approach. This approach must involve DSPs in all phases. As with any of the approaches discussed in this book, the recruitment plan should include specific goals and objectives, a baseline assessment, a time line for implementation, and an evaluation process to identify whether the strategy worked. The tools appearing at the end of this chapter include a form for assessing the relative success of using various recruitment sources; a form for assessing the outcomes of the recruitment and hiring bonus program; and a checklist of recruitment strategies to consider for the plan. These tools can be used in planning and implementing new interventions. Assessing the effectiveness of various recruitment sources can be helpful. A study conducted in 1990 indicated that 73% of service sector companies with 200 or more employees conducted follow-up studies of recruitment sources to determine which sources yield greater proportions of high-performing employees (Terpstra & Rozell, 1993). That same study reported that using recruitment studies was significantly correlated with sales growth and overall organizational performance.

OVERCOMING IMPLEMENTATION BARRIERS

Developing and implementing a recruitment plan and using effective recruitment strategies require changes in organizational practice. Change has the potential to be difficult, producing resistance from those affected. Resistance to change from current employees can be reduced by involving those employees in the planning process from the beginning. For example, current employees may resist playing a role in recruiting their friends because they may not think it will make any difference. Clearly explaining the reasons for wanting to use more inside sources (to improve the chance that new hires will stay) can help overcome this resistance.

Another possible problem that should be avoided is that of emphasizing, recognizing, and rewarding new employees to the detriment of current employees. The challenge is that current employees may feel it is unfair if new employees get access to benefits or rewards that current employees cannot get access to. One way to avoid this problem is to pair a recruitment bonus with a hiring bonus so that both current and new employees have access to the new program. Another strategy is to make sure that the recognition program for current employees (see Chapter 9) is fair and fully operational before specific incentives are offered to new employees.

Another barrier to implementing a recruitment program with specific monetary outlays is that board members or administrators may resist the expenditures. The primary strategies for overcoming this barrier include providing evidence from the organization's own data about the size and impact of the challenge (e.g., turnover rates, vacancy rates, the percentage of leavers who stay less than 6 months), citing research findings about the effectiveness of proposed recruitment strategies, and building an evaluation process into the intervention so that stakeholders can see how well the intervention worked.

QUESTIONS TO PONDER

1. How is your organization different from other similar organizations in the area? Why would someone want to work for your organization instead of for another?
2. Does this organization have an up-to-date marketing plan developed with the input of DSPs?
3. How might your organization's most recent newspaper advertisement be revised to communicate your organization's vision and to enhance your organization's visibility?
4. What is your organization's primary target audience for potential recruits? Has the message been tailored to this group?
5. What new audiences might your organization consider targeting? Why? How might the message be tailored to those audiences?

6. Does your organization welcome and support new immigrants? If yes, how? How might your organization improve its success recruiting and supporting a diverse workforce?

7. What strategies does your organization use to promote the use of inside recruitment sources? How effective are they? What new strategies can be tried to increase the proportion of new hires that have heard about the job from an inside source?

CONCLUSION

A plan to address turnover and retention problems must include attention to the recruitment process. Since most employee turnover occurs during the first 6–12 months after hire, finding effective strategies to reduce early turnover is essential. This chapter reviews both short- and long-term strategies (e.g., using inside recruitment sources and developing a marketing plan, respectively) to address recruitment challenges. Organizations must also modify the marketing approach and make an ongoing assessment of emerging sources of potential new hires to get the word out to people from those emerging groups. As with all of the strategies in this book, assessing the status of current recruitment efforts and the results of changing practices are critical components of an effective recruitment strategy.

RESOURCES

Brounstein, M., & Visconti, R. (1992). *Effective recruitment strategies: Taking a marketing approach*. Menlo Park, CA: Crisp Publications.

This workbook provides practical information and exercises to assist people who are new to the task of recruitment or who want to improve their success. It provides step-by-step instructions on implementing some of the interventions mentioned in this chapter.

Doverspike, D., Taylor, M.A., Shultz, K.S., & McKay, P.F. (2000). Responding to the challenge of a changing workforce: Recruiting nontraditional demographic groups. *Public Personnel Management, 29*, 445–457.

This article describes demographic challenges for recruitment and discusses strategies to focus recruitment on older baby boomers, Generation Xers, and members of racial and ethnic minority groups.

Kazis, R., & Gittleman, M. (1995). School-to-work programs. *Info-line* (Issue 9509). Alexandria, VA: American Society for Training and Development.

This booklet provides guidelines for organizations considering using school-to-work programs to improve recruitment success. It talks about these programs, provides two case study examples, and describes challenges organizations may face in implementing a school-to-work intervention.

Taylor, M., Silver, J., Hewitt, A., VanGelder, M., & Hoff, D. (1997). *Career pathmaker: A toolkit for entering careers in human services and health care*. Cambridge, MA: Human Services Research Institute. (Available from the publisher, 2236 Massachusetts Avenue, Cambridge, MA 02140; 617-876-0426; fax: 617-492-7401; https://ssl23.securedata.net/hsri/index.asp?keywords=career+pathmaker&type=Title&id=pub_search)

See the description of the toolkit earlier in this chapter.

Wanous, J.P. (1992). *Organizational entry: Recruitment, selection, orientation and socialization of new-comers* (2nd ed.). Boston: Addison Wesley.

This academic text reviews research and describes best practices in recruitment, selection, orientation, and socialization.

Worth, W.E., & North, A.B. (1995). Building an internship program. *Info-line* (Issue 9511). Alexandria, VA: American Society for Training and Development.

This booklet provides an overview of the process of designing an internship program. It describes selection techniques, orientation and training guidelines, supervision strategies, and evaluation strategies.

Developing a Marketing Plan

Use these questions to guide the development of a marketing plan. The steps are adapted from Caudron (1999).

1. **Identify the needs and perceptions of current employees and potential new hires.**
   What are the demographics of current employees?
   How do current employees perceive this organization?
   What do the current employees like and/or dislike about this organization?
   What is important to current employees?

2. **Craft an organizational identity.**
   What does this organization want to be known for by its employees?
   Do the current logo and marketing materials effectively communicate the mission and vision of the organization? Do they clearly communicate the identity?
   How have current DSPs been involved in crafting the organization's identity?

3. **Create or update the organization's mission and vision statements.**
   Does the mission statement clearly reflect the vision of the organization?
   How are the mission and vision communicated in marketing activities?

4. **Identify and remove barriers to attracting high-quality recruits.**
   What inconsistencies exist between the articulated mission and vision and the actual employment practices in this organization?
   What do current employees say about barriers and problems?
   What do leavers give as reasons for leaving?

5. **Package the organization's image.**
   What names, logos, colors, and slogans will be used to communicate the image?
   How long has it been since the names, logos, colors, and slogans have been updated?

6. **Spread the word to potential employees.**
   What are the five key messages the organization wants to convey?
   How can various people in the organization be involved in spreading the word?

7. **Enhance the organization's visibility.**
   Is the organization marketing careers in human services, not just specific jobs?
   Is the organization using a range of different mediums to communicate about careers and jobs that are available?
   What three to five new strategies can be used this year to enhance the visibility of this organization?
   How can this organization work together with other human services organizations to promote careers in human services?

8. **Monitor and update the plan as needed.**
   What process can be used to ensure that the marketing plan is updated regularly?
   What should be monitored and how?

Source: Caudron, 1999.

Staff Recruitment, Retention, and Training Strategies for Community Human Services Organizations by Sheryl A. Larson & Amy S. Hewitt.

Assessing the Effect of Recruitment Sources on Hiring

This chart can be used to evaluate the effectiveness of recruitment sources for an entire calendar year. According to recruitment source, track the number of applicants and the number who were hired. Calculate the percentage of applicants from each source who were actually hired. The data recorded on this chart will tell which recruitment source yielded the highest percentage of actual hires. Whenever possible, use a computerized database or spreadsheet to track this information to automate the computations.

Year:			
Referral source	Number applied	Number hired	% hired from source
Inside sources			
Applicant was referred by current or former employee.			
Applicant was referred by person receiving supports from organization or family member.			
Applicant responded to internal posting.			
Applicant worked for organization in past.			
Applicant was an intern.			
Applicant was a volunteer.			
Applicant was a school-to-work participant.			
Applicant was a welfare-to-work participant.			
Applicant was referred by another inside source (e.g., board member, volunteer).			
Total inside sources			
Outside sources			
Newspaper advertisement			
Job fair			
High school or college job board			
Employment or referral agency			
Television or radio advertisements			
Other outside source			
Total outside sources			
Totals			
Total inside sources			
Total outside sources			
Total recruitment source unknown			
GRAND TOTAL			

Staff Recruitment, Retention, and Training Strategies for Community Human Services Organizations by Sheryl A. Larson & Amy S. Hewitt.

Assessing the Effect of Recruitment Sources on Retention

This chart tracks all employees who quit during a calendar year. You will need to know the recruitment source for the people who left the organization in the year and the number of months each person worked before quitting or being fired. Enter the number of people who left who had heard about the job from each type of source. Then enter the number in each tenure group who heard about the job from each source. Finally, calculate the percentage of those who left who had 0–12 month's tenure by referral source (number of leavers with 0–12 months' tenure divided by number who quit or were fired). Referral sources with the lowest proportion of leavers in the first 6 and 12 months are the most effective for retention. Whenever possible, use a computerized database or spreadsheet to track this information to automate the computations.

Year:

Referral source	Number who quit or were fired	Tenure of leavers			% from the referral source who left after	
		0–6 months	7–12 months	13+ months	0–6 months	7–12 months
Inside sources						
Applicant was referred by current or former employee.						
Applicant was referred by person receiving supports from organization or by a family member.						
Applicant worked for organization in past.						
Applicant responded to internal posting.						
Applicant was an intern.						
Applicant was a volunteer.						
Applicant was a school-to-work participant.						
Applicant was a welfare-to-work participant.						
Applicant was referred by someone who works in a similar organization.						
Applicant was referred by another inside source.						
Outside sources						
Newspaper advertisement						
Job fair						
High school or college job board						
Employment/referral agency						
Television or radio advertisements						
Other outside source						
Totals						
Total inside sources						
Total outside sources						
Total recruitment source unknown						
GRAND TOTAL						

Staff Recruitment, Retention, and Training Strategies for Community Human Services Organizations
by Sheryl A. Larson & Amy S. Hewitt.

Assessing the Effect of Hiring Bonuses
and Recruitment Sources on Retention

Use this chart to assess the effectiveness of recruitment and hiring bonuses. For each person hired in the year, you will need to know if he or she received a hiring bonus, whether the organization paid an inside source a bonus when the person was hired, and how long the new hire kept working for the organization. Record the number of people hired during the year that fit in each box.

To determine if hiring bonuses made a difference, compare the proportion of new hires who left within the first 6 months after hire and who received a hiring bonus with the proportion of new hires who left within the first 6 months after hire and who did not receive a hiring bonus. If the number of new hires who received a bonus and left in the first 6 months is smaller than the number who did not receive a bonus and left in the first 6 months, the bonus may have had a positive effect on retention. A similar comparison can be done for the proportion of new hires that left within the first year of being hired.

To compute whether providing recruitment bonuses to current employees made a difference, use the same procedure as for gauging the effectiveness of hiring bonuses.

Intervention	Number hired	Number who left after 0–6 months	% who left after 0–6 months	Number who left after 7–12 months	% who left after 7–12 months
New hire received hiring bonus					
Yes					
No					
Inside source (e.g., current employee) got recruitment bonus					
Yes					
No					

Checklist of Creative Recruitment Strategies

Use this chart to note how many creative strategies the organization is using now and to rate the extent to which those strategies are working, whether the organization would like to start using the strategy in the future, and when to start using the strategy. In the empty spaces at the bottom, add any other strategies you are aware of or are currently using. For strategies that are not effective, consider whether any of the ideas in this chapter could improve the effectiveness of the program. If a strategy is not working and the organization cannot or will not modify it, consider discontinuing it in favor of another strategy. Use the Priority column to identify one or more strategies to modify or start using in the next 3 months.

Strategy	Use now (mark all that apply)	How effective (1, *low*; 5, *high*)	Priority for next 3 months (mark up to 3 choices)
1. Internal recruitment (posting job opportunities internally)			
2. Networking with other managers and supervisors to find internal applicants			
3. Recruitment bonus for current employees			
4. Recruitment bonus for supported individuals and their families, board members, and other referring stakeholders			
5. Hiring bonus for new recruits			
6. Developing relationships with school-to-work, welfare-to-work, and job service staff			
7. Internship programs for high school students			
8. Comprehensive marketing plan development			
9. Development of creating marketing materials			
10. Recruitment videotapes			
11. Television and radio advertisements			
12. Trade show giveaways (e.g., pens, pencils, letter openers with organization name)			
13. Web site recruitment			
14. Marketing to nontraditional sources			
a. Community clubs, civic groups, scouts, and churches			
b. Advertising in ethnic newspapers			
c. Military bases and veterans groups			
15. Presentations about careers in human services			
a. High school and college classes			
b. Workforce centers			
c. Job fairs			
16. Open houses			
17. Volunteer programs			
18.			
19.			

3

WHAT IS THIS JOB ALL ABOUT?

Using Realistic Job Previews in the Hiring Process

SHERYL A. LARSON, SUSAN N. O'NELL, AND JOHN K. SAUER

Realistic job previews (RJPs) improve retention of new employees by providing potential new hires with an accurate picture of the job for which they are interviewing *before* the organization makes a job offer. This hiring practice allows applicants to make an informed decision about whether they wish to accept a job offer should one be made. An RJP includes information on both the positive and the negative aspects of the job. This chapter describes how and why RJPs can reduce turnover and identifies what components should be included in an RJP. Various methods for delivering an RJP are also described.

TARGETED FRONT-LINE SUPERVISOR COMPETENCIES

Competent supervisors incorporate RJP strategies into their hiring practices; this skill is assessed in the Personnel Management competency area. Front-line supervisors (FLSs) use the related skills of seeking input from key stakeholders, including current direct support professionals (DSPs) and individuals receiving supports and their family members. Competent FLSs also use communications skills from the Staff Relations competency area to gather information, develop a plan, and implement an RJP.

Primary Skills

FLSs schedule and complete interviews with potential new staff in collaboration with DSPs and individuals supported and family members.

FLSs understand the importance and components of an RJP in the hiring process and use these methods effectively with potential new hires.

Related Skills

FLSs seek input from other staff and from individuals receiving supports and their family members in making hiring decisions.

FLSs effectively communicate with staff by listening to their concerns, supporting and encouraging their ideas and work, thanking them for their contributions, and providing positive feedback regarding their performance.

FLSs seek staff opinions and input regarding various issues (e.g., program plans, budgets, procedures) and empower staff to make decisions.

UNDERSTANDING THE PROBLEM

Although not all turnover is bad, all turnover is costly. Long-term DSPs who leave their jobs take with them skills and knowledge that are not easily replaced. This is especially true in human services work, in which much of the critical knowledge DSPs take with them is the history and needs of the people they support. The loss of long-term employees typically means the loss of deep knowledge and skills. In addition, from the perspective of the organization, DSPs who leave their jobs take with them a significant investment in time and money spent recruiting, hiring, training, orienting, and supervising.

Turnover rates for DSPs in community residential service settings have averaged around 50% since at least 1981 (see Chapter 1). Even more important than the number of DSPs who leave their positions is how soon after being hired they leave those positions. In a longitudinal study of more than 100 small residential support settings, 45% of DSPs who left the organization left in the first 6 months of employment (Larson, Lakin, & Bruininks, 1998). An additional 23% of all leavers left 6–12 months after hire. Ultimately, the majority of people who leave DSP positions do so within their first year on the job.

Depending on the way in which people are recruited, hired, and trained, the quantifiable cost of getting a new DSP into an organization and ready to start work with even moderate independence can meet or exceed $2,500. Many of the financial costs of filling a position are the same whether the DSP who left was with the organization a day or a decade. The longer the new employee stays, however, the more the overall hiring costs are offset. Recruiting and training new employees are critical organizational investments, and their value can be measured by the amount of time a new employee stays with the organization. Early turnover, therefore, is much more costly to the organization than other types of turnover in terms of financial viability and best use of resources.

The human cost of repeated, early turnover in this industry is significant as well. From the perspective of existing employees, this cost is harder to quantify. There surely is a loss of trust, energy, and the will to support the next new DSP who is hired. In addition, long-term DSPs and supervisors can become jaded toward new DSPs and therefore, directly or indirectly, be less welcoming and willing to share their current knowledge and skills with new DSPs. Often, existing employees believe that it is a waste of time to demonstrate correct job procedures and to encourage the development of new skills because the new DSP is most likely going to be gone within a few days, weeks, or months. Early turnover is also disruptive and detrimental to the individuals receiving supports from the organization. People receiving supports become more vulnerable because they must repeatedly share intimate details of their lives with people they barely know. New DSPs do not always know these individuals' unique needs, desires, and preferences. As a result, new DSPs may make decisions that do not take those needs, desires, and preferences into account and the individuals supported bear the loss of quality in their lives. It is impossible for a new DSP to provide the same high-quality supports as a long-term DSP who more clearly understands the people being supported.

Extremely early turnover, in which the new employees are hired and then resign within a few hours, days, or weeks of accepting a position, is an indicator to existing employees and people being supported that the organization is not being effective in its hiring practices. Early turnover is often caused by poor screening and selection practices, which result in poor job matches and disenchanted and underperforming DSPs. In addition, other employees may believe that the organization does not care about finding the right DSP. People who receive supports and their families may have difficulty believing that the organization cares about the overall quality of support services. To be successful in reducing turnover and increasing retention, and to maintain the viability of the organization overall, the organization must make a commitment to address the problem of DSPs leaving early in their tenure.

RESEARCH SUPPORT FOR SOLUTIONS

RJPs inform potential employees about details of the job that they are unlikely to know, thereby reducing turnover caused by new employees' unmet expectations. Unmet expectations held by newcomers about important aspects of the job and organization cause low job satisfaction (Porter & Steers, 1973). Low satisfaction, in turn, causes newcomers to quit. The principle is that if employers provide better and more complete information to potential recruits and if they encourage those candidates to use the information to make an informed decision about whether the organization and job are a good match, those individuals who do accept positions will have fewer unmet expectations and will therefore be less likely to leave the job. This theory has substantial research support. For example, in a study of newly hired residential DSPs, those who had fewer unmet expectations about their jobs and about the organization were significantly less likely to quit in the first 12 months after hire than those who had more unmet expectations (Larson, Lakin, & Bruininks, 1998).

Several meta-analyses that compared the findings of many studies have reported that providing RJPs to reduce unmet expectations can be effective in reducing turnover. For example, one meta-analysis found that RJPs improved retention rates by 9%–17% (McEvoy & Cascio, 1985). Another meta-analysis found that RJPs increased retention of employees 12% for organizations with annual retention rates of 50% and 24% for organizations with annual retention rates of 20% (Premack & Wanous, 1985). These studies, some of which included research conducted in organizations that support individuals with disabilities, suggest that RJPs have a positive effect and that this effect is larger for organizations with higher turnover rates.

More recent research has provided a more refined understanding of the effectiveness of RJPs. One summary of studies using meta-analysis reported that RJPs delivered after a job offer has been made but before an applicant decides whether to accept a position are more effective in reducing turnover than RJPs offered when an applicant first makes contact with the organization (Phillips, 1998). The reason suggested for this is that applicants who are close to making a decision about the job will pay closer attention to the RJP than would applicants who are just learning about an opening. This suggests that pairing the RJP with the final interview may be most powerful in reducing turnover. That same study also found that RJPs that involve a verbal exchange of information (in which the applicant can ask questions about the RJP) are the most effective in reducing turnover but that written RJPs are also effective. Videotaped RJPs were much less effective in reducing turnover. Interestingly, videotaped RJPs shown after hire, during a socialization or acculturation process for new employees, were associated with improved performance. If done effectively, RJPs also provide a comprehensive picture of the organization and its mission to applicants so that they can make an informed choice about whether they are a good match for the organization and the position.

STRATEGIES FOR RESPONDING TO THE PROBLEM

RJPs help ensure that recruits who accept a position will be less likely to leave due to problems with personal job satisfaction because the recruits have made an informed decision about whether to take the job based on realistic information provided by the organization. Unfortunately not only are RJPs underutilized in the human services profession, but it also could be argued that in these desperate times many organizations have taken the opposite approach in dealing with recruitment. Organizations that were not forthcoming about potentially difficult duties and assignments when a newspaper ad brought a pool of 20 people to choose from might likely be even less forthcoming in times when a newspaper ad brings only 1–2 responses. When learning about RJPs, some organizations will react negatively at the thought of "deliberately chasing away" potential employees, particularly when staring down the barrel of double-digit vacancy rates! This view of RJPs, however, is shortsighted at best.

An examination of an organization's internal data about turnover and vacancy rates will show whether early turnover is a problem. This assumes, of course, that the organization is actually tracking the number of people hired who never show up for training, as well as those who leave in the first few days after hire. Many organizations brush off this early turnover as insignificant and do not see the need for tracking it. An organization might be shocked, however, at the magnitude of resources being used on this early turnover. These resources include the cost of recruitment (including ads; marketing materials; background checks; employee testing; and salaries of those involved in interviewing, screening, and other applicant review) and overtime wages paid to current employees whose workload increases due to vacant positions. Even one person who does not show for his or her first day of work could be costing the organization hundreds or thousands of dollars. In addition to causing increased recruitment and hiring costs, DSPs who actually start working and quit shortly after devastate the overall financial health of the organization, employee morale, and service quality.

In the long run, RJPs are a vital part of the hiring toolkit used by community human services organizations. The RJP approach includes both community education and outreach and specific RJP materials and approaches for use with applicants. Direct support to people with disabilities is part of one of the most invisible industries in the country. Because of this lack of visibility, human services organizations must spend time informing people of the importance and characteristics of available positions. This is especially true as more applicants come from increasingly diverse pools of employees and as consumer-directed community supports continue to be developed. RJPs help people understand the work they are being asked to do and how a particular organization goes about doing it.

For instance, although recent immigrants, displaced workers, and retirees are nontraditional pools of potential employees to which many organizations are reaching out, many people in these potential applicant pools will have little experience in facilitating community inclusion and networking for people with disabilities. Younger employees may have more exposure to regular interactions with their peers with disabilities, especially if they went to an inclusive school. Younger employees, however, may have less experience with and understanding some of the other tasks that are associated with providing support to people with disabilities. Such tasks may include doing laundry, cooking, and documentation. Organizations should understand these potential skill deficits and ensure that job candidates clearly understand that they will be expected to develop and use skills in those areas.

The RJP development process includes keeping the job description up to date, gathering information from new and long-term employees about the positive and negative characteristics of the job, summarizing information that potential recruits are unlikely to know or are likely to have unrealistic expectations about, developing a strategy to present the information to candidates before they decide whether to take the job, and implementing and evaluating the RJP (Wanous, 1992). Because of the relatively low profile of the community human services industry, RJPs must contain information about direct support work in general, the organization specifically, and the specific needs of the people with whom the employee will be matched.

The following subsections describe the components of and the steps in creating an RJP. Figure 3.1 summarizes the steps graphically.

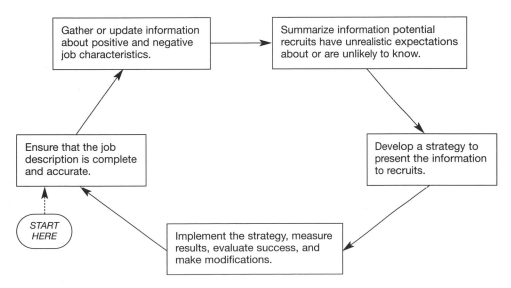

Figure 3.1. The realistic job preview (RJP) process.

Ensure that the Job Description Is Complete and Accurate

Having a job description that accurately summarizes the key functions of the position is critical for many of the interventions discussed in this book. In addition, the very act of providing an accurate, up-to-date job description to all applicants is an important part of the RJP process. Depending on how long it has been since job descriptions have been updated and what process was used, this may require quite a bit of work. (Chapter 11 provides guidance on how to develop job descriptions for FLSs; those principles can be applied to developing meaningful job descriptions for DSPs.) An accurate and complete job description can help the organization to select topics to describe in the RJP.

Gather or Update Information About Positive and Negative Job Characteristics

The next step in developing an RJP is to identify the characteristics that current employees like and dislike about their jobs. There are many ways to accomplish this task. One of those ways is to develop and distribute a job satisfaction survey that asks current employees about their jobs. A variety of questions can be helpful, but here are some of the most effective questions:

- What is the best part of your job?
- What makes you want to stay at this organization or in this job?
- What could your employer do to make your job better?
- What was the hardest part of starting this job? Give specific examples.
- What specific incidents make you want to leave this organization or job?
- What would you tell a friend who was applying for your job?

The responses to these questions can help the organization in determining the information to share in an RJP as well as in identifying issues that need to be addressed by supervisors or managers. An alternative to conducting a survey would be to use focus groups of current employees to discuss these questions. Focus groups or team discussions can be particularly useful when an RJP is being developed for a single site with a small group of employees.

Because relationships between new employees and people who receive services and their family members have an effect on the overall success and satisfaction of the new employee, it is important to gather information from family members and individuals receiving support about their expectations of DSPs and their hiring priorities. They often have a slightly different yet critically important perspective on this issue that will be very illuminating to the potential recruit. In addition, information provided by people who receive services and their family members helps the potential recruit get a realistic feel for the interaction and tone of the relationships they can expect to have with the people they will support.

Another important part of this assessment process is identifying the unique characteristics of the organization and/or the people being supported. Important questions to ask when gathering this information include

- How is this organization different from other organizations (or sites) that provide similar services?
- Why would someone want to work here?

- What organizational and procedural aspects should the candidate be made aware of that will have an impact on his or her ability to perform the job?

A well-rounded RJP will require input from a variety of people affiliated with the organization. People who currently work in the position, however, should provide the majority of the information about the job and its impact on new employees. When creating the RJP, it is best to involve a mix of newer and more experienced employees who work in the position. Relying on people outside of the position, even if they worked in the position for many years (e.g., employees who have been promoted or otherwise reassigned), is not sufficient. Job duties and requirements for DSPs change on a regular basis. In addition, people outside the position are apt to focus on their own needs rather than providing a DSP's perspective.

Summarize Information Potential Recruits Have Unrealistic Expectations About or Are Unlikely to Know

After the information has been collected, the next step is to review the information to identify issues that newcomers are unlikely to know or about which they are likely to have unrealistic expectations. The organization should rely mostly on recently hired recruits to help understand what information to include or emphasize in the RJP for DSP positions. The organization can develop a list of themes, both positive and negative, that will be included in the RJP. Information to highlight might include the following:

- A description of the organization and its vision and mission
- Basic information about the job (e.g., hours and scheduling; pay; paid leave time policies; skill prerequisites such as ability to read and comprehend complex medical information and the ability to lift a certain amount of weight; DSP job prerequisites such as a driver's license, a negative criminal background check, and the need to have a working and insured vehicle to use on the job)
- A description of typical job duties (e.g., cooking; shopping; assisting with personal care; helping people develop and maintain friendships; helping people manage their own behavior; supporting people to use community environments such as restaurants, stores, doctor and dental offices, and recreation venues; keeping records of supported individuals' activities and progress toward personal goals)
- Basic expectations about work behavior (e.g., the importance of showing up and being on time for every shift, the amount of notice required when the employee has a personal conflict with a shift, expectations about respectful interactions, ability to work without daily direct supervision)
- General information about the interests and needs of the people supported
- Testimonies from current employees about why they love their jobs
- Testimonies from current employees about the hard parts of their jobs

The selection of topics to include should be made in conjunction with current employees with the goal of using the most important information applicants need to make an informed decision about whether to take a job if it is offered.

Develop a Strategy to Present the Information to Recruits

Many different strategies can be used to share RJPs with potential employees. Those approaches include structured observations; meetings with current staff, individuals, and family members; videotapes; photograph albums or scrapbooks; booklets or brochures; web-based multimedia presentations; group RJPs; and internships or volunteer programs. Tables 3.1–3.8 review development issues, implementation considerations, cost implications, and advantages and disadvantages of each approach. Each method has strengths, weaknesses, and factors to consider when making a choice about the best type of RJP for an organization. Since the goal of RJPs is to present undistorted information to job applicants about the job and the organization before a job offer has been made, the organization should select the format that will best convey the information in the most affordable and practical manner given current resources and needs. For example, it may be practical and affordable to purchase a professionally done, customized RJP videotape in an organization that hires 500 DSPs each year but not for an organization that hires 5 DSPs annually.

In addition to the eight specific types of RJPs reviewed in Tables 3.1–3.8, an organization could also choose to use a hybrid method that combines two or more of the methods to create a more flexible and comprehensive RJP. The use of multiple methods should be coordinated to avoid overlap as much as possible. A hybrid approach may be advantageous because it provides more perspectives or more comprehensive information than could be covered in a single approach. For example, a hybrid approach might pair an industry-, state-, or organization-specific RJP videotape with site-specific scrapbooks.

This chapter describes several formatting options for an RJP, but organizations should not limit themselves to only these ideas. Other strategies such as developing slide presentations (delivered via a projector, computer, or in print) may also work. The organization can take advantage of creative ideas developed by the project team to develop an RJP to match the organization or site as well as possible. Also remember that the tables in this chapter simply describe formats for delivering RJP information. Regardless of which format is chosen, the content should be developed through the processes previously outlined in this chapter. We encourage organizations to think creatively about what would be the best approach for them based on available organizational resources and needs.

Regardless of the method or strategy the organization uses for its RJP, to be effective the RJP must have the following characteristics:

- The purpose of the RJP must be clear to the applicant (e.g., to help him or her decide whether to take the job if offered).
- The RJP must use credible information (e.g., real people and events, not actors and scripts; testimony from job incumbents rather than a discussion with supervisors).
- The RJP should include information about how current employees feel about their jobs.
- Positive and negative information should be balanced to reflect actual experience (a topical outline can be used to keep this balance when live people are part of the RJP).
- The RJP should be presented before or at the time that a job offer is made.

Several strategies can be used to determine whether an RJP is effective. The first strategy is to review the completed RJP and evaluate the process used in its development. A worksheet to evaluate the RJP is included at the end of this chapter. That tool asks current employees to rate the extent to which the criteria just listed were met from A (*excellent*) to F (*very poor*).

Table 3.1. Structured observation realistic job previews (RJPs)

Overview	Structured observation RJPs occur at a work site and give the applicant a comprehensive overview of job characteristics. For the session to be most effective, the applicant should take primary responsibility for gathering the information he or she needs so that working staff are focused on performing duties in their usual way. Providing the applicant with a checklist and scheduling structured observations during busy but routine activities is one way to ensure that staff and individuals receiving supports act naturally during the observation.
Development considerations	Structured observations should have set criteria and should not be informal processes in which the applicant merely shows up and watches what happens. A checklist or other method for ensuring that important information is gathered should be used (see the Structured Observation Worksheet in the Tools section of this chapter).
	People receiving supports should be consulted about the structured observation before its implementation. They may find the opportunity to prescreen prospective employees appealing. Their advice should be sought on how to ensure understanding of private care duties without intrusion and of other types of duties, such as documentation, that may not be consistently observed.
	Direct support professionals (DSPs) should be involved in identifying critical job components to be highlighted and in deciding how DSPs will be involved in the observations.
Implementation considerations	Observations should be in the exact site the candidate would work, if possible.
	Observations should be at times or in situations that help the applicant get a realistic expectation of what the job responsibilities would be (typically at a mealtime or another busy time when individuals receiving supports and staff are less focused on the visitor and are acting more naturally.)
	The candidate should be prompted to watch for certain information, to ask specific questions, and to provide specific types of feedback about what he or she saw. It is helpful to provide the applicant a written worksheet with a list of the information and questions to answer (see the Tools section of this chapter). It is also helpful to schedule time for the person observing to interact with both the DSPs and the people receiving supports during the observation.
	Observations should be followed by a debriefing to address questions and to provide information about job components not observed.
	The applicant could be asked to turn in the worksheet (or a photocopy of it) as a work sample test so that his or her documentation skills can be assessed.
	Observations should be scheduled with employees and individuals receiving supports in advance and should respect individuals' privacy and comfort level with the process.
	Observations should be scheduled so that the observer sees other DSPs, not front-line supervisors, at work.
Cost effectiveness	Structured observations require thorough planning to make them effective and comprehensive.
	They are the least expensive method to implement because extra staff time is not required during the observation and materials (e.g., checklists) are inexpensive to produce and update.
Pros	Structured observations are inexpensive to develop and implement.
	They are easy to update.
	They are easy to customize to individual sites and individuals receiving supports.
	They directly involve individuals receiving supports and DSPs in the hiring and selection process.
	They provide information to the potential hire from the people who understand the job best.
	The debriefing provides the applicant opportunities to ask questions about job aspects that were not observed and to establish a dialogue about what was observed.
	The structured observation sets the expectations that the DSP role includes supporting and informing new and potential staff and that new staff should seek information.
Cons	The structured observation is potentially invasive to individuals receiving supports and current employees.
	Each visit is different.
	During the observation, it is difficult to show all areas that might be important to new employees (e.g., pay and benefits, personal care, documentation).
	It might be difficult for people to act naturally when they are being observed.
	The observation sessions can be difficult to schedule.
	Structured observations are not portable.

From O'Nell, S., Larson, S.A., Hewitt, A., & Sauer, J. (2001). *RJP overview*. Minneapolis: University of Minnesota, Institute on Community Integration, Research and Training Center on Community Living. Also available on-line: http://rtc.umn.edu/pdf/rjp.pdf; adapted by permission.

Table 3.2. Realistic job preview (RJP) meetings with current direct support professionals (DSPs) and people receiving supports and/or family members

Overview	In these individual meetings, current DSPs and people receiving supports and/or their family members explain in their own words what the job is like; what the benefits and drawbacks are; and what their hopes, needs, and expectations for new hires are.
Development considerations	Current DSPs and people receiving supports and their families who participate should be trained about the purpose of RJPs and coached about how to make the meetings productive.
	It is important to clarify to all involved whether the meetings will be used solely for the purpose of an RJP or whether these participants will also be making recommendations about whether applicants may be a good match for the setting.
	As with structured observations, there should be guidelines for information to be shared during these meetings, and planning time is required to make sure that the organization has identified those criteria.
	The people who will conduct these meetings need to be willing to make a long-term commitment and must be coached on the goals of the RJP and what types of information will be helpful to share with recruits.
Implementation considerations	The prospective employee should be given a set of suggested questions to ask during the meeting.
	These meetings should occur in the actual work setting but in a private location whenever possible.
	These meetings can be scheduled after the job interview on the same day or on another day. The applicant should have the opportunity to gracefully opt out of the hiring process if the RJP reveals job characteristics for which they are ill-suited.
	Individuals receiving supports and their family members may be offered a stipend for their participation.
	People receiving supports who do not speak may wish to put together a collection of photographs or use other methods to show their routines and preferences.
Cost effectiveness	Development costs are similar to those for structured observations.
	Implementing the meetings requires staff time, making this method relatively expensive to maintain long term.
	The cost of bonuses or stipends paid to current DSPs and individuals receiving supports and family members who participate in the RJP should be considered.
Pros	The meetings are portable (if participants are willing).
	The meetings can provide opportunities for individuals receiving supports and their families and DSPs to be directly involved in the hiring process.
	The meetings provide direct information to potential hires from the people who understand the job best.
	The meetings allow candidates to ask questions that might not be answered by a structured observation.
	Each meeting is adaptable to the unique characteristics of, benefits of, and difficulties involved in working at each site.
Cons	Without good training and clear focus, the DSP or person receiving supports and his or her family may not provide adequate information.
	The meetings require that staff spend time away from their regular job duties.
	The meetings can be difficult to schedule.
	Each applicant's experience can be highly variable because each meeting is different.
	Prospective employees may be uncomfortable and less inclined to ask important questions in this form of RJP.
	The meetings may be a burden on current DSPs and people receiving supports and their families.
	The organization may be unable to find DSPs and people receiving supports and their families who are willing to participate.
	If the organization offers a stipend to participating DSPs and people receiving supports and their families, the stipend has to be paid, even if the prospective employee does not show up.

From O'Nell, S., Larson, S.A., Hewitt, A., & Sauer, J. (2001). *RJP overview.* Minneapolis: University of Minnesota, Institute on Community Integration, Research and Training Center on Community Living. Also available on-line: http://rtc.umn.edu/pdf/rjp.pdf; adapted by permission.

Table 3.3. Videotape or DVD realistic job previews (RJPs)

Overview	RJP videotapes or DVDs are often professionally produced and cover all jobs in a particular job classification. Amateur videos specific to a site can also be used, or the two methods may be combined. Videotapes show an applicant what the job is really like. They focus on situations that show the job most realistically or that typically cause early turnover due to lack of information about the job. It is important to include actual DSPs and individuals receiving supports in the video (rather than actors without disabilities) to make the video realistic. High-quality videos produced by groups of provider organizations or other entities may serve as a useful adjunct to other RJP methods.
Development considerations	Videos and DVDs require significant work beyond identifying the critical aspects of the job to include in the videotape. Writing a script; gathering consent forms; preparing settings; and coordinating participants, equipment, and video crews are also necessary. For a professional-quality video or DVD, access to high-end equipment and experts in camera work, sound recording, production, and duplication are needed.
	These RJPs need careful script development to ensure that critical components are present both visually and in words. Consultants or others who are familiar with the job and the organization and who are skilled videographers should develop the script.
	Because of the expense and time involved in production and updates, the planning process should be meticulous, and only the most critical pieces of information should be included.
Implementation considerations	Videos or DVDs can be made accessible at multiple sites but require a TV and VCR or DVD player and a staff person to be present to run the equipment and to answer questions.
	RJPs that are too long can lose impact; those that are too short may not contain all necessary information.
	Research suggests that video RJPs are less effective than other approaches in reducing turnover (Phillips, 1998) but that they may be helpful in improving job performance if shown during initial posthire socialization.
Cost effectiveness	Videos and DVDs are very expensive to produce and to update.
	If a video or DVD is well produced and content is not date sensitive, it can be used for a long time, increasing cost effectiveness. Updates, however, can be nearly as expensive as initial development.
	A TV and VCR or DVD player must be available at every site where the RJP is going to be used.
	Usually staff time is required to use RJP videos or DVDs. This usually will be time taken away from another task rather than additional hours added to the schedule.
Pros	Videotapes and DVDs are portable.
	Videos and DVDs are realistic without being repeatedly intrusive.
	Videos and DVDs can cover a variety of topics that might be concerns to the applicant (e.g., pay and benefits, major job duties)
	A video or DVD provides comprehensive look at the organization.
	This kind of RJP shows people actually engaged in the tasks required by the job, thereby providing credible information to newcomers.
	A video or DVD gives highly consistent information to each prospective employee.
Cons	Special equipment and expert filming and production are required for the video to look polished.
	Developing and updating a video can be very expensive and difficult.
	A TV and VCR or DVD player are needed for the video to be shown.
	Videotapes with poorly developed content will not be effective, and those with poor production quality may be discounted.
	Someone must be present when the RJP is shown to ensure that questions raised by the RJP are answered effectively.
	Capturing special needs or characteristics of people in many different individual sites in a professionally done video is very expensive.
	Videotapes or DVDs do not provide applicants with direct contact with DSPs or individuals receiving supports and their family members

From O'Nell, S., Larson, S.A., Hewitt, A., & Sauer, J. (2001). *RJP overview.* Minneapolis: University of Minnesota, Institute on Community Integration, Research and Training Center on Community Living. Also available on-line: http://rtc.umn.edu/pdf/rjp.pdf; adapted by permission.

Table 3.4. Photo album or scrapbook realistic job previews (RJPs)

Overview	Photo albums or scrapbooks compiled by the people working in and/or supported at a specific site can tell the story, using pictures and words, of what it is like to work at that site. These books are a low-technology option that can be developed and modified at the local level.
Development considerations	Photo albums or scrapbooks need to be carefully designed to attract applicants and maintain their attention and to include all the necessary information.
	Organizations need to be careful to be specific about the tasks of the job and avoid (or explain) jargon that may not be understood by prospective employees. For example, avoid using only generic words such as *personal care;* mention or illustrate specifics such as helping people brush their teeth, helping people use the toilet, and so forth.
Implementation considerations	Simply handing an applicant a scrapbook may not accomplish the intent of an RJP. The person may not read all of the materials or may not fully comprehend them (especially if there are language barriers and if examples are not specific).
	A checklist similar to the one necessary for structured observations (see the Tools section of this chapter) should be used to ensure that the applicant understands the information.
	To be most effective, the applicant should view the RJP in the presence of individuals receiving supports and their family members and/or current direct support professionals (DSPs), who can explain what is pictured in more detail and can answer questions.
	Time with an album or scrapbook should be followed by a debriefing with the supervisor or hiring authority to answer questions and to provide information about job components that the applicant does not understand.
	Outdated information should be removed or replaced. (Using an album or scrapbook with removable pages facilitates this process.)
Cost effectiveness	Film and other supplies must be purchased and used creatively to tell the story effectively.
	This format is very inexpensive overall.
Pros	Photo albums and scrapbooks are highly portable.
	They provide a vehicle to encourage individuals receiving supports and their families and current staff members to share their lives with potential new hires in a relatively nonthreatening format.
	Photo albums and scrapbooks can be developed by current DSPs at a site as a team-building exercise.
	Photo albums and scrapbooks can be adapted to a variety of settings, individuals receiving supports, and so forth.
Cons	A separate album or scrapbook is needed for each site.
	Quality photo albums or scrapbooks require creativity and a significant amount of effort to create.
	Impact depends on the amount of energy the applicant spends engaging with the materials.

From O'Nell, S., Larson, S.A., Hewitt, A., & Sauer, J. (2001). *RJP overview.* Minneapolis: University of Minnesota, Institute on Community Integration, Research and Training Center on Community Living. Also available on-line: http://rtc.umn.edu/pdf/rjp.pdf; adapted by permission.

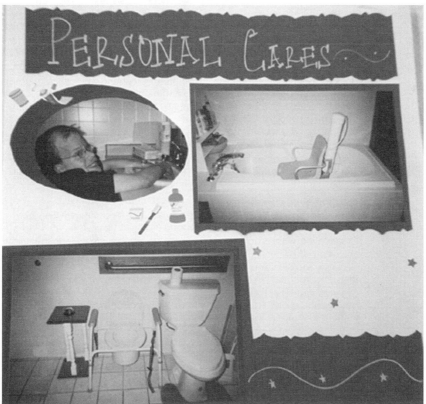

Figure 3.2. Pages from realistic job preview (RJP) scrapbooks. (Top page created by Marcie Grace.)

Table 3.5. Booklet or brochure realistic job previews (RJPs)

Overview	Booklets or brochures can be of varying lengths and levels of sophistication but should include the components of an effective RJP that are discussed in this chapter. Booklets or brochures are typically printed in bulk and given to each applicant.
Development considerations	Booklets or brochures need to be carefully designed to attract applicants and maintain their attention and to include all the necessary information.
	Organizations need to be specific about the tasks of the job and avoid (or explain) jargon that may not be understood by prospective employees. For example, avoid using only generic words such as *personal care;* mention or illustrate specifics such as helping people brush their teeth, helping people use the toilet, and so forth.
	If booklets or brochures contain photographs or identifying details of real DSPs and individuals receiving supports, then consent must be obtained.
Implementation considerations	Simply handing an applicant a booklet or brochure may not accomplish the intent of an RJP. The person may not read all the materials or fully comprehend them (especially if there are language barriers and if examples are not specific.)
	Booklet or brochures should be site specific or should be paired with other information about the site(s) where the person would be working.
	The information presented should be balanced so that there is adequate detail and so that the booklet or brochure is not too long.
	Booklets or brochures should be supplemented with opportunities for applicants to meet people and ask questions or to view videos about the kind of work the job entails.
Cost effectiveness	Professional-quality brochures and booklets are expensive to produce and design. Organizations with staff members who have graphic design skills, however, could tap that talent to produce a good product.
	The organization may need to purchase computer hardware and software and may need to work with layout and design professionals, consultants to help identify what information should be presented and how, and professional printers and photographers.
	Printing decisions need to balance the cost effectiveness of large bulk orders with the potential for waste when it is time to update materials.
	Costs can be reduced by using black-and-white rather than full-color materials; however, such materials may not be received as positively by applicants. Using volunteers to collate, fold, and staple brochures or booklets can also reduce the cost.
Pros	Booklets or brochures are highly portable.
	Booklets or brochures can be distributed by current employees, individuals receiving supports and their families, board members, and others.
	Potential employees can take the booklet or brochure with them to consider further in the privacy of their own home.
	Booklets or brochures can be adapted to a variety of settings, individuals receiving supports, and so forth.
	Even if the organization works with a graphic designer or a consultant, current DSPs can work together to help develop the booklet or brochure as a team-building exercise.
Cons	Expertise is required to create effective and attractive materials.
	Booklets or brochures do not provide opportunity for prospective employees to interact with individuals receiving supports and their family members and DSPs.
	Organization-wide brochures or booklets are not likely to include the unique characteristics of a specific site or individual receiving support.
	Because booklets and brochures are not interactive, they may be less effective than other methods in helping an applicant understand the job (Phillips, 1998).
	Organizations may hesitate to be specific enough with information in this format because the needs and characteristics of supported individuals change over time and because a mass-produced brochure or booklet may not be long enough to provide specific information about particular sites.
	The value of booklets or brochures may not be understood by applicants unless the reason for using them is clearly explained.
	The organization can print a lot of brochures, but if the staff are not committed to using them, the brochures will sit unused.
	Outdated versions may be circulating.

From O'Nell, S., Larson, S.A., Hewitt, A., & Sauer, J. (2001). *RJP overview.* Minneapolis: University of Minnesota, Institute on Community Integration, Research and Training Center on Community Living. Also available on-line: http://rtc.umn.edu/pdf/rjp.pdf; adapted by permission.

Table 3.6.   Web-based multimedia realistic job previews (RJPs)

Overview	A web-based multimedia RJP involves putting comprehensive information about the positive and negative features of jobs on a web site for prospective employees to review. Web sites can be used for more than simply presenting an RJP. They can be developed as part of a recruitment portal that includes items such as on-line applications, postings about current position openings, e-mail contact information, and links to other targeted sites (e.g., public schools, community centers). Web-based multimedia RJPs may include photographs, verbal descriptions, video clips, and/or written information about the organization and about the job.
Development considerations	Web-based multimedia RJPs are most effective if they are well designed. Organizations are advised to work with consultants who understand design issues, such as how to display content most effectively and how to limit access to sensitive materials.
	Organizations need to buy or have the computer hardware and software to produce and maintain a web site and train or hire someone to do updates.
	Organizations may need to rent computer server space and register with on-line search engines.
	Development and quality testing can take a significant amount of time.
	If photographs, video clips, or identifying details of real direct support professionals (DSPs) and individuals receiving supports are used, then consent must be obtained.
Implementation considerations	Organizations should to train current staff (especially those doing hiring) on how to access and use the on-line RJP.
	Web sites need to be checked regularly for dead or inaccurate links. A system should be created to ensure that all information is updated and accurate (e.g., contact person, available positions) and that any e-mail contact is answered promptly.
	Organization must provide access to a computer and assistance to potential new hires who do not have computer access or who are not computer literate.
Cost effectiveness	Web-based multimedia RJPs can be expensive to produce but are relatively inexpensive to maintain and update, especially if they are developed thoughtfully (e.g., automatically updated when new positions are posted).
	Development costs vary but would be no more than and potentially much less than a video, especially if current staff have computer expertise.
	The greatest costs are felt by organizations that do not have any existing hardware, software, or internal expertise.
	Updates can often be made by a person with basic computer skills.
Pros	Web-based multimedia RJPs are flexible in terms of the type and form of information presented.
	These RJPs are highly portable and are easily accessible to job seekers (can be viewed in homes, in libraries, at the organization's sites, and at workforce and community centers).
	Web-based multimedia RJPs can be part of a comprehensive on-line recruitment portal for the organization.
	RJPs in this format are easy and inexpensive to update frequently.
	An on-line RJP provides younger, web-savvy recruits a way to access information in a familiar format.
	Updated information is immediately available, with little chance of outdated materials being accidentally distributed.
	Web-based multimedia RJPs can be customized to the organization's sites and to the needs of the applicant seeking information.
	This kind of RJP can provide potential recruits with direct e-mail contact with DSPs, other organization staff, and (with their permission) individuals receiving supports or their family members.
Cons	To access a web-based multimedia RJP, computer equipment and Internet service are required.
	Existing personnel may hesitate to use this kind of RJP without training and encouragement.
	Creating web-based multimedia RJPs requires expertise in how to use the web environment most effectively.
	Slow or outdated equipment, download times, or server problems may make the process annoying or irritating to people trying to access information.
	Not all applicants have web access or knowledge of how to use computers or the web.

From O'Nell, S., Larson, S.A., Hewitt, A., & Sauer, J. (2001). *RJP overview.* Minneapolis: University of Minnesota, Institute on Community Integration, Research and Training Center on Community Living. Also available on-line: http://rtc.umn.edu/pdf/rjp.pdf; adapted by permission.

Table 3.7. Group realistic job previews (RJPs)

Overview	In a group RJP potential applicants are given information about the job. The meetings can be divided into three or four 5- to 10-minute segments. During each segment, information about the job is provided and questions are answered. A variety of presentation methods including panel discussions, videotapes or DVDs, brochures, and formal presentations, can be used. After each segment, a break allows people to leave if they decide this job is not a good match for them. At the end of 30–40 minutes, those who remain fill out a job application and interviews are scheduled.
Development considerations	Like other RJP formats, planning time is required to identify which aspects of the job to highlight and how.
	This is a method for presenting an RJP and requires that one or more of the other methods (structured observations, meetings, videotapes, photo albums or scrapbooks, booklets or brochures, web-based multimedia presentations) be developed first to communicate the RJP content.
Implementation considerations	Potential applicants should be informed of any job prerequisites before this meeting so that they do not come if they do not meet these requirements.
	People attending the group RJP may be influenced by the behavior of others and may leave or stay depending on how others behave.
	Group RJPs may work best at recruitment fairs or similar presentations at schools, workforce centers, or other places.
Cost effectiveness	Development and implementation costs vary depending on the materials and methods used.
	When direct support professionals (DSPs) and individuals receiving supports and/or their family members are involved and stipends are offered for their participation, it is less expensive to have them meet with a group than to do so with individual applicants and will likely make the process more illuminating as more questions will be asked and explored.
Pros	A group RJP provides information to more than one person at a time, reducing the time commitment per potential applicant.
	This RJP method shows potential applicants that it is okay to decide to not pursue the job.
	The structure can help keep information more consistent than when current employees meet with individual applicants.
	Group RJPs are somewhat portable (but require space to present to a group).
Cons	Group RJPs require prospective employees to be available at the scheduled times (low flexibility).
	Cost–benefit ratio may be low due to the need for planning, scheduling, employee time, materials needed, and so forth.

From O'Nell, S., Larson, S.A., Hewitt, A., & Sauer, J. (2001). *RJP overview.* Minneapolis: University of Minnesota, Institute on Community Integration, Research and Training Center on Community Living. Also available on-line: http://rtc.umn.edu/pdf/rjp.pdf; adapted by permission.

Table 3.8. Internships or volunteer program realistic job previews (RJPs)

Overview	More of a long-term strategy, internships or volunteer opportunities provide people who are not sure whether this job or career is of interest to them a chance to try it out. Some internship programs focus on high school students who are fulfilling course or community service requirements for school.
Development considerations	This method requires a dedicated person within the organization who will guide the program through development and implementation.
	Planning must include consideration of the guidelines regarding what interns or volunteers are allowed to do and what the conditions of the internship or volunteer experience will be (e.g., supervision requirements, whether any compensation will be provided, hours). The guidelines should consider liability and insurance issues and whether background checks are needed.
	Intentional opportunities should be built into the internship or volunteer program to provide specific information about the positive and negative characteristics of the job that are not immediately apparent to individuals interacting with individuals for a short period of time (e.g., interns and volunteers may not experience the full range of duties that paid staff are expected to perform, such as paperwork and assistance with personal care).
Implementation considerations	Internships can be paid or unpaid.
	Providing recognition of people who were interns or volunteers (e.g., at banquets and award ceremonies, in local newspapers) can help generate interest from other people.
	The organization must ensure that there is screening and that information is given to the potential interns or volunteers in advance to ensure the best match between these people and their duties.
	One of the other types of RJPs (structured observations, meetings, videotapes, photo albums or scrapbooks, booklets or brochures, web-based multimedia presentations, group RJPs) may be useful in helping potential interns or volunteers learn more about the organization before they begin.
Cost effectiveness	Internship and volunteer programs are expensive in terms of coordination efforts.
	Internships or volunteer opportunities are a long-term strategy that may not show immediate benefits.
	The program will only be cost-effective as an RJP if it leads to new employees; therefore, efforts should be spent on finding people who have a potential for eventually entering the field full time and/or for providing referrals to people who would become employees.
Pros	Internships or volunteer programs provide additional people to enhance quality-of-life outcomes for individuals supported while also giving the interns or volunteers a good picture of what the job is really like.
	Internships or volunteer programs provide organization staff and individuals receiving supports and their families information about the interns or volunteers.
	Even if not choosing a career in human services, participants leave with a better understanding of the individuals supported.
Cons	Internships or volunteer programs are time intensive.
	The actual yield in terms of new employees can be quite low. That is, it may take many interns or volunteers to yield one new staff member.
	The intern or volunteer may have to go through a "pseudo-hiring" situation (e.g., criminal background checks, training) that may increase the cost to the organization.
	The organization may spend a lot of time on interns or volunteers who are a poor match.
	The program may be invasive to people receiving supports and to current direct support professionals.

From O'Nell, S., Larson, S.A., Hewitt, A., & Sauer, J. (2001). *RJP overview.* Minneapolis: University of Minnesota, Institute on Community Integration, Research and Training Center on Community Living. Also available on-line: http://rtc.umn.edu/pdf/rjp.pdf; adapted by permission.

Additional questions to ask in reviewing the completed RJP include the following:

- Were individuals receiving supports and their families involved in deciding what and how to communicate?
- Was written consent obtained to use photographs or other information about individuals receiving supports that will be shared?
- Have current DSPs reviewed the final product?

Implement the Strategy, Measure Results, Evaluate Success, and Make Modifications

Once the RJP has been developed, the next step is to try it out. This may initially involve a small pilot test in which a small number of new applicants review the materials. This pilot may involve a specific feedback mechanism used to ask the applicants what they thought of the materials and if they had any questions about what they saw (see the Realistic Job Preview Evaluation at the end of this chapter). This pilot can be used to identify minor changes that could make the RJP more effective. Obviously, with materials such as the development of a videotape, piloting may have to take place before final edits are done or at various stages of production to contain costs.

The next step is to implement the RJP for a period of several months to a year. During this phase, the organization can either have all eligible applicants experience the RJP prior to or in conjunction with a preemployment interview, or divide the pool of applicants so that half experience the RJP and the other half (the control group) participate in the hiring practices that do not include the RJP. Piloting the RJP with two such groups is a better way to test the effectiveness of the RJP because the organization can clearly see if the RJP makes a difference in how long new employees stay. If the organization uses this method, it is important to keep records of which applicants and which new hires received the RJP to learn whether their outcomes are similar to or different from others who did not. Minor adjustments can be made along the way to ensure that the process is as refined as possible. For example, if a 30-day follow-up survey shows that new employees continue to have unrealistic expectations about a specific aspect of the job (e.g., scheduling practices), additional information about that aspect can be added to the RJP.

There are several specific indicators of whether the RJP made a difference. The most direct measures of success will probably include tracking the following information:

- How many people experience an RJP? (Count people who are hired as well as those who stopped the application process after using the RJP and were never hired.)
- What proportion of people used the RJP to decide that the job was not a good match for them? (Count the number who applied but stopped the process after using the RJP divided by the total number of applicants.)
- Do people who are hired after receiving an RJP stay longer than those hired without participating in the RJP? (Compare the RJP group with the new hires in the 6 or 12 months before the RJP was implemented.)
- Do new hires who have had an RJP report that more of their expectations about the job were met when surveyed 30 days after hire than new hires who did not receive an RJP? (See the New Staff Survey at the end of Chapter 13 for a tool to assess this.)

To understand how the RJP is working without using a control group, gather data prior to its use, and track the following for all people hired in the 12 months before the RJP was implemented:

- What percentage of people who leave the organization (or site) leave within the first 6 months after hire?
- What percentage of newly hired DSPs remain with the organization (or site) at least 6 months?

If the RJP is effective (and unmet expectations on the part of new employees were the true reason for early turnover before the organization used the RJP), then after the RJP is used, the percentage of people who leave in less than 6 months will decrease and the percentage of new hires that stay at least 6 months after they are hired will increase.

If people who used the RJP still leave in the first few weeks after hire, it is important to ask them what information they wish they had known so that they could have made a better decision about whether the job was a good match for them. This information will then need to be built into the RJP as appropriate. It is also important to ask about other reasons these people may be leaving, such as lack of support on the job in the form of orientation, training, and supervision or other reasons. In this case, strategies such as improvements to the orientation program (see Chapter 5), competency-based training (see Chapter 6), or supervisor training (see Chapter 11) should be implemented to reduce unnecessary turnover that is not related to unmet expectations.

In the Spotlight: Lutheran Social Service of Minnesota—Realistic Job Preview Scrapbooks

Lutheran Social Service of Minnesota (LSS) participated in a multiyear project to assess its workforce challenges and to design interventions to address its most pressing problems. LSS is a large multiservice organization providing services in many parts of Minnesota. The Home and Community Living Services (HCLS) division provides residential services to nearly 700 individuals with intellectual disabilities or developmental disabilities in more than 100 settings, including small group homes (most of which are funded by Medicaid's Home and Community-Based Services Waiver program), parental homes, semi-independent living settings, and small homes supporting senior citizens. In December 2003, the HCLS division employed 1,058 DSPs and 51 FLSs.

LSS designed a comprehensive RJP program to increase the chance that potential recruits would make informed decisions about whether to accept jobs offered to them. In April 2000, twenty supervisors, managers, and DSPs met for an all-day meeting. Participants learned how to develop an RJP and viewed videotape RJPs that had been developed by other organizations. Meeting participants also learned about the advantages, disadvantages, and design characteristics of various types of RJPs. Teams from each region of the state then met to develop an organization plan on how to implement RJPs in their region. After the meeting, newly hired DSPs throughout the state were surveyed to identify the key challenges facing new DSPs that should be addressed in the RJP. Initially, 11 homes agreed to participate as pilot test sites for the RJP project. An additional 6 homes heard about the project and also developed RJPs.

The pilot homes developed several different types of RJP strategies, and several homes used more than one strategy. These homes used photograph preview books (used by 12 sites), formal structured observations (2 sites), informal site visits for all new hires (10 sites), job descriptions included with all applications (11 sites), participation of a current DSP in the recruitment interviews (11 sites), a work sample test composed of a worksheet turned in by the recruit at the end of a structured observation (2 sites), interviews including individuals receiving supports (1 site), and hiring practices that incorporated the results of a parent survey (1 site).

In spring 2001, the results of the pilot test were evaluated. The RJPs yielded striking improvements in the pilot homes. In 2000, 24 new employees were hired with an RJP in pilot study homes. All of those individuals stayed in their new jobs for at least 3 months, and 91% were still employed 6 months after hire. This compares with an organizational benchmark statewide of 79% of new hires staying for 3 months and 53% staying for 6 months.

One supervisor who developed an RJP scrapbook brought it home to show to her husband. When her husband saw the book, he remarked, "In all the years you have been working in this field, I never understood what you really did. Now I get it." Other pilot study homes reported that the very act of developing the RJP scrapbooks turned out to be a great team-building exercise. It provided opportunities for the DSPs to use their creativity in a new way. One administrator who had participated in the training reported that he had been skeptical about RJPs and had decided not to use them. But after noticing the dramatic improvements in retention in other pilot study homes, he changed his mind and decided that the homes he supervised would participate after all.

On the basis of the pilot test results, the LSS management team decided to implement RJPs statewide. Information about the pilot tests and the results was shared at a meeting of all supervisors. Each site was required to use a structured interview for all hiring, a structured observation for all applicants, and at least one other form of communicating information about the job to new applicants (e.g., a photograph album, interviews involving individuals receiving supports). By the end of 2001, the vast majority of units had developed RJPs and structured interviews.

The long-range impact of this intervention has become clearer over time. Between July 2000 and December 2002, 28% of new hires who had used an RJP had left their positions, whereas 69% of new hires who had not used an RJP had left their positions. The biggest impact of the RJP was seen in the first 12 months after hire.

OVERCOMING IMPLEMENTATION BARRIERS

Although effective for reducing early turnover due to unmet expectations on the part of the new employee, RJPs require a significant amount of investment in time and money. An organization may have difficulty sustaining the energy required to create and update an RJP. In addition, there is an inherent desire not to provide potential employees with negative information about the organization or the job, especially in a low unemployment economy. It can be very difficult to help organizations understand that this "airing of dirty laundry" can have a positive impact on the organization as a whole. The reality is that new hires who quit after only a few days not only learn about this negative information but also take with them the negative baggage of not being told the truth about the job before they agreed to accept the position. Organizations that want to develop successful RJPs have to enlist the support of all affected individuals, such as the organization, division, or site leadership team; administrators; human resources professionals; board members; DSPs; and managers and supervisors. When the RJP planning team has good data, enthusiasm, and a persuasive argument, the team will be more likely to gain the support of those affected by the project and those who have to approve the project. Once the organization has decided to create an RJP, the planning team should assign the responsibility of developing the product to a small group of invested, knowledgeable, and dedicated individuals.

In developing an RJP, it is important to consider the privacy of the people who receive services. Developing an RJP should be a collaborative process in which individuals receiving supports and their family members and current staff members work together to decide what information to share and how to share it. This process probably requires educating stakeholders about how RJPs 1) can help reduce the number of people who are hired who don't work out and 2) can increase the likelihood that people who accept positions really want to be there. Certain types of RJPs, including structured observations, meetings, and photograph albums or scrapbooks, provide excellent opportunities for individuals receiving supports and/or family members to participate in the hiring process. If videotapes or photos are to be used in the RJP, individuals who are photographed or filmed or whose life details are used and/or these individuals' legal representatives or guardians should provide consent.

Structured observation RJPs include a time when the applicant spends 30 minutes to 2 hours at a service site. Obviously these visits should not happen without the permission of the people receiving supports and/or their legal representatives. Visits by strangers can be somewhat disruptive. This disruption during visits, however, can be minimized by building in guidelines and expectations for potential recruits. For example, in Career Pathmaker, a toolkit that introduces the human services industry, Taylor, Silver, Hewitt, VanGelder, and Hoff recommended the following guidelines for visitors:

1. You will meet people with disabilities who are receiving support in this service setting. Please do interact in a friendly and respectful manner with anyone you meet. Do greet people warmly—shake hands, have conversations, but don't talk to your host or others about the people receiving services who are right in front of you as if they were not there. It is normal to have questions about the service participants or staff you meet. Ask the person directly or ask your host when you are alone.
2. Do treat adult service participants as you would treat other adults, not as children just because they have a disability or other disadvantaging conditions.
3. Do treat the information you have learned or observed with respect and confidentiality—don't talk about people you have met or what you have observed in public places or to anyone other than your host. Even when discussing your observations, try to use the participant's first name only.
4. Do try to remain quiet and stay in the background when it is clear that service participants are engaged in a work, learning, or medical activity or if they are upset.
5. Do stay with your host or guide at all times. Wandering off without guidance can sometimes be disruptive in a human service setting.
6. Do use "people first" language. This means referring to people you meet by their names and not their diagnoses. For example, "Joan, the woman who uses a wheelchair," not "the paraplegic."
7. Do ask your guide questions about anything and everything that comes to mind. Just remember, do so privately. (1997, p. 33)

When considering the amount of disruption caused by a site visit, compare that with the (usually greater) disruption caused when someone is who is a poor match for the job leaves after working for an hour or a day when they find out what the work is really like. Not only will you have the disruption, but also you will have endured the significant expense of hiring and training someone who ultimately leaves. The goal of an RJP is to stem the tide, to reduce the number of people who are hired who are simply not a good match for the job.

In the Spotlight: Dungarvin Minnesota—From Technological "Dirt Road" to "Superhighway"

Part of a larger national organization, Dungarvin Minnesota is a provider of community based residential services that participated in a project to improve employee retention rates using technical assistance from the University of Minnesota's Institute on Community Integration (ICI). Dungarvin Minnesota chose to develop an RJP that would be delivered in a multimedia format over the web.

The RJP was designed to be viewed by all potential applicants, and the web format was chosen because it provided multiple options for the organization to have people view it, such as in homes, at workforce centers, at the organization, or in libraries. In addition, the web site offered a high-impact format that allowed for quick, inexpensive, and immediate updates, with no fear of outdated versions being disseminated.

The 16-page RJP (http://www.dungarvin.com/Employment/Realistic%20Job%20 Preview/RJP-page01.htm) combines text, photos, and voice clips of people receiving support and their families, DSPs, and others speaking about the aspects of the job that new DSPs should know before applying. Some of the topics described include the need to cook, clean, be on time, attend training, support people with medical needs, support people with behavior challenges, and complete job-related documentation.

Developing the web site required organizing the message and content, writing a script, identifying which software and hardware to use, and gathering media to use in the RJP. People who received services and people in direct support or other roles had to be identified so that photographs and sound clips could be created for the RJP. Permission from the individuals in the photographs and sound clips and/or their legal representatives was needed. The web site was completed nearly a year after its initiation.

A four-question survey about the potential applicant's opinion about the information presented in the RJP and how it related to his or her own attributes was combined with the web site for the following purposes: 1) to make sure the person had actually viewed and paid attention to the information, 2) to ensure there was a match between the person's personality and the qualities required by the job, and 3) to evaluate the effectiveness and message of the RJP.

The process required decisions to be made at various junctures about a host of issues such as design, technology, and content. A significant amount of resources and legwork were needed. Based on previous experience in developing marketing tools, the organization empowered a small group of knowledgeable people to make decisions regarding the RJP. This structure helped keep the project moving along; thus, we recommend it as strategy for development of RJPs.

The organization was concerned that not everyone would have web access and that the file size would create long download times for people without high-speed access. The organization itself did not have web access at every site. This problem was overcome by loading the RJP as a static site onto the hard drive of laptop computers so that the RJP could be viewed on those computers even without web access. This approach, however, introduced some of the problems found with other methods of RJPs, such as the possibility of dissemination and use of outdated versions.

Dungarvin Minnesota started using the web site RJP in 2001. Initially, 3 of 35 program directors used the RJP. They reported some difficulties because most of the candidates spoke English as a second language and were having trouble both with the language and with the technology. Some candidates took an hour to review the material. Another early struggle was that different candidates needed different amounts of time to review the material. This was causing difficulties with the timing for interviews. This challenge was overcome by implementing the RJP after the interview instead of before it.

The process of working on the RJP improved practices in other areas of hiring and orientation. The process of boiling the job down to its essentials helped administrators and supervisors of DSPs to understand that new and prospective employees needed to hear about aspects about the job that seemed obvious (e.g., showing up on time, being nice to co-workers). The organization started to recognize that administrators and supervisors should not assume that people in the workforce have the same perspective and the same understanding regarding job responsibilities.

Upon completion of the RJP project, the staff at Dungarvin Minnesota believed they had made a quick journey from technological "dirt road" to "superhighway." They also knew that the future maintenance of the web site would be a continuing adventure.

QUESTIONS TO PONDER

1. What are your organization's current recruiting practices? Do recruiters minimize or hide significant issues (challenging behaviors, limited resources, unpleasant job duties) in an effort to get new employees in the door?
2. How often do people leave before completing their first day on the job?
3. Does your organization recruit from pools of potential employees who are likely to have little information about your services and needs?
4. When developing an RJP, who can provide an accurate picture of the DSP role within your organization, to ensure that both positive and negative aspects are revealed? How can you get this information in a way the feels safe to current employees and people receiving supports?
5. What are the unique differences, issues, or circumstances that DSPs within your organization or site need to handle (e.g., specific characteristics of people supported and their families, vehicle use), and how can these be addressed in the RJP?
6. What mode or modes of delivery would you recommend for an RJP in your organization or site?
7. How will you encourage stakeholder support for an RJP? What will your board of directors, CEO, administrators, recruiters, individuals receiving supports and their families, and others think about the RJP? How can you help them understand its value and encourage their participation?

CONCLUSION

This chapter provides information about RJPs and the importance of using them. It also provides step-by-step instructions for developing an RJP. If you struggle with turnover of new employees (particularly in the first 6 months), RJPs may help reduce the number of people who leave your organization. If this is your situation, create an RJP and see whether it helps you as much as it has other organizations in similar circumstances.

RESOURCES

Creative Memories (http://www.creativememories.com/home.asp)

This company provides ideas and supplies to create innovative scrapbooks. A search engine shows the names of consultants around the world. Ideas can be used for creating RJP photograph albums or scrapbooks.

University of Minnesota, Research and Training Center on Community Living, Institute on Community Integration. (2004). *Direct support: A realistic job preview* [Customizable videotape or DVD]. Minneapolis: Author. (Available from the author, 612-625-1566; http://rtc.umn .edu/wddsp/tools.html)

This videotape or DVD illustrates the real, everyday work of DSPs in vocational and residential settings supporting individuals with intellectual or developmental disabilities. It provides first-person stories and advice for people considering direct support as a career choice. Topics include what to expect on the job, the rewards and challenges of direct support, qualities of great DSPs, and lessons learned by DSPs.

Your Responses to the Realistic Job Preview

After reviewing the Realistic Job Preview (RJP), we would like to understand your impressions of direct support work and this organization. You will be asked to respond to the following questions regarding the RJP before scheduling an appointment for an interview. (You may want to use the space provided to make notes.)

Based on the RJP, what do you think will be some of the biggest challenges of direct support work

for you? _____

_____

_____

_____

Based on the RJP, what parts of the job do you think you will enjoy the most?_____

_____

_____

_____

What attributes do you have that you think will make you good at direct support work?

_____

_____

_____

Based on the RJP and other information about our organization, what about working for this organi-

zation appeals to you? _____

_____

_____

_____

Adapted from questions developed by the University of Minnesota, Institute on Community Integration, for use with Dungarvin Minnesota's multimedia, web-based RJP (http://www.dungarvin.com/Employment/Realistic%20Job%20Preview/RJP-page01.htm).

Staff Recruitment, Retention, and Training Strategies for Community Human Services Organizations by Sheryl A. Larson & Amy S. Hewitt.

Realistic Job Preview Evaluation

Organization: _____   Type of RJP:_____

Each member of the realistic job preview (RJP) development team should complete this form. Rate each item from A (*excellent*) to F (*very poor*), and list any additional comments that you may have. Scores should be discussed as a team, with the goal of identifying any changes or modifications that should be made to the RJP.

Key criteria	Quick report: A (*excellent*) to F (*very poor*)
1. The RJP makes the *purpose clear* to the applicant (to help people decide whether to take a job if offered). *Comments:*	
2. The RJP provides *credible information* about actual work life (e.g., preparing meals, participating in staff meetings, shopping with individuals receiving supports). *Comments:*	
3. The RJP includes specific *thoughts and feelings of current employees* about the job. *Comments:*	
4. The RJP balances *positive/fun and difficult/unpleasant tasks* to reflect actual experiences (e.g., participating in a 5K run with an individual receiving support, assisting with personal care). *Comments:*	
5. The RJP highlights a *variety of job features* to show the depth and breadth of the work (e.g., salary and benefits, co-worker characteristics, staff training opportunities). *Comments:*	

From O'Nell, S., Hewitt, A., Sauer, J., & Larson, S. (2001). *Removing the revolving door: Strategies to address recruitment and retention challenges* (p. 87 of learner guide). Minneapolis: University of Minnesota, Institute on Community Integration, Research and Training Center on Community Living; adapted by permission.

Structured Observation Worksheet

We would like to give you an idea of the kind of work that goes on in our organization. You will be observing individuals supported and direct support professionals (DSPs) in action. Before your visit, read through the following guiding questions. After your visit, note your observations.

- What are the various job activities that DSPs do?
- What are the personal characteristics of the staff members that make them appear to be good at their job?
- What was the atmosphere of the home/site when you arrived? (e.g., welcoming, clean, institution-like or home-like)
- What kinds of things do the people you observed seem to like?
- What kinds of assistance do the people you observed need or receive?
- Who prepared the meals? Who cleaned up afterward?
- What chores did you observe the staff members doing?
- Did you see anyone hurting him- or herself or someone else or breaking something? If so, describe the event and how the situation was handled.
- How did staff members figure out what a person wanted to eat or to do? Were choices offered?

Questions to ask of the staff members at the home or site of your visit:
- What do you like best about your job?
- What is the most fun part of this job?
- What is the most difficult part of your job?
- What is your least preferred job task?
- What kinds of supervision do you receive?
- What is your regular shift? How are holidays scheduled? What happens if a staff member calls in sick or is on vacation? What are the overtime policies here?

Questions to ask of the people receiving supports whom you observe:
- What do you like to do for fun?
- Who do you like to spend time with?

After your visit take a few minutes to answer the following questions:

In thinking about the conversations and observations of DSPs and activities during this visit, I am

excited about the following: _____

_____

_____

Some things that bothered me about what I observed or heard include the following:

_____

_____

I am confused about the following: _____

_____

_____

I would like to know more about the following: _____

_____

_____

Adapted by permission from Taylor, M., Silver, J., Hewitt, A., VanGelder, M., & Hoff, D. (1997). *Career pathmaker: A toolkit for entering careers in human services and health care.* Cambridge, MA: Human Services Research Institute; and from an internal RJP handbook developed by Lutheran Social Service of Minnesota.

4

SELECTION STRATEGIES
SHERYL A. LARSON AND AMY S. HEWITT

"When you hire people that are smarter than you are,
you prove you are smarter than they are." R.H. Grant

Taking the time to select the best candidates for a job is useful in reducing turnover. When organizations have great difficulty finding applicants, however, they may be tempted to hire anyone who is willing to take the job. This phenomenon is sometimes called the "warm body syndrome" and can have the negative effect of lowering expectations of employees, creating a perception that anything goes among current employees, and lowering the image and status of direct support professionals (DSPs). Hiring just anyone for an open position also exacerbates turnover problems in the long run because a person who is a poor match for the job is more likely to quit or be fired due to performance or attendance problems. The term *selection* as used in this chapter refers specifically to the process of selecting from among all qualified applicants the person who will most likely best meet the needs of the organization for a specific position.

Many techniques are available to assist an organization in this process. This chapter reviews several of these techniques, with a special emphasis on structured interviews.

TARGETED FRONT-LINE SUPERVISOR COMPETENCIES

Competent front-line supervisors (FLSs) use several personnel management skills in the selection process. Key competencies include the following.

Primary Skills

FLSs schedule and complete interviews with potential new staff in collaboration with existing DSPs and supported individuals and their family members.

FLSs seek input from other staff and from individuals receiving support and their family members in making hiring decisions.

FLSs arrange for criminal background checks and (if driving is an essential job function of the position) driver's license reviews for newly hired personnel.

FLSs assess potential staff's functional ability and capacity; ensure that health physicals are completed (if required); and address any identified modifications or accommodations for employees, as dictated by the Americans with Disabilities Act (ADA) of 1990 (PL 101-336).

FLSs can articulate the difference between recruitment and selection and the importance of both.

UNDERSTANDING THE PROBLEM

The hiring process is often one of the most time-consuming parts of a supervisor's job. With a turnover rate of 50%, for example, an FLS would need to hire an average of one new person for every two positions during the course of a year. In addition to having to replace employees who leave their jobs, supervisors also have to hire individuals to meet increased needs or service expansion opportunities and to fill any vacancies remaining from previous years. Because employees are the most important resource in a human services organization, the hiring decisions that are made have a large impact on the quality of the services that are delivered. The challenge for supervisors and managers in the selection process is to select the person from among all of the possible candidates who is the best match for the job, the people he or she will be supporting, and the organization. Valid and reliable selection practices can help organizations to reduce turnover and improve performance (Thomas & Brull, 1993).

There are also several other reasons to use good selection practices. Management journals and newsletters often publish stories about large lawsuits against organizations that hire individuals who later hurt someone (e.g., Greengard, 1995). Avoidance of legal problems caused by negligent hiring, supervision, and promotion and lack of due diligence are cited as key reasons to screen applicants carefully before making a hiring decision.

RESEARCH SUPPORT FOR SOLUTIONS

The career management and consulting firm Drake Beam Morin estimated that according to research, nearly 80% of turnover is due to hiring mistakes ("How to Increase Retention," 1998). Thus, if better selection and hiring practices were used, many problems related to turnover could be reduced. A well-designed selection process ensures that, to the extent possible, the candidates who are hired are able to do the job and are good matches for the organization's culture. Such a process is a powerful tool for FLSs and human resources managers.

Many selection strategies and tools are available. They vary both in terms of how effective they are and how difficult, complex, or time consuming they are to use. One challenge for supervisors is to balance the speed and simplicity of the hiring process (so that good applicants do not choose another job while waiting for a job offer) with the use of strategies that are good indicators of whether an applicant will do a good job.

The research about selection is expansive and complex. Many studies focus on the extent to which various selection strategies are valid. Validity is a measure of the extent to which scores on the selection measure correspond with overall performance or tenure of employees. Validity coefficients range from 0 to 1.0. A coefficient of 0 means that scores on the selection measure do not have any correspondence to job performance or tenure (meaning that the selection measure is no better at choosing applicants than a random drawing of applicants' names from a hat would be). A coefficient of 1.0 means there is a perfect correspondence between 1) the strategy and 2) job performance or tenure. As a point of reference, the correspondence between age and grade in school for children is .88. This chapter points out highlights of the research on the validity of selection strategies that can be used to guide hiring practices in community human services settings.

Several comprehensive reviews discuss the relative merits of various selection strategies. Hermelin and Robertson (2001) reviewed nine different meta-analyses that examined many different studies of the validity of selection strategies (see Table 4.1). Hermelin and Robertson classified each of the strategies as having high (.45 or higher), medium (.25 to .45) or low (0 to .25) validity. Higher predictive validity scores mean that there is a higher correspondence between high scores and excellent performance and between low scores and poor performance. Using strategies with high predictive validity increases the chances of selecting candidates who will be good performers and rejecting candidates who will be poor performers. Table 4.1 describes each strategy, lists the validity category for each, and lists the range of validity coefficients from the studies reviewed.

The findings reported in Table 4.1 are supported by several other studies. Buckley and Russell (1999) reported meta-analysis results showing that the predictive validity of structured interviews was .57, compared with .30 to .40 for cognitive ability tests, biographical data inventories, and assessment centers and .20 for unstructured interviews. Another study reported that structured interviews were more effective than assessments of cognitive ability and conscientiousness (Cortina, Goldstein, Payne, Davison, & Gilliland, 2000). Clearly, structured interviews are one of the most effective, if not the most effective, selection strategies available.

Interestingly, one study found that although cognitive tests were used by 27% of service companies with more than 200 employees and that weighted application blanks (in which responses meeting certain criteria are given particular numeric scores) were used by 23% of such companies, structured interviews were used by only 18% of those companies (Terpstra & Rozell, 1993). When used, however, these selection strategies were significantly correlated with annual profit, profit growth, sales growth, and overall company performance. An on-line survey of businesses revealed that the five most commonly used selection methods are standard applications with verifiable information such as education and experience, reference checks, behavior-based interviewing, manual résumé screening, and situational interviews (Burton & Warner, 2001).

An important consideration in designing selection practices is whether a technique results in illegal discrimination against protected groups of people. Illegal discrimination occurs when people are unfairly turned down for employment or are treated less favorably or more favorably during the hiring process based on age; race; ethnicity; gender; disability status; religion; sexual orientation; or other characteristics

Table 4.1. Comparison of the validity of common selection strategies

Strategy	Basic description	Effectiveness (predictive validity)
Structured interviews	Structured interviews use the same questions for every applicant and score responses using a standardized scoring guide. Two major types are structured behavioral interviews and situational interviews. Both are based on a job analysis and assess skills critical to successful job performance.	High (.48 to .67)
Cognitive ability tests	Standardized tests assess the intelligence or cognitive ability of the candidates. Candidates whose scores most closely match those of successful employees are given preference in hiring.	High overall (.44 to .47) High for very complex jobs (.60) Low for the least complex jobs (.24)
Biographical data (weighted application blanks)	Past work history, education, honors and awards, extracurricular and community service activities, and other social or life experiences are scored, with points awarded for experiences or activities that predict future employment success.	Medium (.36)
Personality and integrity tests	Personality tests assess the personality attributes of candidates. Integrity tests assess attitudes toward counterproductive behaviors or aspects of personality believed to be related to counterproductive behaviors (Hermelin & Robertson, 2001).	Medium (.31 to .37)
Work sample tests or assessment centers	Work sample tests examine an applicant's skill on a work-related task through direct assessment (e.g., a typing test for a clerical applicant). Assessment centers are a behaviorally based managerial selection procedure that incorporates multiple assessments and multiple ratings by trained managers of behaviors related to the job (e.g., in-basket, leaderless group discussion, business games; Cascio, 1987)	Low to medium (.24 to .43)
Unstructured interviews	Unstructured interviews have no constraints on the questions asked and result in only a global assessment of the candidate (Buckley & Russell, 1999)	Low to medium (.23 to .37)
The "big five" personality traits	Tests examining the "big five" personality traits: conscientiousness, emotional stability, extraversion, agreeableness, and openness to experiences. (Of these traits, conscientiousness had the highest predictive validity, .10 to .15)	Low (.00 to .15)

Sources: Nine meta-analyses that included 20 estimates of validity (Hermelin & Robertson, 2001).

that federal, state, or local laws say cannot be the basis for hiring decisions (Roehling, Campion, & Arvey, 1999). Failure to make reasonable accommodations for disabilities (under the ADA) or for religious beliefs and practices can also be the basis for a discrimination charge. Careful review of federal, state, and local laws and consultation with human resources professionals and legal advisors are important to protect against engaging in these illegal practices. Organizational personnel who are involved in recruitment and selection processes should receive training to ensure compliance with relevant established laws.

STRATEGIES FOR RESPONDING TO THE PROBLEM

The hiring process is complex and involves several phases. Before applicants are selected the process involves 1) identifying the knowledge, skills, and attitudes (KSAs) required of people who will accomplish the work (job analysis, see Chapter 6); 2) describing the working conditions, pay, opportunities for promotion, and job training that will be provided; 3) crafting a job description for the specific position to be filled; 4) marketing specific positions to potential applicants (see Chapter 2); and 5) helping applicants make an informed decision about whether a particular position is of interest to them (e.g., through a realistic job preview [RJP; see Chapter 3]). Once these steps are completed and the organization has one or more applicants for a position, the selection process begins. As mentioned previously, *selection* is the process of deciding which applicant best meets the needs of the organization. The selection process includes initial screening of applicants, choosing and implementing one or more techniques to gather additional information about applicants, and using this information to make a final hiring decision.

Given its needs, the organization should decide which strategies make the most sense. Mornell (1998) suggested that each organization or hiring unit develop a flowchart describing its selection process. Figure 4.1 presents one possible example. The remainder of this chapter describes the various steps listed in Figure 4.1, with the exception of RJPs, which are covered in Chapter 3.

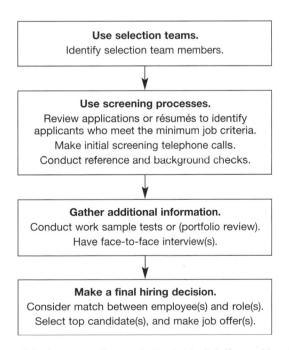

Figure 4.1. Selection process (from application to job offer). (*Source:* Mornell, 1998.)

Use Selection Teams

The selection process can be conducted by one person or by a team of people in conjunction with human resources specialists. Since differences in interview skills and experience can affect success in choosing applicants who will do a good job, pairing skilled interviewers with inexperienced or less skilled interviewers can help to reduce the number of hiring mistakes made (Dipboye & Jackson, 1999; Graves & Karren, 1999). Using a panel or at least a pair of interviewers can also help interviewers reduce or eliminate irrelevant inferences about the candidate that are not job related, eliminate idiosyncratic biases among interviewers, and increase the range of information and judgments on which decisions are based (Tullar & Kaiser, 1999). Selection teams may be involved in only one phase of the selection process (e.g., the structured interview) or may participate from beginning to end. Teams can include two or more supervisors or administrators but also could include DSPs and/or individuals receiving supports and/or their families.

Including DSPs in the selection process can empower them and can lead to greater acceptance of hiring decisions by others (Harris & Eder, 1999). Also, including individuals receiving supports and/or their families in the selection process is important because they have key information about which candidate might be the best fit for supporting their needs. Individuals who receive in-home supports may have strong preferences about the characteristics of people who will provide those supports. Similarly, individuals who receive supports may have specific needs and interests that they would like to address in the selection process. For example, a person with Tourette syndrome whose tics are offensive to some people may want to ask candidates about their responses to tics (or may want see how candidates react if a tic occurs during an interview). People receiving supports and their family members can also be helpful in deciding whether the applicants have the right attitude for the job. They may place a different priority on factors such as having a positive attitude, being flexible, having a sense of humor, or envisioning what is possible than others on the hiring team do. When people receiving supports and their families are excluded from the selection process, they may not get along with the person selected or may not be confident about the person's abilities. This may in turn cause conflicts that increase stress and burnout for staff members.

Use Screening Processes

Application or Résumé Reviews

Before reviewing applications or résumés, the selection team should have a clear idea of the minimum job requirements. Team members can list key minimum skills or characteristics a person must have to perform the essential job functions (e.g., is at least 18 years old; reads and writes English proficiently enough that required documentation can be completed; is willing to submit to criminal background check if required by organization or state; has a driver's license, if driving supported individuals is a DSP job requirement at the organization). The selection team should discard applicants who do not meet the minimum job requirements. The team should also eliminate applicants who have had many different jobs in a short period of time. Previous job behavior is a good predictor of future behavior. A person who has moved from job to job quickly (in a period of months rather than years) in the past is more likely to do so in the future than a person who has stayed with each job for at least a year before moving to the next one. Other characteristics of good performers (e.g., is a team player; respects others; manages time well; demonstrates compassion, empathy, commitment, and cooperation; communicates clearly and listens closely) should be assessed throughout the hiring process.

Screening Interviews

Screening can be done when a person asks for an application. It can also be done after applications have been received, to assist in deciding which candidates to interview. Screening often takes the form of a brief telephone call designed to help the organization find out if the prospective employee meets the minimum job qualifications. Screening activities can include basic RJP information such as pay scale and benefits, general responsibilities and requirements of the job, and hours or locations of the job. The screening process should be consistent for each applicant. Using a checklist and specific set of questions can help in maintaining consistency. Questions that may be helpful in a screening telephone call include the following:

- What experience do you have supporting people with disabilities?
- What is your understanding of the broad responsibilities of a DSP?
- How did you hear about this job?

In addition to general questions like these, this telephone call can be used to confirm or clarify information on the application and whether the applicant is willing and able to work the hours and days the position requires. The organization should come to consensus about what information should be gathered from applicants and shared with applicants at this point. Screening can quickly eliminate people who are not eligible for employment; applicants who are completely unfamiliar with the type of work and, upon learning basic information about the job, decide it is not a good match for them; and applicants whom the organization deems are not a good match for the job because of the location, hours, or other characteristics of the position. A screening telephone call can be used to assess, among other things, how easy it is to reach the candidate, whether the candidate returns the call at the time suggested, and whether the person is an articulate communicator (Mornell, 1998). The advantage of using screening calls is that they can save time by reducing the number of applicants who are interviewed face to face and permit RJP information to be streamlined. Screening may seem like an extra step, but it can greatly reduce the number of no-shows to the interview.

At the end of the screening, one of three decisions is made. Either the applicant is not qualified for the job (in which case a staff member thanks the applicant for his or her time and indicates that the organization does not intend to invite the applicant for an interview), the organization is not sure (in which case a staff member may tell the applicant that it is uncertain whether he or she will be included in the interview and asks for additional information needed), or the applicant is a viable candidate

(Yate, 1994). For applicants who are qualified to continue the application process, Yate suggested communicating the following ground rules for future contacts:

- We expect all interview appointments to be kept punctually.
- We expect to be informed if for any reason the applicant cannot make a meeting.
- We expect application forms to be filled out accurately and completely.
- We intend to check references and conduct all required background checks.
- We will treat any and all information shared with us as confidential.

Using ground rules helps set expectations. Observing whether candidates comply with the expectations can help assess whether the candidates will follow guidelines such as these should they be hired. Adhering to these guidelines can help the organization to avoid making exceptions that lower the organization's expectations of new hires.

Reference Checks

Reference checks involve contacting former employers, academic institutions, and others mentioned on the application or résumé to confirm the accuracy of the information provided and to assess the fitness of the applicant for the position. Reference checks and recommendations can be used to obtain four types of information about applicants: 1) education and employment history (e.g., confirmation of degrees, diplomas, and dates of employment); 2) evaluation of the applicant's character, personality, and interpersonal competence; 3) evaluation of the applicant's past job performance; and 4) whether the person is eligible to be rehired by the organization (Cascio, 1987). Rosen (2001) suggested that before reference checks are conducted, the organization could ask the applicant, "When we contact past employers, pursuant to the release you have signed, would any of them tell us you were terminated, disciplined, or not eligible for rehire?" It may also be helpful to ask the applicant what positive and negative comments a reference might make about him or her (Mornell, 1998).

Potential questions to ask when conducting a telephone reference check include the following (Curzon, 1995; Deems, 1994; Mornell, 1998):

1. *Background:* In what capacity and for how long did you know the applicant? What was his or her specific work assignment? What were the circumstances surrounding his or her leaving?
2. *Technical competence:* Is the applicant competent in communicating with and supporting individuals whom our organization supports? How would you rate his or her overall performance, work habits, problem-solving skills, and ability to work independently? Did this person follow through on assignments? What are the applicant's strengths? What is one skill this person needs to work on?
3. *People skills:* How well does the applicant get along with peers, supervisors, interdisciplinary team members, and individuals supported and their family members?
4. *Motivation:* What motivates this person to do a good job?
5. *Other:* Is there anything I have not asked that I should know about?

Using this as a guide, the organization can develop its own list of questions to use when checking references.

It is important to understand the legal and ethical considerations regarding reference checks. An article on ethical hiring practices suggested the following practices, among others, for conducting reference and other background checks:

- Do not get information without first getting [the] applicant's consent.
- Allow applicants to name sources they do not want contacted and to explain why not.
- Put requests for information from references in writing.
- Tell information sources (e.g., former employers) that all information sought will be made available to applicants.
- Never ask references for opinions (e.g., ask the factual basis for applicants leaving their former employment, not whether their former employers would ever rehire them).
- Verify information given by [references] whenever possible.
- Assess all applicants for the same job or kind of work [in] the same way (Brumback, 1996, pp. 275–276).

One challenge in conducting reference checks is that some people are reluctant or are not permitted by their company's policy to answer questions due to potential legal liability. One strategy that may be helpful is to call the list of people given as references at times they are unlikely to be near their telephone (e.g., at lunchtime, very early in the day). Leave a phone number and a message that says "X person is a candidate for such-and-such position at our company. Your name was given as a reference. Please call me back at your convenience." Most people will return your call if the person is an excellent or outstanding applicant but will not call back if they have significant reservations about the person (Mornell, 1998). It may also be important to check references that are not job related. For example, a person who knows the candidate from volunteer work may have observed the person completing tasks or working on a project.

Biographical Data Verification

Biographical data can be reviewed in several ways. Among the simplest is a verification of the data on the application form or résumé provided by the applicant. Checking information about education, employment, and other job qualifications provides a check of the integrity of the applicant and confirms that the person meets the minimum qualifications for employment (e.g., high school diploma or GED; valid driver's license, if driving supported individuals is a DSP job requirement at the organization). Weighted application blanks can help improve the accuracy of the selection process. These score work history, education, community service activities, and other data based on how well those activities predict performance or tenure.

Background Checks

Many but not all states require applicants for human services jobs to submit to a criminal background study as a condition of employment. People with criminal convictions for certain offenses (e.g., murder, rape, felony assault) are typically disqualified from employment in human services organizations. Some states maintain registries of people who are disqualified from employment due to past abuse or neglect. Other background checks may include a driver's license check (if driving is an essential job function) or a verification of professional licensure (e.g., for a certified nursing assistant). In most cases these checks are pass/fail and determine whether a candidate is eligible for employment. Even in states where background studies are not required, organizations may want to consider them for individuals who will be working with people who are vulnerable to physical, emotional, or financial exploitation. Many tools are available for this purpose. For example, a Social Security trace can verify previous addresses, and a motor vehicle records check shows any violations, convictions, and restrictions for a candidate applying for a job that requires use of a motor vehicle. A credit history review when hiring FLSs and others who manage finances for the organization can show how individuals have handled money and whether they have any judgments or liens against them (Greengard, 1995). Since credit reports often contain errors, an organization using credit reports should give the candidate an opportunity to explain any adverse information before using it to make an employment decision (Mornell, 1998). Whether conducting state-required criminal background or certification checks, reviewing educational transcripts, or checking employment history, the organization should be clear with applicants that a background check will be conducted and should obtain written consent when required (an organization's human resources department or an attorney can provide details). A statement to this effect should be posted on the organization's web site, on job application forms, and in classified ads.

Gather Additional Information

Once applicants have been screened so that the pool includes only those who meet the minimum qualifications for the job, the next step is to gather more in-depth information about the remaining applicants. By doing so, the organization can identify the applicant who best matches the job and the organization. The selection of interview questions or topics for investigation should include at least the following steps (Harris & Eder, 1999):

- Using the job analysis results (described in Chapter 6), identify the most important tasks to be performed in the job (consider the relative frequency of the task, the impact of an error, and the significance to the organization).
- List the knowledge, skills, and attitudes (KSAs) and other requirements (e.g., licensure) necessary for successful performance.
- List work requirements, such as attendance rules and policies on overtime and holiday work, that are important for success in the job.
- List the major motivators for employees in the role (including intrinsic motivators related to the nature of the task and extrinsic rewards offered by the organization) that may match applicant preferences or that may be unique to the organization.
- Identify the top four or five unique values that are held by the organization or that are present in the work environment that can be compared with applicant preferences and values.

The purposes of this phase of the selection process include assessing personal qualities, organizational fit, job competence, and values (Bartram, Lindley, Marshall, & Foster, 1995).

Work Sample Tests

Work sample tests provide an applicant with an opportunity to demonstrate his or her skills in job-related tasks before hire. Using such tests provide at least two advantages to an employer. First, the tests offer an opportunity to observe applicants doing tasks that are required on the job. Applicants who score well on such tests may be more likely to perform well on the job after hire (e.g., Cascio, 1987). Second, work sample tests provide applicants an opportunity to experience a bit of the job before hire. In a sense, a work sample test functions as an RJP (see Chapter 3). One of the more helpful work sample tests for DSPs may be conducted simultaneously with an RJP. Such tests might assess applicants' skill in observing and communicating with individuals who have disabilities and their skill in documenting observations. Setting up a work sample test for these two skills involves two parts. First, an applicant participates in an RJP or an interview that involves interacting with an individual supported in the potential job setting. This interaction could be participating in a meal, viewing an RJP photograph album or scrapbook, or asking or answering questions during an interview with a person with a disability. The following skills could be assessed through such an activity:

- Use of effective, sensitive communication skills to build rapport and open channels of communication by recognizing and adapting to individual communication styles
- Use of augmentative and alternative communication devices to interact with individuals
- Interaction with and support of individuals using active listening skills, acknowledgment of individuals' ideas and concerns, and responding in an appropriate and respectful manner
- Communication in a manner that is culturally sensitive and appropriate

These skills are drawn from the residential DSP competencies identified by Hewitt (1998b).

Another part of the work sample test paired with an RJP involves asking the applicant to complete a structured observation worksheet (see Chapter 3) to describe his or her observations during an RJP. The applicant is asked to turn in the worksheet for evaluation. The following competencies could be assessed (Hewitt, 1998b):

- Reading and completion of daily logging, program charting, and health care notes as needed, using approved abbreviations and objective language
- Maintenance of standards of confidentiality and ethical practice in documentation and communications (e.g., free of bias or judgment)

This part of the combined work sample test and RJP could also be used to assess whether the applicant has adequate written English skills to successfully complete his or her job duties. This particular work sample test brings with it the added benefit of providing a tool to help the supervisor and the applicant discuss any questions or concerns about the job or the applicant's observations. See the end of Chapter 3 for examples of questions to use in a structured observation.

Another type of work sample test, portfolios, is becoming more common as postsecondary education opportunities for DSPs expand. Portfolios are samples of a candidate's work in various competency areas. Portfolios are being used in some states to credential DSPs or to provide access to wage increments. Because portfolios involve a significant amount of work, they are most commonly developed for courses that offer postsecondary or continuing education credits. Although most applicants for DSP positions today do not have a portfolio, it is good practice for organizations to begin asking for portfolios or work samples that could be included in portfolios to encourage the use of portfolios during selection and hiring. For example, a DSP who will be responsible for writing skill development or behavior change interventions may be asked to provide a sample of a program that he or she has previously developed, with an example of how progress was documented.

For any work sample test, the scoring criteria should be determined before the test, and the same criteria should be used for each applicant. Those criteria should be based on the standards used by the organization to differentiate between excellent and poor performance for current employees. A good way to evaluate the test before implementing it for new hires is to try it on yourself and a few excellent performers to ensure that it measures what you think it does (Mornell, 1998).

Structured Interviews

Structured interviewing ensures that the information gathered during the interview yields accurate information about the skills a person has related to the job tasks of the position for which they are interviewing. Elements of structure include asking all applicants the same job-related questions and establishing clear criteria for evaluating responses to the questions (Gilliland & Steiner, 1999). Effective structured interviews pose questions that relate to job requirements as measured by a critical incident job analysis (see Janz, Hellervik, & Gilmore, 1986, for specific instructions on how to use this type of job analysis). Briefly, critical incident job analysis involves collecting examples of both excellent and poor job performance. For example, top-performing DSPs and FLSs may be asked to describe the best and worst examples of DSPs' responses to a certain crisis. Details about what excellent and poor performers did in the situation are gathered until patterns of behavior common to excellent and poor performance in this situation can be discerned. Those patterns form the basis for assessing responses to the structured interview questions. Structured interviews use a behaviorally anchored scoring guide (which gives specific examples of answers that qualify for a particular score) to evaluate the answer to each question in terms of what constitutes an excellent, an acceptable, or an unacceptable answer in a particular organizational setting (Maurer, Sue-Chan, & Latham, 1999).

Developing Questions

Several formats can be used in structured interviewing. The two most common forms are the behavior description interview and the situational interview. Behavior description interviews are based on the premise that the best predictor of future behavior is past behavior in similar circumstances (Janz et al., 1986). Past behavior that occurred recently or that is part of a longstanding pattern of behavior have greater predictive power than behavior that is less recent or that occurred only once. Behavior description questions ask candidates to describe situations they faced, what the candidates did, and what happened as a result. The most effective behavior description questions ask about greatest extent or degree of a situation or job feature using terms such as *most/least*, *best/worst*, or *hardest/easiest* (Janz et al., 1986). Effective questions may also ask about the first or last time something happened or about a person's most significant accomplishments (Brull, 1996).

Situational interviews are based on goal-setting theory, which suggests that intentions are related to actual behavior. They are developed from critical incidents identified in job analyses and ask future-oriented, hypothetical questions (Gilliland & Steiner, 1999). A key characteristic of situational interviews is that they pose situational dilemmas in which the applicant is forced to choose between two or more equally desirable or undesirable courses of action (Maurer et al., 1999). The consistency of interview scores across raters can be increased if questions are based on a job analysis and are closely related to the job, if answers are rated on a question-by-question basis, if the interviewer takes notes during the interview, if an interview panel rather than a single rater is used to evaluate candidate responses, and if a scoring guide for each question is used (Janz et al., 1986; Maurer et al., 1999).

There remains a fair amount of debate about whether questions about past behavior or questions about future intentions are the most valid and best type of questions to use in an interview (Motowidlo, 1999). Studies have found empirical and theoretical support for both types of questions. It is possible that interviews using either type of question can help identify the best candidates if the questions are based on a job analysis; if all candidates are asked the same set of questions; and if responses are scored with behaviorally anchored scoring guides, and, preferably, are used in panel rather than one-to-one interviews. At the end of this chapter is a set of behavior-based questions based on the DSP competencies in the *Community Support Skill Standards* (CSSS; Taylor, Bradley, & Warren, 1996; see also Chapter 6). Table 4.2 shows an example of a structured behavioral interview question, with scoring criteria to assess responses.

Since structured interview questions are based on critical situations that distinguish the behavior of excellent and poor performers, the process of developing a structured interview must include a means to identify critical incidents that define excellent and poor behavior. Fortunately, the CSSS (Taylor et al., 1996) and *The Minnesota Frontline Supervisor Competencies and Performance Indicators* (Hewitt, Larson, O'Nell, Sauer, & Sedlezky, 1998; see also the Introduction and Chapter 1) outline key areas in which competent performance is required. Those standards can be used to identify critical incidents by topical area. Developing a scoring guide for behavioral questions involves convening a meeting of experienced and high-performing experts within the

Table 4.2. Sample structured behavioral interview question and scoring guidelines

Content	
Competency area	Community Living Skills and Supports: Household Management
Competency statement	Direct support professionals (DSPs) assist individuals in completing household routines (e.g., cleaning, laundry, pet care) and are respectful of individuals' rights and ownership of their home.
Interview question	Describe the household chore or duty you like least. How do you ensure that the chore or duty is completed?
Probe questions	How often is that task completed? Who actually does the task? If someone other than you does the task, describe how you communicate with that person about the task.
Scoring examples	
Excellent (5 points)	I negotiate with my roommate or spouse to do a task they strongly dislike in exchange for them helping me with or completing the task I strongly dislike doing. This way the task is completed when needed and is done well.
	I do it right away to get it out of the way before I do more preferred tasks.
Average (3 points)	I do the task as infrequently as possible.
	I hire someone else to do the task for me.
Poor (1 point)	I yell at my kids, my spouse, or my roommate until they complete the task.
	I just don't do it.

organization (both DSPs and FLSs or managers) to reach consensus about excellent (5), average (3), and poor (1) answers to each question (Maurer et al., 1999). This can be as simple as asking experts to think of the best, the average, and the poorest performers they have observed in that situation and to report what those performers did. At the end of an interview, applicants' total scores are used for ranking purposes.

Before interviewing candidates, it may be also helpful to prepare a single-page chart listing 10 most critical job skills and qualifications on which each candidate will be scored. Some skills and qualifications will be scored based on a single interview question; others will be based on an overall assessment of the applicant's performance during the interview or application process (e.g., verbal communication skills), on information provided by references, or on background materials or work samples provided by the applicant (e.g., writing skills). This chart of key job skills can be used to easily compare applicants.

Structured interviews may also include factual questions regarding a person's work history or education or questions to clarify information gathered through other selection strategies. These questions can help to verify information, clarify questions that arose during application review and reference checking, address omissions in the application, and assist the organization in making a final decision about the candidate who is the best match for the job (Harris & Eder, 1999). Common types of such questions and their purposes are listed in Table 4.3.

In evaluating the responses to these additional questions, the organization should consider the following factors (Bruce & Moore, 1989):

- Does the information provided in the interview match or conflict with data on the application or from other sources?
- Did the candidate show discomfort in discussing certain facets of his or her background?
- Did the candidate provide vague or general answers that do not document accomplishments or otherwise answer the question?

The interviewers may want to note whether the applicant was on time and prepared for the interview. This factor, along with responses to structured interview questions about showing up for work on time, can be used to predict whether promptness is likely to be a problem if the person is hired.

Conducting and Scoring the Interview

When the interview is conducted, several prompts can be helpful in eliciting more complete information from applicants who do not elaborate sufficiently for the interviewers to assess their skill in the area. Common types of prompts include the following (Maddux, 1994):

- Clarifying questions (e.g., "What do you mean by . . . . ?")
- Seeking new information to build on a previous statement (e.g., "Could you tell me more about . . . . ?")
- Repeating a question that was asked but not answered
- Clarifying what has been said that seems to be inconsistent
- Summarizing key ideas

Table 4.3. Factual and other examples of various types of interview questions and their advantages and disadvantages

Experience and activity descriptions

Purpose: Putting candidate at ease, providing overview of past experience, and setting stage for other questions

Advantages

  These descriptions are easy for the person to provide.

  They establish rapport.

  They give a shy applicant an opportunity to warm up to the interview.

Disadvantages

  These descriptions put candidates with no previous relevant experience at a disadvantage.

  The descriptions may falsely imply that if a candidate has done a task before, he or she can perform it well.

Examples

  "Please describe your primary duties in your last job."[a]

  "Describe the most important responsibilities you had in your last position."[a]

  "What do you typically do when you have a difference of opinion with your boss?"

  "Describe a typical day in your most recent position."

Technical knowledge questions

Purpose. Testing an applicant's knowledge

Advantages

  Technical knowledge questions can provide direct information about whether the applicant has the knowledge, skills, and attitudes (KSAs) needed in the position.

Disadvantages

  It is difficult to construct questions that are valid (that measure what you think they measure) and reliable (that yield the same result when asked on different occasions or under different circumstances).

  Tests using these questions can raise employment law issues if the tests unfairly discriminate based on protected characteristics not related to actual performance of the job (e.g., age, race, gender, disability).

  Some candidates are intimidated by these types of questions or do not test well but are actually good employees.

Consideration

  It is difficult to craft questions with the right degree of relevancy and difficulty.

Examples

  "Please give an example of positive reinforcement."

  "Describe the most complex work task you have used a computer to complete."

Questions about biographical facts, credentials, and achievements

Purpose: Obtaining information about a person's education, employment history, and past achievements that is verifiable using other sources

Advantages

  Biographical questions are usually easy for the applicant to answer.

  They help establish the applicants' past experience and achievements.

Disadvantages

  These questions require verification as some applicants lie or exaggerate their credentials.

  These questions may falsely imply that people with certain education or achievements will be better employees.

Examples

  "What licenses or certificates do you hold in this state?"

  "What special recognition have you received?"[a]

  "What postsecondary degrees have you earned?"

  "Describe the most recent job you had that is related to this position."

(continued)

Table 4.3.   *(continued)*

Self-evaluation opinion questions

Purpose: Asking what the applicant thinks about a topic

Advantages

   Self-evaluation questions reveal areas for probing.

   The questions provide information the applicant thinks is important.

Disadvantages

   These questions invite the applicant to say what he or she thinks you want to hear.

   They make a candidate who thinks quickly and speaks fluently seem very competent.

   The questions do not provide any evidence about what the candidate has done.

   These kinds of questions may falsely imply that if a candidate likes a task, he or she can perform it.

Types of questions[a]

   Likes and dislikes

   Strengths and weaknesses

   Statements of goals, attitudes, and philosophies

   Hypothetical or speculative statements

Examples

   "What did you like best about your last job?"[a]

   "What are your biggest weaknesses?"

   "Why did you apply for this job?"

   [a]*Source:* Janz, Hellervik, & Gilmore, 1986.

Negative balance questions can be helpful when the applicant seems too good to be true or gives few or no examples of struggles. The interviewer can ask a negative balance question as a follow-up to a structured interview question (Yate, 1994), for example, by saying, "That is very impressive. Now, will you describe a situation that did not work out quite so well?"

Interviewers should be careful to avoid the following common errors in scoring interviews:

- Leniency—giving high scores to all applicants
- Halo effect—giving applicants who score highly on one question higher scores on other questions than are warranted
- Central tendency—clustering scores around the average rather than giving reasonable numbers of the highest or lowest scores (e.g., not giving any 1s or 5s on a 5-point scale).
- Range restriction—using only a small subset of possible scores to rate candidates instead of using the whole range (e.g., giving all applicants 4s or 5s on a 5-point scale).

Other biases, such as being influenced by physical attractiveness, should also be checked. Table 4.4 lists several other suggestions to improve the overall interview process (Brull, 1996; Curzon, 1995; Deems, 1994; Harris & Eder, 1999; Maddux, 1994; Mornell, 1998).

During the final round of interviews, it can be helpful to end each interview by asking the candidate to call back in a couple of days (set a specific time and date). During that call, ask if the candidate has any new questions or thoughts about the job. The point of this is to put another test of reliability in the process. Approximately 15% of final candidates miss this call (Mornell, 1998). Using this strategy can help screen out people who will not reliably complete assigned tasks.

Table 4.4. Suggestions for improving the interview process

The interview should promote goodwill between the candidate and your organization regardless of whether the candidate is offered employment.

Having too many questions will frustrate both the interviewer and the person being interviewed. In a 1-hour interview, only 8–12 questions can be comfortably covered. Shorter interviews should include fewer questions.

Warmly greet and introduce yourself to the applicant; ask the applicant what name he or she prefers.

Begin the interview with small talk.

Listen more than you talk.

Start with the assumption that the candidate has no skills and allow him or her to demonstrate capabilities.

Share the purpose of the interview and explain that the applicant will have a chance to ask questions about the job.

Begin with relatively familiar topics, such as previous work or education, to help the applicant become comfortable with talking.

Use silence to prompt more complete answers.

Maintain occasional eye contact and a pleasant facial expression.

Do not assume that people are better at the things they like to do than at the things they do not like to do.

Do not take information on strengths and weaknesses at face value. Probe for examples; check with references.

Avoid asking questions that can be answered by a single word such as *yes* or *no*.

Keep in mind that statements of attitude and philosophies are poor predictors of people's actual behaviors.

Be sure to spend time giving the applicant information about the position, but do not do this until near the end of the interview. Incorporating a realistic job preview (RJP) can be a very effective strategy to do this.

Give a 5-minute warning before the interview ends to provide the applicant a chance to mention any important information that has been missed.

End the interview on a pleasant note.

Tell the applicant what to expect next in the process.

Sources: Brull, 1996; Curzon, 1995; Deems, 1994; Harris & Eder, 1999; Maddux, 1994; Mornell, 1998.

Formal Assessments

Persuasive arguments have been made in the research literature (cited earlier in this chapter and summarized in Table 4.1) that job performance is strongly predicted by general intellectual ability. Researchers have argued that this is true for almost all types of jobs (Behling, 1998). The reality, however, is that few community human services organizations have the capacity to directly assess cognitive ability through, for example, intelligence tests. In the absence of such tests, organizations interested in this trait for potential employees may look to other information gathered through the selection process. For example, grades in school and completion of postsecondary education correlate (although not perfectly) with general intelligence, which in turn is associated with better job performance, job knowledge, and success in on-the-job training (Behling, 1998). Other indicators of cognitive ability include vocabulary and problem-solving success, which may be assessed in interviews. Although cognitive ability may be highly related to job performance, however, job performance is not the only factor to consider when selecting DSPs. Retention, or stability of employees, is just as important as or more important than performance. In that context, it is critical to remember that studies of DSPs (e.g., Larson, Lakin, & Bruininks, 1998) have repeatedly shown no correlation between education and the length of time a person remains on the job. Another argument against the broad use of cognitive ability testing is that applicants may not see how the test is relevant to the job and may take offense to having to take the test (Janz et al., 1986).

It is relatively uncommon but not unheard of for community human services organizations to use formal testing of prospective employees. One intriguing test may have practical relevance for community human services settings. This test measures the extent to which the applicant's values match those of the organization (Brumback, 1996). The exercise is crafted by having the organization first identify its top five values that guide its activities (e.g., assisting the people the organization supports to direct the course of their own lives). Then the organization identifies 15 other values that are either of no or of low importance to the organization. Each of the 20 values is written on a separate index card. Each applicant is asked to sort the cards into four piles, each containing 5 cards according to how important the applicant feels the values to be a significant part of the organization's culture. Applicants are given one point for each card in the *most important* pile that matches the organization's top five values.

Make a Final Hiring Decision

At the end of the hiring process, if two or more qualified applicants remain, the organization has to decide which of those candidates to hire. Hopefully, the selection process has effectively narrowed the field to just a few excellent candidates. Using multiple hurdles to get to this point can improve hiring success. For example, to get to the reference check stage of the process, the applicant must have the required education and experience. To get to the interview, the applicant must have a positive reference check. To get to a work sample test, the applicant must pass the interview. This approach does not necessarily require that an extended amount of time pass between the various steps, but it does require that the organization use very specific criteria about who is eligible to continue to the next stage. Often, these important steps are forgotten or exceptions to the rule are routinely made in the interest of filling positions. It is important to stay with the process that has been developed. Doing so will save much trouble later on and will ensure that all candidates are evaluated on the same criteria.

There are several factors to consider when deciding among the top candidates for the job. Candidates can be evaluated on how they score on the various selection strategies identified previously. One approach is to simply hire the candidate who scores highest on the interview. Other possibilities include picking the top two or three candidates based on the selection procedures and then evaluating factors such as the personality match of the candidate with the job, the candidate's interest in the job, the behavior of the applicant during the selection process (e.g., on time, neatly and appropriately dressed, polite, friendly). Remember that skills can be developed but that attitudes rarely change (Curzon, 1995). It may be better to hire someone with fewer skills whose values and attitudes are a good match for the organization than to select a highly skilled person who has a negative attitude.

Job Carving

Job carving is a strategy to examine the total skills required to provide supports in a particular work site and to craft job descriptions for an individual employee based on the strength of the employee. Rather than requiring all DSPs to develop expertise in all skill areas, specialist roles are created based on the skills each DSP brings to the job. The full array of skills is available by combining the skills of the team of employees. Job carving may be a helpful strategy when many otherwise qualified individuals are not hired because they cannot or will not meet certain skill requirements. For example, a current job description may require all DSPs to cook, drive a car, and dispense medications. Individuals who cannot do all of these things are often not considered for employment. An organization that uses job carving may be able to reserve some of its positions for people who do not meet one of these skill requirements by ensuring that others who work similar hours at the location do.

When there are fewer applicants than there are jobs, employers may need to be more flexible with respect to prerequisite skill requirements to maintain a full complement of staff. Job carving does not mean hiring people who are incompetent. Instead, it means looking more closely at the minimum job requirements to see if there are ways to get the job done without requiring each employee to be able to do all components of the job.

Job carving may also be useful in the performance review and retention process. Organizations that lose employees because of burnout or because employees strongly dislike certain job tasks may find that redefining job roles for excellent performers may help. In this case the team of employees could negotiate to reallocate tasks among team members. One member may prefer to dispense medications while another may want to take responsibility for program writing or charting.

An alternative approach to job carving for a specific position might be to combine recruitment and selection activities across multiple work sites. Under this scenario, an organization documents the essential job functions in each of the sites and matches applicants to sites based on their strengths and skill needs. For example, a man who could not provide personal care to women could work at a site where the individuals supported are independent in their personal care, or he could work at a site supporting only men. A person who does not have a driver's license could work at a site where most community activities are within walking distance or can be reached by bus.

Matching Employees

A final stage in the selection process is to make sure that the candidates selected are a good match for the specific role they will work in. This means working hard to match new employees with individuals receiving supports based on individual characteristics and interests. Placing a new employee who hates rock music in a home where he will be supporting young men whose passion in life is to attend rock concerts may not be the best match. This also means looking at geography so that commutes can be minimized and so that people who take public transportation are not unduly burdened.

Making the Decision and Extending a Job Offer

The next phase in the hiring process is deciding based on all of the information gathered which candidate will be the best match for the position. Success in selecting the best candidate is enhanced if the selection process has been thorough and unbiased and provides the organization the information needed to identify the best candidate. Once a candidate has been selected, the person should be notified, preferably by telephone with an offer. The offer should include the name of the position, the name of the supervisor, the salary and benefits being offered, and a deadline for getting a decision from the applicant. The person making this call should know whether the salary and benefits are negotiable and within what parameters in case the candidate asks.

Candidates who were excluded during the hiring process as not eligible for employment or not suitable for a position can be notified (usually in writing) as soon as such a determination has been made. If more than one finalist for the position could potentially fill the job, however, these people should be informed of their finalist status but should not be sent a rejection letter until the job offer has been accepted by the top candidate. This makes it possible to offer the job to another candidate if the organization's first choice is no longer available or turns down the offer.

The selection process is not over when an offer has been extended and accepted. The hiring authority still must document that all applicants were fairly evaluated and that the decision to hire or not to hire a person was based on legal criteria. It is important to keep a simple list or form naming each candidate; whether a job offer was extended to the person; whether a job offer was accepted; and, if an offer was not extended, the reason for that decision. Common reasons for rejecting candidates include the following: The person does not meet the minimum job specifications, the person meets minimum specifications but is not the best qualified, the applicant has no prior related experience, the person has less prior experience than other candidates, the candidate cannot meet physical standards for essential job functions of the position (e.g., lifting), the person has fewer skills than the person selected, the candidate has less direct training or experience than the person selected, the applicant cannot work the schedule or hours required, and the applicant withdrew from consideration (Maddux, 1994).

When the position is filled, unsuccessful candidates should be notified as soon as possible. Candidates who were interviewed should be contacted by telephone and sent a follow-up letter, whereas candidates who are not interviewed can be notified by mail or e-mail. One common way to notify unsuccessful candidates is to say that the candidate whose qualifications best fit the job specifications was selected (Maddux, 1994).

In the Spotlight: Franciscan Health System Skilled Nursing Facility

A skilled nursing facility operated by the Franciscan Health System reduced turnover from 146% to 51% in 2 years by introducing a 90-minute assessment prior to hire (see Thomas & Brull, 1993, for a complete description of this intervention). The organization assessed cognitive skills (e.g., understanding directions), administrative skills (e.g., being organized), interpersonal skills (e.g., likeability, cooperation, compassion, consideration), motivation (e.g., personal pride, quality orientation, enthusiasm, commitment), and adjustment (e.g., reliability, responsibility). The assessment used three separate tests: the Personnel Decisions Inc. Employment Inventory (Personnel Decisions, Inc., n.d.-a), the Guilford-Zimmerman Temperament Survey (Guilford & Zimmerman, n.d.), and the Personnel Decisions Inc. Job Preferences Inventory (Personnel Decisions, Inc., n.d.-b). The organization also used a structured interview process to assess applicants' behavior and values to find a match to the organization's values. Applicants were divided into three groups according to score. Applicants with scores in the top third were considered green-light candidates and were hired immediately. People scoring in the bottom third were given a red-light score and were not hired. People in the middle third were considered yellow-light candidates. The organization tried to hire only green-light employees but also hired yellow-light employees when there were too few green-light candidates or when there was an urgency to fill a certain position. This process resulted in substantial cost savings due to increased productivity and reduced turnover and in FLS reports that the quality of nursing assistants had improved substantially.

OVERCOMING IMPLEMENTATION BARRIERS

Although structured interviews (both situational interviews and behavioral interviews) have considerable research support, they are relatively uncommon in human services settings. There are several barriers to implementation of these techniques. First, the interview protocol requires scoring of each response as the interview progresses. Although this enhances the accuracy of the process, it can be tedious for the interviewer. Second, situational interview questions can frustrate less-qualified applicants. Third, the process requires time to conduct a job analysis, identify critical situations, develop questions, and create a scoring guide (Maurer et al., 1999). Like all of the research-based techniques described in this book, this intervention is not a quick fix. Time and effort are required to do it well. The advantage of using a well-defined strategy such as structured interviewing is that solid research evidence suggests that the payoff is increased success in hiring candidates who can actually perform the job well.

Considerations for Developing and Using Selection Strategies

It is important to involve DSPs throughout the process of developing and using selection strategies. They can provide valuable assistance in identifying critical incidents that define excellent and poor performance. In addition, by testing interview questions with current excellent performers, the organization is able to gauge whether the criteria established for good versus poor answers are realistic.

Evaluating Selection Success

The key element in evaluating selection success is assessing whether the people who got high scores on the selection criteria actually turn out to be excellent performers who stay in their positions. To assess success, the organization can keep a record for each employee of his or her hire date, termination date, scores on the selection criteria, and reason for leaving. One important point to consider is the percentage of people who leave the organization who were terminated involuntarily. A related consideration is the percentage of people hired in the previous year who were terminated. One study that followed new hires in more than 80 organizations found that 15% of new hires were terminated within a year of starting (Larson, Lakin, & Bruininks, 1998). That termination rate is quite high and probably means that many people were hired who should have been screened out in the selection process. It is very costly in terms of hiring costs, exposure to risk, unemployment costs, and so forth, to use involuntary terminations to "fix" a selection error. Organizations that terminate large numbers of new employees may want to reevaluate selection practices to screen out applicants who are a poor match with the organization or the job.

Another more sophisticated approach to assessing the success of the organization's selection process involves measuring performance indicators for new hires. For example, the organization can track the scores new hires got on selection criteria, divide those new hires into high- and low-scoring groups, and then check whether the average performance ratings are higher for the high-scoring employees than for the low-scoring employees. For more technical information about this topic, consult a textbook on personnel management (e.g., Cascio, 1997).

QUESTIONS TO PONDER

1. Are there components of the selection process that your organization is skipping? How could they be better addressed?
2. Has your organization succumbed to the "warm body syndrome," hiring all applicants just to fill vacancies? If yes, what steps could your organization take to change this?
3. What specific changes can your organization make to improve the questions it asks in the interview process? Does your organization use structured behavioral interview questions? Why or why not?
4. What changes are needed in your interviewing practices to make them conform more closely to the structured interview techniques described in this chapter? What will you do first?
5. Has your organization developed set selection criteria for all applicants? Are these criteria used consistently across applicants and across different parts of the organization?
6. Is job carving a strategy your organization could use? Why or why not?
7. What proportion of staff members who leave your organization are involuntarily terminated? What selection strategies can reduce that proportion?

CONCLUSION

This chapter reviews the components of an effective selection process. The literature suggests that strategies such as structured interviews can be very useful in selection. Each organization should review its policies and practices regarding selection to decide whether those practices are consistent with what research suggests is best practice and to identify ways to improve success in selection and hiring. Selection is hard work, but it is a necessary part of the recruitment and retention process. If it is done poorly, the selection process can cause even the best recruitment, retention, or training intervention to fail; if done well, the selection process can substantially improve success with recruitment and retention.

RESOURCES

Curzon, S.C. (1995). *Managing the interview: A how-to manual for hiring staff.* New York: Neal-Schuman Publishers.

Curzon's book provides specific suggestions and easy-to-understand examples about how to improve selection practices, categorized into the following sections: preparing for the interview, creating questions, using a group or panel interview process, conducting the interview, extending the interview process, choosing the candidate, offering the job, and wrapping up.

Deems, R.S. (1994). *Interviewing: More than a gut feeling* [Videotape and handbook]. West Des Moines, IA: American Media.

This videotape and handbook provide a good overview of the interviewing and selection process. It provides specific instructions on each phase, specific examples to illustrate the main points, and exercises that allow users to apply the new learning. Topics covered include identifying needed job skills, preparing questions, conducting the interview, evaluating candidates, handling difficult interview situations, and implementing behavior-based interviewing.

Eder, R.W., & Harris, M.W. (Eds.). (1999). *The employment interview handbook.* Thousand Oaks, CA: Sage Publications.

This textbook contains 21 high-quality literature reviews about the employment interview process. One of this book's goals is for readers to become informed consumers of employment interview research. Its target audience is researchers and graduate students, instructors in industrial/organizational psychology and human resources management, and experienced supervisors and administrators.

Janz, T., Hellervik, L., & Gilmore, D.C. (1986). *Behavior description interviewing: New, accurate, cost effective.* Boston: Allyn & Bacon.

This classic text reviews the reasons for using behavioral interviewing, explains how to analyze a position and create appropriate structured interview questions, describes how to move through the interview, contains several job aids such as checklists for improving interviewing skills, and gives many examples of structured interviewing questions.

Mornell, P. (1998). *45 effective ways for hiring smart: How to predict winners and losers in the incredibly expensive people reading game.* Berkeley, CA: Ten Speed Press.

This book provides concrete information about effective selection strategies, in an expanded list format. Sections include the following: pre-interview strategies, strategies during the interview, strategies after the interview, reference-checking strategies, and final strategies. The book has a helpful summary chart of the 45 strategies and their benefits and also includes helpful examples of various forms needed during the selection process.

Sample Interview Questions for Direct Support Professionals

Following are sample interview questions for organizations supporting individuals with disabilities. This list includes both behavior description questions and situational interview questions. The questions are based on direct support professional (DSP) competencies in the *Community Support Skill Standards* (CSSS; Taylor, Bradley, & Warren, 1996; see Chapter 6 for more information on the CSSS). We recommend that the organization choose questions that suit its needs and the needs of the people to be interviewed. The organization should ask the same set of questions of all applicants for a particular position.

Competency Area 1: Participant Empowerment
1. Describe a situation in which you assisted an individual to recognize that he or she had several choices in how to handle a difficult problem. What was the situation, what did you do, and what was the final outcome?
2. A participant at the group home in which you work has told you she thinks she might be a lesbian and would like to meet other women in the gay community. What steps would you take to empower her?
3. Describe a situation in which you have encouraged someone to advocate for him- or herself. What was the situation, what did you do, and what was the result?
4. You and a person with disabilities you support are at a local restaurant. The server taking your order looks and speaks only to you. The person you are with can give his or her own order. What would you do?

Competency Area 2: Communication
1. Describe ways in which you have communicated with a person who does not communicate verbally.
2. Your new co-worker, Mohamed, is Muslim. During Ramadan he fasts during the day and has asked you to change duties with him for the month so that he will not have to cook for the people who live in the group home. You cook a great deal already, and do not want to take on the extra duties for him. How do you respond to him?
3. Your co-worker has a habit of interrupting you at staff meetings. In the past you have waited for her to finish and bring up your point again, only to have her interrupt once more. As a result, you often leave staff meetings feeling frustrated because your ideas were not discussed. How do you address this issue?
4. Describe a situation in which your attempts to communicate with someone were ineffective. What was the situation, what did you do, and what happened as a result?
5. Describe the worst misunderstanding you were involved in at your last job. What was the situation, what did you do, and what happened as a result?

Competency Area 3: Assessment
1. Sally's mother expresses concern to you that Sally, whom you support, may be hard of hearing and tends to ignore her when she is talking. You have noticed this but have also found that when Sally is around friends or watching television, her hearing appears to be fine. You suspect that Sally is choosing to not listen to her mother. Sally's mother recently told you she wants her daughter's hearing tested and asks you for your thoughts. How might you share your assessment of the situation with Sally's mother?
2. Tell us about a time when someone whom you supported was injured and you had to make an immediate judgment about what needed to be done to help the person. Describe the injury and your steps in making the assessment.
3. Describe a situation in the past in which you participated in a team assessment process. What was your role? What was the outcome?
4. Tell me about the last time you solved a problem that required a lot of hard thinking and analysis. What difficulties did you encounter, how did you overcome them, and what was the result?

(continued)

Funding for the development of these questions was provided by the Partnerships for Success Grant funded by the U.S. Department of Labor (Grant No. N-7596-9-00-87-60). The opinions and assertions contained herein are the opinions of the authors and are not to be construed as official or reflecting the view of the U.S. Department of Labor.

Interview questions were developed by Talley Sjonberg, Karen Pederson, Amy S. Hewitt, and Sheryl A. Larson (University of Minnesota, Institute on Community Integration, Research and Training Center on Community Living) and have been adapted by permission. Other sources of questions include Julie Stocker (Hiawatha Homes, Rochester, Minnesota) and Homberger (1990).

Competency Area 4: Community and Service Networking

1. A person you support tells you that when he was a child, his family went regularly to a Catholic church and that he would like to become active in the faith again. How do you support him in this goal?
2. Michele is quiet and doesn't leave the house. She is not involved in any activities and has no personal relationships. Michele claims she has no areas of interest and seems unhappy with her life. How might you assist Michele in recognizing and developing areas of interest?
3. Please describe some community resources in your neighborhood. How might a person with a disability use those resources?
4. Think about the last time you moved to a new community. What strategies did you use to find places to engage in your favorite leisure activities? How did you go about meeting people with interests similar to yours? John recently moved from a large institution to a supported living setting. How might you assist John to learn about and become part of his new community?
5. Describe the most embarrassing situation you have experienced when you were with a person with a disability. What was the situation, what did you do, and what happened as a result? What, if anything, would you do anything differently if you were in a similar situation in the future?

Competency Area 5: Facilitation of Services

1. Tell me about a time when you had to practice professional confidentiality. What was the situation? What did you do? What was the outcome?
2. Think about the closest working relationship you have had with a person with developmental disabilities. What did you do to make that relationship work?
3. A few weeks after developing her support plan, Rachel changes her mind about wanting to get a job. What are the first two things you would say or do to respond?
4. Describe a situation in which you helped a person set a goal and then supported the person to achieve that goal. What was the goal, and how did you help?
5. Describe a situation in which you or someone you know needed a medical, psychological, or other support service but was having trouble getting it. What was the situation, what did you do, and what was the result?

Competency Area 6: Community Living Skills and Supports

1. Describe the best meal you have ever prepared for a group of people.
2. Describe the household chore or duty you like least. How do you ensure that the chore or duty is completed?
3. Describe the household chore or duty you like most. What strategies do you use to ensure that the chore or duty is completed?
4. What actions would you take if you recognized a person showing signs of having an allergic reaction (e.g., hives)?
5. Kamol, a resident in the group home where you work, was raised in a Thai community. Lately, he has expressed how much he misses his mother's cooking and talks about Thai dishes he loved as a child. How might you respond to this situation?
6. Describe a time when you were required to provide medical assistance or treatment to another person. What was the situation, what did you do, and what happened as a result?
7. If you were in a store and the person you were supporting sat down and refused to move, what would you do?

Competency Area 7: Education, Training, and Self-Development

1. How have you kept up on relevant resources and information about a topic of interest to you?
2. What else besides your education and job experience qualifies you for this job?
3. Describe the last thing you did for self-improvement.
4. Tell me about the best class you have ever taken. What was the class? Why was it good?
5. What is the next thing you want to learn how to do or how to do better? What is your plan for accomplishing this?

Competency Area 8: Advocacy

1. What advocacy organizations and services are available in this community that might assist people with disabilities?
2. Tell me about a situation in which you have advocated on behalf of another person or a time when someone else has advocated on your behalf. What made that advocacy successful or unsuccessful?
3. Describe a time when you witnessed a person with disabilities being teased by a co-worker or other person. What did you do? What could you have done to assist that person?

(continued)

Competency Area 9: Vocational, Educational, and Career Support

1. Mali would like to join a Hmong quilting group, but she has no method of transportation other than the bus, which is a long and confusing ride. What could you to do as her DSP to support her in gaining access to this program?
2. Describe a time when you have supported another person in a vocational or education program or with his or her career development. What did you do, and what was the result?
3. Describe the things you have done in the last couple of years to advance your career. What supports did you receive? What was the most helpful assistance you got?
4. Describe the first job you ever had. What would you do to adapt that job so that it could be performed by someone who could not walk (or talk, see, or hear)?
5. Wilma has been attending a traditional day training center for 15 years. She works only 2 hours each week and earns less than $1 every 2 weeks. Wilma expresses an interest in finding a real job. What are the most important things you will do in the next 2 weeks to help Wilma?

Competency Area 10: Crisis Intervention

1. Betty, a person living in the home where you work, is sensitive to loud noises. One afternoon, the maintenance crew comes to the house to do yard work and the sound of the riding mower sends her into a panic. She begins pacing rapidly while crying and covering her ears. She picks up a nearby object in attempt to throw through the window toward the maintenance employee. How would you handle this situation?
2. Describe the last time you became involved in a conflict or a crisis. What was the situation? What did you do? How well did it work? What would you have done to prevent the situation from occurring?
3. Describe the most difficult person you remember ever dealing with at work or at school. Describe the most difficult situation you remember encountering with that person. How did he or she react to you? How did you deal with the situation? What did you do about your own feelings? Did you ever discuss your differences with this person? If not, why not? If yes, what happened?

Competency Area 11: Organization Participation

1. Tell me about the mission of the last company you worked for. Did you agree or disagree with that mission? Explain why.
2. Describe a situation in which you played a role in making a change within your last place of employment (or place of worship, community center, or club). What was the situation, what did you do, and what was the result?
3. Describe a situation in which you had a conflict with a co-worker. What was the issue, what did you do, and what was the outcome of the conflict?
4. Describe the most memorable situation in which you had a conflict with your supervisor. What was the issue, what did you do, and what was the outcome of the conflict?
5. What was the best experience you have ever had as a member of a team? What was your role on the team? What made it a good experience?
6. Describe the worst supervisor you have ever had. What made that person a poor supervisor? How did you work with that person to complete your job duties?
7. Tell me about the last time you found yourself trying to do too many different things at the same time. How did you handle the situation?
8. Describe the co-worker whom you most appreciate. What characteristics or qualities of that person do you most appreciate?
9. What behaviors do you think are most important or most valued by team members or co-workers in the workplace? Of the behaviors you just listed, which is your strongest or most positive behavior with co-workers? Which might be a possible improvement area for you?
10. What does teamwork mean to you? Give some examples of things you have done to be a good team member or to improve teamwork.

Competency Area 12: Documentation

1. Tell me some of the reasons you think that documentation is important.
2. Describe a situation in which someone you know used words to describe a person or a group of people that showed disrespect. What, if anything, did you do in that situation?
3. Describe a situation in which you were asked to document an event. Describe what occurred, what information was documented, and why you documented the things you did.
4. What was the best thing you ever wrote? What was the topic? What made this piece the best you ever wrote?
5. Describe the most difficult writing assignment you have ever had. What was the assignment, and how did you handle it?
6. Describe the last paper or writing assignment you completed in school or at work. What was the assignment, what did you do, and what was the outcome of the assignment?

(continued)

Experience, Credentials, and Self-Evaluation Opinion Questions

1. Describe a typical day in your most recent job.
2. Please describe your present job responsibilities. Which are most difficult and why? Which are most enjoyable and why?
3. Describe any classes, experiences, or training you have received to prepare you for the job you are applying for.
4. Describe the most difficult job you have ever had. What made the job so difficult? How did you overcome the difficulties?
5. What is the most common misperception that other people have about you?
6. Most of us have more than one reason for leaving a job. What are some of yours, from past or present experience?
7. What one or two words would most or all of your previous supervisors use to describe you?
8. What part(s) of your last or present position did you like least? What did you do to try to overcome the situation? What would you think if you were to know in advance that this situation would be present in your new job?
9. What accomplishment in your present job are you most proud of? What was your best idea (whether it was implemented or not)?
10. Under what circumstances might you seek out a co-worker or peer for advice or suggestions? Provide examples of times that you did in the past.
11. Describe your ideal job. Explain your preferences, the amount and type of supervision, amount of contact and kinds of relationships with co-workers, job tasks, and freedom to work or to make decisions.
12. If you had the authority or power, what one thing would you change about your current or last position?
13. Other than money, what rewards, benefits, or work situations are most important for you?
14. How much time did you miss from work last year? The year before?
15. What suggestions has your supervisor given you for performance improvement or development?
16. We have all made mistakes on the job, some of which are bigger than others. Tell me about the biggest workplace mistake you ever made. What were the circumstances, and how did you deal with the situation? What did you learn from the experience?
17. Tell me about your schedule flexibility and your work schedule preferences.
18. If you were offered this position and you were to accept it, what one or two major contributions would you make to the organization, in the short term (in the first few weeks) and in the long term (after a year or so)?

II

SOCIALIZING AND TRAINING EMPLOYEES

5

ORIENTATION, SOCIALIZATION, NETWORKING, AND PROFESSIONALIZATION

Amy S. Hewitt, Sheryl A. Larson,
Susan N. O'Nell, and John K. Sauer

Direct support professionals (DSPs) who are new to an organization need a variety of supports to be successful. They need to understand how things work at the organization and how to perform their specific job roles. They also need to know whom they can turn to for assistance and support, both when they first begin the job and as they become longer-term employees. This chapter focuses on strategies organizations can use to welcome and help DSPs new to the organization find the supports they need to be successful. Three subsequent chapters (Chapters 6–8) focus on specific training and mentoring interventions that organizations can use to help DSPs learn the specific skills and competencies they need in their jobs.

DSPs at all phases of their employment need opportunities to network and to learn from one another. Providing these opportunities is an effective training and retention strategy. This chapter describes why it is important for DSPs to meet with and learn from other DSPs. It also provides case examples of associations and alliances that have formed specifically for this purpose. In addition, professionalization for DSPs is discussed.

TARGETED FRONT-LINE SUPERVISOR COMPETENCIES

Primary Skills

Front-line supervisors (FLSs) network with people working at other service organizations to learn new ideas and strategies for supporting individuals.

FLSs understand the purpose of orientation and implement strategies to welcome new DSPs and help them feel comfortable in their new positions.

FLSs coordinate, schedule, and document DSP participation and performance in orientation and completion of self-directed learning and development.

UNDERSTANDING THE PROBLEM

Many organizations use orientation as a way to cover annual and mandated training requirements. Often the word *orientation* translates into approximately a week of classroom training that rapidly covers mandated topics and sends new employees to perform job duties with little ongoing support. Many people work their first shift without any co-worker or FLS present. Given that early turnover is so pervasive (Bachelder & Braddock, 1994; Colorado Department of Human Services, Office of Health and Rehabilitation Services, Developmental Disabilities Services, 2000; Larson, Lakin, & Bruininks, 1998), existing staff justifiably feel cautious about extending themselves to new employees until the new employees have proven capable. Therefore, what little contact new employees have with existing employees and supervisors can sometimes be less than welcoming. In addition, in places where turnover is high, existing staff and supervisors may still be in the orientation and/or probationary phase of employment as well.

Orientation is not the same as training. Whereas training focuses on task performance, the focus of orientation is learning the context of the job (e.g., knowing how to fit in and relate to co-workers and supported individuals; handling routine problems; understanding expectations regarding helping and cooperating with others; following organizational rules; appreciating the politics, power, mission, vision, and values of the organization; understanding the organization's special language; supporting or defending organizational objectives) as well as learning how to cope with stress and learning about the interpersonal skills needed to succeed within the job context (Ostroff & Kozlowski, 1993; Wanous & Reichers, 2000). Moreover, orientation occurs during a time of high stress related to the newcomer's transition to a totally new culture, whereas training occurs throughout the person's tenure in the organization (Wanous & Reichers, 2000).

The period in which an employee is learning the ropes of his or her new job is often much longer than the industry is willing to wait. To fully socialize an employee to a new job can take 6–12 months (Hutchins, 2000b; Larson, Lakin, & Bruininks, 1998). This amount of time can seem daunting to an industry that considers a tenure of 3–6 months to be long term. Many organizations do not even have a truly discernible orientation period, choosing to lump new DSPs with experienced DSPs in the same classroom training sessions. Given that this so-called orientation comes with merely a few hours to a few days of on-the-job training and supervision, new DSPs are often on their own to fend for themselves the best they can. Newly hired DSPs commonly describe orientation as sink or swim, trial by fire, boring, nonexistent, overwhelming, or redundant (Larson, Sauer, Hewitt, O'Nell, & Sedlezky, 1998).

This approach to providing orientation for new employees is at the root of much of early turnover. In the rush to get people through mandated training so that they can work without supervision, many organizations have completely lost sight of the true purpose of orientation, which is to help new employees become familiar with the company and the job at a comfortable pace and to ensure that they feel welcomed and that the choice of employment was a good one (Spruell, 1987; Wanous, 1992). Although it is understandable that organizations may feel pressure to fill DSP positions that have been vacant for a long time and may rely on overtime and use of temporary staff, the result is an ongoing circular problem. Rushed orientation practices combined with haphazard recruitment and selection strategies are part of a system in which many organizations do not expect new employees to stay on the job very long. Consequently, little effort is put into helping new employees adjust and feel welcomed and comfortable, and therefore even many people who have found the job to be a good match end up leaving because they do not develop the necessary organizational commitment or confidence in their ability to do the job well.

To lose one high-potential employee due to inadequate support in the first few weeks of employment (or at any point in employment) is a recruitment crisis and a waste of significant magnitude. Organizations need to use the orientation period to cultivate in new employees a sense of satisfaction and commitment to the organization and the DSP job. By the end of the first day, the employee should have a strong sense that he or she has made the right choice in taking the job (Hutchins, 2000b). By 30 days after hire, the employee should have a defined sense of commitment to the job and the organization; if not, he or she is unlikely to still be there a year after hire (Larson, Lakin, & Bruininks, 1998). Improving how DSPs are oriented to their organization and their role as a DSP and training them to develop needed skills are essential solutions to the challenge of keeping new employees in community human services.

RESEARCH SUPPORT FOR SOLUTIONS

Employee-Centered Orientation

In human services, an industry that regulates most aspects of service provision, it is easy to consider orientation the time period in which regulation-mandated training must be provided and to consider success as having spent the designated time addressing the designated topics. Employee-centered orientation, in contrast, is designed to help newcomers cope with the stress of starting the new job. Its goal is to welcome new employees; promote positive attitudes about the job; establish open communication between the organization and the new employees; and to acquaint new employees with the organization's history, philosophy, structure, mission, vision, values, goals, policies, and procedures (Benson & Cheney, 1996; Dipboye, 1997; Goldstien, 1993; Holland & George, 1986). Providing planned opportunities for new employees to get to know other employees and the people they will be supporting before the first solo shift can be helpful in the orientation process. Pacing the information provided during orientation can also help to reduce the likelihood that a new employee will become overwhelmed with the information.

Realistic Orientation Programs for new Employee Stress

Another important line of research suggests the need to identify early possible stressors of the job and ensure that new hires are given effective strategies to respond to these stressors (Wanous, 1992). Realistic Orientation Programs for new Employee Stress (ROPES) is a research-based approach to supporting new employees (Wanous, 1992). The goal of ROPES is to reduce stress among new employees and to encourage them to stay in the organization. Effective socialization using ROPES should do the following:
* Provide realistic information about job stresses.
* Provide general support and assurance (one-to-one or in small groups).
* Help new employees demonstrate, discuss, and rehearse various coping skills.
* Teach self-control of thoughts and feelings.

Reducing stress for newly hired employees can reduce turnover. Research also suggests that providing realistic information about job stresses to new employees after hire can reduce turnover (Hom, Griffeth, Palich, & Bracker, 1998). Implementation of ROPES is discussed later in this chapter.

Socialization

Socialization is the ongoing process of learning the social culture of the organization and how to get along with others in the organization. For DSPs, socialization includes becoming familiar with routines and getting to know co-workers and the individuals receiving supports. It also includes developing an understanding of the mission, vision, and values of the organization. New employees often find it is difficult to get to know the routines, traits, and behaviors of their co-workers and the people to whom they provide supports (socialization) and to learn and complete their job duties and routines of their daily work (orientation) (Larson, Lakin, & Bruininks, 1998). Support from co-workers is important to assist them in this. A study of newly hired DSPs found that DSPs who were supported by their co-workers were more likely to stay than those who were not (Bachelder & Braddock, 1994). Six aspects of co-worker support were identified:

- Co-workers go out of their way to help new staff members adjust.
- New DSPs can understand their role by observing co-workers.
- Co-workers are personally supportive of new staff members.
- Experienced staff see advising or training newcomers as a main job responsibility.
- Experienced staff guide newcomers about how to perform the job.
- Training expands and builds on knowledge gained in previous training.

These researchers suggested that organizations design DSP orientation and work roles around groups rather than around individuals to support relationships between new and more experienced staff members; assign a specific person to assume primary responsibility for preparing, instructing, and advising new employees during the orientation period; and have supervisors and co-workers communicate a personal interest in new employees actively and directly during their initial period of employment. Co-workers were reported in another study to be the most available source of socialization information and the most helpful (Louis, Posner, & Powell, 1983). New employees who have mentors are able to learn more about organizational issues and practices than those who do not have a mentor during their early organizational socialization (Ostroff & Kozlowski, 1992).

Supervisor Support

Although co-worker support is critical to successful orientation and socialization of newcomers, support from FLSs also plays a key role. Research on socialization outcomes suggests that the information provided by supervisors about the tasks and roles of new employees is the most important factor in positive socialization outcomes such as newcomers' commitment, feelings of adjustment, and satisfaction with the job and the organization (Ostroff & Kozlowski, 1992). After peers, supervisors were rated by new employees as the most available and most helpful sources of socialization information (Louis et al., 1983). Furthermore, the helpfulness of supervisors in the socialization process was significantly correlated with employees' job satisfaction, organizational commitment, and tenure intentions (Louis et al., 1983).

STRATEGIES FOR RESPONDING TO THE PROBLEM

Improve Orientation Practices

As pointed out earlier in this chapter, existing organization-centered orientation practices are contrary to the true purpose of orientation, which is to welcome and begin socialization for new employees, get them committed to the organization, and give them a clear understanding of their job and the roles within the organization. To minimize early turnover of employees who are a potentially good organization match, organizations must redesign orientation to ensure that organizational commitment and employee satisfaction with the job choice is high and that new employees develop a basic level of job competence at a pace that is comfortable for them. Some businesses have found success in thinking of the orientation process as starting during the recruitment and selection phase (Hutchins, 2000a). Providing a realistic view of the position, the stresses, and the duties before an applicant is officially hired or is even interviewed is critical (see Chapter 3, which describes realistic job previews).

It is very important that everyone in the organization (including FLSs, current DSPs, new DSPs, and individuals supported and their families) understand the purpose and value of the orientation process. Once candidates are officially hired, orientation should be clearly distinct from training. Opportunities for new employees to meet supervisors, co-workers, and people receiving services in a friendly and calm atmosphere are important during orientation. It is also important for the new employee to get familiar with new environments and routines. Table 5.1 describes other important characteristics of effective orientation.

For orientation to be most effective, everyone in the organization needs to be supportive and assist new employees to adjust to the demands of the job and feel good

Table 5.1. Characteristics of effective orientation

Effective orientation should

Be distinct and separate from skills training

Welcome the new employees

Provide information on the organization's history, mission, philosophy, structure, values, and goals and what makes it different from other agencies

Help new direct support professionals (DSPs) understand the human services field and the political context of their job

Assist newcomers in understanding their roles and job duties

Describe essential policy and procedures

Provide information to help new employees to manage stressors of the job

Be a supportive and fun experience

Enable new employees to connect with people who will be there to help them when they need it

---

about their employment choice. Co-workers and supervisors need to stop setting up situations in which "only the strong survive." This often occurs when existing employees distance themselves from new recruits because of a belief that the new recruit will soon be gone. It results in a testing of sorts and is counter to the goal of having a stable set of competent co-workers. Even if existing employees are not doing anything consciously to drive new DSPs away, co-workers and FLSs may need training and development on how to welcome, support, and interact with new employees. Understandably, existing employees may need some assurances from managers and administrators that better screening and selection is part of this new expectation, especially if these employees have been subjected to a number of new recruits that were a particularly poor match for the organization. In addition, co-workers and FLSs can be more welcoming of new recruits if they are given honest information about the training needs of the new recruits and if they understand that support will be provided up front. Administrators and managers need to be present during the orientation for new employees. They need to learn each person's name, take an interest in his or her work, and give the new recruit the message that they are excited that he or she chose to become a part of the organization. In addition, the people who receive supports and their families need to know when new people are starting and should be encouraged to welcome them.

Because of the structure of human services jobs, it is not uncommon for new employees to go a long time without meeting all of their co-workers or even their supervisor. This practice should be minimized, and creative techniques should be applied to work introductions around employees' schedules. Alternative methods can help co-workers get to know each other and at least match names with faces. Providing a personalized staff book to new DSPs with each employee's picture, name, and brief biographical or job information can be helpful. Other industries that deal with extreme geographic dispersal of employees have presented this information on a computer intranet network (Hutchins, 2000a). Using the staff log to welcome and introduce new employees is also a possibility.

Supervisors need to take the time to meet with new employees immediately after hire. Depending on the particular set-up of the organization, an FLS or a senior staff member should be assigned to help each new employee during his or her transition. Building in structured time for the supervisor to meet with the employee and observe his or her work is important. It will minimize the employee's stress about unclear job tasks and provide an opportunity for the employee to ask the supervisor questions. Table 5.2 describes some useful orientation strategies.

Switching from organization-focused orientation practices to employee-centered orientation practices can be difficult. As with most strategies designed to remove the revolving door of turnover, orientation requires organizations to make an investment in changing practices. This investment can have many positive returns. Employees who bond with the organization and feel welcomed and wanted will most likely end up being long-term employees and being successful in providing high-quality supports.

As with any other intervention mentioned in this book, is important for the organization to evaluate the effectiveness of its orientation practices. This evaluation can be formal or informal, with the supervisor asking the newcomer if all of his or her

Table 5.2.   Useful orientation and socialization practices

Start orientation during the recruitment and selection process.

Provide new employees with realistic information regarding stresses they may encounter and how to manage those stresses.

Make sure that new employees understand on the first day where, how, and from whom to get help if they need it.

Present information effectively using innovative principles, methods, and strategies.

Let new employees meet their supervisors and co-workers in person in a calm and friendly way, very soon after hire.

Spread out learning activities over longer time frames.

Acknowledge new employees at different points (e.g., on the first day, after the first week, after the first 30 days).

Reunite orientation cohorts and provide other socialization and networking opportunities.

Provide a peer or other mentor for the first 1–6 months. (One mentor could work with multiple mentees, if needed.)

Plan times to check in to discuss problems or issues routinely during the first several weeks of employment.

questions have been answered and whether the orientation adequately prepared the newcomer for the job. Table 5.3 shows some of the questions that can be used to evaluate the orientation process. Chapter 13, which discusses assessment and evaluation, contains surveys that could be used or adapted to assess satisfaction with the orientation process (e.g., New Staff Survey, Staff Satisfaction Survey). The evaluation results should be used to update the orientation process and materials periodically.

Create an Intentional Socialization Process

Whereas orientation typically occurs in a new employee's first week to month on the job, socialization takes much longer (Wanous & Reichers, 2000). Rushing new employees into their work roles without attending to the socialization process is not an effective practice and can lead to these employees' feeling unprepared, unsupported,

Table 5.3.   Questions to evaluate orientation using employee and supervisor opinions

Employee reactions

Did the orientation prepare you well for the job?

Which components were most important?

Was enough, too little, or too much time devoted to key topics?

Did the sequence, timing, and duration of orientation fit your schedule and information needs?

Do you have suggestions for improving orientation?

Supervisor reactions

Did the orientation affect the job performance of the new employees?

Are new workers comfortable with the organization?

Are you comfortable with your role in the process?

Do you have any suggestions for orientation topics, activities, materials, trainers, time on topics, or scheduling?

overwhelmed, and underappreciated. Organizations can use several interventions to ensure that new hires are appropriately socialized into their new positions.

Welcoming Activities

The socialization process begins at hire and continues for months or even years as a newcomer learns the nuances of the mission, vision, and values of both the organization and the industry. Much of the early socialization process occurs as part of orientation. It is important that new hires get an immediate sense from their employer that they are appreciated and welcomed. New employees should know from the beginning that their employer recognizes that it is a privilege to have them as an employee and will provide all of the support they need to have a successful employment experience. Executive directors, managers, and FLSs should go out of their way to make new employees feel special and to let them know that they recognize that the newcomers have chosen to work for this organization instead of another. A simple handwritten welcome note can go a long way in conveying excitement about a new employee to that person. Some organizations also create welcome baskets. These baskets are given to new hires and may include items with the organization's logo and mission on them (e.g., T-shirts, coffee mugs, pens, balloons); survival items (e.g., chocolate bars, coffee, gift cards); or other items, such as a bouquet of flowers, that are designed to say "We are glad you are here" and "You are now part of our team." It is also common for organizations to plan a welcome dinner or lunch for new employees. If the employee is hired to work at a group living environment, supported individuals and their family members and co-workers from that site might get together for a welcome barbecue or dinner. A welcoming event might be similarly organized at an organization's offices during lunch.

Opportunity to Understand the Organizational History, Values, and Purpose

New employees need to feel connected to the organization to act in accordance with the organization's purpose and mission. During the initial introduction to their new job and roles, it is important for the new hires to learn about the organization's history: when it started, how it has changed over time, the types of services it provides, its value to the people it supports and to the community, and what others have to say about the organization. It is not enough for new employees to read a mission, vision, or values statement. New employees need to see how these are lived in the organization. One way to share this is for people who receive supports, their family members, or their friends to provide testimony and stories. For example, an organization's mission is to provide opportunities for community inclusion to people with disabilities, it would be powerful for a current DSP to describe how she has helped a person to be included in a neighborhood intramural soccer league. Some organizations develop videotaped interviews with supported individuals and their family members, board members, and DSPs telling stories.

During the socialization period, it is also important for the organization to show new employees everything the organization does for its employees. Of course, this means pay, benefits, bonuses, and the like, which have probably been discussed before hire, but it also means the more qualitative aspects of employment. For example, the organization should convey how it seeks and listens to the voice of each employee. It is also important to share the organization's representative and participatory management with new hires so that they recognize that the organization is deeply committed not only to them as individuals but also to the group of employees of which they are a member.

Immediate Connection to a Person in a Similar Role or to a Mentor

It is critical that each new DSP have access to a co-worker or a mentor who can provide support on the job from the very beginning of his or her employment. This person can be selected through a formal program such as the one described in Chapter 8 or can be a volunteer who informally takes the new person under his or her wing. In either case, it is important that a specific person be designated to assist the new employee. This designated person should be someone who has volunteered for the role and who is easily accessible to the new employee for the first weeks and months of employment. This person's role is to model for the newcomer how the organization does things.

Implementation of Realistic Orientation Program for new Employee Stress

As mentioned earlier in this chapter, ROPES (Wanous, 1992) is a research-based orientation approach designed to reduce stress among new employees, provide realistic information about the job to these newcomers, and encourage them to stay in their jobs. If an organization implements ROPES, the information about factors that cause stress for new employees should be identified by current employees because they are in a better position to know what causes stress in their position than are others who may not work in that same situation. In community direct support work, possible stressors include not knowing the people who receive supports, not knowing what the typical day or routine is, having to provide medical interventions and treatments, supporting people with unpredictable behavior, working with peers who sometimes are not supportive of new people and new ideas, and being criticized by supported individuals' family members who are not satisfied with the supports provided.

Once these stressors are explained to newcomers, it is important to let these employees know that these are common experiences and that they are not alone. Their supervisor can let them know that it is common to feel fear, frustration, disappointment, and sometimes even anger in their new positions. More important, in the very early phase of employment, newcomers should have an opportunity to talk with other new employees about their feelings, fears, anxiety, and so forth. Sharing both the difficulties and the successes of the job is one of the best ways to alleviate stress.

Early in the socialization process, it is also important for the organization to provide new employees the opportunity to demonstrate, discuss, and rehearse ways they can cope with the stressors they will encounter in their jobs. This needs to occur before they encounter the stressors so that the employees feel competent that they have strategies to use when stress arises. Stress management is not a new concept; however, it is not often included in typical orientation and socialization programs for DSPs in community human services settings. Stress management techniques such as the following should be taught to new hires:

- Deal directly with the stress (e.g., get a written schedule of your workday so that you know what to expect as the day goes on, ask other staff the five things the people you support like the most or least).
- Change your perception about the stress (e.g., reappraise the situation; remember that everyone makes some mistakes at the beginning; keep in mind that everyone else is stressed, too).
- Manage the symptoms of stress (e.g., exercise, meditate, use deep breathing).
- Recognize that what stresses one person out might not stress you out; therefore, not all of the job stressors that others describe to you may be stressful to you.

The life and work experiences brought to a new job by each employee are unique. ROPES may need to be modified to acknowledge these differences and to provide specific ideas for people with various backgrounds. For example, a person who has never worked with individuals with disabilities might be most stressed about how to communicate with a person who does not talk, whereas another person might be more stressed about how to fit in with other staff members.

Support Networking Opportunities

Networking is the next step in building a successful career in direct support. With a good orientation and with opportunities for socialization, a DSP is prepared to continue learning and growing in his or her career. Supervisors reported that opportunities to gather with people in their own organization or with supervisors in other organizations were a very helpful component of learning their new job (Larson, Sauer, et al., 1998). DSPs can also benefit from having networking opportunities. Networking with colleagues can help DSPs to get professional advice on how to provide certain supports, to get a different point of view when dealing with a difficult situation, to help find funding or services that are beyond the organization's scope, and to maintain contacts in the event that one needs to leave an organization and find another direct support job. Networking opportunities can take many different forms, including developing relationships with mentors; participating in organizationwide staff meetings or celebrations; and participating in external conferences, trainings, and professional growth opportunities. Opportunities to network with DSPs in other units or divisions of an organization can help a DSP better understand his or her own work in the context of the organization as a whole. For example, a DSP in one organization was invited to attend a statewide meeting of organization staff as a reward for excellent performance during her first 12 months in the organization. By networking with other staff and listening to the speakers, she learned many new things about her employer. She reported after the meeting that she had had no idea that the organization did so many different things with so many different kinds of individuals. Attending this statewide meeting helped her put her work within the organization into better perspective. Similar advantages can be conferred by making it possible for DSPs to attend state or regional conferences (either those developed specifically for DSPs or those on topics that the DSPs are particularly interested in).

In the Spotlight: Mid-Hudson Coalition

The Mid-Hudson Coalition for the Development of Direct Care Practice, Inc. (MHC), created in 1992, is a working partnership of governmental, educational, and private institutions; individuals; and international groups. MHC is a membership organization consisting of DSPs, students, supported individuals, and organizations from the Hudson Valley region of New York State. It has more than 30 member organizations and several hundred individual members. The coalition is founded on the principle that providing quality care is a responsibility that all citizens share. MHC is committed to improving the quality of life for supported individuals through an educated and competent direct support workforce.

MHC's mission statement is as follows:

MHC's panoramic vision of the future forecasts a society where services are readily accessible through the aid of a professional direct care staff member whether in the home, the community, [or] a residential center or via a public assistance program. Such a caring society is built upon effective partnerships among specialists, direct care professionals, and persons with disabilities.

To meet this mission, MHC works collaboratively across organizations and communities to

- Develop new higher education programs for the direct support workforce
- Provide scholarships (paid for with membership dues, conference proceeds, and other resources) for tuition and books to DSPs who are enrolled in approved, participating educational programs
- Establish effective methods of direct support practices representing the diversity of direct support work in the Hudson Valley (across human services types and populations)
- Sponsor forums for DSPs throughout the year and an annual conference for DSPs to explore recommended practice in direct support and to network
- Sponsor an annual forum for executive directors and human resource personnel, to offer relevant training and networking and support opportunities to attendees
- Provide a newsletter to keep members connected with the coalition and its activities
- Offer leadership roles for DSPs within the organization and respond to the needs expressed by DSPs in the Hudson Valley region

This organization has proven that through commitment, collaboration, and a common mission, DSPs can and will become better educated and more committed to the field of community human services work. According to MHC, its organizational members have remarkably low annual turnover rates of DSPs when compared with other organizations in the region and state. Their leaders are committed to improving the working conditions and public image of DSPs. Most member organizations have found ways to build career paths and pay competitive wages. For more information, contact MHC, 36 Violet Avenue, Poughkeepsie, NY 12601; 845-452-5772 x119; fax: 845-452-9338; e-mail: info@midhudsoncoalition.org; http://www.midhudsoncoalition.org/

Encourage the Professionalization of Direct Support Professionals

Welcoming and supporting new employees also includes socializing them into the profession of providing direct supports. As with networking, professionalization is relevant throughout a DSP's career. It is important for DSPs to understand that they are part of a profession that extends well beyond the home or site in which they provide supports and even beyond the organization for which they work. Helping new-comers to the direct support profession to understand the national context of their work is critical. Unfortunately, in most settings, although DSPs are expected to dem-onstrate professional skills, they are often not treated in a professional manner, nor do they have opportunities that are typically granted to most professionals (e.g., training, education, networking, adequate wages).

Sometimes organizations fear providing networking opportunities because they fear that DSPs will jump ship or form a union. This thinking is shortsighted. Provid-ing professional recognition and opportunity may actually cause employees to be more committed to the organization. It is critical to create the opportunities that em-ployees need to be challenged and to help them grow (Harvey, 2000).

Professions such as nursing, social work, physical therapy, and teaching share several components. For example, to work within these professions, a person must have a certain amount and type of accredited training, they must pass a test or main-tain certification to be able to practice, and they must obtain continued education. Each profession has a body of knowledge that is reflected in the literature and a pro-fessional association that one can be affiliated with. In addition, in each of these pro-fessions, a professional can lose licensure or certification if he or she behaves in an unethical or illegal manner. Most often, members of these professions are able, through their credentialing body or professional association, to sanction other mem-bers for this type of behavior.

To create a direct support profession, a group of individuals and the organizations they represented formed the National Alliance for Direct Support Professionals (NADSP) in 1994. This group of interested individuals and organizations has worked hard to begin to build the foundation for the profession of direct support. Figure 5.1 identifies the goals and objectives of the NADSP.

The NADSP is committed to the well-being and full participation of all people, including people with disabilities, in everyday life in American neighborhoods and communities. The NADSP recognizes that DSPs are crucial to this commitment and that that employment conditions must be improved throughout the United States to

---

The NADSP mission is to promote the development of a highly competent human services workforce which supports individuals in achieving their life goals. We have organized our mem-bership into committees to address each of the following goals (in order of priority):

1. Enhance the status of direct support professionals.
2. Provide better access for all direct support professionals to high quality educational expe-riences (e.g., in-service training, continuing and higher education) and lifelong learning which enhances competency.
3. Strengthen the working relationships and partnerships between direct support profession-als, self-advocates, and other consumer groups and families.
4. Promote systems reform which provides incentives for educational experiences, increased compensation, and access to career pathways for direct support professionals through the promotion of policy initiatives (e.g., legislation, funding, practices).
5. Support the development and implementation of a national voluntary credentialing process for direct support professionals.

Figure 5.1. Mission and goals of the National Alliance for Direct Support Professionals (NADSP). (From National Al-liance for Direct Support Professionals. [n.d.]. *NADSP guiding principles.* Retrieved from http://www.nadsp.org/about/princip.html; reprinted by permission.)

ensure the continuity and quality of support necessary for the self-determination and community inclusion of all people.

The NADSP has been instrumental in developing several important products that align with bringing professional identity to the DSP: *Frontline Initiative*, The Moving Mountains Commitment, and the NADSP Code of Ethics. *Frontline Initiative* (see Figure 5.2) is a national newsletter written by and produced for people working in direct support roles. Its purpose is to codify the exact body of knowledge required of and used by DSPs.

The Moving Mountains Workforce Principles (see Figure 5.3) were developed by the NADSP to encourage organizations and individuals to adopt policies and practices that result in a competent, committed direct support workforce. The NADSP asks organizations to pledge to advance the workforce principles.

The NADSP Code of Ethics (see Figure 5.4) is a set of ethical practice guidelines to support people in direct support roles to make solid decisions based on ethical practice.

In addition to developing these important products, the NADSP has challenged its member organizations to embrace DSPs as leaders. For example, the NADSP worked with the American Association on Mental Retardation (AAMR) to develop a division on direct support and to offer *Frontline Initiative* to AAMR members. NADSP encourages and mentors new state and local chapters of AAMR. The following In the Spotlight segment overviews one such statewide organization in Missouri.

Figure 5.2. *Frontline Initiative,* a newsletter of the National Alliance for Direct Support Professionals (NADSP). Reprinted by permission of the NADSP.

Actively shape conditions of employment to enable direct support professionals (DSPs) to sustain themselves and their families in a self-sufficient manner by working to

- Provide health care benefits to all employees (pro-rated for part-time employment).
- Support employees in acquiring resources to meet basic life needs (e.g., housing, transportation, child care).
- Provide a living wage indexed to the cost of living that is regularly adjusted by geographic region.
- Offer flexible employee benefit plans (e.g., cafeteria plans).
- Support employee assistance programs and work conditions that encourage health and wellness and prevent job burnout.
- Prevent excessive administrative costs (e.g., salaries, bonuses, overhead) from draining resources for adequate DSP salaries and benefits and high-quality support.
- Work vigorously to raise both public and private funds necessary to provide adequate supports for participants and favorable salary and benefit conditions for DSPs.
- Ensure equity and fairness in determining salary, benefits, and bonuses for employees at all levels within the organization.

Promote ethical practice in direct support and partnership with support participants by working to

- Ensure that direct support practice is consistent with the NADSP Code of Ethics.
- Promote the empowerment and advocacy of people receiving support and their families through education.
- Rigorously screen job candidates to eliminate those who have committed acts of abuse, neglect, exploitation, or other criminal activity.
- Include the voices of support participants and their families and DSPs in the governance and evaluation of support activities.
- Honor committed DSPs by actively striving to coach, discipline, or terminate ineffective employees.

Value and empower DSPs by working to

- Ensure active and comprehensive participation of DSPs in organizational practices, policy development, and decision-making.
- Include DSPs in developing plans of support for people who receive services.
- Promote a professional identity for direct support.
- Develop organizational cultures that recognize and celebrate the accomplishments of direct support.
- Promote public awareness of the achievements of DSPs.

Ensure continuity and quality of support by working to

- Modify existing or develop new organizational practices to enhance recruitment and increase retention through the use of effective interventions.
- Track employee recruitment and retention statistics to improve outcomes.
- Provide high-quality, consistent supervision.
- Assist DSPs to overcome the isolation of decentralized environments by providing opportunities for peer support and interchange.
- Provide mentors to DSPs.
- Emphasize DSP performance outcomes that are aligned with what support participants want in their lives.

Develop a career focus regarding direct support by working to

- Identify career and educational paths for DSPs and support DSP advancement along these paths.
- Provide incentives for DSPs to pursue professional development opportunities.
- Develop and use multilevel skill and knowledge frameworks that result in recognized awards or credentials tied to advancement (e.g., on-the-job certification, credential and apprenticeship programs, postsecondary certifications and diplomas).
- Provide professional development opportunities such as job readiness, basic skills training, and advanced and specialized direct support.
- Use valid skill, knowledge, and ethical practice sets as the foundation for professional development.
- Provide high-quality educational experiences by using quality materials and effective instructional methods.

Figure 5.3. National Alliance for Direct Support Professionals (NADSP) Moving Mountains Workforce Principles. (Adapted by permission of the NADSP.)

Direct support professionals (DSPs), organization leaders, policy makers, and people receiving supports are urged to read the NADSP Code of Ethics and to consider ways that these ethical statements can be incorporated into daily practice. The beliefs and attitudes associated with being an effective human services professional are the cornerstones of this code.

Person-Centered Supports

As a DSP, my first allegiance is to the person I support; all other activities and functions I perform flow from this allegiance.

Promoting Physical and Emotional Well-Being

As a DSP, I am responsible for supporting the physical and emotional well-being of the individuals receiving support. I will encourage growth and recognize the autonomy of these individuals while being attentive and energetic in reducing their risk of harm.

Integrity and Responsibility

As a DSP, I will support the mission and vitality of my profession to assist people in leading self-directed lives and to foster a spirit of partnership with the people I support, other professionals, and members of the community.

Confidentiality

As a DSP, I will safeguard and respect the confidentiality and privacy of the people I support.

Justice, Fairness, and Equity

As a DSP, I will promote and practice justice, fairness, and equity for the people I support and the community as a whole. I will affirm the human rights, civil rights, and responsibilities of the people I support.

Respect

As a DSP, I will respect the human dignity and uniqueness of the people I support. I will recognize each person I support as valuable and help others understand his or her value.

Relationships

As a DSP, I will assist the people I support to develop and maintain relationships.

Self-Determination

As a DSP, I will assist the people I support to direct the course of their own lives.

Advocacy

As a DSP, I will advocate with the people I support for justice, inclusion, and full community participation.

Figure 5.4. National Alliance for Direct Support Professionals (NADSP) Code of Ethics. (Adapted by permission of NADSP.)

In the Spotlight: Direct Support Professionals of Missouri

Don Carrick

Direct Support Professionals of Missouri (DSPM) began in 1997 after a series of person-centered change meetings were held in the northwest Missouri area. Attendees realized DSPs were not represented well at the meetings and that without them, real and effective change could not occur. Other meetings were organized by DSPs to provide enhancement training and a chance for direct support to discuss the difficulties and successes in their jobs. The first DSP meeting was well received, and the organizers began looking for ways to continue.

With the help of a grant from AAMR, DSPM grew. The organization held several conferences, bringing together DSPs from across the northwest Missouri area and sponsoring presenters, including Dave Hingsburger, an internationally known writer and speaker about disability rights and advocacy. Due to the popularity of these meetings, and interest from other areas, the core group involved in the overall direction of DSPM began to look at ways to expand across the state.

DSPM's mission is to elevate the lives of the people supported through their staff of DSPs. The organization does this by getting DSPs together, promoting the communicating of ideas, and providing training and information to this segment of human services. DSPM has also become an advocating force for direct support in Missouri. DSPs can voice their concerns and are listened to at small, local meetings, and their comments are brought to the attention of the leaders in the human services industry. DSPM participated in a successful campaign to increase direct support wages by $1 an hour and continues to fight for additional wage increases in Missouri.

Since its inception, DSPM has also worked with the Missouri branch of the AAMR, and DSPM continues to assist with conferences and other projects. DSPM has begun to work with People First of Missouri on ways to inform direct support applicants about what the job entails and what it means to the people being supported. In addition, the organization has become an affiliate of the NADSP. DSPM is proud of its participation in assisting NADSP to form a nationwide code of ethics for direct support (see Figure 5.2).

DSPM's web site (http://www.dspm.com) gives basic information about the group and provides news and links on direct support issues both in the state and nationwide. DSPs can become members of DSPM at no cost. Members have access to a message board on the web site where they can discuss their jobs and receive important news updates. DSPM hopes to expand across Missouri. For further information please contact DSPM, Post Office Box 454, Maryville, MO 64468; 660-582-7113, fax: 660-582-3493; e-mail: dspm@asde.net.

OVERCOMING IMPLEMENTATION BARRIERS

Probably the biggest barrier to success in implementing effective orientation, socialization, networking, and professionalization practices is the pressure organizations face to fill vacant positions as soon as possible because staff turnover rates are too high. This chapter has presented both research support and practical information to demonstrate that rushing through orientation and ignoring socialization are mistakes. Instead of fixing the problem of vacant positions, organizations risk making turnover and vacancy rates even more of a problem. Successful retention requires attention to the practices described in this chapter.

Several barriers are common for organizations wishing to improve networking or professionalization opportunities for DSPs. For example, providing good networking opportunities requires creativity and financial resources. Organizations that are considering professionalization efforts often worry about the cost of employing individuals with increased training or credentials. There is not an easy answer to this concern. Organizations that have created higher standards and that have paid correspondingly higher wages have found, however, that the benefits of doing so in terms of quality of services and retention are great.

QUESTIONS TO PONDER

1. When a newly hired employee starts working at your organization, what steps does your organization take to make him or her feel welcomed and supported?

2. What stressors do DSPs experience when they start new positions in your organization? What is your organization doing to support new staff in coping with these stressors?

3. How do you communicate your organization's mission, vision, and values to new employees?

4. Does your organization have a specific socialization plan in place to assist new employees and employees who have recently been promoted to learn the roles and expectations of their new positions?

5. Does the first week on the job for DSPs focus on orientation and socialization, or is a year's worth of training crammed into that time instead?

6. What opportunities exist within your organization or community for DSPs to network to share ideas, provide support, and learn from one another?

7. Does a professional organization exist for DSPs in your area? If not, what could you do to start such an organization?

CONCLUSION

Addressing recruitment, retention, and training challenges requires careful attention to the experiences of DSPs from the time they learn about a potential job in your organization until the time they leave your organization. This chapter has focused on interventions and practices that can help people who are newly hired or those in new positions to learn the ropes of the organization and those new positions. This chapter also describes strategies to support employees throughout their tenure in the organization through networking opportunities and professionalization. If new employees are leaving in the first 3 months after being hired, then the orientation and socialization interventions described in this chapter may remedy that situation. If current employees are dissatisfied with their jobs because the organization does not offer adequate opportunities for career development, the networking and professionalization interventions in this chapter may be helpful.

RESOURCES

National Alliance for Direct Support Professionals (NADSP) (http://www.nadsp.org/)

The official web site of the NADSP contains information from local chapters across the United States with tips and resources for how to start a local, regional, or state professional association for DSPs.

Wanous, J.P. (1992). *Organizational entry: Recruitment, selection, orientation and socialization of newcomers* (2nd ed.). Boston: Addison Wesley.

This book provides a comprehensive overview of the organizational entry process. It synthesizes the research in a manner that provides concrete ideas about how to implement recommended-practice interventions. Written for both academic and practitioner audiences, this book may be somewhat technical, but it is an essential tool for readers who want to understand more about the theory behind the strategies.

In the Spotlight: Harry Meyering Center

Traci L. LaLiberte

The Harry Meyering Center (HMC) in southern Minnesota serves 145 individuals receiving supports through semi-independent living services (SILS), in-home services, supportive living services, and intermediate care facilities (ICFs). As staff work together to address issues of DSP recruitment and retention, they welcome and connect with newly hired staff.

Each new staff person is immediately assigned a peer mentor who assists in welcoming the staff member to the organization and offers an ongoing support to that staff member. The initial connection between mentor and mentee is made through face-to-face contact. Mentors are assigned to every new hire and are selected by their supervisors for their skills.

To connect new employees to current staff throughout the organization, a digital photograph of each new hire is posted in the staff lounge for approximately 2 weeks. After the photos are removed from the staff lounge, they are placed in a staff photograph album, which allows for continued connections and recognition between staff members. Staff members who work opposite shifts or at separate sites can also use the photo album when trying to swap shifts.

A formal staff welcoming program presents new hires with a welcome basket. The employees receives a brightly wrapped basket containing a coffee mug that says "Welcome to HMC," a can of soda, a bag of popcorn, and candy. In the basket is a note from the staff development director, welcoming the individual to the organization. In addition, the executive director of the organization includes a personalized note for each new hire. She may comment on a particular strength or skill the employee brings to his or her new position or acknowledge the education pursuits of a new employee who is also in school. Reaction to these personalized notes has been very positive.

As new employees settle into their new position, the efforts to make them feel welcome continue. The newcomers receive a recent HMC newsletter in their mailbox. This external newsletter is widely distributed to supported individuals and their families and other key stakeholders. Occasionally, new hires also find candy in their mailboxes. During the first 2 days of orientation, the organization also provides new hires with lunch. The first day is a working lunch, but the second day is a social lunch attended by management staff and mentors.

For some new hires, the organization provides business cards and appointment books because these new staff members will be out in the community networking and using their cards to recruit. People have reported that they *really* like this perk.

Checklist for Orientation,
Socialization, Networking, and Professionalization

Orientation and Socialization

_____ Have the newcomer's direct supervisor greet and welcome the new DSP in person the first day (keep this as social as possible).

_____ Give a note of welcome from the CEO or executive director.

_____ Provide welcome baskets.

_____ Let the supported individuals and family members know about the new hires and encourage them to call or send notes to the newcomers to welcome them.

_____ Hold a welcome dinner or lunch where newcomers will be working, attended by people who receive supports and co-workers

_____ Challenge supervisors, co-workers, and supported individuals and their families who work with newly hired staff to each give at least one positive comment regarding performance or attitude to the new DSP in the first week of employment.

_____ Assign an experienced peer to the new employee. Arrange a face-to-face meeting early in the orientation week. Let this person be the first point of contact for questions about the company.

_____ Set up face-to-face meetings in the first several weeks of employment between the FLS and the new employee(s). Use this time to check in regarding what is and is not working from the perspective of the new DSP.

_____ Create a computer-based orientation and networking environment that helps people keep in touch with each other and feel connected to the organization. Consider some of the following:

- An e-mail system that alerts current staff and supported individuals and their families that a new DSP has been hired and urges them to call or send a note of welcome

- A page on the web site listing people associated with the organization, with photographs and short biographies listing areas of specialty and roles in the organization. Include when, how, and why to contact this person. Get a digital camera and post new DSP information on the first day of orientation. Display it as you show newcomers this section of the web site during the orientation period.

- An on-line list of questions frequently asked by new employees. Have an interactive and supervised on-line bulletin board for new questions.

- An e-mail address for each new staff to communicate with others as needed for organization business. Clarify do's and don'ts for computer use, e-mail use, and web access up front to avoid misunderstandings or misuse.

Networking and Professionalization

Internal Opportunities

_____ Hold weekly open brown-bag lunch conversations with the director.

_____ Have a social hour once a month for all staff following staff meetings.

_____ Ensure that all staff meetings for DSPs are run by and for DSPs.

_____ Have DSPs take part in cross-functional work teams and action committees at the organizational level.

_____ Create logical work teams connecting people who have regular contact with each other. Teams should consist of organization employees and individuals supported and their families. On a periodic basis, randomly assign each person another person's name. Within 1 week, each person is to post on the web site or other designated spot a positive comment about the person whose name he or she received.

_____ Have DSP appreciation events in which administrators, FLSs, and supported individuals cook, serve, and share a meal with DSPs. Provide small but personalized tokens of appreciation for each DSP.

_____ Have experienced DSPs create and deliver their own training to each other.

External Opportunities

_____ Sponsor and send DSPs to local conferences and workshops designed for DSPs.

_____ Create a local professional association for DSPs.

_____ Have a statewide DSP day of celebration endorsed by the governor.

_____ Use DSPs as organization representatives in community action committees, industry associations, or informational forums.

_____ Provide a paid volunteer day to all employees once or twice a year. It gets employees out into the community and builds their esteem. Give employees a chance to share their good works with others.

_____ Give DSPs business cards, organization literature, and any other trappings of professionalization that are provided to other organization staff. This helps DSPs to share information with others and helps community members and others take DSPs and the organization seriously.

_____ Create public service announcements (for television, radio, billboards, and so forth) that highlight and thank committed, competent, and caring DSPs for their contribution to the community.

From O'Nell, S., Hewitt, A., Sauer, J., & Larson, S. (2001). _Removing the revolving door: Strategies to address recruitment and retention challenges_ (p. 87 of learner guide). Minneapolis: University of Minnesota, Institute on Community Integration, Research and Training Center on Community Living; adapted by permission.

6

LINKING TRAINING AND PERFORMANCE THROUGH COMPETENCY-BASED TRAINING

SUSAN N. O'NELL AND AMY S. HEWITT

The harder it is to find new staff to fill vacancies, the more critical performance issues are for employers. Employers are struggling with hiring from a shrinking pool of available employees, some of whom do not have the needed basic skills. Yet, few employers have a clear idea of how to improve performance. A typical solution is to provide more training opportunities. Despite expending significant effort and resources, however, organizations often do not achieve desired results from this additional training. Employee performance is a multidimensional issue. Employers do not always know how to develop and use performance criteria or how to support and reward employees to positively influence performance. This chapter explores the components of performance and the link between performance and training, including the importance of creating an ongoing competency-based training cycle of setting clear performance expectations; coordinating job analyses; assessing performance; providing feedback; and supporting and training employees in developing necessary knowledge, skills, and attitudes (KSAs) and the importance of weeding out underperforming employees and rewarding employees who meet or exceed performance expectations to attract and retain high-quality employees.

TARGETED FRONT-LINE SUPERVISOR COMPETENCIES

Front-line supervisors (FLSs) have variable responsibility for training depending on the organization for which they work. Many organizations see training as firmly in the purview of the "organization trainer" or other human resources personnel. In other organizations, supervisors and managers are the primary or only trainers of direct support professionals (DSPs). For example, in one study, 97% of FLSs reported conducting performance reviews, 94% reported providing house orientation, and 92% reported providing ongoing training to DSPs, but only 65% reported providing organization-level orientation (Larson, Lakin, & Bruininks, 1998). Either way, FLSs at a minimum must take an active interest in providing feedback to employees regarding performance and acting as role models and resources for DSPs.

Primary Skills

FLSs teach and coach DSPs using various approaches so that DSPs achieve required direct support competence.

FLSs observe, monitor, and provide feedback to DSPs regarding the implementation of individualized support plans.

FLSs provide coaching and feedback to DSPs regarding performance.

FLSs coordinate, schedule, and document DSPs' participation and performance in orientation and in-service training and completion of other self-directed learning and development.

FLSs observe and solicit feedback from DSPs and supported individuals and their families regarding DSPs training needs and desired opportunities.

FLSs share with DSPs resources and information related to supports, technology, intervention, and other issues for supporting the individuals served.

FLSs identify potential trainers and provide resources, coaching, and opportunities for DSP training.

Related Skills

3 FLSs identify necessary resources for individuals served and DSPs and advocate for these resources with their managers.

5 FLSs review, provide follow-up on, and discuss issues with DSPs regarding incident or accident reports.

FLSs provide necessary disciplinary action, including demonstrating correct performance of job tasks as indicated.

FLSs monitor for medication errors and review as indicated with DSPs.

6 FLSs support DSPs in learning how to use a computer, e-mail, and the Internet.

UNDERSTANDING THE PROBLEM

Because the labor pool is shrinking, organizations have started hiring people who have fewer or different skills from the previous pool of employees. Serious skill gaps in basic reading and math continue to grow, but employers are pulling back from testing for basic skills, not believing they can be as selective as they once could (Rottier, 2001). To fill vacancies, organizations are tapping new pools of employees by recruiting from older people (retirees), younger people (high school students), immigrants, displaced employees, and people making the transition from welfare to work. This increased diversity in the workforce means that employers can no longer rely on a common language, understanding, or skill base to shore up employee performance. For instance, some employees may have only a rudimentary understanding and use of English, whereas others may be inexperienced in typical home care activities such as laundry or cooking. Still others may need training on basic job skills, such as how and when to inform a supervisor regarding an unscheduled absence from work or how to interact with people. If a job candidate meets other important criteria, such as having a positive attitude toward engaging in direct support work, training and orientation can be adjusted to assist him or her with these skill gaps so that he or she will succeed in direct support work. The organization, however, must consider how much of this can be accomplished internally with existing resources and what other strategies need to be used.

Direct support work is viewed as entry-level work by the general public, mostly due to the wages associated with it, but to be effective, DSPs must possess and be able to implement a wide variety of complex skills without benefit of on-site supervision (Hewitt, 1998a, 1998b; Taylor, Bradley, & Warren, 1996). Many employees admit to not having these skills, and they point to their own lack of competence and that of their co-workers and supervisors as negatively affecting job satisfaction, which in turn causes turnover (Hewitt, Larson, & Lakin, 2000; Larson, Lakin, & Bruininks, 1998).

Employers often view training as one of the primary solutions to employee performance issues. Many employers take the approach that if an employee is not doing a job properly, additional training is all that is needed for the person to become a competent employee. However, an employee's completing a specified number of hours of training does not guarantee improved performance.

There are numerous federal and state mandates regarding training for DSPs in the community human services industry (Hewitt & Larson, 1994). As a result, most organizations require DSPs to undertake a significant amount of training on various prescribed topics. Yet, many current DSPs still do not have the skills necessary to do their jobs effectively, and organizations feel increased pressure to beef up training as new recruits are hired without essential skills (Gardner et al., 1983). Newly hired DSPs also report that they are not receiving the training and support they need to be successful (Sedlezky et al., 2001).

Employers must set clear expectations for performance. Despite the need for new and existing employees to develop skills, however, organizations report having significant problems getting DSPs to attend even required training (Larson, Lakin, & Bruininks, 1998; Larson, Lakin, & Hewitt, 2002). Organizations admit to reducing expectations out of the fear of having to replace people or of not finding people to fill vacancies (ANCOR, 2001b). As the skill gaps between employees and job expectations grow, the threat to people receiving supports, whose basic health and safety needs may no longer be met, grows as well (Anderson & Hewitt, 2002). DSPs have reported becoming frustrated by the low standards of performance of the new employees, and some are leaving as a result (Larson, Lakin, & Bruininks, 1998). This turnover of otherwise satisfied employees is certainly a challenge to the industry. For increased employee retention to be meaningful, organizations must work to keep their most competent and qualified employees.

In some communities, organizations are pulling back from developing much-needed new support services due to the lack of adequate employees to fill DSP positions (Kansans Mobilizing for Workforce Change Stakeholder Advisory Group, 2004). This inability to create new and timely services results in people who need support services remaining on waiting lists, to the detriment of those individuals and their families. Industry stakeholders acknowledge that this lack of qualified employees is a significant barrier to person-centered support services and that a high-quality workforce is essential in creating a system that provides high-quality support to everyone (Hewitt & Lakin, 2001; National Association of State Directors of Developmental Disabilities Services, 2000b). There is also concern that the increasingly complex needs of people who receive supports in home- and community-based settings cannot be met by the people who are currently being recruited and employed in the field (Greene, 2000).

Although the lack of qualified DSPs has a profound effect on the lives of the people being supported (Anderson & Hewitt, 2002), the human services industry has been slow to calculate the actual financial cost of low employee performance. Like any other business investment, decisions about training should be based in part on return on investment. In an industry in which training is mandated so heavily and in which training is primarily funded by federal and state governments, it is surprising that accountability for training results has not been part of the discussion, especially given the public support for decreasing government waste.

There are various indicators of the cost of poor performance in traditional businesses or in nonprofit organizations or government agencies (Bowsher, 1998; Carr, 1992). The most frequently cited indicators of poor performance include the following:

- Loss of customers (or individuals supported) due to low satisfaction
- Higher operating costs (e.g., overtime pay, increased insurance premiums due to employee accidents)
- Loss of employees due to low job satisfaction
- Increased need for supervision of employees (resulting in supervisor stress, turnover, and/or inability to complete other critical tasks)
- Increased recruitment and hiring costs (e.g., advertising, hiring bonuses, screening, time to interview)
- Increased need for training of new employees and retraining of existing employees and related costs (e.g., instructor time, materials, overtime for other employees covering training hours)

Poor performance in community human services has huge costs in real dollars and in the human and societal costs of not providing adequate care and support to people with developmental disabilities and to other people who rely on DSPs. The financial losses associated with poor performance are perhaps most distressing in an industry that currently does not provide a livable wage to the bulk of its employees (ANCOR, 2001b; Braddock & Mitchell, 1992; Hewitt & Lakin, 2001) because such losses mean that organizations have less money available for wages.

The question remains: How can the community human services industry have all of the signs of attrition and financial loss due to poor performance and simultaneously spend large amounts of money on staff training aimed at ensuring competence? Understanding the depth of this problem includes understanding two important concepts: 1) Training is only part of the performance equation, and 2) to be effective in improving employee performance, training has to designed and delivered properly.

There are many problems with the methods and to some extent the topics used for training DSPs. Even if every trainer were to become proficient in effective training techniques and topics were completely in line with current best practices, training would not necessarily improve employee performance. Performance is the product of many variables at various levels within the organization and within the employee. Training alone, no matter how well designed, cannot compensate for barriers within organizations or employees that decrease or impede employee performance. The following are some critical barriers to performance that no training program, no matter how well designed, can overcome:

- A poor match between the employee and the specific job (e.g., personality, hours available, transportation problems; see Chapter 4, which discusses how to select employees who are a good match for the job)
- Lack of needed resources to do the job (e.g., high-quality, person-centered supports arc not likely to happen in an environment with one DSP to support eight people with significant support needs)
- Lack of clear vision and expectations by supervisors, administrators, quality assurance monitors, and others (e.g., person-centered support will not happen if feedback and expectations are focused exclusively on other aspects of support; see Chapter 12, which discusses articulating an organization's mission)
- Absence of recognition and reward for improved performance (see Chapter 9, which discusses employee recognition)
- Incompetence accepted and perpetual in the organization (e.g., unsatisfactory performers are maintained)

To create and maintain high-performance work environments, organizations must incorporate a variety of strategies designed to improve and maintain the skills and performance of the organization's best employees. The organization must work from the outset to recruit and select new employees who will enjoy the available work and to weed out undesirable candidates, such as those who may be a threat to the people whom they support or those who do not have a desire or capacity to perform well (see Chapter 4 for strategies on selecting employees). Once high-potential employees are hired, they need to be reinforced, supported, rewarded, and held accountable for job skills in order to maintain these skills.

If performance problems are due to skill gaps (the difference between what employees know and what they need to know to do the job) rather than other factors, high-quality training programs can improve employee performance and help these employees gain critical skills. High-quality training is competency based and is part of a comprehensive system that identifies skill gaps and provides needed supports to the employee to develop and maintain critical skills.

Competency-based training (and performance reviews) are critical, for although organizations may still be focused on whether they are meeting training mandates, to meet the promise of person-centered supports, organizations will have to have a much higher level of confidence in their employees' knowledge, skills, and attitudes (KSAs). It is one thing to satisfy regulators, organizations, and quality assurance monitors evaluating compliance issues in the short term by demonstrating attendance at training. It is another thing altogether to have confidence that an employee knows how to handle a wide variety of situations appropriately and with confidence.

RESEARCH SUPPORT FOR SOLUTIONS

One approach that is being increasingly used in United States business and industry is competency-based training (Blank, 1982; Goldstein, 1993; National Governors Association Center for Best Practice & Mid-Atlantic Workforce Brokerage, 1999). Competency-based programs provide a systematic approach to training that is designed, monitored, and adjusted with work performance and results in mind. Competency-based programs for DSPs are based on specific, precisely stated outcomes (usually called *competencies* or *tasks*) that have been recently verified as essential for successful employment. These competencies describe exactly what a DSP should be able to do upon completion of the training program. Competency-based training programs provide the DSP with high-quality, individual-centered learning activities and materials carefully designed to help the learner master each task. Within these models, the DSP is given enough time to fully master one task before moving to the next. Competency-based models also require each learner to perform each task to a high level of proficiency in a joblike (or real work) environment before receiving credit for attaining the task (Blank, 1982). These training programs typically avoid dictating the method of instruction, thus allowing for more flexibility within organizations and educational institutions (Fiorelli, Margolis, Heverly, Rothchild, & Krasting, 1982).

Research support for competency-based training methods include large-scale evaluations. One such study showed that competency-based training in vocational education made significant contributions to employers because that learning can be acquired on the job (Mulcahy & James, 2000).

In the Spotlight: Dungarvin—A New Perspective on Training

Sandy Henry, Orville Williamschen, and Dawn Smith

Dungarvin provides a wide range of services across an equally wide range of geography. As owner and manager of 12 corporations in 12 states, Dungarvin provides residential, case management, Medicaid waiver, day habilitation, and supported employment services, employing 1,700 DSPs nationwide. With such a large and diverse workforce, orientation and training of DSPs is an enormous task. To transform current practices and develop a new competency-based training program is monumental, even overwhelming. Everyone in the organization has to change the way they think, talk, and act about training.

The traditional model of training DSPs is an initial orientation and periodic in-service sessions. This model meets regulatory requirements but often fails to motivate staff or really address what DSPs need to know. Employees often leave orientation and training not understanding how to apply classroom learning to real work situations. Or, if they are experienced employees, they may leave bored and frustrated because they have not learned new or valuable information.

This is an especially critical issue at Dungarvin, which offers a wide variety of services in many different locales. Some states have an employment pool with many experienced DSPs; others have fewer experienced employees. Dungarvin needs to meet the training needs of a staff with diverse skills and experiences, ensure that they are always learning and growing professionally, and make a direct connection between training and better services to supported individuals. For these reasons, Dungarvin is moving toward competency-based training.

When Dungarvin decided to make this companywide shift to competency-based training, it set up a committee of members from four states with representation from different levels of management. This committee used the results of focus groups of DSPs, on-site observations, and a needs assessment survey to determine what their DSPs do, what they need to do to be good at their jobs, what they liked and didn't like about the current training model, and what KSAs the DSPs needed. The organization also established a mission and charge for the committee and drew up a 1-year work plan. Each member of the committee shared his or her specific knowledge, experience, and ideas regarding what competencies were required of Dungarvin employees during orientation. They started with the *Community Support Skill Standards* (CSSS; Taylor, Bradley, & Warren, 1996).

In using the CSSS as a tool, the committee identified those standards that all Dungarvin DSPs needed during the orientation period. Once the base competency areas and skill standards were established, the committee developed more specific performance indicators for each skill standard. These were reviewed and refined by Dungarvin managers across the country. The committee then identified how the various competencies would be measured using assessment strategies such as direct observation by peers or supervisors, written documentation or testing, employee self-reporting, or verbal discussion. These assessments may enable some staff to test out of areas of training in which they are already competent, whereas others may receive additional training until they achieve competence.

The committee is currently reviewing existing curricula and hopes to find a mix of appropriate curricula already available, developing only limited additional curricula. Dungarvin pilot-tested the competency measurement and evaluation tool in four states. The committee is making revisions and expects the system to be completed soon. All states will then add to the national standards and curricula for unique services in their areas.

The mission of Dungarvin, Inc., is "Respecting and responding to the choices of people with developmental disabilities." Living by this mission also means that as an organization we must also respect and respond to the needs of our DSPs.

Sandy Henry is Senior Director, Orville Williamschen is Regional Director, and Dawn Smith is Director with Dungarvin, Inc., St. Paul, Minnesota. They may be reached at 612-699-6050 or 690 Cleveland Avenue South, St. Paul, MN 55116. From Henry, S., Williamschen, O., & Smith, D. (1998, Winter). A new perspective on training at Dungarvin. *IMPACT: Feature Issue on Direct Support Workforce Development, 10*(4), 16; adapted by permission.

STRATEGIES FOR RESPONDING TO THE PROBLEM: DEVELOPING COMPETENCY-BASED TRAINING

So that DSPs can enhance and maintain their performance, they must have access to a system of competency-based training. In essence, competency-based training is designed to facilitate the development of specific, well-thought, applicable competencies. *Competence* is generally defined as having the needed KSAs to do something that is designed or required to yield certain outcomes. Thus, competency-based training is purposeful and is intended to develop specific skill sets as well as certain knowledge and attitudes. Figure 6.1 illustrates a seven-step training process through which compe-

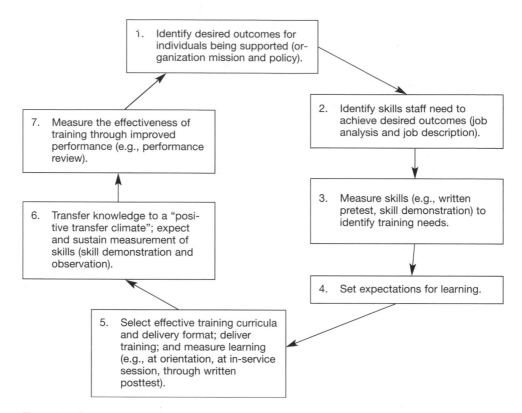

Figure 6.1. Competency-based training model. (From Hewitt, A., & Larson, S.A. [1994]. Training issues for direct service personnel working in community residential programs for persons with developmental disabilites. *Policy Research Brief, 6*(2), 10; adapted by permission.)

tence can be achieved (Hewitt, 1998a; Hewitt & Larson, 1994). The rest of this chapter explains this competency-based training model and discusses potential barriers and methods of evaluation of the model in community human services organizations.

Step 1: Identify Desired Outcomes (Organization Mission and Policy)

"To ensure that each employee is physically present for all state and federally mandated training." Unfortunately, this is often the message employees get from their training experience. Regardless of how well crafted an organization's mission statement and business goals are in relationship to person-centered supports and quality of life, employees can lose their focus on what is important to everyday job functions during mind-numbing, in-depth explorations of first aid; medication administration; local, state, and federal regulations; CPR; blood-borne pathogens; emergency procedures; cleaning checklists; and other process-focused training.

Although most of these topics are critical parts of the foundation on which to build high-quality, person-centered supports, without additional training and development opportunities, DSPs will not develop the skills necessary for more sophisticated supports. Also, depending upon the message and focus of the training, often

DSPs learn only that there are *a lot* of regulations and that if they are not followed, employees and the organization will get into trouble. Most organizations, however, do not move beyond training mandates as a method for identifying employee training needs. To understand what training employees need, it is important for an organization to identify the competencies that they need. This has to be done within the context of the organization's mission and vision. The focus on the mission and vision needs to permeate competency-based training so that employees have a clear understanding of what the organization considers important and why.

Step 2: Identify Skills Staff Need (Job Analysis and Job Description)

The first step to creating effective training is job analysis—identifying what people need to know to do their jobs and understanding when they need to develop these skills and abilities. Many organizations have outdated or inaccurate job descriptions and performance reviews and unclear expectations for DSPs. This lack of clarity comes primarily from changes in the expectations for DSPs, brought about by changing paradigms in support (e.g., use of individual instead of congregate support models; increased focus on self-determination, choice, empowerment, and person-centered supports).

As hard as it has been (and remains) to change the physical location in which support services are provided (as happened in deinstitutionalization), the move to smaller, more individualized support settings has been a great success compared with the industry's response to the changing roles of the DSP. New paradigms of support require a different set of skills for the successful DSP, including being able to manage health and safety concerns in balance with supporting individuals served to achieve personal goals and address individually defined quality-of-life issues. Knowledge and skills in the areas of advocacy; community building; and facilitating choice, empowerment, and self-determination are important, yet few curricula or models for teaching these skills exist. Mandated training primarily focuses on health and safety topics and has not been adequately updated to reflect these new concepts in supports (Hewitt & Larson, 1994). A job analysis of residential direct support competencies (Hewitt, 1998a) shows clearly that many residential DSP duties and skills include tasks well beyond meeting basic health and safety standards (see the Tools section of this chapter for examples)

Another unheralded and often ignored change is that not all direct support positions are identical. As increased skills are needed, increased specialization can be expected and is desirable. It is reasonable to expect that employees who are new to the field have more direct supervision. Full maturity of a DSP often requires years, not days. To stay current, DSPs need ongoing development opportunities.

These perspectives of direct support work fly in the face of industry practices that treat DSPs as if they were a "dime a dozen" and as if "anyone" could do the work. For example, these perspectives call into question organizational practices such as hiring DSPs, regardless of previous experience, at the same wage or providing raises based solely on employee tenure rather than on development of specific skills and experiences that contribute to the organization's mission. Another questionable practice is using repetitive "cookie-cutter" training as the only kind of training opportunity available to DSPs.

Conduct Job Analysis and Apply Results to Training and Performance Appraisal

The lack of definition regarding actual DSP job duties makes it difficult to assess what skills people have and to develop and offer training that meets these people's needs. To fully understand the KSAs needed by DSPs, an organization should conduct a thorough job analysis identifying what employees do and what they should do to effectively complete their job duties. Use of job analysis is one characteristic of high-performing organizations; regular use of job analyses is associated with lower turnover and higher productivity (Huselid, 1995). By taking the time to identify the necessary KSAs required of employees in each position, an organization can ensure that employees are trained to do what they are supposed to and that their performance is measured against the critical elements of the job.

Job analyses can be conducted in a variety of ways (Camp, Blanchard, & Huszczo, 1986; Wiant, 1993). Basically, what is important is that periodically (every 1–2 years), the organization uses a structured and purposeful way to gather information from several sources (e.g., employees, supervisors, individuals served) about what employees are doing that works well, what employees are doing that is not working well, and what employees need to be doing to be the best at what they do. This information can be gathered from written surveys, interviews, focus groups, on-line forums, reviews of incident reports, letters in employees' personnel files recognizing excellent performance, and other sources. Important questions to ask or consider when conducting a job analysis are included in Table 6.1.

At least two comprehensive job analyses have been designed for DSPs who support people with disabilities in community settings. The first is the *Community Support Skill Standards* (CSSS; Taylor et al., 1996), which describe competencies needed by

Table 6.1. Job analysis questions

People to ask	Questions
Employees	What do you do on your job? What tasks or duties do you complete every day, every week, or every month?
	What do you feel you should be doing to be the best at what you do?
	What are the challenges you face, or what are the hardest tasks related to your job?
Supervisors/managers	What do direct support professionals (DSPs) do at their jobs? What tasks or duties do they routinely complete (e.g., daily, weekly, monthly)?
	What should DSPs be doing to be the best at what they do? What should they be doing to fully embrace and carry out the organization's mission and values?
	Describe incidents that illustrate excellent performance for DSPs.
	What mistakes do DSPs in your organization make routinely? Describe critical incidents that illustrate poor performance for DSPs.
Individuals and family members supported	What do the best DSPs do to support you well?
	What do the worst DSPs do that is not supportive of you or that you feel is not effective direct support work?
	What do you think DSPs should be doing to provide the very best possible supports?

DSPs across a variety of community settings, including residential, educational, and vocational, and many different populations, such as people with mental health needs, older adults, and people with developmental disabilities. The second is the *Community Residential Core Competencies* (CRCC; Hewitt, 1998b), which are specific to community residential supports for individuals with developmental disabilities. In addition, job analyses have been developed for FLSs (Hewitt, Larson, O'Nell, Sauer, & Sedlezky, 1998; see Figure 1 in the Introduction) and executive directors of community support organizations for people with disabilities (Oregon Rehabilitation Association, 1999). Overviews of and samples from the CSSS, CRCC, and the job analysis for executive directors are included at the end of this chapter.

Using an existing job analysis as a jumping-off point can expand an organization's understanding of the skills needed by DSPs (or FLSs or executive directors) and can greatly reduce the time needed to do a job analysis. Rather than start from scratch, the organization can select the competencies needed for the job from an existing job analysis and add any other skills that may be specific to the organization or the position. Organizations that use this process may find that DSPs actually need skills that have not previously been identified or that training efforts to date have not addressed several important categories of skills. Another benefit of building a job analysis on existing skill sets is that many state and national initiatives have linked these skill sets to innovations in postsecondary education, voluntary credentialing, and apprenticeship programs as a way to professionalize direct support and retain competent DSPs and FLSs. By building training and assessment opportunities around these existing job analyses and the skill sets within them, an organization could have an advantage in terms of providing real career opportunities and being considered an employer of choice. (For more on professionalization of direct support work, see Chapter 5.)

Use the Identified Competencies in Job Descriptions and Performance Appraisals

Once the skills needed to perform a job have been identified through job analysis, the next step is to develop up-to-date job descriptions and corresponding performance appraisal protocols. The job descriptions should be comprehensive enough that an applicant for the position, if hired, would not be surprised by the duties he or she is asked to perform and specific enough that supervisors evaluating performance can discern whether current employees are competent in the core areas of their job assignment. One way to accommodate DSPs with different skills is to create multiple direct support positions within the organization. These different positions can be based on clusters of skills that are considered entry level, intermediate, and advanced. They can also be differentiated based on areas of specialization, such as mentoring employees, making community connections, or keeping abreast of health or behavioral supports. Compensation should vary, with advanced and specialized employees being compensated at higher levels than entry-level employees. Performance appraisals should be customized to accurately reflect the skills required of each position. For performance appraisals to be effective, employees must clearly understand the requirements of their positions and participate actively in self-assessment of their skills when completing performance reviews.

Although it is important for organizations to be aware of individual desires for promotions that will take employees into supervisory roles and to nurture those interests through development opportunities and timely promotions, in most community human services organizations, more than 80% of the employees work in direct support roles (Larson, Hewitt, & Anderson, 1999). Many people find direct support work to be more satisfying than supervisory or management work. By providing varied opportunities for DSPs and acknowledging their expertise through fair compensation, an organization can increase retention of highly qualified employees in positions that are still primarily direct support roles. Organizations should not be afraid to develop positions that let different employees capitalize on their strengths and interests. For instance, one location may have three positions requiring primarily direct support, with some supervisory components (e.g., acting as a family liaison, scheduling visits or supports, peer mentoring). Organizations can think creatively while also being clear about job expectations.

Step 3: Measure Skills to Identify Training Needs

When a new employee is hired, an initial skills assessment is needed to ensure that the employee has the basic skills necessary to perform his or her assigned job. Some skills may be assessed during the hiring process, but much of this work will occur after an employee has been hired. Because many training topics are mandated by federal or state law, organizations often send all new employees, regardless of competence, through the full gamut of mandated training within the first few weeks of employment. This approach is not likely to inspire much confidence in an experienced employee who may become bored by having to retake training on topics he or she has already mastered and is not likely to provide enough assistance to the inexperienced employee in initial skill development. Such a strategy should not be confused with orientation, which, as discussed in Chapter 5, is about welcoming employees to the organization and helping them understand how things work at the organization. Orientation covers topics such as how to complete time cards, where supplies and equipment can be found, and whom to talk to for questions about a variety of topics.

For an organization to meet training mandates, it is important to consider providing reasonable options for new but experienced employees to "test out" to be exempted from training on mandated topics. Since so many mandated topics relate to health and safety or regulatory topics, developing effective tests of this knowledge is usually not difficult. Simple demonstration combined with paper-and-pencil tests can provide a good idea of an employee's level of competence and knowledge related to most mandatory training requirements, such as medication administration or understanding of rules and regulations. Certifications and credentials earned prior to hire can help in identifying new employees who should be offered a test-out option.

For employees who come to an organization with little work history in community human services, the organization should avoid making assumptions about what these employees can or cannot do or what they know or do not know. It may be useful to ask all new employees to fill out a self-assessment of their knowledge or skills about direct support work. Generally employees will make a good-faith effort to identify their skills and past training completed. Once exemption tests and self-assessments have been completed, it is important to next compare what employees know and can already do, using job analysis results (the list of necessary KSAs for their positions).

Immediate and ongoing training opportunities should be identified and should flow directly from the assessment of skills gaps between an employee's current competence and those required of his or her position. Assuming that training is needed and has been identified as a result of a skills gap assessment, prioritizing training needs is important. Those skills that will be required first in the course of the individual's employment should be the target of initial training. Training on topics that are important but less critical should not be covered until the person has had a chance to become acquainted with his or her work site and has begun to see why and how this later training is relevant to his or her work. Training should not occur on topics unrelated to the actual job tasks and duties of the employee's current position or a position that he or she aspires to fill in the future.

Steps 4, 5, and 6: Set Expectations for Learning, Deliver Training, and Transfer Knowledge to Job Performance

Once training needs are identified and prioritized, it is important for the organization to determine how the employee will be trained. Chapter 7 focuses on effective training practices for adult learners and offers detailed information about training techniques, that is, the "how" of training delivery (Step 5 of the competency-based training model).

Organizations must also pay close attention to where and when learners will be trained. To effectively train employees in meaningful job skills, organizations must consider giving up their loyalty to classroom delivery of training. Although an estimated 78% of all corporate training is done in the classroom (Caudron, 2000), organizations that provide community residential services to people with developmental disabilities rely on classroom learning for an even greater proportion of training experiences (Braddock & Mitchell, 1992). Classroom training has many drawbacks. The direct support workforce is geographically dispersed, works odd hours, and has other constraints that make attending classroom training difficult, so classroom training should not be the primary way in which organizations expect to train their employees. Classroom training is the least flexible alternative in terms of location and scheduling. Because people retain more information when they practice a skill in the setting where it will be used (O'Neill, 1998), one of the most effective options is structured on-the-job training. Other alternatives include self-paced training modules (written, videotaped, or computer based), skill mentoring, or a combination of these options with classroom-based training.

Step 7: Measure the Effectiveness of Training Through Improved Performance

Training programs in organizations often focus on tracking *seat time*, or the amount of time a staff person is physically present in a training session. In fact, there may be no other record of the person's training other than the title or topic of the training; the duration of the training session; and the staff person's signature, indicating attendance at the session. Organizations measure the relative success or failure of their training programs by the number of employees who attend training sessions of their own initiative. Unfortunately, as organization trainers can attest, participants might not be awake for the entire training session. In addition, sometimes training time is padded (e.g., if the session is scheduled to last 3 hours and the material is covered in 2 hours, employees still get credit for 3 hours of training). This strange method of evaluating training is the result of maintaining a focus on meeting training mandates rather than ensuring that employees have actually gained competence in the KSAs on which the training has focused.

Typically, beyond checking completion of hours on various topics, there is limited assessment of posttraining competency at all, and when it does exist, it is usually done through response to multiple-choice or other paper-and-pencil tests. The benefits of these kinds of testing are that they can be standardized and are quick and easy to administer and score. On the other hand, a passing score on a written test may not necessarily reflect a person's actual ability to perform the skills in a real setting.

Enhanced assessment, such as asking the learner to provide responses to problem-solving scenarios, or portfolio assessment, in which the learner gathers work samples that are evidence of his or her effectiveness as an employee, are better options. These assessments are usually richer than true/false or multiple-choice tests, but they, too, have limits. These measures are difficult to develop, harder to reliably assess, and require greater resources (e.g., time, people). To be considered effective by performance and competency standards, training must result in improved performance on the job. Performance appraisals and assessment methods should thus be designed to incorporate direct observation of skills in the actual work setting as the primary method for assessing the employee's competency. This direct observation of skills call on a variety of sources, including people receiving supports and their family members; co-workers; supervisors; and even neighbors or friends of the people being supported, if they are willing.

Because DSPs often work alone and people with developmental disabilities may have limited experience or skills in providing well-rounded performance evaluations, someone else charged with assisting an employee in his or her development and performance—such as a supervisor—will have to be available to observe employee performance. Supervisors often spend so much time hiring and orienting new employees, dealing with scheduling issues, and providing direct support because of vacant positions that they are left with little time to monitor, assess, and train staff. Efforts must be made to provide direct guidance and feedback to employees regarding their performance, particularly entry-level employees who are learning basic job duties and who may or may not be able to perform accurate self-assessments.

One option to enhance this observation opportunity is to create lead DSP positions or peer mentors. More experienced employees who are working on advanced skills should be encouraged to use more sophisticated methods of demonstrating their skill. Presentations to other employees or governing boards, development of portfolios or useful products, and other creative methods can be used to demonstrate competency in higher-level skills as well as to provide additional professional development opportunities to employees. For a review of various performance assessment and evaluation options, see Table 6.2.

Developing and maintaining a highly competent workforce requires ongoing assessment of skills gaps and provision of needed training. Compartmentalizing training

Table 6.2.   Performance assessment and evaluation options

Assessment or evaluation type	Pros	Cons
True/false or multiple-choice test		
Written test of knowledge	Easy to score Less costly to implement Easy to use with large numbers of people Familiar to most supervisors and employees	Difficult to design valid questions Difficult to measure application to what occurs on the job Some people do poorly on written tests.
Scenario-based problem solving		
Learner is presented with a real-life situation in a vignette and is asked to respond.	Presents actual situations and focuses on what the learner would do Provides opportunity for in-depth responses	Difficult to ensure scenario is an accurate portrayal of the learner's job Time-consuming to develop Difficult to train scorers to reliably assess Vulnerable to desirability bias; learner may give socially desirable answer rather than what he or she would actually do Learner may give the right answer but may then fail to do it on the job.
Portfolio development		
A collection of work samples selected by the learner as a demonstration of his or her competence in a given area	Provides real work examples and experiential learning Can provide portable evidence of competence for employees seeking career advancement Allows evidence to be presented by learner in various formats and creatively	Time-consuming to develop Difficult to train scorers to reliably assess Unfamiliar to most employees, meaning that training must be provided on how to develop a portfolio Learner has to be self-motivated.
Self-assessment		
Assessment of an individual's own skills using behaviorally anchored rating scales	Allows assessment of hard-to-observe behaviors Provides a chance for individuals to provide input into the assessment process Can help individuals better understand skills gaps and future training needs	More chance than with other methods for false or misleading responses Individuals may not understand the skill well enough to assess themselves.
Direct observation		
Observations made of the employee actually doing their job or demonstrating a skill (these observations can be made by a supervisor, manager, co-worker, peer mentor, person who receives supports, or other person)	Employee is observed demonstrating actual skill on the job.	Hard for evaluators to be around to observe Reliability of sources can be challenging. Observers must have a good understanding of what good performance looks like.

and performance evaluation to specific times and places discourages employees from actively participating in their own development and from holding themselves to higher standards. In contrast, providing ongoing opportunities to learn and develop encourages high-potential employees to continue to enhance and cultivate skills. Although quarterly, semiannual, or annual evaluations may help ensure that the gamut of skills are assessed and may be used in annual compensation adjustments, performance feedback and related training and development opportunities should be scheduled for when employees need them.

In the Spotlight: ELM Homes

ELM Homes is a large organization in south central Minnesota that employs approximately 475 staff members to support individuals across 10 counties in three intermediate care facilities, 50 supportive living services homes, and approximately 100 semi-independent living situations and in-home support locations. ELM Homes has used the CSSS (Taylor, Bradley, & Warren, 1996) in its job analyses since October 1999. ELM Homes's job descriptions and performance evaluations are based entirely on the CSSS competency model. ELM Homes has found great success in its approach to job analysis and is on the cutting edge within the profession. Although challenges have surfaced, the significant advantages have made the process worthwhile and rewarding.

The many advantages of a competency-based work environment are rooted in gains to the individuals involved. First and foremost, supported individuals receive a higher quality of service from DSPs who achieve increased levels of competency as a result of ELM Homes's commitment to this approach. ELM Homes's staff members embrace the competency-based model because they can experience career advancement through the process. Career advancement is built into their job descriptions. Staff members decide for themselves if they want to move forward by achieving higher competency levels in their work. Regardless of the choice regarding advancement, each employee is paid in relation to his or her level of competency.

ELM Homes's employees report that when they attend conferences, they are more knowledgeable and better prepared than some of their colleagues from other organizations. In addition, when employees begin advanced education through a vocational program (also based on the CSSS), they experience greater success. They credit this success to the competency-based approach at ELM Homes because the terminology and concepts, and ultimately the professional competencies, are encompassed in their daily job tasks. These employees express pride in working for a leading organization and in their personal levels of achievement and knowledge.

From the administration's vantage point, a competency-based program affords the opportunity to provide employees targeted feedback, whether complimentary or corrective, in a timely and accurate fashion. The organization is better equipped to handle staffing issues as they arise and to hold employees accountable to their skill competency levels. Employee performance evaluation is objective and less vulnerable to subjective errors and challenges.

The competency-based approach has not come to ELM Homes without resistance, however. Although the challenges have been few, they are worth noting. The creation of job descriptions took considerable time, energy, and resources from the organization. Once completed, the job descriptions were lengthy. This length is, however, necessary to carefully address each competency area in depth. The next challenge is that a lengthy job description subsequently results in a lengthy performance evaluation. Last, the vocabulary used in the competency-based program and in the organization environment is advanced, and many of the entry-level employees are unfamiliar with this specialized vocabulary when they begin working at ELM Homes. It is time consuming, albeit necessary, to train new employees in the language and concepts inherent in a competency-based program.

Overall, ELM Homes benefits tremendously from implementing the competency-based program with its employees. It is rare that an organization can implement change that results in satisfaction of administration, employees, and consumers. The competency-based program seems to be the key.

OVERCOMING IMPLEMENTATION BARRIERS

The most noteworthy barrier to aligning current training practices with higher performance is the need to significantly revise practices throughout the organization. Enhancing performance may not be business as usual for most direct support organizations. Organizations may fear that turnover of poor or barely adequate performers will be too much to handle or that new training and assessment methods will be too complex.

DSPs and trainers may initially resist a new training paradigm. Employees may resist being responsible for identifying their own training needs and seeking necessary training opportunities. Trainers may resist the transition from being the ones who deliver all of the training to coordinating and communicating about training resources (including such information sources as staff members who have expertise on various topics, and Internet-based resources), especially if the benefits of helping with training are not made clear. Supervisors and co-workers may resent what are perceived as additional responsibilities in welcoming, mentoring, and training new employees. DSPs may not enjoy or feel secure in having training outcomes measured in terms of job performance, and they may not agree with trainers on which competencies are important. In addition, trainers may not like having to adapt their training styles to those of trainees as opposed to trainees adapting to the trainers' preferred styles.

Revamping an outdated and ineffective training and orientation system takes a significant amount of planning time and ongoing effort. It is critical to anticipate barriers to implementation and to seek and build necessary support and buy-in from everyone involved. Organizations are wise to educate governing boards, employees, and people receiving supports about the need to make these changes and to help them understand the parameters and to seek their input in developing and maintaining the new system.

Across industries, only an estimated 15% of training courses are evaluated based on performance on the job (Caudron, 2000). Ultimately the mark of an effective training program is that performance on the job improves. Evaluating the effect of improved training practices is not as hard as it seems. The costs of poor performance should serve as important indicators for tracking the success of performance-based training systems and other changes to improve performance: greater satisfaction on the part of individuals supported and employees, reduced need for remedial supervision, and significant cost savings over time through reduced operation costs and less money spent on hiring new employees and providing remedial training to employees.

QUESTIONS TO PONDER

1. Are your organization's mission, vision, and purpose clear at all levels of performance, including during training opportunities? Do employees and trainers know how training relates to the mission, vision, and purpose of your organization?
2. Is yours a learning organization (an organization that continually strives to better itself by seeking new information and ways of doing things)? If not, how can ongoing learning become part of your organization's culture?
3. Do all employees have and understand their current job description, which is based on the results of a job analysis? Do the job descriptions reflect the actual skills people need to accomplish the organization's mission and vision? Are training opportunities, resources, and evaluation tools in line with these critical skills?
4. Are all DSPs working under the same job descriptions and pay scales, despite having different responsibilities, skills, and abilities?
5. How are employees trained? What flexible training opportunities could be developed?
6. At your organization, who is responsible for conducting an employee's training: the employee, his or her supervisor, or the human resources department? How can you empower and support employees to take initiative for identifying and meeting their own training needs?
7. How does your organization identify environmental factors that impede training? How are these resolved?

CONCLUSION

Developing, using, and evaluating a competency-based training program is complex and challenging. Identifying needed skills and competencies by conducting a job analysis is critical. All training for and evaluations of employees should be directly related to the KSAs indicated in the job analysis. Careful consideration of what employees need to learn and how they will apply that learning on the job is an important part of effective skills evaluation. Though implementing competency-based training is a challenge, the payoff of a competent workforce is well worth the effort.

RESOURCES

Hewitt, A. (1998). *Community residential core competencies: Necessary competencies for direct support staff working in community residential services for people with developmental disabilities.* Minneapolis: University of Minnesota, Institute on Community Integration, Research and Training Center on Community Living (Available on-line: http://www.rtc.umn.edu/pdf/analysis.pdf)

This is a job analysis completed for the role of DSPs who work in small community residential services supporting people with developmental disabilities.

Hewitt, A., Larson, S.A., O'Nell, S., Sauer, J., & Sedlezky, L. (1998). *The Minnesota frontline supervisor competencies and performance indicators: A tool for agencies providing community services.* Minneapolis: University of Minnesota, Institute on Community Integration, Research and Training Center on Community Living. (Available from the publisher, 612-624-0060; http://www.rtc.umn.edu/pdf/flsupcom.pdf)

This booklet contains the results of a comprehensive job analysis for community FLSs. It describes the characteristics of a contemporary community support organization; the mission, vision, and values that underlie the competencies; and the 14 broad FLS competency areas, competency statements within these areas, and performance indicators for each of the competency statements.

Oregon Rehabilitation Association. (1999). *Competencies for executive directors.* Salem: Author.

This document lists the skills needed by executive directors in community human services settings. It is designed to assists boards of directors as well as current and aspiring executive directors to understand the key skills and competencies that executive directors need to be successful.

Taylor, M., Bradley, V., & Warren, R., Jr. (1996). *Community support skill standards: Tools for managing change and achieving outcomes.* Cambridge, MA: Human Services Research Institute. (Available from the publisher, 2236 Massachusetts Avenue, Cambridge, MA 02140; 617-876-0426; fax: 617-492-7401; http://www.hsri.org/)

The *Community Support Skill Standards* (CSSS) are a job analysis of the roles and competencies of DSPs who work in community human services organizations.

Excerpts from the *Community Support Skill Standards*

The *Community Support Skill Standards* (CSSS; Taylor, Bradley, & Warren, 1996) reflect the results of a job analysis for community human services practitioners in direct support roles. The standards are organized first by broad competency areas, which describe competencies needed to be effective in direct support roles. Within each broad competency area are multiple skill standards that describe specific competencies required of DSPs. In addition, each broad competency area contains work activities that describe specific job duties or tasks and performance indicators that provide ways to determine if an employee has demonstrated the competency.

Provided here are excerpts from the CSSS, including all 12 broad competency areas and a sampling of the skill standards within some of these areas. Also included are a sample of various work activities and performance indicators for the first competency area. To get a clearer picture of the comprehensiveness of these standards, readers should review them in their entirety.

COMPETENCY AREA 1: PARTICIPANT EMPOWERMENT

The competent community support human services practitioner (CSHSP) enhances the ability of the participant to make decisions and to lead a self-determining life by providing the support and information necessary to build self-esteem and assertiveness.

Skill Standard A: The competent CSHSP assists and supports the participant to develop strategies, make informed choices, follow through on responsibilities, and take risks.

Activity: Assists the participant to identify alternatives when faced with making a decision
Performance indicator: The participant reports the staff person has helped him or her identify alternatives when making decisions.
Activity: Assists the participant to understand the potential outcomes of all alternatives and helps identify potential barriers
Performance indicator: Given a scenario, cites barriers that limit choices for participants and describes ways to overcome those barriers

Skill Standard B: The competent CSHSP promotes participant partnership in the design of support services, consulting the person and involving him or her in the support process.

Activity: Assists the participant to make informed choices about the design of supports by encouraging the participant to explore a range of options and to think about his or her ambitions, aspirations, and hopes for the future
Performance indicator: Demonstrates, through role-play, techniques and effective strategies to enhance the participant's ability to make decisions about support, treatment, or services

Skill Standard C: The competent CSHSP provides opportunities for the participant to be a self-advocate by increasing awareness of self-advocacy methods and techniques, encouraging and assisting the participant to speak on his or her own behalf, and providing information on peer support and self-advocacy groups.

Activity: Provides information to the participant regarding options for peer support and self-advocacy groups and the potential benefits of participation
Performance indicator: Can identify several major self-help and self-advocacy organizations that are relevant to the needs of the participant
Activity: Encourages the participant to participate in opportunities that will facilitate assertiveness and self-esteem
Performance indicator: Given specific scenarios, can describe activities that will enhance the participant's assertiveness and self-esteem

Skill Standard D: The competent CSHSP provides information about human, legal, and civil rights and related resources; facilitates access to such information; and assists the participant to use information for self-advocacy and decision making about living, work, and social relationships.

Activity: Seeks current information on human, legal, and civil rights and relevant resources
Performance indicator: Describes the relevant legal and civil rights provisions that affect participants

COMPETENCY AREA 2: COMMUNICATION

The CSHSP should be knowledgeable about the range of effective communication strategies and skills necessary to establish a collaborative relationship with the participant.

(continued)

From Taylor, M., Bradley, V., & Warren, R., Jr. (1996). *Community support skill standards: Tools for managing change and achieving outcomes.* Cambridge, MA: Human Services Research Institute; adapted by permission. (Available from the publisher, http://www.hsri.org/)

Skill Standard A: The competent CSHSP uses effective, sensitive communication skills to build rapport and channels of communication by recognizing and adapting to the range of participant communication styles.

Skill Standard B: The competent CSHSP has knowledge of and uses modes of communication that are appropriate to the communication needs of participants.

Skill Standard C: The skilled CSHSP learns and uses terminology appropriately, explaining as necessary to ensure participant understanding.

COMPETENCY AREA 3: ASSESSMENT
The CSHSP should be knowledgeable about formal and informal assessment practices in order to respond to the needs, desires, and interests of the participants.

Skill Standard A: The competent CSHSP initiates or assists in the initiation of an assessment process by gathering information (e.g., participant's self-assessment and history, prior records, test results, additional evaluation) and informing the participant about what to expect throughout the assessment process.

Skill Standard B: The competent CSHSP conducts or arranges for assessments to determine the needs, preferences, and capabilities of the participants using appropriate assessment tools and strategies, reviewing the process for inconsistencies, and making corrections as necessary.

Skill Standard C: The competent CSHSP discusses findings and recommendations with the participant in a clear and understandable manner, following up on results and reevaluating the findings as necessary.

COMPETENCY AREA 4: COMMUNITY AND SERVICE NETWORKING
The CSHSP should be knowledgeable about the formal and informal supports available in his or her community and skilled in assisting the participant to identify and gain access to such supports.

Skill Standard A: The competent CSHSP helps to identify the needs of the participant for community supports, working with the participant's informal support system and assisting with or initiating identified community connections.

Skill Standard B: The competent CSHSP researches, develops, and maintains information on community and other resources relevant to the needs of the participant.

Skill Standard C: The competent CSHSP ensures participant access to needed community resources coordinating supports across organizations.

Skill Standard D: The competent CSHSP participates in outreach to potential participants.

COMPETENCY AREA 5: FACILITATION OF SERVICES
The CSHSP is knowledgeable about a range of participatory planning techniques and is skilled in implementing plans in a collaborative and expeditious manner.

COMPETENCY AREA 6: COMMUNITY LIVING SKILLS AND SUPPORTS
The CSHSP has the ability to match specific supports and interventions to the unique needs of individual participants and recognizes the importance of friends, family, and community relationships.

COMPETENCY AREA 7: EDUCATION, TRAINING, AND SELF-DEVELOPMENT
The CSHSP should be able to identify areas for self-improvement, pursue necessary educational and training resources, and share knowledge with others.

COMPETENCY AREA 8: ADVOCACY
The CSHSP should be knowledgeable about the diverse challenges facing participants (e.g., human rights, legal, administrative, financial) and should be able to identify and use effective advocacy strategies to overcome such challenges.

COMPETENCY AREA 9: VOCATIONAL, EDUCATIONAL, AND CAREER SUPPORT
The CSHSP should be knowledgeable about the career- and education-related concerns of the participant and should be able to mobilize the resources and support necessary to assist the participant to reach his or her goals.

(continued)

COMPETENCY AREA 10: CRISIS INTERVENTION
The CSHSP should be knowledgeable about crisis prevention, intervention, and resolution techniques and should match such techniques to particular circumstances and individuals.

COMPETENCY AREA 11: ORGANIZATION PARTICIPATION
The CSHSP is familiar with the mission and practices of the support organization and participates in the life of the organization.

COMPETENCY AREA 12: DOCUMENTATION
The CSHSP is aware of the requirements for documentation in his or her organization and is able to manage these requirements efficiently.

Excerpts from the *Community Residential Core Competencies*

The *Community Residential Core Competencies* (CRCC; Hewitt, 1998b) represent the core skills DSPs need when working in small community residential services organizations supporting people with developmental disabilities. This section includes excerpts from the results of this job analysis. Included are all 14 competency areas, samples of the skill standards within some of these areas, and specific job tasks and duties within the skill standards for the first competency area. This includes only a small portion of the results of this job analysis. It is important to obtain the entire job analysis (see the Resources section in this chapter) before using it to develop a competency-based training program.

COMPETENCY AREA 1: HOUSEHOLD MANAGEMENT
Assists the individual with household management (e.g., meal preparation, laundry, cleaning, decorating) and transportation needs to maximize his or her skills, abilities, and independence

Skill Standard A: Coordinates necessary shopping activities
1. Assists individuals in purchasing personal need items (e.g., health and beauty supplies, clothing)
2. Purchases groceries based on planned menu in accordance with individuals' preferences
3. Purchases needed household supplies and items
4. Puts supplies away
5. Supports individuals in choosing clothing styles based on their likes and dislikes rather than on staff likes and dislikes
6. Assists individuals to prioritize their personal needs and developing individual budgets
7. Prepares a grocery list based on each individual's food preferences
8. Assists individuals to purchase gifts and presents as needed and within budget
9. Purchases items after comparing prices and quality and selecting the best value
10. Involves individuals in deciding whether they want to go shopping and in choosing the location
11. Assists individuals with making decisions regarding purchases
12. Notifies appropriate staff when various supplies are low in the house
13. Knows and adheres to household spending limits (e.g., groceries, supplies) and follows organization financial procedures

Skill Standard B: Assists with meal preparation and ensures that meals are prepared
1. Assists individuals as needed in preparing for and cooking meals
2. Follows menus and recipes
3. Assists individuals in recognizing safety precautions and issues regarding food preparation and cooking
4. Assists individuals in following special diets (e.g., soft, puree, low calorie, sodium free, low fat)
5. Assists individuals with eating or feeds individuals as needed and identified in their individual plans
6. Washes hands before and after handling food items and/or touching another person or item
7. Stores leftover food appropriately (e.g., dating food, throwing out old food)
8. Handles food properly
9. Assists individuals as needed in planning meals and developing menus based on their preferences (e.g., being creative, offering a variety of foods, providing menu options, using substitution lists)
10. Assists individuals as needed in cleaning up after food preparation, cooking, and meals
11. Assists individuals as needed in preparing individual lunches
12. Uses kitchen equipment correctly (e.g., dishwasher, food processor, oven, stove, microwave, blender)
13. Assists individuals as needed in presenting the meal and eating environment in an appealing manner
14. Cleans out the refrigerator and cabinets as needed

Skill Standard C: Assists with financial planning and management for individuals served
1. Knows the balance of individuals' personal funds and assists individuals as needed in making appropriate expenditures based on the availability of funds
2. Uses household petty cash and individuals' spending money in accordance with organization policies and procedures
3. Organizes and keeps receipts
4. Completes accurate audits of individual consumer funds as indicated by organization policies and procedures
5. Assists and supports the individuals in banking (e.g., making deposits and withdrawals, cashing checks)

(continued)

From Hewitt, A. (1998b). *Community core residential competencies: Necessary competencies for direct support staff working in community residential services for people with developmental disabilities;* adapted by permission. Available on-line: http://www.rtc.umn.edu/pdf/analysis.pdf

6. Documents and records all financial transactions
7. Knows the balance of household funds and makes appropriate expenditures based on the availability of funds
8. Balances various accounts (e.g., petty cash, individuals' checkbooks)
9. Completes cash on hand sheets accurately and when necessary
10. Completes medical assistance paperwork and submits it in a timely manner

Skill Standard D: Completes household routines
1. Assists individuals as needed with cleaning (e.g., cleaning bathroom, dusting, dusting blinds, cleaning kitchen, washing windows, emptying and cleaning refrigerator, sweeping, mopping, vacuuming, carpet cleaning)
2. Assists individuals as needed with laundry
3. Assists individuals as needed in decorating the house for celebrations
4. Knows the home is the individual's and is respectful of this (e.g., knocks on the outside door before entering, refrains from calling it "my home")
5. Knows the household routines and shift flow
6. Knows where cleaning and household items are stored in the house
7. Assists individuals as needed with making beds
8. Assists individuals as needed in washing the dishes or running the dishwasher
9. Stores and uses cleaning and household products appropriately
10. Assists individuals as needed in recycling
11. Assists individuals as needed with pet care (e.g., feeding, bathing, providing health care)
12. Completes house walk-through checklists to identify needs
13. Assists individuals as needed in maintaining plants and wall hangings

Skill Standard E: Ensures maintenance of household is completed
1. Completes simple home repairs
2. Schedules needed repairs and home maintenance
3. Knows and uses the maintenance on-call system
4. Identifies accessibility and accommodation issues for individuals within the house
5. Maintains proper temperature in the refrigerator
6. Changes light bulbs
7. Maintains proper temperature in home as determined by individuals' preferences and needs
8. Assists and supports individuals in completing lawn care and yard work

Skill Standard F: Provides transportation and maintains vehicle
1. Uses approved gas purchasing procedures for company vehicles
2. Ensures that individuals use seat belts and that people who use wheelchairs are secured in the vehicle
3. Uses lifts on vehicles appropriately
4. Assists individuals in arranging transportation for appointments and events
5. Maintains legal driver's license and informs organization immediately if license is revoked
6. Knows individuals' needs while riding in a vehicle (e.g., behavior management, safety)
7. Drives vehicle safely (e.g., is aware of weather conditions, practices defensive driving)
8. Understands and follows vehicle maintenance lists
9. Washes company vehicle
10. Supports consumers in using public transportation systems
11. Knows local community routes, roads, major sites, and attractions
12. Communicates with day program regarding transportation needs or problems
13. Uses hazard lights in vehicle as needed (e.g., in case of flat tire or breakdown)
14. Knows what equipment and supplies are located in vehicle and when and how to use them

COMPETENCY AREA 2: FACILITATION OF SERVICES
Staff member has knowledge sufficient to fulfill his or her role related to individual service plan development, implementation, and review.

Skill Standard A: Understands individual service planning process

Skill Standard B: Maintains collaborative professional relationships with the individual and all support team members (including family and friends), follows ethical standards of practice (e.g., confidentiality, informed consent), and recognizes own personal limitations

(continued)

Skill Standard C: Implements an individual service plan based on the individual's preferences, needs, and interests

Skill Standard D: Assists and/or facilitates the review of the achievement of individuals' outcomes

COMPETENCY AREA 3: HEALTH AND WELLNESS
Promotes the health and wellness of all individuals supported

Skill Standard A: Administers medications accurately and in accordance with organization policy and procedures

Skill Standard B: Observes and implements appropriate actions to promote healthy living and to prevent illness and accidents

Skill Standard C: Uses appropriate first aid and safety procedures when responding to emergencies

Skill Standard D: Assists individuals in scheduling, keeping, and following through on all health appointments

Skill Standard E: Assists individuals in completing personal care (e.g., hygiene, grooming) activities

Skill Standard F: Assists with identifying, securing, and using needed adaptive equipment (e.g., augmentative and alternative communication devices, walkers) and therapies (e.g., physical, occupational, speech, respiratory, psychological)

Skill Standard G: Assists individuals in implementing health and medical treatments

COMPETENCY AREA 4: ORGANIZATIONAL PARTICIPATION
Is familiar with the organizational mission

Skill Standard A: Is aware of the organization's mission and priorities and how they relate to job roles and responsibilities

Skill Standard B: Is aware of and implements all organizational policies and procedures

COMPETENCY AREA 5: DOCUMENTATION
Is aware of the requirement for documentation in his or her organization and is able to manage these requirements efficiently

Skill Standard A: Maintains accurate records: collects, compiles, and evaluates data and submits records to appropriate sources in a timely manner

Skill Standard B: Maintains standards of confidentiality and ethical practice

COMPETENCY AREA 6: CONSUMER EMPOWERMENT
Enhances the ability of individuals to lead a self-determining life by providing the support and information necessary to build self-esteem and assertiveness and to make decisions

Skill Standard A: Assists and supports individuals in making informed choices, following through on responsibilities, and trying new experiences

Skill Standard B: Promotes individuals' participation in support services, consulting each person and involving him or her in the support process (e.g., daily support of the individual's emotional needs)

Skill Standard C: Provides opportunities for individuals to be self-advocates, encouraging and assisting individuals to speak on their own behalf

Skill Standard D: Provides information about human, legal, and civil rights and related resources; facilitates access to such information; and assists the participant to use information for self-advocacy and decision making about living, work, and social relationships

COMPETENCY AREA 7: ASSESSMENT
Is knowledgeable about formal and informal assessment practices to respond to individuals' needs, desires, and interests

(continued)

Skill Standard A: Is knowledgeable of assessment and processes used to discover individuals' needs, preferences, and capabilities and how they are used in development and review of the service plan

Skill Standard B: Discusses both formal and informal findings and recommendations with the individual in a clear and understandable manner

Skill Standard C: Assists, completes, or arranges for assessments to determine individuals' needs, preferences, and capabilities by gathering information, informing individuals about what to expect throughout the assessment process, using appropriate assessment tools and strategies, reviewing the process for inconsistencies, and making corrections as necessary

COMPETENCY AREA 8: ADVOCACY
Is knowledgeable about the diverse challenges facing individuals (e.g., barriers to human rights)

COMPETENCY AREA 9: COMMUNITY AND SERVICE NETWORKING
Is knowledgeable about the formal and informal supports available in the community and is skilled in assisting individuals to identify and gain access to such supports

COMPETENCY AREA 10: BUILDING AND MAINTAINING FRIENDSHIPS AND RELATIONSHIPS
Supports the participant in the development of friendships and other relationships

COMPETENCY AREA 11: COMMUNICATION
Is knowledgeable about the range of effective communication strategies and skills necessary to establish a collaborative relationship with each individual

COMPETENCY AREA 12: CRISIS INTERVENTION
Is knowledgeable about crisis prevention, intervention, and resolution techniques and should match such techniques to particular circumstances and individuals

COMPETENCY AREA 13: STAFF SELF-DEVELOPMENT
Pursues knowledge and information necessary to perform job duties

COMPETENCY AREA 14: VOCATIONAL, EDUCATIONAL, AND CAREER SUPPORT
Is knowledgeable about the career- and education-related concerns of individuals supported

Excerpts from the *Competencies for Executive Directors*

The following competency areas and statements are adapted from the *Competencies for Executive Directors* (Oregon Rehabilitation Association, 1999), which boards of directors of organizations can use when hiring and appraising the performance of executive directors.

A. Personal Skills and Behaviors
A1 Demonstrates a deep commitment to the individuals we support and serve
A2 Models personal integrity and requires the same from others
A3 Takes responsibility for own actions and actively works to correct errors
A4 Strives to develop personally and professionally
A5 Shows a restrained response about personal accomplishments by sharing credit with others

B. Communication Skills and Behaviors
B1 Listens actively
B2 Communicates with staff and management in an open, forthright, and clear manner
B3 Consistently speaks from personal and organizational values
B4 Speaks effectively
B5 Writes effectively

C. Consumer-Centered Programs and Services
C1 Plans, designs, and delivers an individual-centered service system
C2 Puts the individual first
C3 Collects information about and understands the needs of the individuals and customers served by the organization
C4 Integrates services
C5 Measures client satisfaction

D. Leadership and Planning
D1 Creates and communicates a compelling and inspiring sense of purpose in the organization
D2 Builds a mission to guide the decisions of the organization
D3 Initiates and leads a strategic plan that will accomplish the vision of the organization through its mission
D4 Responds to change as a fact of life
D5 Makes tough decisions with information available

E. Organizational Management
E1 Supports the board
E2 Obtains and uses input from the individuals receiving supports and other stakeholders
E3 Plans practical implementation of strategic initiatives
E4 Designs, implements, and evaluates program, fiscal, and human resources development policies and procedures
E5 Knows the process of fundraising and recognizes those who give

F. Human Resources Development
F1 Sets and follows appropriate human resources policies and procedures
F2 Maintains a competitive compensation package that attracts and retains qualified staff
F3 Increases the capacity and competency of staff
F4 Identifies staff recruitment and retention issues, develops and implements intervention strategies, and evaluates the results to inform future decision-making
F5 Addresses disciplinary actions, employee grievances, and employee litigation in a systematic, legal, respectable, timely, and responsible manner

G. Financial Management
G1 Protects the financial resources of the organization
G2 Budgets the resources of the organization effectively, meetings its strategic goals

H. Community Partnerships
H1 Promotes community understanding of the organization and its activities
H2 Understands public policy terminology and process
H3 Builds positive relationships with peers
H4 Resolves conflict with positive outcomes

From Oregon Rehabilitation Association. (1999). *Competencies for executive directors.* Salem: Author; adapted by permission.

7

OUT OF THE CLASSROOM AND ON TO EMPLOYEE TRAINING PROGRAMS THAT WORK

SUSAN N. O'NELL, AMY S. HEWITT, AND JOHN K. SAUER

Current methods for training employees often do not work. Industry challenges that add to the struggle include a highly dispersed workforce, a need for people to work odd hours, and complex state and federal mandates. In Chapter 6 the link between training and performance is discussed. The competency-based training cycle is introduced in that chapter to clarify the need to incrementally develop and assess skills as they are performed in the actual work setting. In order to help people develop these competencies, a variety of methods must be used that meet employees' unique training needs. This chapter provides information on ways to structure training to encourage better retention of information and in ways that are customized to employee needs. Adult learning principles; how to develop and maintain ongoing training opportunities; and the use of innovative training practices such as just-in-time training, on-the-job training (OJT), emerging technologies in training, mentoring, and intentional learning are reviewed. The implications of training a diverse workforce are also discussed.

TARGETED FRONT-LINE SUPERVISOR COMPETENCIES

Front-line supervisors (FLSs) and managers are often tempted to provide most training through lectures given in a classroom. The competent FLS takes an active role and interest in ensuring that what is taught to DSPs is transferred to the actual job performance. The FLS does this by providing opportunities for DSPs to learn actively in the work environment or by finding other effective methods that help the employees learn. The FLS provides feedback to the employee regarding performance and acts as a role model and resource for DSPs. Listed here are primary and related training competencies that supervisors and managers need.

Primary Skills

FLSs teach and coach DSPs in effective approaches to master required direct support competencies.

FLSs observe, monitor, and provide feedback to DSPs regarding the implementation of individualized support plans.

FLSs provide coaching and feedback to DSPs regarding performance-related issues.

FLSs coordinate, schedule, and document DSPs' participation and performance in in-service training and completion of other self-directed learning and development.

FLSs observe and solicit feedback from DSPs and supported individuals and their families regarding DSP training needs and desired opportunities.

FLSs share with DSPs resources and information related to supports, technology, intervention, and hot issues for supporting the individuals served.

FLSs identify potential trainers and provide resources, coaching, and opportunities for DSP training.

Related Skills

FLSs identify necessary resources for individuals served and DSPs, and advocate for these resources with their managers.

FLSs review, provide follow-up on, and discuss issues with staff regarding incident or accident reports.

FLSs provide necessary disciplinary action, including demonstrating correct performance of job tasks for staff as indicated.

FLSs monitor for medication errors and review as indicated with DSPs.

FLSs support DSPs in learning how to use a computer, e-mail, and the Internet.

UNDERSTANDING THE PROBLEM

There is no doubt that the human services industry has significant training challenges. Lack of basic employee competence and poor training attendance, despite provider requirements and state mandates, are chronic problems for provider organizations and their training staff. The most difficult training issues are arranging training times so that DSPs can attend the sessions (according to 70% of FLSs who responded to a survey); providing training that results in changes in job performance (53%); finding conferences, courses, or workshops that are reasonably priced (42%); and finding incentives to motivate staff to attend training (41%) (Larson, 1996). These challenges make sense given the changes the industry has seen since the mid-1970s, but they also point to the major source of the problems. An estimated 78% of all corporate learning, across industries, takes place in the classroom (Caudron, 2000). A full spectrum of training opportunities can be presented in a classroom, and certainly some topics (e.g., teamwork) are best learned in a group. The successful organization, however, lets go of its classroom training in favor of other methods. That is no doubt a shocking proposition for an industry that relies primarily on classroom training as its only sanctioned method for training employees, but times have changed and it is time to change training methods to meet new needs.

When institutional care and other large congregate care services were virtually the only direct service option, classroom training, although still dependent on the quality of the instructor and curriculum, at least made sense logistically. At any given time, dozens of employees were scheduled to work in the same location in which training was being held. Staffing was primarily shift focused. Classes could thus be conveniently scheduled before or after direct support shifts so that employees not working during the class could be expected to attend most sessions. This is not the case, however, for community providers today because of the continual dispersal and individualization of support settings.

This move to more customized supports, although invaluable to the individuals and families who need supports, has created a situation in which provider organizations have difficulty gathering employees in one setting at a common time for classroom training. Congregate care settings often had a designated room where training could be held. In community settings, this is not typically the case. Training sessions occur in varied locations, and often employers do not have well-equipped training rooms. Training that is scheduled in program locations often displace or impose upon the people who live or work in that location. Training provided in administrative offices or even in the support setting can impose a severe hardship on low-wage employees who may be asked to spend more on transportation or babysitting than they would receive as compensation for attending the training.

Dispersal of services has meant more than just changing the location of where supports are provided. DSPs are expected to have a much richer set of skills than ever before (Hewitt, 1998a; Taylor, Bradley, & Warren, 1996) and to apply them with much less direct supervision and support from peers or other professionals (e.g., nursing professionals) (Jaskulski & Ebenstein, 1996). To provide consumer-directed, person-centered supports, DSPs must have the same skills and knowledge regarding health, safety, and growth and development for people with developmental disabilities as before but within a different context. In addition, today's DSPs need to have other skill sets. They need to have good written and verbal communication skills, be creative problem solvers, be capable of independent judgment and reflection, and have a good awareness of when and from whom to seek further support. Ideal DSPs need to be savvy about providing culturally competent and natural supports; fostering self-determination; balancing choice with risk; encouraging advocacy; building community capacity; and working both independently and in partnership with the person receiving supports, support teams, and other community members (Taylor et al., 1996).

This may seem to be a long wish list given the low-wage, low-status nature of the DSP position, which is often referred to as entry level by the industry. Employers are beginning to require new skills of DSPs but are often not modifying and improving the methods or content of their training and development programs. Also, employers are increasing skill requirements while facing other challenges. For instance, to enlarge the pool of potential new employees, organizations are tapping into new groups of people, such as recent immigrants or retirees. Revised training methods will need to address the skill gaps that new pools of employees may have. For instance, when hiring from the traditional pool of workers—American-born women between the ages of 18 and 44—most human services recruiters could count on new employees' being familiar with the common domestic duties associated with many direct support roles. Now, however, recruits may have variable levels of experience with American-style household chores and other skills.

In addition, across industries, American companies are struggling to find new employees with basic literacy and math skills. This is the result of a combination of decreasing abilities in the pool of applicants combined with increased job responsibilities (Rottier, 2001). Increased diversity of the workforce means that corporate expectations in dress, grooming, language, and timeliness have to be examined for bias. Once a comfortable standard is developed for these areas, the standards need to be clearly and proactively shared with new and existing employees and potential applicants. (To learn more about the specific skill sets needed by DSPs, refer to Chapter 6.)

Within community human services, components of training practices are dictated by regional, state, and federal requirements; in some states the actual curriculum to be used by an employer is prescribed. This often leads organizations to develop prescriptive, limited training programs in which the number of hours and topics for training are predefined for the employee (Hewitt, Larson, & O'Nell, 1996). Most often this training is done in a classroom because the curricula are usually developed to be delivered this way. Although the topics may be based on important direct support skills and the curriculum itself may be of a high quality, this training is unlikely to meet the needs of all employees, whose backgrounds vary greatly. Mandates are often well intended and almost always include minimum standards. Training for DSPs, however, must go far beyond what is prescribed to be comprehensive enough to develop the full complement of skills that a new employee may need.

Employers face a multitude of issues regarding training DSPs. Some issues are well beyond the capacity of individual organizations to change; however, improving internal training and staff development practices is something that individual organizations can and should do to improve retention of DSPs.

Unfortunately, training often does not take into account established adult learning principles (Lieb, 1991) or accommodate individual learning styles and areas of need. Organizations often ask DSPs to take responsibility for their own training, but in practice this usually means that DSPs are responsible for signing up and attending standard, repetitive, annual trainings, which is a far cry from DSPs actually identifying their own skills gaps and development needs and seeking out training that meets those needs in a timely manner. Many training topics and curricula are outdated or meet the needs of only a small portion of the direct support workforce. Training events are held at times and places that are inconvenient for most DSPs. Worse, most training does not review transfer of the skills learned to the actual work environment. Current training practices are most certainly discouraging, as most organizations put a significant amount of time and resources to their training programs; however, in absence of necessary innovations, this activity is not successful.

Although many organizations think that DSPs do not show a lot of drive to attend organization-sponsored training, training plays an important role in retention of employees. DSPs point to their own lack of confidence in their competence and that of their supervisors and co-workers as primary reasons for experiencing dissatisfaction with their jobs (Larson, Lakin, & Bruininks, 1998). American employees in general are very concerned with their co-workers' and their own competence. Feeling that they work on an effective team is critical to job satisfaction (Laabs, 1998). Despite the fact that relationships with co-workers and supervisors are commonly cited reasons for turnover, organizations rarely offer DSPs training on team-building or professionalization. New employees do not know what is expected of them and therefore experience increased stress and job dissatisfaction, which in turn makes them more likely to resign (Hewitt, 1998a). In addition, there is decreased job satisfaction on the part of competent employees, who feel they have to bear the brunt of co-worker incompetence and that they have reached a plateau in their own development (Hewitt, 1998a).

In the Spotlight: Ark Regional Services

Traci LaLiberte, Mary Arnold, and Jackie Walker

Ark Regional Services is a nonprofit organization serving adults with developmental disabilities in Laramie, Wyoming. Ark is committed to training, developing, and supporting its DSPs and other staff. The goal for the competency-based training system is to ensure that staff are competent and confident and can deliver the highest quality of care to the individuals receiving supports. All newly hired DSPs go through new employee orientation. New hires are given training on the Ark mission, history, and policies; safety training; CPR and other first aid; and Mandt crisis interaction training. They also are introduced to eight competency-based skill areas, Ark's professional standards, and Ark's educate, model, observe, and evaluate (EMOE) training program. Ark has adapted and customized EMOE from a training method developed by Perry Samowitz, Director of Training at YAI/National Institute for People with Disabilities.

After orientation, DSPs continue their skill development both at Ark's Center for Professional Development and at their job site. New DSPs are scheduled to complete online training modules on Ark's skill competency areas and some of the modules from the College of Direct Support. Supervisors are given classroom and site training on how to observe the skills of DSPs, how to develop skill development plans, how to give constructive feedback, and how to evaluate their programs and staff performance. Supervisors are supported by mentors who work extensively with the supervisors on-site to ensure that each DSP can develop the eight skill areas and be successful as a DSP.

It is important that Ark's supervisors also be competent because they are the models and they support their staff's success. It is important that each supervisor and DSP can see what the skills look like as experienced staff members model them on site. After modeling, the supervisor and DSP discuss strategies that are effective in the actual work setting. Ark strongly believes that only by observation and feedback on a regular basis will DSPs work in a competent manner and ensure that the individuals they support really enjoy quality of life.

A key aspect of Ark's training program for both DSPs and supervisors is the use of creative training techniques. The first technique is using organization-made video vignettes. Short, prerecorded role plays are used to demonstrate a point or concept clearly. The videos promote lively discussion, and often new staff members ask to be in the next videos that are scheduled to be recorded. Staff are also recorded completing the skills required in their daily jobs. Every staff member, whether a supervisor or a DSP, must be videotaped at least once per year. The videotapes are then reviewed by a levels committee that uses the tape as one component in determining awarding pay increases. Ark has also designed skill development plans for each of the eight skill areas so that each DSP is being supported to develop skills for successful relationship-building with the individuals whom he or she supports. This is an opportunity for DSPs to build success in partnership with their supervisors. At Ark, it is crucial that staff not only gain new knowledge but also be able to demonstrate the skills associated with that new knowledge.

RESEARCH SUPPORT FOR SOLUTIONS

See Chapter 6 for research support for competency-based training.

STRATEGIES FOR RESPONDING TO THE PROBLEM

Current direct support training practices need a major overhaul if the promise of high-quality person-centered supports is to be achieved. To stop the loss of good employees due to inadequate training and support, organizations are going to have to become training innovators that use the best of what is available to meet the needs of each employee. Many of these training innovations are summarized in the first column of Table 7.1.

Provide Innovative Training

Providing innovative training is a lot more than applying new "bells and whistles" to the same old training methods and materials. Innovative training is really about getting away from ensuring that each employee is in the classroom to complete a certain number of required training hours on a certain list of training topics and, instead, developing more productive, competent, and satisfied employees focused on achieving the organization's mission, vision, and business goals. The following points are important to consider when revamping training:

- Training should meet individual employees' needs in terms of location, time scheduled, topics, pace, and learning style.
- Training should be offered close to the time when the employee can use it, that is, "just in time."
- Training should improve actual competence on the job.
- Training should provide employees with new challenges and opportunities (promotions, new duties, pay increases, further educational opportunities).
- Training should be a collaborative process between employee and employer, with both having roles and responsibilities for employee training. Employees also should be encouraged to acquire skills outside of formalized training.
- Training and development should focus on helping the organization meet its mission, vision, and business goals (as opposed to focusing only on meeting legal mandates).

Table 7.1. Training do's and don'ts

Do	Don't
Align training with applicable competencies, job descriptions, and employee skill gaps as identified by job analysis, performance appraisal, and competency-based assessment	Train for the wrong reasons (e.g., solely to meet legal mandates for a certain number of hours per year)
Integrate skill development and training in a system of recruitment, selection, and corporate culture that expects, supports, and rewards employee competence	Expect training to take care of all performance problems (Laabs, 1998; Caudron, 2000)
Use adult learning principles and competency-based assessment	Use only lecture-based or classroom training and knowledge-based assessment
Provide training that meets the individual needs of employees	Repeatedly train employees on knowledge and competencies they already have
Provide opportunities for employees to learn at a comfortable pace	Overwhelm trainees with too much, too fast, or demean them by providing too little, too slowly
Train on a variety of skills, including "soft skills" such as teamwork and communication	Train only on technical skills such as medication administration or documentation
Expect employees to take responsibility for identifying their own training needs	Assume that the organization knows what employees need to know and mandate all training
Use a variety of training formats to meet the time and location constraints of employees	Set training schedules that meet only the trainer's needs
Encourage employees to seek and capitalize on naturally occurring training opportunities	Compartmentalize training to specific times and places
Accurately assess employees' training needs	Assume that some training topics are "just common sense"
Keep training and orientation separate. Use orientation to help reduce stress among new employees, help them develop initial skills, and enhance their commitment to the organization.	Ignore the needs of new employees and/or use orientation to meet annual training needs
Make a clear connection between training and the organization's mission, vision, values, and goals	Train employees without helping them understand how the training relates to higher-quality supports

The training setting (e.g., on the job rather than in the classroom) is only one component of innovative training. Employers can choose whatever setting will work best for individual employees. For instance, if a state mandates the use of a certain curriculum, it is important to ensure that employees understand and can apply the content included within that curriculum. The curriculum does not necessarily have to be taught in a classroom setting, even if it was developed to be taught that way. There is nothing preventing an organization from developing self-paced training modules around the content of the curriculum or permitting employees with previous experience to test out training on the content by demonstrating the skill. Although the regulating agency might seek indicators in a personnel file that training has been accomplished, defining indicators focused on actual competence in the work setting is probably all that will be needed. It is unlikely that state or federal oversight agencies would insist on a record of classroom attendance if alternative documentation of competence exists. Similarly, for organizations in states that mandate a certain number of annual training hours and set of topics, evidence that each employee understands and can apply knowledge in topic areas is critical and should be documented. Annual hours of training do not necessarily have to be on the state-mandated topics. Furthermore, if the mandated hours are not enough for an employee to achieve satisfactory competence in essential job skills, the organization should not stop training once the hours have been reached. Remember, mandates are usually geared toward minimal standards, not what is needed to truly get the job done. Organizations need to move beyond just offering these topics. Experienced staff should be urged to participate in annual test-out of competence in mandated topical areas. Performance evaluations that are well-written, combined with a short knowledge-based test, should serve as ample evidence that employees have competence in most mandated areas. Additional training can be then selected from a literally infinite list of exciting possibilities. (See the section in Chapter 6 that describes Step 7 of the competency-based training model for more information on linking performance measures and training.)

Along with reconstructing the way in which training is provided, organizations are urged to reconsider the breadth of topics that they offer to their employees, particularly DSPs. Often seminars, advanced education opportunities, and conferences on the most innovative concepts in community human services are offered almost exclusively to administrative staff. Opportunities to gain exposure to exciting new developments in the field are rarely offered to DSPs, who most surely would benefit from understanding the changes in values and strategies that are affecting and changing support systems. Contemporary direct support requires a wide variety of skills, from an understanding of home economics to an understanding of self-determination. Activities on topics such as stress management, diversity, sensitivity, facilitation of services, development of natural supports and community readiness, organizational participation, foreign language, computer skills, and cross-cultural supports, as well as basic skills training in literacy, motor vehicle safety, and grocery shopping, are all legitimate staff development activities. Because direct support is about supporting better lives, almost any training topic or development activity is justifiable if it translates into increased worker competence and longevity.

Put Innovations into Practice

Contrary to popular misconception, innovative training does not have to be more expensive or require more energy than current training practices. But, to be successful, it does require cost shifting and a change of focus. Using innovative training does not mean ignoring training mandates, but it does mean understanding how to creatively apply them in ways that meet the real needs of employees. Although supervisors in small organizations may feel at a disadvantage because of having fewer resources to allocate to training and development, many smaller organizations have the advantage of quicker decision-making processes, easier assessment of the success or failure of training innovations, and a better understanding of the needs of each employee.

To be most effective, training needs to be part of an overall organization design that is focused on employee performance and one in which a system for defining, assessing, and supporting employee competence pervades the organization. The competency-based training cycle (Hewitt, 1998a; Hewitt & Larson, 1994) and its relationship to overall performance issues is discussed in depth in Chapter 6. The remainder of this chapter describes specific training techniques and methods that enhance learning retention and success.

Revamp Training Practices

Most organization training is instructor focused. That means the timing, location, format, content, and method of delivery are selected for the convenience of the instructor. This is a fine system if the goal is simply to gather signatures on a page to put into personnel files but is not a good system to ensure employee competence and job satisfaction. Training calendars that vary little from year to year may be easier for the trainer but often exacerbate attendance problems. Although many organizations perceive lack of attendance as an intrinsic flaw in the DSP work ethic, the truth is many employees want to be competent and feel good about how they do their work. But instructor-focused training is not the path to increased competence. With that kind of training, combined with sometimes extreme inconvenience in scheduling and location, it is no wonder that these training sessions have low or no attendance.

To maintain employee motivation for training, employees must perceive that the training has value. Some ways to provide training that meets learners' needs include group training, on-the-job training (OJT), computer-based multimedia training, intentional learning and learning contracts, mentoring, and job aids; these methods are discussed later in this chapter. Remember, however, every training method can be executed well or badly, depending on whether it is learner or trainer focused.

Creating a learner-focused training system may seem overwhelming to trainers and supervisors, but employees by definition have to become more involved in defining and identifying training needs. This takes a huge burden off trainers and supervisors who feel responsible for identifying training needs and enforcing attendance. Although the organization still has significant responsibility for defining the competencies necessary for each employee and assessing skill gaps, the responsibility for developing skills becomes a partnership between the employees and employer. If the goal of training and development activities is meeting the mission, vision, and goals of the organization, then employees and trainers alike have a point of focus to help them make sense of employee training and development. In addition, employees become more adept at identifying their own skill gaps and needed resources for achievement.

Adult Learning Principles and Learning Styles

Adult learners have physiological differences from child learners, including decreased vision and hearing, decreased short-term but increased long-term memory, less energy, and slower reaction speed (Miller, 1998). Adult learners are goal oriented and quickly become impatient with material that seems irrelevant to their needs. They like and need to apply information rapidly to retain it. Even if they are completely new to a job, they come with a host of life experiences that they are ready and eager to apply to the setting, and they thus expect to be treated with respect and to be heard during training.

Learning styles vary from person to person and within the same person, depending on the content or timing of the training or other aspects of the training or the person's development. Thus, no one instructional format will ever meet the needs of every employee. The instructor needs to vary training styles and methods of presenting information and check for understanding at frequent intervals, ideally through demonstration of skill in the actual environment. The key is not to peg a person as one type of learner or another but to always show respect for the learner and his or her individual needs.

During training sessions, the instructor should assist learners in reflecting on learning. To facilitate this, goals of the learning opportunity should be made clear to the learners up front. In addition, an assessment by the instructor or a self-assessment done by learners of current understanding should occur so that training can be customized to each learner and so that each learner is aware of his or her own training goals and skill gaps. In large groups, instructors can do this by asking participants to share what they know about the training topic; after this, instructors provide supplemental information in line with the instructional goals.

The training should have learners use a combination of reading, hearing, seeing, and doing (and touching and smelling, if they are appropriate to the content). Materials should be a mix of instructor presentation and learner application to ensure participants' full understanding, retention, and ability to apply their learning. See Table 7.2 for advice on ensuring that training addresses multiple learning styles and is effective with adult learners.

There are many sources of information on adult learning principles and learning styles, and new information will always become available, especially as workforce diversity increases. Some studies have suggested that workers from various immigrant groups may have very different training preferences. For instance, although most adult learning principles are based on the premise that adult learners are self-directed, some cultural data on training suggests that people from certain cultural backgrounds prefer training in which directions are clear and specific and the instructor defines what is right or wrong over training that is self-directed or open ended (Thayer, 1997). In addition, any inventory tools used to identify trainer or learner styles may have some cultural, gender, or other biases. Although some of the specifics may change, much of what is known about adult learning styles will likely remain valid for some time to come.

Table 7.2. Principles for providing training to adults

Use some or all of the following training methods: lecturing, demonstrating techniques or giving examples, encouraging the learner, testing, questioning, providing resources, modeling, providing feedback, interacting with the learner, listening, negotiating, and evaluating the learner.

Make materials easy to read and hear.

Provide immediate reference to how the learning will be used and applied in the work setting and how it will meet a learner's needs or skill gaps.

Provide opportunities for learners to share their experiences, ideas, and suggestions.

Set clear but flexible goals and objectives for the learning.

Provide opportunities for learners to see, hear, do, and (if applicable) touch and smell during learning.

Provide opportunities for learners to evaluate their own learning and to assess their skills and levels of understanding.

Provide immediate and informal feedback on performance.

Provide additional and relevant resources related to the topic at hand.

Include individual and group activities in the training.

Just-in-Time Training

Just-in-time training (done within minutes or hours of being needed in the actual setting) is completely foreign to many organizations. One quick test of an organization's current capacity for just-in-time training is this question: How far in advance is the training calendar posted? If an organization usually knows in January what training will be available in December, chances are that this organization does not use just-in-time training.

Employees have to use the information they learn from training to retain it. Organizations that train people in 40-hour blocks or according to the trainer's schedule are wasting a lot of effort. In fact, training and development professionals should be considered part of an organization's inventory. If it isn't used, then it is a waste of a product that has potential costs (Carr, 1992). Think of it this way: When a person is hungry, a meal is prepared to suit his or her appetite. It wouldn't make much sense to serve a year's worth of meals in one week. The person could not eat it all, it would not keep the person from being hungry later on, and the amount of waste would be huge. Yet, the approach of "force-feeding" training to DSPs is almost standard practice in the human services industry. A DSP who receives training that is too distant from the point of using it will not retain the skills. This means that the organization will need to spend more money and time retraining the employee or that the employee will lack essential skills. Either scenario will cause frustration on the part of the employee and his or her co-workers and may put the people receiving supports at risk.

Identifying just-in-time training needs is usually part of a comprehensive organizational environment that regularly assesses employee skill gaps. It is likely that the employee can provide good feedback about his or her most pressing skill need at the moment. Supervisors, co-workers, and people being supported and members of their support teams, as well as written documentation and direct observation of employee performance, are other good sources for identifying immediate employee skill needs. These immediate skill gaps provide the foundation for just-in-time training.

The more competent the employee, the more additional evaluation and exploration will be needed to help the employee identify just-in-time training needs, but for workers new to direct support, and particularly those in the orientation phase, just-in-time training is a critical component to success. An example of just-in-time training in the community human services industry is training on how to use a Hoyer lift with an individual who has extremely limited mobility, such as for helping to transport the individual from his or her bed to a wheelchair. Although the employee may be introduced during the first week or day of training to the use of the lift, the actual instruction on the lift's use should happen *exactly* when the employee needs to use it. This means that using the Hoyer lift may appear on a list of OJT topics but that the time of the actual training must match the need of the employee being trained and not the employee or supervisor doing the training. In practice this means that if due to other training needs, the employee will not be in a situation to use the lift independently for some weeks, training should not happen until then. Many organization and OJT trainers, however, will demonstrate the use of the lift in the first few days of employment and assume that the employee will retain the knowledge until he or she uses the lift independently for the first time a few weeks later. In this scenario, there is a high chance that the employee will not use the lift correctly and potentially injure him- or herself and the person being lifted.

Just-in-time training is an excellent method to teach specific skills related to the needs of people being served. Moving from classroom modeling and role playing to the actual work environment where the learning will occur is at the foundation of just-in-time training.

Create Real Staff Development Opportunities

Employees want to feel competent performing their jobs. For some employees in direct support positions (often employees who have other career goals or who plan to leave after a period of time), this feeling of competence may be enough to keep them from prematurely leaving a position. Community human services organizations must nurture the potential long-term employee who is seeking to create a profession out of direct support and shorter-term employees who might stay longer in the field given development opportunities that are intentional and appropriate to the employees' needs. The future of the direct support industry as well that of as individual organizations may depend on constructing and offering effective staff development.

To create effective staff development, training must have a greater purpose than meeting immediate organizational needs and regulatory mandates. To maintain employee motivation, training must lead employees to new opportunities (e.g., promotions, new duties, pay increases, higher quality of life, increased recognition, personal satisfaction, enhanced skills, further education). A lack of such incentives is one of the reasons that long-term employees dread repetitive organization training. They have nothing to gain from attending the exact same training they attended the year before, and the year before, and so forth. Jazzing up the content of stale training by creating cute games and serving food does not hurt, but the training still will not lead to any desired outcomes for the employee. It's the same old stuff—just served up in a slightly different way.

Creative linking of training to real development opportunities is important. The development can be personal or professional. The National Alliance for Direct Support Professionals (NADSP; http://www.nadsp.org/) can provide more information about what is going on nationally in this area. Organizations should let employees guide the identification of what opportunities are most meaningful to them. For example, organizations can support staff development in areas such as

- Achieving educational goals such as completion of a GED or postsecondary credit-bearing coursework
- Developing literacy in English or in another language of interest
- Passing driver's licensing tests
- Joining a social club or sports league
- Learning a new skill such as ethnic cooking, painting, or yoga

A staff development questionnaire or plan is another way to solicit information from and engage DSPs in their own learning and development. A simple DSP training development plan is included at the end of this chapter.

The support that organizations provide for these opportunities may range from providing stipends and time off to complete learning goals to offering the training on site. Because the employees' abilities to provide direct support are enhanced the more they are connected to their communities and the more they feel positive about their own opportunities and lives, organizations can enhance employee satisfaction, commitment, and diversity of skills and experiences by providing richer development opportunities. Knowing that committed, personally satisfied employees stick around longer is an added benefit (Griffeth, Hom, & Gaertner, 2000).

Make Best Use of Available Methods

Organizations can use many different training methods to teach employees necessary skills and knowledge. The choice of method has to do with the content and the practicalities of meeting people's individual needs. The following subsections describe various training methods and how each can best be used to maximize its effectiveness.

Group Training

If the competencies to be developed are best learned in a group setting and if several employees need to develop these skills at the same time, then group training can be the way to go. A prime example of this is the development of a new support site where several employees need training all at once.

Topics that may be best in a group setting are ones that are less tangible or hands-on and more about teaching attitudes or values (e.g., diversity, team building, or sensitivity, as opposed to medication administration or first aid). Such topics are enriched by a variety of perspectives, and the human experience, as opposed to specific job experience, is valuable fodder for group discussion and learning. Often it is expected that group learning begins and ends with the time spent together. For many topics, however, a group kick-off to develop basic levels of understanding, with independent work and practice in the real world and then a return to the group for people to share experiences and discuss applications of their learning, is terrific for developing deeper understanding of complex materials. This is sometimes referred to as a cohort model. This instrumental approach keeps the group learning sessions fresh and provides opportunities for members to share, rethink, and learn from one another.

In group or cohort training situations, trainers should see themselves as guides, resources, and facilitators, and they should work to create a group experience that helps employees learn from each other and that provides a rich experience. Like every form of training, group training should include a mixture of instructional strategies to meet the needs of a full spectrum of learners. The training experiences should have learning objectives and should be evaluated for effectiveness in terms of transfer and application of skill in the actual work environment.

On-the-Job Training

People learn most of what they do on the job as they face work situations. When this learning is unstructured, people may learn the wrong way, the least efficient way, the less respectful way, or they may not learn at all. Common pitfalls of poorly designed OJT include the following:

- The people who do the OJT training (whether DSPs, FLSs, or managers) do not know how to train. The ability to train others requires understanding how to present and teach materials and how to assess for understanding. Most people do not naturally have these skills, especially when instructing a learner who has limited literacy or special learning needs.
- The OJT trainer does not have the necessary skills to do the job task he or she is teaching (Dipboye, 1997). It seems obvious, but if the OJT trainer does not know what he or she is doing, he or she cannot train anyone else how to do it. The trainer will either skip the material or will make something up.
- The OJT trainer is resentful and grudging. A person doing on-site training needs to be excited about training the new DSP and needs to be focused on teaching new skills, not on catching people's mistakes. Even extremely dedicated DSPs and supervisors or managers burn out and may feel that it is a waste of valuable energy to train a new staff person who most likely will soon leave the organization.

Despite the ways in which OJT can go wrong, OJT has a number of benefits, including being inexpensive, convenient, and providing natural settings for employees to practice and demonstrate actual competence. OJT can be offered as just-in-time training and can help build staff relationships when done right (Carr, 1992).

Effective OJT is structured so that the people doing the training are qualified and competent. Keep in mind that seniority doesn't always mean the employee is the best trainer. For example, few DSPs' job descriptions list providing training to other DSPs, despite the fact that DSPs often are qualified to do so by virtue of their training and experience on the topic. OJT trainers should be given the time and resources to do the training properly, and they should be acknowledged and rewarded for their role.

Regardless of how qualified trainers are selected, it is important that OJT time not be used to read policies and procedures unless they are immediately important to the specific setting (e.g., read emergency procedures at the support setting and in conjunction with the first practice drill). Otherwise, organization policies, such as those that govern leave time, holidays, and how to sign up for benefits should be addressed during orientation (see Chapter 5). OJT opportunities should be short and modularized. OJT works best with concrete duties such as bathing someone and conducting a fire drill. As much as possible, the new employee should perform the tasks learned while the trainer is present to observe the new employee's performance. As with other kinds of training, it is also important to pace learning and OJT schedules to meet the needs of the employees.

OJT checklists can be effective tools to structure this type of training. These checklists, however, need to be focused on behavior outcomes. Before using them, OJT trainers need to learn how to use the checklists and should explain their purpose to the learner. A sample OJT checklist is provided at the end of this chapter. The list is only a sample and is not intended to be inclusive of all needed skills, as checklist items would vary across organizations, sites, and skill competency areas.

Computer-Based Multimedia Training

Computer-based multimedia training has been widely embraced by certain industries with similar training challenges to those faced by the community human services industry (Benson & Cheney, 1996). When people have trouble coming together for training and when people are at different skill levels, computer-based multimedia training can provide customized training that is accessible to employees at home, at work, or almost anywhere there is a computer. Multimedia training offers a number of advantages over other types of portable training such as videotapes or books. For example, if multimedia training is done well, it can be customized to each learner, it presents material in a variety of ways, and it checks for understanding. Studies show that learner retention with multimedia training is higher because learners can pace themselves at a comfortable rate and materials are presented through pictures, text, videos, and learner interaction (Hall, 1995; IBM Multimedia Consulting Center, 1994; Ouelette, 1995; Williamson, 1994).

The biggest barrier to computer-based multimedia training has been the related expense of hardware and software. Today, however, high-capacity computers should easily fit in to the training budget of even small organizations. In addition, public libraries, schools and workforce centers often have computers available for use. The College of Direct Support has developed an exciting new national curriculum available over the web that is aimed at critical skills specifically needed by DSPs. This curriculum has made accessibility to high-quality training anytime and anywhere a reality in the community human services industry (see the In the Spotlight segment about the College of Direct Support).

In the Spotlight: The College of Direct Support

The web and computer technology offer new and exciting ways to make high-quality training opportunities available to people in their own homes, at the work site, or anywhere that they have access to a computer and the web. The College of Direct Support is a place to find these high-quality training opportunities (http://www.collegeofdirectsupport.com).

The College of Direct Support offers modularized courses in topics that are important to DSPs, their employers, and the people they support. Courses cover positive behavioral supports, health and safety, first aid, and empowerment, self-determination, and many more topics. DSPs can pick the courses or even individual lessons that are most meaningful to them and their employers, and DSPs can participate in training when and where they want. For example, a DSP who needs to learn how to support a person with challenging behavior can get the information when he or she needs it and can then apply it instead of waiting for the training to be offered by the organization.

The courses in the College of Direct Support are based on state-of-the art knowledge in the field and on a set of nationally validated competencies, the *Community Support Skill Standards* (CSSS; Taylor et al., 1996), as well as on established ethical guidelines for DSPs, the NADSP Code of Ethics (see Figure 5.4). Content is self-paced; each lesson is approximately 30–60 minutes long and contains opportunities for DSPs to reflect on and interact with the material throughout the learning experience. A record of training is kept in the College of Direct Support database so that each learner can measure his or her progress. Assessments that can be used with the courses include multiple-choice pre- and posttests as well as suggested on-the-job assessment and portfolios. After successfully completing all of the lesson posttests in a course, the DSP receives a certificate of completion listing the stated course objectives and related competencies from the CSSS.

The College of Direct Support is a collaboration between MC Strategies, a multinational company experienced in computer-based training; the University of Minnesota,

Institute on Community Integration, Research and Training Center on Community Living, a leader in research and training in DSP recruitment, retention, and training; and the Sertoma Center, an organization that provides support services for more 150 individuals in the east Tennessee area. The College of Direct Support was originally funded by the U.S. Department of Health and Human Services. After initial development of 11 core courses, updates and new development have been maintained through customer fees and supple-mental grants.

Intentional Learning and Learning Contracts

As explained earlier in this chapter, the best training is identified and achieved through a collaborative process between employee and employer. Intentional learning, in which the employee defines the process by which he or she will achieve learning goals, helps the employee understand how to identify training needs and takes responsibility for seeking resources as needed. Learning contracts are one way to set up intentional learning. The employee and supervisor agree to the goal of the learning, the resources needed, and the timelines; then the employee takes responsibility to achieve necessary learning utilizing whatever method works best for him or her.

Because of limited resources, regulatory mandates, and high turnover in human services, training for DSPs is often punitive. Employees are told that they are required to attend training and are given ultimatums. An intentional learning environment sets a totally different tone for learning. The organization has a purposeful plan or means for the employee to acquire knowledge and skills—but the employee is a part of the plan. The organization assists in determining the when, where, why, and how regarding the learning.

Skill Mentoring

Skill mentoring can be used to help DSPs develop technical skills or to enhance DSPs' socialization and therefore commitment to the organization. Like OJT, mentoring provides a chance for DSPs to develop skills in the actual job setting and to learn from experienced employees. Mentoring has similar pitfalls to those of OJT in regards to who is selected as a mentor (for the mentoring experience to be useful, the mentor has to be qualified and competent). Unlike OJT, a mentor–mentee relationship is for a specified period of time and is focused on relationship building and skill building. The mentor assists the newer employee in understanding the ins and outs of the job and fosters the development of essential problem-solving skills. Much of the work of the mentor involves supportive listening, guidance, and support. Mentoring programs take time and effort up front to develop. Chapter 8 focuses on mentoring and describes how to design and implement mentoring programs.

Job Aids

Job aids are checklists or other environmental prompts that help employees remember the steps of tasks that are complicated or used infrequently. They are typically used as supplements to more in-depth training on the procedure and should not be used in absence of structured training. These aids are often used and developed by conscientious employees who find methods to remind themselves of the critical steps they must take to ensure they are doing something correctly. In the community human services industry, job aids could describe, for example, how to conduct safety checks before driving, how to complete medication administration, or how to add the proper amount of thickener to a food item. Other areas may be quick "cheat sheets" on the daily routines of people supported or the recipes that need to be prepared. It may be useful for an organization to prepare job aids in an employee's native language. Organizations that employ many individuals with limited English reading skills often use picture- or icon-based lists. In general, job aids are inexpensive, reasonably quick to produce and are effective tools for learning and remembering many tasks.

OVERCOMING IMPLEMENTATION BARRIERS

Developing an effective training program is not easy. A substantial investment of time and resources may be required to revise current practices. The rewards, however, of having a successful program are impressive. A common obstacle to success is resistance to change from the people who have developed the current system. In addition, trainers may lack skills in using the new training techniques and may have a limited understanding of how to actually implement the needed changes.

It is not wise to plan to radically and suddenly change a current training system. Like other interventions, changes in training require the investment of the stakeholders, in this case, the people who are being trained, who are doing the training, and who are developing the training, as well as the individuals being supported and those in charge of resources. An organization can bring people on board by offering them training and resources on best practices in training. The organization can let these people develop energy around necessary changes and guide them as needed. The organization can keep the parts that are successful in the existing program and supplement as needed. Incremental development and implementation keeps people from becoming resentful and overwhelmed. It allows them to learn from mistakes and make improvements in a manageable way.

QUESTIONS TO PONDER

1. Does your organization have an annual training calendar? Does it usually include the same topics year after year?
2. What formats does your organization currently use to train employees? What flexible training opportunities could be developed? Does your organization permit employees to test out of training? What new topics have been recently introduced?
3. How fast are new workers expected to be prepared to take on full responsibilities of the job? Has this time increased, decreased, or stayed the same as the skills of candidates have changed?
4. To what extent are existing employees and people receiving supports involved in your organization's attempts to reduce turnover, including training efforts? How

might people in various roles behave differently during orientation and training of new employees?

5. Who is doing training in your organization (e.g., existing DSPs and FLSs)? Are all of the trainers competent in providing training to others?

CONCLUSION

It is clear that current training methods do not always work, as evidenced by organizations that consistently admit (often behind closed doors or off the record) that they have serious concerns about worker competence and the ability to sustain growth in developing community supports for the individuals served. Organizations, however, can and should take action to improve their current training practices. Organizations that are going to survive and thrive in the changing direct support environment are going to have to become training innovators that can take the best of what is known about training and apply it in multiple formats that meet individual employee needs. Ultimately innovation in employee training in the community human services industry is much like innovation in support services. It requires the understanding of individual needs and then the application of individualized supports and resources to create a positive training experience that translates into real worker competence and increased retention of high-quality employees.

In the Spotlight: Special People In Northeast

Special People In Northeast (SPIN) is a nonprofit human services organization founded in 1970. Today SPIN supports more than 2,000 people in a variety of settings, with 634 staff members, 72 students, and 320 volunteers. In 1998, during a major reorganization, a leadership position in direct support called *home life coordinator/community life coordinator* was developed. The position requires an associate's degree and has a $28,000 per year starting salary. More than 50 DSPs are now working in these roles. Simultaneously SPIN worked with its union and staff to articulate a mission, values, and expectations for a new position called direct support professional (DSP).

To help staff obtain the new skills necessary to become DSPs, SPIN develop a curriculum of six new training courses. From September 1999 to May 2000, all habilitation instructors and coordinators and managers completed the courses. In July 2000, 300 habilitation instructors were recognized as DSPs in a celebration ceremony. Even though the organization highly valued education and offered tuition reimbursement, in 1998 only seven DSPs had college degrees or were currently enrolled in college courses. To improve this, SPIN created several new educational opportunities:

- With the Community College of Philadelphia, SPIN offers college-level instruction at job sites. Employees can earn an 18–credit hour Certificate of Recognition, a 33–credit hour Academic Certificate in Human Services, or associate's degree in human services with links to a bachelor's degree.
- With Pierce College, SPIN offers an on-site business degree program.
- With Arcadia University, SPIN offers on-site graduate courses in special education and leadership development.
- SPIN pairs each student with a mentor to support study skills, test preparation, and organizational skills and to provide encouragement and recognition for achievements.

- SPIN supports and recognizes students through study skills workshops, babysitting assistance, and computer workshops and access.
- SPIN provides bonuses to students for each 15 credits completed and provides organizationwide recognition for accomplishments.

Now, 56 SPIN DSPs have bachelor's or associate's degrees, and 19 are enrolled in college.

SPIN's initiatives are not limited to formal education. The organization also trains all managers in Joe D. Batten's (1989) "tough-minded leadership." This training teaches a values-based management philosophy that involves providing clear expectations and stretching them; using a "time with" approach to support DSPs; and focusing on strength discovery, development, and deployment. Seventy-five managers have completed the 48-hour course and are invited to attend monthly Batten leadership seminars to sharpen their skills.

Other recruitment, retention, and training initiatives at SPIN include the following:

- Cross-functional quality council groups for staff, consumers, and families to develop, initiate, and implement change
- A five-county, 60-organization image marketing campaign to attract DSPs and to improve their status
- Spin Traditions, an orientation program that integrates the mission, values, and expectations at SPIN with personal stories from families, consumers, and staff, and focuses on welcoming new staff members
- A leadership path that gives exemplary DSPs an opportunity to earn more money for taking increased responsibilities in staff recruitment and development (roles include ambassador, strengths development peer, team leader for new staff orientation and socialization, and traditions presenter)
- A "right-fit" philosophy that is used in the hiring and preservice training to ensure that new employees share SPIN's values and mission and can meet expectations
- A recruitment and retention plan that provides increased pay for positions, longevity bonuses, recruitment bonuses, and leadership opportunities at all levels
- Staff recognition efforts such as rewards for achieving tenure benchmarks starting at 1 year

These efforts have helped SPIN to maintain a turnover rate for adult services employees of less than 33% since 1998. For more information, contact Kathy Brown-McHale, Special People in Northeast, 10521 Drummond Road, Philadelphia, PA 19154; 215-613-1000; http://www.spininc.org.

RESOURCES

American Society for Training & Development (ASTD), 1640 King Street, Box 1443, Alexandria, Virginia, 22313-2043; 703-683-8100, 800-628-2783; fax: 703-683-1523; http://www.astd.org/

A professional association for people working in training roles. ASTD has many resources to help trainers be more effective at what they do.

National Alliance for Direct Support Professionals (NADSP), http://www.nadsp.org.

The NADSP web site contains information from local chapters across the United States. In many cases, NADSP chapters have emphasized education and training of DSPs.

Training trainers towards excellence: A day of interaction and dialogue for people who train, or are interested in training, direct support professionals. Conference proceedings from a statewide training conference cosponsored by the Minnesota Department of Human Services State Operated Services and the University of Minnesota, Institute on Community Integration (ICI), Research and Training Center on Community Living, St. Cloud, MN. (Available from the ICI publications office, 150 Pillsbury Drive, SE, Minneapolis, MN 55455; 612-624-4512)

This report is a short conference summary that contains many useful tips for training. It includes tips on how to use overhead transparencies and other visual aids, how to use different training styles, and how to work with adult learners.

Taylor, M., Bradley, V., & Warren, R., Jr. (1996). *Community support skill standards: Tools for managing change and achieving outcomes.* Cambridge, MA: Human Services Research Institute. (Available from the publisher, http://www.hsri.org/)

The *Community Support Skill Standards* (CSSS) are a job analysis of the roles and competencies of direct support practitioners who work in community human services organizations. (See Chapter 6 for more on job analysis.)

Direct Support Professional Training Development Plan

Date: _____   Your name: _____

Dates of employment at [insert organization name]: _____

Current work location: _____

1. What are your personal interests (e.g., yoga, stained glass, weight lifting)?

_____

_____

_____

_____

2. What training or learning is required for these personal interests? _____

_____

_____

_____

3. What are your professional goals (e.g., to become an employment specialist, to become a support

coordinator, to be a teacher)? _____

_____

_____

_____

_____

4. What training or learning is required to meet these professional goals? _____

_____

_____

_____

5. What are your educational goals (e.g., GED, A.A., B.A., M.S.W.)? _____

_____

_____

_____

(continued)

Staff Recruitment, Retention, and Training Strategies for Community Human Services Organizations
by Sheryl A. Larson & Amy S. Hewitt.

6. What training or learning is required to meet these educational goals? _____

_____

_____

_____

7. What are the special needs or interests of the people whom you support (e.g., takes multiple psy-

chotropic medications, wants to learn family genealogy)? _____

_____

_____

_____

8. What training or learning is required to support these individuals in their needs and interests?

_____

_____

_____

_____

9. What are three priority learning or training goals for you? List each goal and timeline for achieving
that goal.

	Goal	*Timeline*
1.	_____	_____
2.	_____	_____
3.	_____	_____

Employee signature: _____

Supervisor signature: _____

Structured On-the-Job Training Checklist
for Newly Hired Direct Support Professionals

Competency area: Safety at home and in the community

Purpose: The purpose of this on-the-job training (OJT) checklist is to guide your learning on the health and safety for the people to whom you provide supports. Our expectation as your employer is that you will schedule a time to meet with your supervisor or skills mentor and receive training in the skills identified in this checklist. You will also be expected to demonstrate these competencies.

Your name: _____

Address: _____

Home telephone number: _____   Cell phone number: _____

Your work site: _____   Your supervisor or skills mentor: _____

- ☐ The direct support professional (DSP) identifies what is considered high-risk behavior for the people he or she supports.
- ☐ The DSP identifies real and perceived vulnerabilities for the individuals he or she supports based upon each individual's personal history.
- ☐ The DSP implements safety policies at home, at work, and in the community, based on individual needs and universal best practices.
- ☐ The DSP identifies and ensures resolution of safety issues in the home of the individual supported when they occur.
- ☐ The DSP completes formal and proactive assessments of potential safety hazards in the home environment based on the needs of the individuals who live there.
- ☐ The DSP knows where to find and how to use the fire safety plan where he or she works.
- ☐ The DSP identifies and rectifies any potential fire hazards where he or she works.
- ☐ The DSP periodically practices fire drills with individuals supported.
- ☐ The DSP uses planned fire escape routes when conducting drills.
- ☐ The DSP understands and follows state and organization fire safety standards.
- ☐ The DSP describes the specific action he or she would take in the event of a fire at the place in which he or she works. This action would include specific detail about how to adequately protect the people who receive supports in this setting.
- ☐ The DSP accurately assesses the day's activities for the people he or she supports with regard to community safety precautions that need to be taken.
- ☐ The DSP accurately identifies current and potential risks in the community for the individuals he or she supports.
- ☐ The DSP teaches and models safe behaviors in the community for the people he or she supports.
- ☐ The DSP drives safely and avoids risky behavior while driving.
- ☐ The DSP teaches and models appropriate traffic and automobile safety behavior when working.
- ☐ The DSP implements individual safety protections for the people he or she supports while riding in vehicles.
- ☐ The DSP washes hands using correct procedures at all appropriate times while working.
- ☐ The DSP uses universal precautions as appropriate when in contact with bodily fluids.
- ☐ The DSP correctly cleans and disinfects contaminated surfaces while working.
- ☐ The DSP appropriately cleans and disinfects food contact surfaces while working.
- ☐ The DSP appropriately handles contaminated laundry as needed.
- ☐ The DSP uses appropriate steps when exposed to blood or other bodily fluids.
- ☐ The DSP follows organization procedures regarding incidents in which people have been exposed to the bodily fluids of another person.
- ☐ The DSP completes documentation as needed and accurately in response to incidents and accidents.

8

FOSTERING COMMITMENT AND SKILL THROUGH MENTORING PROGRAMS

AMY S. HEWITT, TRACI L. LALIBERTE,
JODY KOUGL-LINDSTROM, AND SHERYL A. LARSON

Throughout time, mentor–mentee relationships have proven to be effective and meaningful partnerships. In Greek mythology, Homer wrote of a man named Ulysses who went to fight the Trojan War. In his absence, Ulysses asked his trusted friend, Mentor, to guide and advise his young son (Bell, 2002; Brounstein, 2000). The wisdom that Mentor possessed can be seen in other mentors over the years, whereas the eagerness and openness of Ulysses' son can be seen in other mentees. Socrates mentored Plato, and Aristotle mentored Alexander the Great. Henry David Thoreau found a mentor in Ralph Waldo Emerson, and Helen Keller found her mentor in Anne Sullivan. In politics, we have seen Dr. Martin Luther King, Jr., mentor Jesse Jackson. In athletics, Bob Kersee gave mentorship to Florence Griffith Joyner. Even in movies and television, we have grown to admire and appreciate the strength of the mentoring relationships between Yoda and Luke Skywalker (*The Empire Strikes Back*); Professor Helinger and John Forbes Nash, Jr. (*A Beautiful Mind*); and Richie Cunningham and Arthur Fonzarelli (*Happy Days*) (Carr, 2002). This chapter identifies the importance of creating and implementing mentoring programs in community human services organizations. It describes the essential components of a good mentorship program and explains the benefits of a successful quality mentorship program. It provides suggestions for how to develop, build commitment to, implement, and monitor effective mentoring programs. It also examines the roles of stakeholders in supporting mentorship programs.

TARGETED FRONT-LINE SUPERVISOR COMPETENCIES

Front-line supervisors (FLSs) are responsible for ensuring that direct support professionals (DSPs) are well trained and competent. FLSs also coordinate personnel to ensure that what needs to get done gets done.

Primary Skills

FLSs coordinate and participate in DSP training and in-service sessions by orienting new staff, arranging for staff to attend training and in-service sessions, maintaining training records, and supporting ongoing staff development.

FLSs provide orientation and answer questions from new staff through a variety of formal and informal instructional and learning activities.

177

FLSs identify potential trainers and provide resources, coaching, and opportunities for DSP training.

Related Skills

FLSs coordinate personnel management by hiring new staff, conducting performance reviews, facilitating teamwork and staff meetings, creating job descriptions, delegating tasks and responsibilities, encouraging effective communication, defusing crises and conflicts between staff, and implementing grievance and formal contract procedures.

FLSs may complete salary reviews or make recommendations regarding pay increases. FLSs may also identify other means of compensation, opportunities for promotion, and staff celebrations and discuss these with managers, depending upon the management structure at their specific organization.

FLSs attend and actively participate in organization management, planning, and cross-functional work group meetings.

UNDERSTANDING THE PROBLEM

One of the biggest challenges in reducing turnover is to address leaving among newly employed staff members. Employee turnover is most common among newly hired DSPs. One study found that 23% of new employees in small group homes left in the first 3 months after hire and a total of 53% had left within the first year (Larson, Lakin & Bruininks, 1998; see also Chapter 3). Another study found that lower satisfaction with informal co-worker support was strongly correlated with higher turnover among part-time employees with less than 12 months of service in community residential support settings (Bachelder & Braddock, 1994). This chapter examines mentoring as a specific strategy to improve socialization of newcomers and to improve support for skill development for inexperienced employees.

Most people have observed or participated in various mentoring relationships during their lifetime. But, for many people, these relationships did not occur in work environments. In a study discussed by Chip Bell (2002), 35% of employees reported they were not receiving mentoring opportunities from their employer and that they were planning to obtain a different job within a year. Another study reported that 45% of newly hired business graduates had a mentor or sponsor available to them (Louis, Posner, & Powell, 1983). In New York City, 12 of 24 organizations supporting individuals with disabilities used peer mentoring with at least some employees (Ebenstein & Gooler, 1993).

Bell (2002) reported that when he began to study mentoring in the 1970s, there was virtually nothing written about the topic. He began his discovery of mentorship after reading an article called "Much Ado about Mentors" (Roche, 1979), which stated that four of five CEOs of Fortune 500 companies attributed a significant proportion of their success to having had a mentor (Bell, 2002). Approximately 20 years after

Roche's article was published, Brounstein (2000) reported that there were still very few books dedicated to this important area of staff support and cultivation. Instead, mentorship information is tucked in the crevices and corners of various management, leadership, and personnel resources. Brounstein suggested that what people want are books with specific strategies and techniques presented in a clear and concise manner to assist them in starting mentoring programs at their own organizations.

In considering the application of mentoring principles in community human services, it is important to review the context for such progress. Supervisors are often viewed as the crux of quality in a given program. Supervisors affect whether DSPs stay or leave (see Chapter 1). Supervisors have difficult jobs that sometimes feel impossible because employees are geographically spread out and work different shifts. For many supervisors, training, supporting, and developing employees are overwhelming tasks. Developing mentors who can support, train, and develop DSPs can be a tremendous help to supervisors.

Definition of Mentoring

There are numerous types of mentoring and various reasons to have mentoring programs within organizations. The two primary purposes of mentoring are 1) to support and socialize an employee to have a successful employment experience and to move toward certain career goals and 2) to support an employee in developing certain skills. Mentoring programs are used within many types of organizations and businesses, including religious organizations, Fortune 500 companies, nonprofit organizations, as well as community human services settings.

For the purposes of this chapter, we define mentoring as "a deliberate pairing of more skilled or experienced professionals with a lesser skilled or experienced [professional]. . . . to help the lesser skilled person grow, become socialized into his/her new role within the agency, and to develop specific competencies" (O'Nell, Hewitt, Sauer, & Larson, 2001, p. 4 of the Introduction to the Learner Guide). Mentoring provides natural and safe opportunities for the mentee and mentor to share positive and negative experiences, fears, thoughts, mistakes, and knowledge and creates an open and honest learning and teaching environment for mentee and mentor alike.

RESEARCH SUPPORT FOR SOLUTIONS

Organizations that use mentorship programs in which all levels of the organizations actively participate, regularly evaluate, redefine, and commit themselves to the program have greater success in keeping their employees (Taylor, Sauer, Hewitt, O'Nell, & Larson, 2001). Imagine that you are a newly hired employee in an organization that operates 10 supported living programs. On your first day you meet your supervisor, receive an employee handbook, and watch a 30-minute welcome video. Your supervisor explains to you that the organization requires 3 full days of training before working in a home. You appreciate the thoroughness of the organization's training plan and eagerly attend the 3-day training. On your first day after training, the supervisor assigns you to a home and tells you where the files are and that you will find everything you need in the staff cabinet. Feeling isolated, scared, and unsure of what to expect, you venture to your new work site alone. You find the staff cabinets but there is little information about which tasks you are responsible for or how to go about doing them. You suddenly think to yourself that you do not like this job and that you feel uncomfortable without any support or further help from the organization. Wouldn't it be better if you were to have someone to call or to work with for the first couple of days? Of course it would! A mentorship program is designed to prevent the feeling of isolation and confusion described in this type of situation.

The benefits of mentorship programs are numerous. Although organizations each implement mentorship programs differently, many of the benefits described in Table 8.1 are generalizable across organizations. One of the greatest benefits is that mentoring programs can be effective at reducing turnover and preventing burnout. A study of a mentoring program for 120 beginning teachers in Los Angeles documented that retention in the first 3 years increased from 78% to 95% for teachers who had mentors (Colbert & Wolff, 1992). When employees feel supported and listened to and when they have the skills they need to do their job, they stay with the organization longer. In addition, mentoring programs provide a sense of community among new employees and help them to learn the organization's values, mission, and vision. When employees understand and are committed to striving for the desired vision, the people who receive supports are more likely to experience a better quality of life.

New employees also have much to gain by participating in a mentoring program. Feelings of isolation, uncertainty, and fear can be greatly reduced when these employees have a mentor from whom they can seek guidance. A person who is experienced and "in the know" looks out for them and helps them not only learn needed skills to do their job but also learn "the ropes" or how things are done at the organization and the other informal processes and procedures that are never described in policy manuals. Mentors are helpful in providing information about employees' roles and organizational features such as politics, procedures, and policies. Studies have found that employees with mentors had more information about their roles and the organization than those who did not have mentors (Lankau & Scandura, 2002; Ostroff & Kozlowski, 1993). A study of 1,162 people who had a mentor found that mentees who had a highly satisfying informal or formal mentoring relationship reported greater job satisfaction, organizational commitment, and career commitment and less intent to quit than those who reported marginal or dissatisfying mentoring relationships and those who did not have a mentor (Ragins, Cotton, & Miller, 2000).

Employees with mentors also have a place to turn when things go wrong. In community services, crises may occur and unusual circumstances may pop up unexpectedly. Truly no day is ever the same as the day before. Having a mentor can help employees when they are faced with new experiences that may cause anxiety, fear, anger, or frustration. Such experiences often result in employees' deciding to leave an organization. When a mentor is there to listen, draw on his or her experiences, and provide advice to employees, those anxieties and fears are reduced.

Mentors also benefit from mentoring programs. Being called on to share experiences and offer support to others may feel like a vote of confidence. Being a mentor is a way to be recognized for being excellent at what one does. Often this reward can spark a new interest in the work and prevent burnout. This is more likely to occur if

Table 8.1. Benefits of mentorship programs

Key stakeholder	Benefits of mentorship to those key people
Organization	Low-cost method to communicate vision, mission, and recommended practice
	Better-quality supports
	Development of employees
	Increased retention and reduced turnover
	Stronger employee commitment
New hires	Accumulated knowledge and experience of mentor
	Safe opportunity for feedback
	Occasion to discuss anxiety and concerns
	Social connections with others
	Decreased feelings of isolation
	Access to information
	Guidance on norms
Mentors	Recognition for skills and abilities
	Opportunities to develop new skills and advancement
	Renewed interest in job
	Raises, bonuses, and rewards
Supported individuals	Better services
	Less turnover
	Positive long-term relationships

Source: Taylor, Sauer, Hewitt, O'Nell, & Larson, 2001.

the mentors are carefully selected from a group of volunteers and if they are rewarded with a bonus, an increase in pay, or another tangible item.

In the end, when organizations, employees, and mentors gain, the people who receive support gain as well. When employees have the skills they need, are supported, and are rewarded, organizations function better and the people who receive services are much more likely to experience quality support.

STRATEGIES FOR RESPONDING TO THE PROBLEM

To set up a successful mentorship program, first the organization must clearly define in writing the mission, goals, and outcomes of the program. Next, the organization must build commitment to the mentorship program by developing the needed training, incentives, flexibility, time, and supports for employees to participate in the program. The organization should define the roles and responsibilities of key stakeholders in the mentorship program. Only after doing all this is it time to actually develop and implement the program. The final step is to evaluate the program as needed.

Define the Mentoring Program's Mission, Goals, and Outcomes

Developing a mission for a mentoring program helps to focus its purpose. A possible mission for an organization's mentoring program could be "to enhance DSPs' skills, competence and commitment to the organization by providing support, guidance, and training through a planned mentoring program." Another relevant mission could be to reduce turnover. Defining the mentoring program's goals also includes describing what changes (outcomes) are desired and how that change can be measured and documented. The goal may be to reduce turnover, improve employee job satisfaction, or increase the knowledge of DSPs.

Build Commitment

It is one thing to talk about and plan for a mentoring program. It is much more difficult to actually make it happen. For a program to be effective, it must have buy-in from all stakeholders and must have the full support of the people within the organization who make decisions and control resources. Important stakeholders include DSPs, FLSs, managers, people who receive supports and their families, and human resources personnel. Stakeholders in positions of power, such as administrators, managers, and boards of directors, must show their commitment by providing financial support, creating incentives, allowing time away from work duties for mentorship participants, and so forth. Following are some suggestions for securing commitment from these groups of people:

- *Ensure that someone from upper management or administration is involved in the development process for the mentoring program.* Doing so will prevent much time and energy from being wasted. If decision makers are involved from the beginning, they will likely be more comfortable during the implementation and evaluation phases.
- *Seek to identify the financial resources available for marketing, training events, and incentives to mentors and mentees early in the development process.* As with any new program, there are various and hidden costs. The costs may be for program marketing (e.g., fliers, informational meetings), introductory training for mentors (e.g., replacements on the job while mentors are training, refreshments, mentors' training time), and for incentives for participants (e.g., bonuses, raises, other tangible items). Figure out the budget, and build the program within these means.
- *Schedule for the mentors and mentees to have time away from their duties to get together.* Mentors and mentees will need time to meet and to share. In community human services, this likely means that the desired outcome of the mentorship program will have to be authorized by someone in the organization or that a certain amount of flexible time will need to be built into participants' weekly schedules. If there is no time for mentors and mentees to get together, the relationships will not be effective, and the mentoring program will fail.
- *Involve DSPs and individuals receiving supports and their family members in planning and implementing the mentoring program.* If DSPs are to be mentors, it is important to get their input throughout the planning and implementation process. This can be accomplished by including DSPs in planning groups and evaluation activities and getting feedback from focus groups. It is also important to get input from individuals receiving supports and their family members because they are affected by the quality of supports provided by the organization.
- *Solicit short news briefs or newsletter articles from the CEO or administrators regarding the mentoring programs.* One way to convey commitment on the part of the administrators is to ask them to participate in the making of the mentoring program. They can be invited to write about it, share their experiences with mentoring relationships, or be involved in informational sessions about the program.

Building commitment toward the mentoring program is critical because different people within the organization may have very different ideas about the program's purpose. Ensure that everyone agrees on the purpose or desired outcome of the program.

Outline Roles and Responsibilities

Organizations with successful mentorship programs clearly define the roles and responsibilities of program stakeholders at all levels of their organizations (Taylor et al., 2001).

Organization

The organization's role is to promote and foster the development and growth of the mentorship program to the fullest extent by demonstrating commitment to the mentorship program in all actions. Organizations are responsible for educating all staff about the mentorship program, providing participation opportunities, and continually identifying mentors and mentees for the program. Organizations also support their mentorship program by allowing time for the mentor and mentee to meet. The organization's role includes selecting people to become mentors. In doing so, it is important to convey to the chosen mentors that they have been identified to be mentors based on their previous experience and excellent professional conduct. Some organizations require mentors to have had at least a year of experience in their current position, to have not been subject to negative disciplinary action within the past year, to have demonstrated competence in all aspects of their current position, and to show a willingness to participate in the program. When communicating to mentors that they have been selected, the organization should let them know that they are among the few who were chosen and that it is an honor to have been selected. The mentor selection process should instill a shared sense of accomplishment, pride, and ownership among the chosen mentors.

Managers

Managers' support for the mentorship program can make or break the success of the program (O'Nell, Hewitt, et al., 2001). The role of the management team is to be an active participant in the mentorship program by 1) talking positively about the mentoring program and encouraging support for it, 2) encouraging supervisors and DSPs to volunteer to become mentors, 3) encouraging supervisors to foster the mentoring relationships between DSPs and their mentors, and 4) scheduling time for mentors and mentees to meet. All managers' actions model their commitment to and the value that they see in the mentorship program.

Supervisors

The role of an FLS in a mentorship program is similar to that of a manager. Supervisors are to be active participants in the mentorship program by 1) encouraging DSPs to participate in the program; 2) communicating a willingness to provide support, if needed, during the development of the mentor–mentee relationship; and 3) evaluating whether mentees are developing the skills needed to perform the identified roles and responsibilities related to their direct support positions.

Mentors

The role of a mentor is to create and foster a safe and open atmosphere in which the mentee feels comfortable to share his or her dreams, fears, concerns, and experiences.

Mentors' active listening skills create and foster teaching and learning experiences. Following are some other skills needed by mentors:

- Mentors possess clear understanding of their organization's mission statement, values, policies, and procedures.
- Mentors act in accordance with the organization's mission statement and values in their daily work conduct.
- Mentors continually demonstrate appropriate professional skills, abilities, and judgment.
- Mentors have good problem-solving skills and can see multiple solutions and options for protégés when they are faced with a problem.
- Mentors know when and why to refer a mentee to his or her supervisor for direction.

Mentors provide feedback to mentees, celebrate the successes of mentees, and share what worked in similar situations. Mentors share information about particular approaches or techniques that work better to enhance the quality of life for people they support. Mentors can help mentees figure out new or different approaches to use with the people they support, their co-workers, or their supervisor. Mentors also provide role modeling, acceptance, counseling, and friendship (Kram, 1983).

Mentors create opportunities for mentees to learn from experiences by identifying how these experiences relate to the organization's mission, values, policies, and procedures. Successful mentors have a goal of building the mentees' motivation, drive, and commitment to reaching the next level of professionalism in providing respectful, meaningful, and quality supports to the people they serve. Each mentee has different social support needs. When a mentor provides the amount and kind of social support the mentee expects, the mentee is more likely to perceive the relationship as effective and to trust the mentor (Young & Perrewe, 2000). In striving to reach this goal with the mentee, the mentor may use several techniques, including active listening, sharing of professional experiences, shadowing, role-playing, role-modeling, posing questions, giving research and educational assignments, and referring the mentee to other resources. Mentors may need training to develop these skills.

It is important for mentors to understand that mentees need varying amounts of time to feel safe to share fears, mistakes, concerns, and other matters. A mentor cannot control how quickly and to what extent a mentee will exhibit this openness. Mentors can use certain methods, however, to increase the likelihood that mentees are willing to share experiences. One strategy is to explore previous experiences a mentee has had with mentoring. This may generate conversations regarding what the mentee understands about mentorship programs and his or her expectations for the program, and it may open the door for the mentor to explain to how the organization's mentoring program may differ from other programs. The mentor may also share some of the difficulties she or he experienced when starting the job and briefly describe how he or she overcame these difficulties. Another strategy is for the mentor to consistently convey that the relationship between him or her and the mentee is safe, open, and confidential. The mentor can explain to the mentee that what is said between them will not be part of the mentee's performance appraisal, even though at times the mentor may review with the mentee the organization's procedures, expectations, and policies.

The mentor can use many strategies to increase the effectiveness of the mentoring process. Asking the mentee to set up the first mentorship meeting with his or her mentor and supervisor ensures that the mentee takes ownership for the process. The purpose of having the mentee's supervisor at the first meeting is to make sure that a sound foundation is created by reviewing roles and responsibilities and defining the outcomes that are expected from the mentoring process. One important clarification is for the supervisor and the mentor to clearly explain that the mentor will not be reporting to the supervisor what the mentee discusses or how the mentee is doing. Mentorship meetings should be held in a room that is private, quiet, and free from interruption, thus encouraging open, honest sharing and interactions. Mentors may ask their mentees to come to scheduled meetings with a list of items they would like to discuss. Such a strategy helps the mentees to know what to expect. The mentor needs to ensure that sessions remain focused and target the development of new skills and assimilation into the organizational culture.

Last, to facilitate a trusting and open relationship, the mentor should make an effort to follow up on requests and tasks requested of the mentee. Mentors will know they are being successful in their roles when they see a trusting relationship developing, with the mentees "disclosing their own professional challenges, mistakes, and insights they have gained from their mentors and their professional experiences" (Taylor et al., 2001).

Mentees

The roles of the mentee are that of learner, listener, and active participant in his or her professional development as a DSP.

- Mentees clearly identify their professional goals.
- Mentees identify professional areas in which they need or want to grow.
- Mentees share professional experiences with their mentors.
- Mentees complete and review all assignments or tasks that are required in the mentoring program.

Mentees who are open to sharing their experiences and their fears, thoughts, and concerns about their positions as DSPs report gaining more from their mentors than those who are more hesitant (O'Nell, Hewitt, et al., 2001).

An important component of a successful mentee–mentor relationship is that the mentee understands that his or her role includes asking questions on an ongoing basis and soliciting professional suggestions from the mentor. Mentees seek and remain engaged in learning opportunities by making observations, seeking new information, and trying new strategies or skills. Often, mentees seek support from their mentors by expressing what they see as their own personal needs, goals, and desires and then getting suggestions from mentors on how to fulfill these.

A mentee may use the mentoring program to learn about organization protocols, procedures, and informal organizational cultural rules, and he or she may learn problem-solving techniques that are effective within his or her work environments. Often mentees use their time with mentoring to seek suggestions for how to interact with the people to whom they provide support. Understanding the history of the people supported, their network of friends and family, and how each person is supported by the organization are all common topics associated with mentoring relationships. The mentoring time is also often spent problem-solving co-worker conflict.

Develop and Implement the Program

Once sufficient commitment from organization stakeholders is acquired to develop and support a mentoring program, it is time to begin crafting the actual program. There are a number of important components for any given mentoring program (see Table 8.2).

Evaluate the Mentoring Program

The evaluation of the mentorship program must be part of the program's routine up-keep and maintenance. As the organization experiences changes in staff, individuals supported, workforce issues, and legislative mandates, the mentorship program may need modifications to preserve its high-quality results and effectiveness. The development of the program evaluation should begin *prior* to the commencement of the program. This strategic approach to evaluation means that the organization measures what it truly intended to measure rather than whatever data are available at evaluation time. In other words, the organization should be purposeful in collecting data instead of just measuring random outcomes as an afterthought.

When developing evaluation for a mentoring program, the organization should look at why the mentoring program has been implemented (the program's mission and goals). The organization should be sure to specifically define how progress toward these goals will be measured. Once the areas of measurement have been decided upon, the organization must determine a way to collect the data that it is interested in. Chapter 13 provides detailed information about how to measure and assess desired outcomes.

Cost-Effectiveness

Determining the cost-effectiveness of the mentoring program is one way to evaluate the program. An ongoing account must be kept of all expenses that the organization incurs to implement the mentorship program. These expenses could include the training hours for mentors, the payroll amounts attributed to time spent away from job tasks for meetings between mentors and mentees, bonuses or rewards paid to mentors, the training or shadowing time that mentees spend during their orientation, time spent in mentee–mentor meetings, and so forth. With this information, the organization can calculate the total cost of implementing the mentorship program. Next, the organization must determine whether staff turnover rates were reduced and how much money this reduction saved. As retention increases, organizations are able to save considerable amounts of money that would otherwise have been spent on recruiting, hiring, and training new staff. The organization can subtract the cost of implementing the mentorship program from the total savings due to reduced staff turnover; the result shows the cost-effectiveness of the mentorship program.

Staff Knowledge

Evaluating the increase in staff knowledge or in staff satisfaction may be more difficult than evaluating cost-effectiveness in some circumstances. For this type of information,

Table 8.2. Essential components of successful mentorship programs

Middle managers and supervisors understand the purpose and procedures of the mentorship program and show support for the program. Middle managers and supervisors are very influential in the work lives of their employees. They need training in how to select mentors, how to schedule mentorship sessions, and how to offer time for commuting and other tasks associated with the program. It is essential for middle managers and supervisors to be familiar with the program.

A coordinator has been selected to market the program, screen mentors, arrange and track matches, train mentors and mentees, monitor and support program activities, evaluate the program, and advocate for ongoing program support. Implementing a mentoring program requires a significant investment of time and energy. Having a designated coordinator who will champion the program is a critical component of an effective program.

Mentors and mentees understand why they were chosen for participation. They know the purpose behind the program. When the program is being developed, it is critical for mentors and mentees to understand why they were chosen. The program description and guidelines should clearly state the selection standards. There should be a basis for determining who is invited and who is not. If certain positions or sites in the organization involve high stress programs, all people who work in these positions or sites may be assigned a mentor.

Careful consideration is given to how to match mentors with mentees. Mentors and mentees can be matched in many ways (e.g., work location, characteristics of people supported, demographic characteristics). Consider all of the options and give some thought to the matching process. Planning ahead for the matches will improve the overall mentoring program.

Mentors, mentees, supervisors, and managers have a clear understanding of their roles. It may be helpful to create mentorship job descriptions for everyone involved in the program. People need clear explanations to do what they are supposed to do. Mentors and mentees may want to create a time-limited professional development plan with an agreement about mutual responsibilities, developmental goals, meeting frequency, and length of mentorship and an outline of activities to help the mentee to meet his or her goals.

Mentors and mentees make a solid commitment to participate in the program. In developing a program, be sure to figure out how the mentor and mentee can pledge their commitment. For example, they may simply sign a form that says they agree to these new roles for a certain period of time. Whatever the format, be certain that this written commitment exists. This written commitment can screen out participants who are unlikely to fulfill their obligations to the program.

Mentors have regular opportunities to meet one another to get support and training and to celebrate program successes. Monthly or bimonthly gatherings for mentors in which they discuss challenges, reflect on their experiences, celebrate their successes, and strengthen and improve the overall mentoring program are important.

Implementation is carefully planned and piloted before organizationwide implementation occurs. Organizationwide implementation can be difficult. It is often helpful to pilot the program in a small number of sites before implementing it organizationwide. When selecting pilot sites, consider excitement and level of support and commitment to the mentoring program.

The mentorship program is evaluated, and the program is modified regularly based on evaluation findings. No program remains the same over time. Decide up front what aspects are important to evaluate and how these features will be evaluated. Then as the program evolves, refer back to those goals to be sure that the changes are consistent with the original intent.

See *The Peer Empowerment Program* (*PEP;* Taylor, Sauer, Hewitt, O'Nell, & Larson, 2001) for details about the tasks described in this table.

an organization cannot simply rely upon numbers and calculations; instead, it must design a way to collect information about the areas that it is interested in. Two ways to collect such data are through surveys and/or exit interviews. The organization can collect this data through verbal interviews or by using paper- or computer-based questionnaires. Two examples of exit interview questionnaires for peer mentoring programs are provided at the end of this chapter.

As the organization gathers data from the exit interviews, specific areas of strengths and weakness of the program may begin to appear in the participants' responses. If an aspect of the program is continually receiving negative feedback in the exit interviews, the organization can reevaluate how that part of the program is being run and can make the necessary adjustments. For example, if the majority of mentor interviews result in feedback concerning a lack of preparedness, the organization will need to provide mentors with increased training on their roles, responsibilities, and available resources. If feedback from exit interviews show that mentees didn't feel they saw their mentor often enough because the mentor worked at a different site, perhaps the organization needs to change its matching process to include the work site as a criteria for the matching of mentors and mentees.

In the Spotlight: Hammer Residences

Traci LaLiberte

Hammer Residences is located in the Twin Cities Metro area of Minnesota. Currently, Hammer Residences serves over 140 individuals with developmental disabilities through its residential services program. In addition to residential services, Hammer Residences also provides in-home support services, support coordination services, and supported employment services.

The mentoring programs for supervisors and DSPs at Hammer Residences are coordinated by a full-time staff member in the human resources department. The mentoring process begins with a 4-hour training session for anyone wishing to be a mentor. During this training, trainers discuss what mentoring is and is not. Trainers use role plays so that participants can learn about boundaries and understanding the concerns of the mentee. It is emphasized that the mentor is *not* a trainer, although some training does naturally occur during the mentoring sessions. Mentors receive a one-time $200 incentive, as well as a small amount of petty cash for activities with their mentee, such as going out for coffee. A mentor–mentee pairing is designed to last 6 months. During this period, mentors keep a log of activities and time spent with the mentee. Hammer Residences also uses an evaluation form that the mentor and mentee complete at the end of the 6-month time frame.

When a new supervisor is appointed, Hammer Residences' program directors pair a trained mentor with the new supervisor based on personality; personal interests; and organization elements, such as which home the new supervisor will be working in and which home the mentor has previously worked in. An ideal match occurs if the mentor was previously a supervisor in the home where the mentee will be working because the mentor is well equipped to assist the mentee in assimilating into his or her new role and surroundings.

Hammer Residences has been fortunate in that it has encountered little to no challenges. Staff were able to learn, however, from challenges they have faced in the mentorship program for DSPs. Participating DSPs and mentors found it difficult to find time to meet with one another. Some DSPs reported that they felt offended that a mentor was automatically assigned to them as they felt they knew what they were doing in their role as DSP and did not want a mentor. Hammer Residences reevaluated its DSP mentoring program and whether all newly hired DSPs should be assigned a mentor. When DSPs are matched with mentors, consideration is also now given to each DSP's self-esteem and how the mentoring relationship is introduced.

Overall, Hammer Residences is committed to its mentoring programs and has found great success in the relationships formed and the retention of those completing the 6-month program. The mentoring program has become an integral part of the organization's plan for hiring, training, and retaining employees.

For additional information about Hammer Residences's mentoring program, contact Kim Hansen at 952-473-1261.

OVERCOMING IMPLEMENTATION BARRIERS

Although the benefits far outweigh the challenges of creating a mentorship program, the challenges are worth mentioning here so that organizations can be mindful of them and plan accordingly. First, diversity plays a role anytime staff members get together for partnerships. Diversity should be part of the mentor–mentee matching criteria, either by matching people who are different from one another or by matching those who have similar life experiences. DSPs are individuals and therefore bring with them many different ways of communicating, learning, and dealing with problems. Mentors and mentees do not necessarily have to be paired with someone who has the same learning style or communication style, but it is important for the organization to be aware of differences while creating matches.

Second, the organization needs to be aware and committed to the amount of time and resources required to create a successful mentorship program. A study conducted in New York City reported that only 33% of organizations with mentoring programs said their program was extremely or usually effective (Ebenstein & Gooler, 1993). Major challenges included lack of advancement opportunities for those who were mentored (88%), not enough time for the mentoring experience (33%), and resentment from others who did not have a mentor (33%). Clearly, an organization that expects a successful mentorship program but resists providing the appropriate time and resources to make it succeed will have difficulties. Without a true commitment to the mentoring program up front, including commitment from the organization's decision makers, it might be prudent to delay development of the mentoring program to cultivate the required support.

Another obstacle faced by some organizations is a tendency to start too big and without thought. When creating a mentoring program, it is important to remember that mentors need training, processes have to be developed, the program has to be marketed, and so forth. Starting with a small pilot program and then making organization-wide change may help prevent the organization from having a big "kickoff to failure." Working out the glitches in small numbers is always easier than in large numbers.

The *Peer Empowerment Program* (Taylor et al., 2001) includes a helpful list of do's and don'ts for a mentoring program (see Table 8.3). One common mistake is to force people to be involved in the mentoring program. If an organization forces people to be

Table 8.3. Do's and don'ts of implementing and evaluating a peer mentoring program

Do	Don't
View mentors as leaders	Expect the program to run on its own
Provide incentives to mentors	Use mentoring to replace orientation training
Offer frequent opportunities for celebration and recognition of mentors and mentees	Use mentoring to replace supervision
Create time-limited partnerships	Ask people to mentor without preparation
Ensure that partners have specific goals	Force people to become mentors (this invites sabotage or ineffectiveness)
Empower mentors and mentees to direct the program	Expect mentors to do the extra work of participating without incentives
Ensure CEO support of mentoring activities	
Coordinate and support the mentoring program	
Provide ongoing support to mentors	
Publicly announce criteria for selecting program participants	

From Taylor, M., Sauer J., Hewitt, A., O'Nell, S., & Larson, S. (2001). *The peer empowerment program (PEP): A complete toolkit for planning and implementing mentoring programs within community-based human service organizations* (p. 8 of facilitator guide). Minneapolis: University of Minnesota, Institute on Community Integration, Research and Training Center on Community Living; adapted by permission.

mentors, they may be less motivated, and if it forces new employees to have a mentor, the new employees may not value the experience as much. Making the program voluntary and strongly encouraging its use avoids these potential obstacles. The challenges noted in this chapter are just a few examples of those that a mentorship program might face during design and implementation. Remember to plan for potential challenges so that they are less likely to become barriers to establishing a successful program.

QUESTIONS TO PONDER

1. If your organization were to initiate a mentoring program, who would be responsible for the facilitation and oversight of the program?
2. How could your organization provide the best support to mentors so that they are encouraged to participate and strive toward the program goals?
3. What resources (direct and indirect costs) are you prepared to invest in training and supporting mentors and mentees?
4. With an increase in workforce diversity, what can your organization do to best meet the needs of new employees through the mentor program?
5. How will you know if your organization's mentoring program is successful?

CONCLUSION

Peer mentoring programs can help to improve both socialization and training for DSPs in community human services settings. Good mentoring relationships are consistently associated with lower turnover, increased job satisfaction, and improved organizational commitment for mentees. Well-developed mentorship programs require planning and commitment on behalf of the organization. A program's mission, goals, and outcomes should be defined. The roles and responsibilities of the mentor, mentee, and the organization should be established *prior* to implementation of the program. Finally, program evaluation plans should also be designed prior to the commencement of the mentorship program.

RESOURCES

A Guide to the Mentor Program Listings, http://www.mentors.ca/mentorprograms.html

This web page has a comprehensive list of mentor programs being implemented in a variety of settings. Interested readers can search the descriptions of mentor programs by category of interest. Each entry lists contact information for the mentor program.

Brounstein, M. (2000). *Coaching and mentoring for dummies.* Foster City, CA: IDG Books Worldwide.

This straightforward and easy-to-read reference book is available in most bookstores.

Kaye, B., & Scheef, D. (2000). Mentoring. *Info-line.* Alexandria, VA: American Society for Training and Development. (Available from the publisher, http://store.astd.org/product.asp?prodid=1264&deptid=4)

This easy-to-read handbook provides a quick overview of what constitutes an effective mentoring program and provides suggestions for successful program development.

Taylor, M., Sauer, J., Hewitt, A., O'Nell, S., & Larson, S. (2001). *The peer empowerment program (PEP): A complete toolkit for planning and implementing mentoring programs within community-based human service organizations* (Program coordinator, facilitator, and learner guides). Minneapolis: University of Minnesota, Institute on Community Integration, Research and Training Center on Community Living. (Available from the publisher, 612-624-4512; http://rtc.umn.edu/wddsp/dol.html)

This curriculum is designed to train supervisors and managers to design, implement, and evaluate peer mentoring programs. The program coordinator guide provides the information and tools needed to plan and develop the program. The facilitator guide contains the materials needed to orient and train mentors and mentees. The learner guide contains worksheets and handouts for the orientation session and provides a workbook for mentors who participate in a training workshop.

Mentoring Program Exit Interview for Mentors

Please tell us a little bit about yourself and your career.

Where do you work? _____

How long have you worked there? _____

How long were you a mentor? _____

How long has the person you mentored been working for the organization? _____

Please tell us about your experience with the mentoring program.

Do you feel you were an effective mentor? _____

_____

Did you have enough support from your organization to be an effective mentor? _____

_____

Did the training adequately prepare you for your role as a mentor? _____

_____

Do you feel that the person you mentored is better prepared for his or her role? Why or why not?

_____

What benefits did _you_ experience as a mentor? _____

_____

What would help make the experience better or more effective? _____

_____

Would you consider being a mentor again? _____

_____

From Taylor, M., Sauer, J., Hewitt, A., O'Nell, S., & Larson, S. (2001). _The peer empowerment program (PEP): A complete toolkit for planning and implementing mentoring programs within community-based human service organizations_ (p. 29 of program coordinator guide). Minneapolis: University of Minnesota, Institute on Community Integration, Research and Training Center on Community Living; adapted by permission.

Mentoring Program Exit Interview for Mentees

Please tell us a little bit about yourself and your career.

Where do you work? _____

How long have you worked there? _____

How long were you a mentee? _____

How long has the person who mentored you been working for the organization? _____

Please tell us about your experience with the mentoring program.

Do you feel your mentor was effective? _____

_____

Did you and your mentor have enough support from your organization to have an effective partnership?

_____

Do you feel that you are better equipped for your job as a result of being mentored? _____

_____

What benefits did you experience as a mentee? _____

_____

What would help make the experience better? _____

_____

Would you consider being a mentee again? Do you plan to become a mentor? _____

_____

From Taylor, M., Sauer, J., Hewitt, A., O'Nell, S., & Larson, S. (2001). *The peer empowerment program (PEP): A complete toolkit for planning and implementing mentoring programs within community-based human service organizations* (p. 30 of program coordinator guide). Minneapolis: University of Minnesota, Institute on Community Integration, Research and Training Center on Community Living; adapted by permission.

III

MOTIVATING AND SUPPORTING EMPLOYEES

9

STAFF MOTIVATION AND RECOGNITION

TRACI L. LALIBERTE,
AMY S. HEWITT, AND SHERYL A. LARSON

The job of supervising direct support professionals (DSPs) can be difficult, challenging, and at times frustrating. It is, however, also rewarding, stimulating, and important. This chapter focuses on how to keep staff. Motivating staff and providing recognition can often make the difference in whether staff members remain with the organization. It is essential for front-line supervisors (FLSs) and managers to acknowledge employees' accomplishments and positive work performance. An employer that develops satisfying jobs that allow staff members to meaningfully contribute will produce employees who are highly motivated (O'Nell, Hewitt, Sauer, & Larson, 2001).

TARGETED FRONT-LINE SUPERVISOR COMPETENCIES

Competent FLSs understand the importance of employee recognition and can match specific recognition techniques to the unique needs of individual DSPs. Supervisors also effectively communicate with staff by listening to their concerns, supporting and encouraging their ideas and work, thanking them for their contributions, and providing positive feedback regarding performance. Specific recognition and motivation skills needed are listed here.

Primary Skills

FLSs recognize the need for and plan celebrations with staff.

FLSs treat DSPs as professionals and acknowledge DSPs' unique skills and contributions.

FLSs effectively use organizationwide recognition plans and personal ways of acknowledging others for work well done.

Related Skills

FLSs know how to develop and implement a plan for reducing unwanted turnover and vacancies at their own site or across the organization as a whole.

FLSs support other FLSs in understanding and learning about recruitment and retention strategies and why they are important.

FLSs monitor turnover, recruitment success, and employee satisfaction and use the results to improve personnel practices.

FLSs identify necessary resources for individuals supported and DSPs and advocate for these resources with their managers.

UNDERSTANDING THE PROBLEM

Defining Employee Motivation

Experts have not yet agreed on a single definition of motivation (Reid & Parsons, 1995). Perhaps this is because every person is motivated differently. For this chapter, motivation is defined as a willingness of an individual to put forth high levels of effort toward organization goals while simultaneously satisfying his or her needs (E. Lightfoot, personal communication, 2002). Motivation is related to both performance and enjoyment of one's work life (Reid & Parsons, 1995).

Different things motivate different people. Some people are motivated by praise. Others are motivated by knowing they did a good job. Still others are highly motivated by being able to cross off all of the items on their to-do list at the end of each week. Motivation can be an internal process, or it may come from external sources. Motivation can come in the form of concrete and measurable interventions, or it can be intangible. Motivation can be either formal or informal. Effectively motivating staff requires taking the time to get to know what motivates each individual staff member.

Importance of Motivating Staff

Why bother motivating staff? Figuring out what each person prefers as a motivating strategy and integrating it into daily work culture are essential. Motivation is a cornerstone in each employee's success within an organization. If an employee is not motivated to do a good job or to deliver high-quality services to supported individuals, everyone suffers, including the employee.

Having employees who are excited to come to work every day and who anticipate their duties breeds a positive work environment. An employee who meets the workday with enthusiasm and vigor can also meet the needs of a supported individual who has challenging behaviors or can face the occasional disappointment of unmet goals. A highly motivated employee performs his or her job duties in a manner that promotes the mission of the organization. People who receive support services will get the best support from motivated staff. A highly motivated staff can influence numerous stakeholders to effect change and to create an overall positive environment. When one organization builds a highly motivated staff, other organizations want to know its secret.

Employees who lack motivation and dread coming to work are less likely to come to work every day. The organization may begin to experience problems such as poor work attendance and poor quality of work performance, and eventually the organization will see an increase in its turnover rates. Motivated employees, on the other hand, come to work routinely and on time, meet and exceed performance goals, and remain with the organization despite challenges.

To fully understand how to use motivation strategies, it is helpful to first understand why many employees feel demoralized and work without a sense of motivation. Reid and Parsons (1995) argued that in human services, staff performance objectives are difficult to measure. It is difficult for staff to ever *really* know how well they are performing their jobs because they rarely have direct contact with and observation from their supervisors. The missions of many organizations cannot easily be measured in a performance-based manner, which means that there is further ambiguity in the message to staff about their performance (Reid & Parsons, 1995). This is because mission statements often focus on quality of life for people who receive supports, and just as people are individually motivated, quality of life is individually measured. Thus, it is often difficult to quantify and codify whether the mission of increasing quality of life is being met. In addition, several external factors contribute to demoralization, low morale, and the need for motivation. Such external factors include legislative shortcomings regarding funding for wages or new services, poor depiction by media sources of who DSPs are and what they do, low pay standards across the field, lack of professional identity for DSPs, and lack of community resources for support.

RESEARCH SUPPORT FOR SOLUTIONS

Since motivation is not easily defined in human services settings, there is no single recipe for supervisors and managers to use for motivating employees. It is not possible to provide a sure-fire method of motivating each staff member (O'Nell, Hewitt, et al., 2001; Reid & Parsons, 1995). Organizations, however, can use several general theories and specific strategies to motivate employees.

Internal Motivation

Internal motivation is described by three complementary theories that are based on job satisfaction elements: hygiene, needs fulfillment, and expectancy. Hygiene and needs fulfillment theories are based on Maslow's hierarchy of needs and how they influence job satisfaction. Hygiene is based on the lowest two levels of Maslow's hierarchy: physiological needs and safety needs (Russell, 1999). Maslow's theory identifies human needs and presents them in order of their importance for humans. Two of the most basic needs according to Maslow's theory are physiological and safety needs; these represent the most fundamental of all human needs. At the top of Maslow's hierarchy is self-actualization, which all humans desire but do not necessarily need in order to survive. In the work environment, the basic elements that employees need in order to survive relate to aspects of the job such as supervision, policy and administration, working conditions, interpersonal relationships, status, job security, and salary (Russell, 1999). Thus, hygiene theory suggests that good supervision, working conditions, and positive relationships with co-workers and supervisors influence motivation. Also, sound policies, decent pay, and a sense of security can be motivational influences for employees. Certainly the literature within the human services field suggests these factors do matter. Common reasons DSPs give for wanting to leave their positions are difficulty with co-workers, poor supervision, and low wages and few benefits (Larson, Lakin, & Bruininks, 1998).

Needs fulfillment theory suggests that work satisfaction is also associated with the highest three levels of Maslow's hierarchy: belongingness, esteem, and self-actualization. An employee's satisfaction and ultimately motivation depends on recognition, task completion, level of responsibility, advancement, and growth potential (Russell, 1999). According to needs fulfillment theory, people will be internally motivated if they are recognized for their accomplishments and have opportunities for growth and advancement. It can be challenging for community human services organizations to provide internally motivating factors. DSPs often are not recognized for the varied responsibilities and roles they play within an organization, and there are few career ladder opportunities for DSPs who want to advance but who also want be in direct support roles (Jaskulski & Ebenstein, 1996).

Last, expectancy theory relates to an individual's expectation that an act will result in an attractive outcome or reward (Kanfer, 1990; Russell, 1999). The theory is focused on the following three relationships: effort–performance, performance–reward, and reward–personal satisfaction (E. Lightfoot, personal communication, 2002). The premise behind this theory as it applies to an employment setting is that a person's effort directly affects that person's work performance. The quality of that work performance then influences the rewards that the person may or may not receive. And finally, the reward gained or lost by an individual clearly affects his or her personal satisfaction with his or her job. Within community human services, DSPs rarely receive bonuses, and the outcomes of their work are often vague and unclear. The more supervisors can clearly articulate desired outcomes, perhaps the more motivated employees will be. Also, moving toward systems in which staff members are recognized for their outcomes based on expectations theory may influence staff behavior. Clearly, in expectancy theory, there must be a link between effort, reward, and personal satisfaction.

External Motivation

External motivation theory suggests that the key to an employee's satisfaction is controlled outside of the individual. Three external motivation theories include reinforcement, goal setting, and equity. The most general of these is reinforcement theory, made popular in the 1930s by B.F. Skinner. Skinner set forth that an individual's behavior (here, work performance) is determined by stimuli outside of the person (Russell, 1999). The integral aspect of a reinforcement approach to motivating staff is rewarding the person for desirable performance and punishing him or her for undesirable performance (Luthans & Kreitner, 1985). For example, employees who show up to work every day on time and as scheduled are given the chance to be randomly selected to get dinner for two at a local restaurant. However, if they are late, they may be disciplined, and if they do not show up, they may be fired.

Goal-setting theory is based on the use of written performance goals to motivate the employee (Locke & Latham, 1990). Employees may be increasingly motivated if they participate in the goal setting and receive supervisory feedback during their process of achieving the goal (Russell, 1999). Theorists believe that specific and challenging goals lead to higher performance (Locke & Latham, 1990). A general goal, such as one that asks an employee to "do your best," typically results in smaller increases in performance levels. One caveat in applying goal-setting theory to supervisory practices is that setting goals too early in the learning process can draw attention away from learning, causing learning to be hindered. Thus, motivational manipulation through goal setting may be more effective after basic tasks have been mastered (Kanfer & Ackerman, 1989). This is especially true for employees with fewer overall skills and abilities. It may be advisable to have employees participate in setting their own performance goals and be individually measured against these goals instead of using standard performance rewards in which all staff work toward the same goals and are measured in the same way.

Equity theory is based on the idea of fairness. In many organizations, the issue of fairness is an important focus. Often employee morale suffers and turnover rates are affected when employees do not perceive that their supervisor is fair. For example, if one staff member feels as though another is treated better or is given additional rewards that are not given to all employees, he or she may feel frustration, anger, or burnout, all of which can lead to the employee quitting the job. Equity theorists put forth that employees will form their opinion about their treatment by an employer based on how other employees are treated by the employer (Russell, 1999). To determine fairness of financial benefits, an employee will compare his or her pay with that of an employee of a similar skill level and position. Based on his or her findings, the employee may or may not be motivated to continue to perform at a high level. The concept of equity and fairness comes into play with DSPs routinely. Because most organizations only have one level of direct support positions, DSPs often compare themselves with one another. When rewards and reprimands for performance are not given fairly and equitably or are not used at all, DSPs are more likely to compare among themselves their levels of pay, scheduled hours, and access to benefits. This can lead to unhappiness and feelings of unfairness and inequitable treatment. Organizations that have fair and equitable practices will likely have fewer DSPs who become disgruntled enough to leave their positions.

Summary of Motivation Theories

Internal and external motivational theories relate to all employees. One employee may be very invested in equitable treatment, whereas another employee may care more about his or her level of responsibility. The key point is that each employee is different and will desire different forms of motivation. The remainder of this chapter explores three areas in which FLSs and managers can make a significant impact in the motivation of their employees: training and staff development, performance goals, and employee recognition.

STRATEGIES FOR RESPONDING TO THE PROBLEM

Use Training and Staff Development

Supervisors and managers can use training and staff development practices that influence both motivation and recognition. Training and staff development can support the level of confidence a DSP feels related to his or her job duties. If an employee is unsure about how to do his or her job, his or her motivation is likely to suffer. For the purposes of employee motivation, employee orientation and initial skill development must be supplemented by ongoing training for long-term professional development. Providing opportunities for DSPs to gain advanced knowledge and skills of their interest and those related to recommended practice within the industry can be a motivating influence on the employee.

Many employees will seek opportunities for continuing education and advanced training; however, other employees may need to be encouraged and supported in this pursuit. Supervisors and managers must be prepared to assist employees by having up-to-date knowledge of the available training and educational opportunities. The professional development of employees may take place through professional conferences, training workshops, or professional networking. These opportunities should supplement the mandatory annual training requirements imposed by regulations or organization policy, which often are not adequate to train DSPs to do what is expected of them on the job.

Staff development opportunities should be treated as rewards and growth experiences and should not be required. Organizations can be creative in designing development opportunities. For example, if an employee has always wanted to enhance his or her cooking skills and a person who receives supports loves gourmet food, the organization can find an opportunity to send the employee (maybe along with the person who receives support) to a culinary institute or a gourmet cooking class offered by a local restaurant. Or, if an organization has just started supporting a person who has fragile X syndrome, an employee could attend a national fragile X conference to become the organization's expert on the topic. Organizations can challenge employees to use the Internet to find and report new and exciting information relevant to direct support or the individuals supported.

Whether an organization financially supports the professional development of employees, supervisors can do so by seeking inexpensive and creative options (e.g., providing information from the Internet, sharing books and other resources, hosting information-sharing sessions at staff meetings), recognizing people who have acquired learning, providing opportunities for employees to share new learning with others, and acknowledging expertise. Supervisors also may be able to provide a flexible schedule or make changes in an employee's assigned shift to accommodate an academic schedule. The support and respect shown to employees who are seeking additional training or professional development is instrumental in fueling them to strive for high work performance. More information about how to develop and implement effective training programs is available in Chapters 6 and 7.

Set Performance Goals

The second area for supervisors and managers to concentrate on is the collaborative development of performance goals or a performance checklist with employees. In any employment situation, some form of evaluation of employees must take place. If an employee knows that he or she is doing a good job and that the employer appreciates the work that the employee does, he or she will generally be more motivated to continue performing at a high level. And, if an employee has a clear understanding of what he or she needs to do to meet expectations and feels supported in making this effort, he or she likely will be more motivated to improve job performance.

It is important to communicate to new employees, upon hire, basic expectations regarding job performance. To be most effective, this communication should be both verbal and written. Providing employees with a written copy of their job expectations allows them to reflect on the expectations at various points throughout their employment. It provides employees a benchmark of initial and ongoing expectations. Explaining basic expectations, however, is not enough with regard to employee motivation. Since each employee has different interests, skills, and strengths, performance goals must also be individualized. For example, if an employee masters the basic expectations in the first 3 months of employment, his or her goals need to immediately be modified to reflect these achievements. Otherwise, the employee may lose motivation to perform if he or she spends the next 9 months with nothing to strive for. Conversely, if an employee is struggling to reach all of the initial expectations, it may be important to break them down into achievable components so that the employee experiences success.

Supervisors should work collaboratively with each employee to generate performance goals. These goals should be specific, measurable, and observable, much like the goals that are written for individuals who receive supports. Something is measurable if it can be counted and observable if it can be seen. It is critical for the employee to be directly involved in the goal setting. It is the supervisor's responsibility to help the employee set challenging goals that offer the opportunity to stretch to attain a higher level of performance. It is equally important, however, that the supervisor help the employee to set realistic and attainable goals. Thus, the employee's motivation in his or her job comes from trying to meet and possibly exceed their goals.

Long-range goals can seem overwhelming or intimidating to some employees. For these employees, performance checklists could be useful. To create a performance checklist, the supervisor and employee should brainstorm to develop a list of the duties that the employee performs each day. The employee may feel motivated by using that checklist and feeling good when he or she is able to cross every item off the list each day. Over time the supervisor and the employee may negotiate adding things to the checklist that pertain to a special skill or interest that the employee has. Adding or changing the checklist may likely maintain the list's motivational properties. Supervisors should remember, however, that not all employees are alike and that some may be annoyed by the use of a checklist. Some employees may feel the checklist is an indication that the supervisor has no confidence in them as employees. In such cases, longer-range goals may be adequate. Chapter 13 contains more information about measuring competence and assessing performance.

Recognize Employees

Supervisors and managers can also have an impact on employee motivation through the recognition of positive employee efforts and accomplishments. Recognition is an important aspect of keeping employees. Unfortunately, although it is a simple and cost-effective strategy, it is often overlooked as a viable solution to retention problems. Employers often focus on wages as the primary incentive they can offer employees. This solution, however, is shortsighted. Employees often identify less tangible aspects of their jobs as the most motivating and important (Nelson, 1994). Employees need concrete feedback and appreciation for what they do. They want to feel they are an important part of the organization's success, and they desire for managers and co-workers to notice and acknowledge their performance. Most people are not attracted to the human services field for the wages and future earnings. The job is never done, and few DSPs ever become wealthy. Therefore, it is important to take notice of and seek opportunities to acknowledge the value of the work DSPs do every day in their jobs. Because organizations have limited financial resources, it is all the more important for them to offer other forms of recognition for employee skill and contribution to the organization. The next several subsections describe many ways in which supervisors and managers can acknowledge or recognize employees for their efforts and contributions.

Use Various Forms of Recognition

In one study 58% and 76% of employees reported that they had not received verbal or written thanks from their supervisors, respectively (Nelson & Economy, 2003). Employees desire the appreciation of their supervisors. A word of thanks or a quick handwritten note from a supervisor gives meaning to an employee's work. Saying thank you is not the only form of recognition, but it is a great place to start. It is simple, costs next to nothing, and for many employees is very important. When sharing gratitude with an employee, it is important to be specific so that the employee knows what behavior they demonstrated is being recognized (e.g., not just "Good work," but "Great job on dealing with that crisis last week" or "I know things have been a little stressful recently, and I wanted to thank you for how well you've been handling everything at the work site").

Recognition also can be more formal, such as in contests, reward or point programs, or advancement opportunities (Dykstra, 1999; Nelson 1994). In a formal approach to recognizing employees, it is important to create a ritual, a way for everyone to become involved and develop an appreciation for that particular reward program (Dykstra & Gustafson, 1999). Demonstrating consistency and fairness throughout a formal recognition process is essential. If careful consideration is not given to fairness and consistency, DSPs will become frustrated and the recognition program may backfire. In *The Exemplar Employee: Rewarding and Recognizing Outstanding Direct Contact Employees*, Dykstra and Gustafson (1999) described a formal ritual of recognizing exemplar employees (e.g., employee-of-the-month award). They describe the process of developing a ritual as one that takes time and needs continual maintenance. The ritual must have set criteria from which to operate. The organization must develop rules and guidelines with regard to how each exemplar employee is chosen (i.e., a nomination process) and how employees are notified (Dykstra & Gustafson, 1999). The reward itself should also be consistent, whether it is a financial reward, dinner for two, or tickets to a play or a sports event. When formal recognition programs exist, supervisors and managers have important roles in informing employees about the programs, encouraging participation, and deciding if the formal recognition program will be competitive or noncompetitive. Competitive recognition events may include rewarding the employee with the fewest documentation errors or the best attendance record. Noncompetitive formal recognition events include giving an award for average tenure at the organization, providing recognition for completing orientation or probation, and so forth.

Recognition may also be provided through less formal means such as an organization's annual banquet, by the authorization of additional time off (paid or unpaid), or the offering of flexible time (Dykstra, 1999; Nelson 1994). Informal recognition is often more satisfying than formal recognition to some employees. Informal recognition can take the form of no-cost, low-cost, or higher-cost rewards. Table 9.1 provides some ideas for informal recognition strategies.

Supervisors can provide recognition to employees as individuals or as teams (Dykstra, 1999). Employees are often motivated when they can work collaboratively to achieve a goal. When reflecting on the different ways to recognize employees, an organization can be creative and recognize people not only for their individual efforts within the organization but also for their efforts on a work team. Nationally

Table 9.1. Informal recognition strategies

No cost	Verbal thank you
	Verbal praise for a specific action
	A note of thanks on organization letterhead or on the supervisor's business card
	Certificates of achievement
	Inclusion of recognized direct support professional (DSP) in decision making for the organization
	Newsletter article describing staff accomplishments or important personal events (e.g., graduation)
	Recognition of birthdays or anniversaries
	Delegation of tasks (doing so says "I believe in you")
	Congratulations to someone who handles a really tough situation well
	Recognition cards completed by co-workers or individuals supported posted on a bulletin board
	Acknowledgment of concern for personal circumstances (e.g., death, birth, graduation from college, illness, child graduation)
	Having the supervisor or manager do the DSP's job for 1 hour or 1 day
	Respect given to DSP the same way other professionals would be respected
	Recognition of tenure benchmarks (starting at 6 months or 1 year)
Low cost	Clothing with company logo
	Dinner with the supervisor or manager
	Gift certificate
	Plaques, trophies, and awards
	Team dinner or outing
	Tickets to a concert
	Fees paid to attend a local professional conference
	Flowers
	Baked treats
	A bunch of balloons
	Day off for individual or the entire group
	Paid time off to take a college class
Higher cost	$25 check on each person's birthday
	Small pay raise
	Small cash award ($20–$50) with a personal thank-you note
	$100 for the best innovative solution to a problem at a staff meeting
	Organizationwide celebration (picnic or holiday party)
	Promotion to a new position
	All-expenses-paid weekend at a bed and breakfast
	Fees paid to attend a professional conference in another city or state

Sources: Harvey, 2000; Nelson, 1994.

recognized management expert Bob Nelson (1994) recommended that supervisors "catch . . . employees doing things right." He also suggested that it is important to notice the small things that employees do well and to make a *big* deal out of them. It is also important to make sure that efforts are made to "feed" employees regularly with praise and recognition for the things that they do well. This extra effort is sure to result in employees who are happier and more motivated.

When considering the recognition of an individual employee, it is important to focus on the employee's performance (Nelson & Economy, 2003). It is also important to link the recognition of an employee's performance to the organization's goals and objectives (Dykstra, 1999; Nelson & Economy, 2003). A supervisor may find that recognizing employees becomes easier if the supervisor knows them as people and understand the ways in which they like to be recognized (Dykstra, 1999; Harvey, 2000; Kaye & Jordan-Evans, 1999; Nelson, 1994; Nelson & Economy, 2003). For example, when recognizing an employee for volunteering to cover a vacant shift time after time, it would be nice to reward the employee with something that *the employee* would really appreciate. It would be ineffective and embarrassing to purchase Neil Diamond tickets for an employee as a reward only to find out later that he or she prefers AC/DC, *NSYNC, or Michael W. Smith. Or, perhaps recognizing birthdays of employees with a cake, balloons, and singing at staff meetings is a cultural norm within the organization. If the employee, however, is embarrassed or is uncomfortable being the center of attention in large groups, this practice will backfire. The recognition will be a negative experience instead of a positive one for that employee. Taking the time to know how employees would like to be recognized and what types of rewards they would like makes recognition effective and fun.

Several times within this chapter, we have stated that each employee is motivated by different things and likes to be recognized in different ways. One way to ensure that employees get the kind of recognition they desire from supervisors and managers is to ask them early on in their employment (perhaps as a component of new hire paperwork) how they are best motivated and how they like to be recognized. The tools at the end of this chapter include an inventory that supervisors and managers can give to employees to discover what employees want and need in order to effectively be recognized and motivated.

Incorporate Recognition into the Organization's Culture

Organizations need to create recognition within their daily operations. Recognition for good work needs to become routine. In addition to annual events such as employee dinners or monthly events such as naming an employee of the month, more frequent recognition is needed to recognize newer employees. Employees and managers need to develop awareness of the importance and power of recognition and motivation opportunities.

Supervisors play a fundamental role in influencing managers and employees. It is important for supervisors to advocate for the inclusion of employee recognition into daily operations. One way to accomplish this is to make employee recognition part of the organization's strategic plan, supervisor and manager training curricula, and policy development. Supervisors should be prepared to discuss different personal experiences of how the recognition of employees has benefited the organization and ultimately affected staff retention.

Follow the Basics of Effective Recognition

Though many recognition strategies are pretty simple, recognition is not likely to occur just because an organization or a supervisor wants it to. Too often, many workers feel as though they do not have time or energy to look for every opportunity to provide recognition to co-workers or employees. Supervisors, co-workers, and even administrators need training and suggestions about how to do recognition well. To be effective, recognition needs to have criteria. Ultimately, it cannot be mandated; rather it should be sincere, specific, heartfelt, and based on accurate information. It is often more demoralizing for employees to receive insincere, general, or rote recognition than to receive none at all. When recognition is given, it is usually provided to employees that are in good standing and are liked by all; however, recognition is also critical for employees who are not performing well. In these situations, the added positive recognition may be all it takes to motivate a poorly performing employee to improve performance.

Opinions vary about what constitutes effective recognition. Some basic tenets, however, apply to delivering effective recognition to employees (Deeprose, 1994; Dykstra, 1999; Harvey, 2000; Kaye & Jordan-Evans, 1999; Nelson & Economy, 2003; Russell, 1999):

- Recognition must be sincere.
- Recognition must be heartfelt.
- Recognition must be specific.
- Recognition must be purposeful.
- Recognition is best when it is immediate.
- Recognition may be given publicly or privately.
- Recognition can be spontaneous.
- Recognition must be positive.
- Recognition must be geared to the individual (personalized).

Don't Forget Long-Term Employees

It is easy to focus only on finding ways to enhance recognition for new employees to encourage them to stay. But to do so without first recognizing long-term employees is a recipe for disaster and will alienate long-term employees and undermine efforts to build teamwork and camaraderie. Before a bonus or incentive program to find or keep new hires is implemented, be sure that the current staff members have been adequately recognized. If an organization creates a new welcoming program to provide new hires with T-shirts, pens, or mugs bearing the organization, the organization should be sure that current staff receive their T-shirts, pens, or mugs first. Other strategies that can be used to recognize long-term employees include the following:

- Provide bigger year-end bonuses for longer-term employees (e.g., $10 per year of service, paid in December).

- Make sure that there is a reasonable salary spread between new and long-term employees. It is very disruptive to morale to hire new employees at only 25 cents an hour less than employees with 5 or more years of experience.
- Reward years of service (but don't wait for a person to have 5 years' experience— start with 6 months or 1 year of service).

Programs of recognition that favor new over longer-term employees can have serious detrimental effects on longer-term employees. It is important for organizations to consider the potential ramifications of any new recognition program.

Watch Out for Pitfalls!

Defining the guidelines for recognition programs, providing training on how to select recognition activities, and carefully planning how to effectively use recognition to improve employee motivation are all important components of any company-sanctioned or -sponsored recognition program. If an organization does not attend to these issues, the recognition program may fail. An example of a recognition program gone bad is one that recognizes a long-term employee for her 10 years of service with a pen bearing the organization logo (valued at $30) and provides a new hire who has made it through his first year of employment with a $500 retention bonus.

When recognizing employees, the organization should be certain to reinforce only the behaviors the organization wants repeated (Dykstra, 1999; Harvey, 2000; Kaye & Jordan-Evans, 1999; Nelson, 1994; Nelson & Economy, 2003). If the goal is to increase the quality of on-the-job performance, the organization should reward and recognize employees for improved performance, not simply for maintaining performance (Nelson & Economy, 2003). Recognizing people for solely doing their basic job requirements may not improve performance or increase motivation. Carefully thinking through what types of employee behaviors should be recognized is critical for success.

It is important to be aware of other pitfalls to recognition programs (Russell, 1999; see Table 9.2). Organizations can use the worksheet called Identifying Effective Recognition Events, Activities, or Processes that appears at the end of this chapter to determine the effectiveness of its existing recognition efforts and to develop other strategies for employee recognition.

Use Other Strategies for Recognizing Employees

Creating new and doable challenges for staff and providing opportunities for employees to recharge and renew are important strategies for supervisors to employ. Helping employees prevent burnout, stay focused, and remain charged in an everchanging field is an important role for supervisors and managers. This support is especially important for long-term employees, who often are overlooked by employers and supervisors.

Supervisors can be creative in providing employees with fresh challenges and renewal opportunities. As employees' individuality becomes clearer, supervisors can pay attention to the things that the employees enjoy doing the most. Supervisors should learn about their employees' hobbies and how they pass the time. Then, supervisors can create ways in which employees can use their skills. For example, if a DSP enjoys bike riding, consider having that employee hold a bike maintenance class for individuals he or she supports who also enjoy bike riding. If an employee appreciates boats

Table 9.2. How to avoid common pitfalls of employee recognition programs

Keep in mind that money and other financial rewards are not always the most successful ways to recognize and motivate employees.

Make recognition an important part of the job, or employees will not value it that
much.

Dissuade an employee's sense of entitlement with regard to rewards; if an employee expects the recognition, he or she may not see it as a reward anymore.

Do not delay the recognition of someone who is doing a good job; let him or her
know right away!

An effective form of recognition or reward is one that is personalized and meaningful. Avoid generic and mundane rewards.

Sources: Harvey, 2000; Kaye & Jordan-Evans, 1999; Nelson, 1994; Nelson & Economy,
2003; Russell, 1999.

and cars, consider having that employee attend a boat or automobile show with an individual whom he or she supports who has similar interests. If employees seem simply
"fried" and exhausted from working so much overtime, make arrangements with the
local school of massage for employees to have free or low-cost massages.

Opportunities for employees to learn about new things that are happening in the
field may also be sources of recharge and renewal. Chances for DSPs to network with
employees from other organization sites or with employees from other local organizations also can be invigorating. Perhaps an employee could attend a local or state conference as a reward or as part of an incentive program. Or, maybe a sponsor or manager could skip attending a conference so that a DSP could attend. The connections
made validate what the DSP does, permit the DSP to meet new colleagues and learn
new strategies, and give the employee a sense of professionalism and purpose (see
Chapter 5 for further discussion of networking and professionalization).

Providing staff more autonomy in their work and fostering a sense of pride in the
success of the organization is also essential to retention of employees. Managers and
supervisors should ensure that DSPs are always involved in the process of reassessing
and modifying the organization's mission and vision. Organizations should challenge
themselves to see DSPs as the ambassadors of the organization to the outside world.

In the Spotlight: Happy Notes

This activity, created and used by REM Central Lakes, of St. Cloud, Minnesota, encourages people to work together, to attend staff meetings, and to recognize the good deeds
team members are doing for each other as a routine part of their job.

The idea is to get co-workers to recognize each other for what they do to support
each other. Starting with the FLS, who usually has to set the example, have the employees who work together write little thank-you notes (Happy Notes) for helping each other
out. For example, "To Mary — Just wanted to say thanks for picking up that extra shift. It
really made my job easier. Signed, Bob," "To Jessie — Thanks for doing the laundry; it
was great to come on duty and not have to worry whether I would have time to get it
done or not! Signed, Selma," and so forth.

Then the notes are placed in a Happy Notes box. (Use a cardboard box that is about
one foot square, with a slit cut in the top so that staff can deposit the Happy Notes. Make

sure you can reuse the box and that it is easily opened.) Instruct the staff to put their notes into the Happy Notes box and to write as many Happy Notes to each other as possible before the next staff meeting.

At the next staff meeting, either before or after dealing with items on the business agenda, the supervisor opens the Happy Notes box and reads each of the Happy Notes out loud. Then the notes are put back in the box along with slips of paper with the names of each person at the staff meeting, and one is drawn as the winner. Some supervisors require staff to be present to win. The winner receives a small thank-you gift. It can be a $5–$10 gift certificate, a small candle, a flower, a box of candy, or something similar. After the staff meeting, the employees are encouraged to continue writing Happy Notes to each other, and the process starts over.

This idea was provided by Kristine Wainright-Tadych, Regional Director for REM Central Lakes, St. Cloud, MN, 320-259-6022.

OVERCOMING IMPLEMENTATION BARRIERS

Numerous factors can be barriers to the use of effective recognition and motivation strategies:

- Supervisors and managers treat all employees the same and use identical strategies of motivation and recognition for all.
- Recognition is mandated but not supported at all levels of the organization.
- There is unfair and inconsistent use of recognition and motivation strategies.
- New programs of recognition are implemented without consideration for long-term employees who may not have had similar opportunities.
- Recognition occurs during annual events instead of also being incorporated into daily operations.
- Recognition is provided for meeting basic expectations rather than for going above and beyond minimal expectations.

To overcome these barriers, organizations need to train supervisors about the principles of effective motivation. Furthermore, managers and administrators should model effective recognition approaches. For motivation and recognition strategies to work, supervisors and managers need to understand and learn from their employees how they like to be recognized and provide recognition designed to motivate that individual employee. Organizations must ensure that any formal recognition programs are implemented fairly and with similar levels of commitment and enthusiasm by all supervisors and managers. It is also important for organizations to consider how long-term employees may feel when new recognition programs are put into place. Finally, for recognition programs to be most effective, they need to be developed with input from DSPs and should never be forced upon any employee.

QUESTIONS TO PONDER

1. What motivates you to do more or better work?
2. How do you like to be recognized?

3. How do you motivate and recognize the people you supervise?
4. What formal recognition programs exist within your organization? Are they fair, equitable, and consistently used? Explain why or why not.
5. Is recognition a part of daily operations within your organization? In what informal ways do your organization's supervisors, managers, and administrators recognize employees?
6. How are long-term employees motivated and recognized within your organization?
7. What professional development opportunities exist for employees who are motivated by growth and new learning?

CONCLUSION

Recognition is a critical component of an effective workforce intervention strategy. Encouraging and supporting effective recognition practices can result in improved workforce outcomes. Developing motivation and providing recognition to employees are relatively simple and inexpensive retention strategies. Employees are motivated by different intrinsic and/or extrinsic factors. An organization should get to know its employees and tailor the ways in which recognition and motivation are provided to each individual. When efforts are made to create organizational cultures that expect and support recognition, employee commitment to the organization and motivation are more likely to increase.

RESOURCES

Kaye, B.L., & Jordan-Evans, S. (1999). *Love 'em or lose 'em: Getting good people to stay.* San Francisco: Berrett-Koehler Publishers.

This book has one chapter for each letter of the alphabet, with advice for supervisors and managers about how to support and recognize employees. Chapters discuss topics such as knowing what employees want; helping employees find growth and challenge within the organization; helping employees find the work they love without leaving; and offering balance and support to employees who are sick or tired.

Nelson, B. (1994). *1001 ways to reward employees.* New York: Workman Publishing.

This book is great for supervisors or managers who know they should be recognizing their employees but are not quite sure what to do. The premise of the book is that "money isn't everything." The book lists many low- or no-cost strategies and is full of examples and stories about recognizing staff for doing a good job. Book sections include informal rewards, awards for specific achievements and activities, and formal rewards. Appendices share where to get specialty reward items; profile companies that arrange unusual reward activities; and list incentive travel coordinators, motivational and incentive companies, and associations.

Nelson, B., & Economy, P. (2003). *Managing for dummies* (2nd ed.). New York: Wiley.

This easy-to-read book provides comprehensive information on management. Its six main sections are So You Want to Be a Manager?, Managing: The People Part, Making Things Happen, Working with (Other) People, Tough Times for Tough Managers, and Tools and Techniques for Managing. A seventh section, The Part of Tens, provides top-ten lists related to management issues, such as Ten Common Management Mistakes, the Ten Best Ways to Recognize Employees, and Ten Classic Business Books that You Need to Know About. As in all of the "for Dummies" books, icons in the margins call your attention to important information.

Reid, D.H., & Parsons, M.B. (1995). *Motivating human service staff: Supervisory strategies for maximizing work effort and work enjoyment.* Morganton, NC: Habilitative Management Consultants.

This book has valuable information about motivating employees and creating an enjoyable work environment. The authors have a positive perspective, focusing on strengths and opportunities rather than deficits and problems. The 10 chapters are separated into 3 sections; Introduction to Motivation, Enhancing Diligent and Competent Work Performance, and Enhancing the Work Environment. This book is a great addition to the library or "tool box" of all human services supervisors, managers, and administrators!

Sharpe, C., & Bruen, A. (Eds.). (1997). How to motivate employees. *Info-line*(Issue 9108). Alexandria, VA: American Society for Training and Development.

This booklet provides a short but useful overview of strategies to motivate employees. It examines theories such as Theory X/Theory Y, motivation, and hygiene as explanations for employee behavior. It provides many suggestions for improving motivation practices in an organization and lists an array of other available resources.

Recognition and Motivation Inventory

1. What gets you excited about your job and makes you want to come to work every day?

_____

_____

2. What things demoralize you on the job and make it difficult for you to come to work every day?

_____

_____

3. When you do a good job, how would you like your supervisor to acknowledge you?

_____

_____

4. Describe the last time someone told you that you did a good job. How did you feel about that? What, if anything, would you have changed about the way that person told you that you were doing a good job?

_____

_____

5. From this list of "rewards" please circle the ones that are meaningful to you. Put a line through any that would specifically make you uncomfortable or that you would not want. List additional rewards that are meaningful to you.

Balloons	Personal note
Bonus check	Plants
Candy	Private praise
Chocolate	Professional conference registration
Clothing with organization logo	Professional journal subscription
Consumer electronics (CD player,	Public praise (staff meeting, newsletter)
MP3 player, personal digital assistant)	Recognition ceremony/banquet
Day off	Serious cards
Flowers	Special snacks at work (What?) _____
Funny cards	
Gift certificate (Where?) _____	_____
Jewelry with organization logo	
Lunch out with co-workers	Sports tickets
Lunch out with supervisor	Other ideas:
Membership in a professional association	
Movie tickets	_____
Mug with organization logo	
Office supplies with organization logo	_____
(e.g., pens, paper)	
Overnight lodging to attend conference	
or training	

6. When your performance needs to be improved, how would you like your supervisor to let you know? What kinds of assistance help you improve your performance?

_____

_____

From O'Nell, S., Hewitt, A., Sauer, J., & Larson, S. (2001). *Removing the revolving door: Strategies to address recruitment and retention challenges* (p. 153 of learner guide). Minneapolis: University of Minnesota, Institute on Community Integration, Research and Training Center on Community Living; adapted by permission.

Identifying Effective Recognition Events, Activities, or Processes

As a supervisor or manager, evaluate your organization's current recognition activities to determine their effectiveness. First, identify a recognition event or program that you want to review (e.g., employee-of-the-month award). Next, place an *X* under the appropriate frequency column (*Always, Sometimes,* or *Never*) that most describes how your organization uses each characteristic in the targeted recognition program. Last, complete the questions that follow.

Recognition activity to be reviewed: _____

Characteristic	Frequency		
	Always	**Sometimes**	**Never**
Sincere			
Heartfelt			
Specific			
Purposeful			
Immediate			
Public			
Private			
Spontaneous			
Positive			
Individualized			

1. In reviewing how you evaluated the occurrence of each characteristic, do you feel as though the targeted recognition event or program is effective? If so, why? If not, why not?

   _____

   _____

2. What changes could your organization make to the existing event or program to make it a more effective form of recognition? _____

   _____

   _____

3. Can you identify any other forms of recognition that your organization uses that would be more effective than the one you selected for this exercise? Repeat the exercise to evaluate that program.

   _____

   _____

10

FROM GRUMBLING TO GETTING ALONG

Creating and Using Teams to Enhance Retention

AMY S. HEWITT, JOHN K. SAUER, AND LORI SEDLEZKY

Josette was an excellent employee. She had worked for the organization for a couple of years. Her supervisor appreciated her enthusiasm, creativity, and compassion for her work. She really had a natural talent for working with people who had challenges, and she was focused on connecting with families as well. Abruptly, Josette decided to quit working for the organization. Her supervisor was shocked. Not until a few months later did the supervisor realize that Josette had quit because she had been having conflicts with another staff person at the organization. The supervisor felt bad — had she known about the issues perhaps she could have retained Josette as an employee and the people who Josette supported would not have had to be disappointed by her absence.

This chapter provides information and concrete strategies to assist supervisors faced with the kind situation just described. Having a group of people who get along and do not grumble is critical to successful teamwork in community human services. This chapter describes the importance of teams in increasing retention of direct support professionals (DSPs). Basic information about what teams are, how they form, and how to enhance team functioning and team building is included in this chapter. Specific strategies for evaluating the effectiveness of existing teams are also provided.

TARGETED FRONT-LINE SUPERVISOR COMPETENCIES

Competent front-line supervisors (FLSs) are the leaders of the groups of DSPs they supervise. These supervisors are responsible for coordinating and maintaining effective teams. Often when DSPs leave organizations, they do so because of difficulty with their co-workers. The competencies listed here are connected to the need for FLSs to be effective team developers and facilitators.

Primary Skills

FLSs facilitate teamwork and positive interaction and attitudes among DSPs.

FLSs plan, facilitate, evaluate, and follow up on team meetings.

FLSs use knowledge about the status of team development to further team growth.

FLSs help team members build a common definition of *team* to use as a framework for their work.

FLSs increase team awareness about the qualities that make teams effective and successful.

FLSs build an effective team through being organized, identifying and dealing with conflict, setting and monitoring goals, and evaluating and celebrating results.

Related Skills

1 FLSs effectively communicate with DSPs by listening to their concerns, supporting and encouraging their ideas and work, thanking them for their contributions, and providing positive feedback regarding performance.

FLSs provide counseling and support to DSPs when conflicts arise.

FLSs provide formal communication to DSPs by using log books or memos and by facilitating effective meetings and purposeful interactions.

FLSs encourage staff to maintain appropriate boundaries regarding personal and professional issues.

3 FLSs coordinate and facilitate annual, quarterly, and as-needed planning meetings for supported individuals or assist DSPs in this process.

FLSs communicate necessary information and maintain positive working relationships with staff from other organizations that provide supports to individuals served.

6 FLSs coordinate, facilitate, and teach and support DSPs to lead meetings.

1 FLSs recognize the need for and plan celebrations with DSPs.

4 FLSs attend and actively participate in organization management, planning, and cross-functional work group meetings.

UNDERSTANDING THE PROBLEM

Finding, keeping, and training DSPs are significant problems for community human services organizations (ANCOR, 2001b; Rosen, 1996; Test, Solow, & Flowers, 1999; see also Chapter 1). Often people think that poor pay is the main reason DSPs leave their positions. Although pay makes a difference in how long DSPs stay in their positions, it is not the only factor that makes a difference. In fact, DSPs often report that they leave their positions because of conflicts with their supervisor or co-workers (Larson, Lakin, & Bruininks, 1998; Stremmel, 1991). Many DSPs have little contact with co-workers except through staff communication logs, during shift overlaps, and at staff meetings and training sessions. Infrequent contact with co-workers can make it difficult to develop relationships, form cohesive teams and work groups, and resolve conflicts. Problems that arise may not come to the attention of the supervisor. Often, by the time that the supervisor realizes there is a problem, the conflict has already driven an employee out the door. The extent to which a supervisor can facilitate positive interactions between and among DSPs can significantly affect how long DSPs stay in their positions. Facilitating the development of teams and using positive problem-solving skills are critical tasks for supervisors as they try to retain good employees.

Within human services and other disciplines, the use of teams and work groups has become commonplace. Almost all human services organizations have groups of DSPs who work together as a team to support the individuals who receive services and to carry out the daily responsibilities of the job. Human services organizations also have teams or support networks that plan for the supports an individual might receive from the organization and that develop procedures to address challenging behavior. Most organizations also have work teams that address such issues as the allocation of space, employee benefits, grievances, and human rights issues. Thus, supervisors and DSPs have many opportunities to participate in team processes.

RESEARCH SUPPORTS FOR SOLUTIONS

In community human services there has been a notable shift in how supports are delivered. One significant change is that people receive supports in their own homes rather in congregate care settings (Prouty, Smith, & Lakin, 2004). As a result DSPs work in dispersed settings without direct guidance from a supervisor. Some organizations are thus relying more heavily on the work of groups of DSPs or teams. In some cases these teams are guided and directed by a team leader or supervisor and in other situations they are self-directed work teams with a rotating team leader.

There are several documented reasons that teams are used in human services organizations, including 1) to increase productivity, 2) to improve quality, 3) to maximize the potential and skills of all employees, 4) to improve morale and job satisfaction, and 5) to reduce the need for high levels of management (Nelson & Economy, 2003; Sauer et al., 1997; Senge, Roberts, Ross, Smith, & Kleiner, 1994). Perhaps one of the most important reasons to promote teamwork, however, is that high-quality, well-functioning teams could reduce staff turnover by lessening conflict among co-workers, supervisors, and other team members and by improving communication and team functioning.

In considering the use of self-directed teams, it is assumed that a group of people working together who are focused, organized, and trained can be more productive and creative than an individual working alone (Sauer et al., 1997). Synergy—the ideas, attitudes and creativity of the individuals in the team working together—often results in greater productivity and develops a broader and deeper level of knowledge that the team can draw on to support the individuals receiving supports (Sauer et. al., 1997). One commonly held belief about moving to work teams is that initially it costs more money and takes more time to get work done (Nelson & Economy, 2003). Although this is initially likely, the benefits often far outweigh the downside.

In community human services organizations there are numerous ways in which DSPs and others participate in teams. They often work with their co-workers to provide targeted services and supports to the people who receive their services. They may also be a part of ongoing committees or task forces (e.g., quality assurance teams, human rights committees). DSPs are also likely involved in individual support teams (networks) for people who receive services. These support teams often include the individual and his or her family and/or friends; include other staff from the organization and other organizations; and, quite often, include professionals in targeted professions (e.g., nursing; psychology; speech-language, occupational, or physical therapy). Because DSPs are exposed to and asked to be a part of many types of teams, it is critical that they develop the skills and attitudes necessary for them to be effective team players (Taylor, Bradley, & Warren, 1996).

STRATEGIES FOR RESPONDING TO THE PROBLEM

Although supervisors and managers are asked to facilitate team processes and DSPs are asked to be members of various types of teams, these groups rarely receive training on how to develop, facilitate, and evaluate team processes. The following section focuses on the skills and strategies needed by supervisors to effectively manage teams.

Develop Effective Teams

Develop Knowledge, Skills, and Attitudes About Teams and Team Building

Team building and understanding team processes do not come naturally to most team members and leaders. Every team member has a different personality and brings unique experiences, talents, and attributes to the team. Without specific knowledge, skills, and attitudes (KSAs) about why teams are important and about how to facilitate and manage teams, supervisors may experience struggles that are typical to team development yet may have little understanding of team dynamics and how to deal with conflicts. It is critical for supervisors to understand what a team is, the common stages of team development, characteristics of effective and ineffective teams, team-building strategies, and ways to evaluate team effectiveness.

Explore Definitions and Types of Teams

Each team looks and acts differently. Consider the numerous types of teams that exist in any organization or community. The actual word *team* comes from the Indo-European root *deuk*, which means *to pull*. Thus, the concept of pulling together as a group is inherent in the original meaning of the word. Today, a team is any group of people who need each other to accomplish a specific desired outcome (Senge et al., 1994).

As mentioned previously, in community human services organizations, there are many types of teams. Certainly the most common is a person-centered support team.

This type of team focuses on helping the person for whom the plan is being done. The team is composed of people—such as family members, friends, and neighbors of the individual receiving supports; DSPs; an FLS; a program manager; and others—who care about and are committed to the growth and development of the individual who needs support. Together team members work to define the person's dreams, set and prioritize goals, identify potential barriers, search for resources, and commit to supports that help the person achieve his or her dreams and goals. In a person-centered support team, the group members with an organization affiliation also have other responsibilities that relate to organization expectations and individual professional development.

In some community human services settings, there are also interdisciplinary planning teams. These teams are focused on the professionals involved rather than on the individuals supported. These teams meet regularly to develop an individual program plan that is designed to help a person meet goals that will enable him or her to live a more meaningful life in the community. This type of team functions more frequently in ICF/MR (intermediate care facilities for individuals with mental retardation) residential settings or in larger congregate vocational programs. Interdisciplinary planning teams usually include a service coordinator (case manager), a program manager, specialists (e.g., nurse, behavioral support specialist, speech-language pathologist), and the person who receives supports and his or her family and friends; these teams also often include an FLS and sometimes include DSPs. Interdisciplinary team meetings can be confusing to DSPs if their role and purpose in the meeting and their relationship to other team members have not been clearly defined.

Supervisors and managers need to invite DSPs to person-centered and interdisciplinary team meetings, assist them in understanding their role or purpose on these teams, and promote positive team interactions. DSPs often have a unique understanding and knowledge of each person they support and therefore have much to contribute. DSPs on person-centered and interdisciplinary teams often serve as advocates and information specialists.

Another type of team of which a DSP or supervisor might be a member is a cross-functional or project-related team. This type of team brings together people from various roles and positions within the organization for a shared purpose or project. Within community human services settings, cross-functional teams include human rights task forces, quality assurance committees, employee recognition committees, and celebration planning groups. DSPs are often poorly represented on cross-functional teams: It is common for a committee of 10–15 people to include no DSPs or only one. In this situation, DSPs often feel intimidated by the team process and perceive that they have no influence on team decisions and outcomes.

Supervisors and managers need to invite DSPs to become members of teams and train them about the stages of team development, their role within the team, and the overall purpose or function of the team. Then all team members will feel empowered to contribute in the team environment and help the individuals to whom they provide support to become empowered and lead more satisfying and better lives.

Understand Stages of Team Development

Understanding the dynamics of team development processes is an important step in learning how to build and support teams. Table 10.1 provides one model of the stages of team development. Although all teams develop at their own rate and in their own manner, most teams go through similar developmental processes.

At the initial phase, *getting together*, the team is coming together for the first few times and is establishing its purpose, goals, tasks, and rules or norms (Scholtes, 1988; Tuckman, 1965). This is often a time when group members size up one another to see where and how they will fit into the group. Team members may be asking themselves the following questions during this initial stage of development:

- Am I going to be accepted as a part of this group?
- Am I in control of certain things related to this group, or am I controlled by other members?
- Will I have a chance to make valuable contributions to this group by using my talents and skills?
- What is my specific role on the team?
- Who are the other team members, what are their roles, and what do they expect of me on this team?

During the second phase of group development, *doing together*, conflict may occur (Scholtes, 1988; Tuckman, 1965). People are learning about the other members of the group and are forming initial opinions about whether they like them and whether they value their opinions and beliefs. Groups at this stage have defined their tasks and roles and are beginning to tackle the achievement of their goals. When interpersonal and style differences are expressed, conflict can occur. Every team member has a preferred way to approach the specific tasks of the team. When these work styles are not compatible, teams can experience difficulty. For example, the leader of team redesigning orientation to be more accepting of recent immigrants to the United States may use two different strategies in approaching this task: 1) to meet with or interview employees who are immigrants to ask how they might prefer the orientation to be modified or 2) to modify the orientation based on the knowledge of the team members and then have employees who are immigrants provide feedback. The first is more open and participatory; the second, more closed and reaction oriented. When team members approach tasks from differing perspectives and work styles, they need guidance from the facilitator and the involvement of all team members to determine a process that works best for the team to reach the desired outcome. Without this team leadership and team member participation, conflict is likely to arise as the task is implemented because not all members have buy-in to the process. Conflict will probably be more intense if it is not acknowledged and dealt with in the early stages of team development.

During the *becoming together* stage of group development, team members begin to feel like they are actually a group (Scholtes, 1988; Tuckman, 1965). The processes the team will use to achieve its tasks have been agreed on and are implemented. Any conflict that arises for the team members now will likely be identified and acknowledged. The team operates effectively and productively now. At this stage members often define their team with a name.

In the *performing together* stage, team members work on their tasks and seek support from other team members when they need it. When a conflict or barrier is identified, the team is able to resolve it quickly and effectively. Members of the group have developed positive relationships and begin to have trust and respect for each member's

Table 10.1. Stages of team development

Team stage	What occurs
Getting together	Introductions are made. Group members learn about one another, establish goals, develop rules, identify desired outcomes, and define processes. Members consider one another's personalities and characteristics. Some members may test each other's boundaries during this stage.
Doing together	Members begin work on tasks, differences in processes related to task are identified, different opinions are voiced, interpersonal feelings about members develop, and conflict occurs.
Becoming together	Conflicts are worked out, processes are agreed on, effective communication systems are developed, and the group begins to feel like a team.
Performing together	Group members develop positive relationships and respect, problem solving occurs quickly, and tasks are completed.
Rejoicing together	Goals are met, tasks are completed, and the group terminates its meetings.

Source: Tuckman, 1965.

contributions. A supported living program at this stage of group development, for example, operates smoothly, has staff members who complete their assigned tasks well, and openly acknowledges and effectively resolves conflict, and the desired outcomes of the people who receive supports from this program are reached.

The final stage of team development is the *rejoicing together* stage. At this stage the group's tasks are all completed, and group members thus stop working together as a group (Scholtes, 1988; Tuckman, 1965). It is a time to celebrate the team's accomplishments. Many groups in which DSPs and supervisors participate, however, do not have a defined end point. More commonly, team membership turns over frequently or the group tasks change. These ongoing changes significantly affect team processes. Since these conditions are often known ahead of time, it is important for the team to discuss this issue in the early stages of team development. In addition, the team could discuss how celebrations for certain milestones will occur since the group will not have a defined end point.

As the team develops, team members need to consider the fluid nature of the team and discuss how changing membership will be addressed in the team process. Without this discussion, many negative side effects could occur. New team members may not be accepted, the team may not move beyond the initial stages, and some team members may leave the team because they are frustrated with slow progress in achieving desired outcomes. Any of these negative effects of changing membership can lead to an ineffective team. With strong leadership and a proactive approach to this concern, a team can still operate effectively in this environment, avoiding premature termination of team members from the team or organization and other frustrating team outcomes.

If the team's task or function changes, the team may need to reassess its previously identified team rules and process. This can lead to a revisitation of previous stages or the end of the team process. Ideally, the team members enter the *rejoicing together* stage when they have completed their identified tasks and have not found other issues to address as a team. During the *rejoicing together* stage, they focus on summarizing team results and celebrating their accomplishments.

Be Aware of the Characteristics of Effective and Ineffective Teams

Some teams do very well together, and others struggle through all stages of team development. Effective teams are able to generate output, achieve their desired outcomes, and complete identified tasks. Teams that develop supports for people with disabilities often have goals related to the lives of the people they support. For example, a common goal for a person-centered support team might be to assist a person in reducing challenging behavior over 1 month. An effective team would set and reach realistic goals that make this happen or would identify areas that may need to change in the person's environment for this person to reach the desired outcome.

Effective teams communicate well with one another and openly deal with conflict when it arises (Minnesota Department of Human Services, 1993; Ness, 1994; Ness & Krawetz, 1999). For example, members of a person-centered support team who have differences of opinion about how to support a person in reducing challenging behavior can communicate openly and respectfully when discussing these differences and can come to a quick and effective solution. For example, at one meeting of a person-centered support team, a DSP suggested that offering choices during activity time might reduce one individual's challenging behavior. The program manager challenged this idea, but the DSP listed several specific incidents of challenging behavior when choices were not offered. The program manager apologized to the DSP and agreed that offering more choices during activity time might be a useful strategy.

Effective teams usually have a defined structure (e.g., roles, norms, process) and often reach decisions through consensus (Sauer et al., 1997). Table 10.2 summarizes the qualities of effective teams. Team meetings are organized, and members serve specific roles. Meetings generally have stated purposes and an agenda. Common roles for team members during meetings include facilitator, recordkeeper, and timekeeper. Members have completed assigned tasks before each meeting and participate in the meeting.

Even though many teams are effective, it is important for supervisors and managers to be able to recognize the signs of a troubled team. If team members are not aware of the problems a team is having, it is impossible to identify strategies to improve the team process. Every team is different, based on membership, purpose, and

Table 10.2.   Qualities of effective teams

Effective teams . . .

- Set clearly defined mission, vision, and goals, and expect these to be achieved
- Develop a means to determine how well the team is meeting the mission, vision, and goals
- Identify roles and discuss the expectations and activities of those roles
- Solve problems together
- Openly address conflict
- Provide support to all team members, and show appreciation for each member's contributions
- Provide ongoing feedback to one another on how the team is doing; evaluate the team's process and outcomes
- Celebrate the team's successes and accomplishments

processes, but there are some common problems that could be at the root of a team's lack of productivity (see Table 10.3).

Once a supervisor or manager recognizes that a team is operating ineffectively, he or she can help the team to correct the problems. Some of the strategies that might be used include

- Facilitating a dialogue about team perceptions
- Reaching consensus about what is wrong and ways to deal with the issues
- Providing training
- Suggesting the use of periodic feedback and performance checks
- Supporting and recognizing the team's progress

Implementing these strategies in a planned and consistent manner will help the team on its journey to becoming effective or regaining effectiveness.

Establish Group Norms and Rules

Group norms and rules are standards that team members develop through brainstorming or other processes so that the team runs more smoothly and effectively and so that team members have guidelines to follow in meetings. For example, some group norms address how team members will treat each other (e.g., with respect, using active listening), what is expected for meeting deadlines or communicating with each other between meetings, attendance expectations and how absences will be handled, and what processes are to be used for resolving issues or conflict (e.g., creative problem solving).

Supervisors and managers have many opportunities to form new teams and to work with new groups of people. Considering the previously mentioned elements of effective teamwork each time a new group of employees comes together is important. Because teams in community human services often encounter frequently changing mem-

Table 10.3. Common signs of troubled teams

There is a lack of communication. People are afraid to communicate and are guarded.

Team members use impersonal communication. Members do not talk in meetings but follow up with negative e-mails or memos.

Members often criticize other members and say hurtful and disrespectful things.

There is no discussion or disagreement during meetings. All members go along with everything and never share differences of opinion.

Meetings are poorly organized, and everyone dreads coming to them.

Competition among team members is obvious and disruptive.

The team's mission and goals are unclear to team members.

Everyone shows up to the team meetings, but nothing gets done.

Decisions are always made by the facilitator or the leader, not by all team members.

Members are confused or disagree about their roles.

Team members lack diversity (e.g., age, gender, race, religion, level of productivity, type of work).

The team does not talk about itself as a team and rarely evaluates its effectiveness.

Sources: Scholtes, 1988; Varney, 1989.

bership, having processes in place to welcome, support, and inform new members about the team norms is essential for the health of the team. Also, when new members are added to the team, it may be useful to review the team's purpose, goals, and roles; the responsibilities of team members; and the informal ways the team operates. This will assist new members in understanding the team norms as quickly as possible. Table 10.4 lists several questions that teams can answer as they establish team norms and roles.

Establish Team-Building Strategies

Several team-building strategies can assist in the development of effective teams, including 1) planning and conducting effective meetings, 2) using ice breakers and other tools to help team members get to know one another better, 3) using good communication skills, and 4) celebrating team accomplishments.

Plan and Conduct Effective Meetings

Many times people complain about having to go to meetings that are ineffective or not worth their time. Assigning a team facilitator is important to ensure the effectiveness of the team's meetings and outcomes (Nelson & Economy, 2003; Sauer et al., 1997). All team members, but in particular the team facilitator, should be skilled in planning, conducting, and evaluating effective meetings. A team facilitator keeps the team on track with discussion and tasks, informs the group about the time allotted for each agenda item, and takes the pulse of the team's process and progress. Often the role of the facilitator is rotated, enabling other people to share in the responsibility and to better understand and observe which facilitation strategies work for the team.

Another important element of effective team meetings is ensuring that each meeting has an agenda. Agendas should have designated items for discussion and decision making, and these items should be allotted a specific amount of time. Team members often appreciate being informed of the purpose of the meeting and the agenda items before the meeting. Often team members want to add items to the agenda; the facilitator can solicit this information by asking team members to review and add any needed items to the agenda before the meeting.

Table 10.4.   Establishing team norms and rules: Questions to ask

What are our mission, vision, and goals?

When, where, and how frequently should we meet?

Who will serve in what roles on the team? Will they serve in these roles throughout the duration of the team, or will we rotate these roles?

When a new member comes into the group, how will we welcome this person and assign him or her roles?

When a person leaves the group, how will we handle this transition?

How will we reach decisions within this team? By consensus? Majority rules? Leader decides?

When conflict arises within our team, how will we handle it?

How will we keep members informed about our activities after we meet and between meetings?

Are we a time-limited group or an ongoing group?

How will we support one another?

How will we celebrate our accomplishments?

In addition, it is important for the team to determine if each meeting should be recorded in some way. Sometimes, team members decide to keep their own notes; other times official meeting minutes are kept and disseminated. Whatever process is used, it is important for teams to have a way to keep track of critical decisions and individual or group assignments.

Have Team Members Get to Know One Another

As mentioned previously, team members all come to the group with unique expectations, experiences, skills, attributes, strengths, and work styles. It is important for teams to take the time to identify the unique qualities in all team members and explore who could use specific strengths in specific situations. For teams that have been working together for a while, revisiting these differences may be useful. Some teams find it helpful to use simple team-building activities at the beginning of any meeting. This can be as simple as answering questions such as the following:
- "What animal do you most identify with and why?"
- "What is one thing that others in the group likely do not know about you?"
- "What is your favorite color?"

Some teams may choose to use a more formal assessment tool such as the Myers-Briggs Type Indicator (Myers & Briggs, n.d.). Whatever method a team chooses, team members should get to know one another, understand and talk about the differences among group members, and capitalize on the strengths of team members.

Use Good Communication Skills

Team members and team facilitators need to understand and use effective communication skills. These skills may be difficult to develop but are essential to effective teamwork. All team members need to be able to listen, paraphrase, and provide constructive feedback to other team members. Conflict or ineffectiveness in teams almost always relates back to team members' inability to effectively communicate with one another. Table 10.5 provides some essential definitions and tips to assist team members in enhancing their communications skills.

Celebrate Team Accomplishments

Celebrating team accomplishments is an important aspect of team building (Nelson, & Economy, 2003; Rees, 1997). It conveys to group members that their contributions are valued and appreciated. Without celebrations and purposeful acknowledgement of the team's contributions, the work environment can sometimes feel depressing, oppressive, or unforgiving. Simple acknowledgments of team events and accomplishments, such as the arrival of new members, completion of an assigned task, or supporting a person served to achieve a desired goal, can make the difference between an exciting or a stale and stagnant work environment.

Acknowledging team members through celebrations can be simple, direct, and not very time consuming. Some celebrations ideas include 1) going out for lunch together; 2) identifying and discussing milestones at team meetings; 3) acknowledging team accomplishments together and sharing them with others (e.g., managers, administrators, organization leadership team); 4) writing a quick note for the organiza-

Table 10.5. Effective communication skills

Communication skill	Definition
Active listening	Active listening involves sensing, understanding, evaluating, and responding. Active listeners keep an open mind and hear out the person who is speaking. Active listeners make a point to understand the position of the person who is speaking. They observe verbal and nonverbal cues, and they do not interrupt a speaker. Active listeners pay attention when the speaker is talking, and they make a point to look at the person who is communicating.
Paraphrasing	Paraphrasing is saying back to the speaker what you thought he or she said using your own words. The purpose of paraphrasing is to clarify for the speaker what you heard and to allow him or her the opportunity to tell you if what you heard is what the speaker thought he or she said. This interaction helps to ensure that what was said is understood in a way that the person communicating intended. Some common ways to start paraphrasing are "What I heard you say was . . . " or "Do you mean . . . ?"
Constructive feedback	Constructive feedback is a way to tell the person who is communicating how you perceived his or her statement and what you think about it. When providing constructive feedback it is important to focus on how the communication affects you. This type of feedback should be objective, descriptive, and timely and should provide the person with useful information with which he or she can do something. When providing constructive feedback, you are trying to help the person. Constructive feedback is not about trying to hurt someone or achieving personal gain. It is designed to be respectful and to focus on the behavior or statement that has been communicated, not on the person. Some possible ways to start constructive feedback are "I wanted to give you some feedback on what I observed in the meeting," or "When you said *X*, I felt *Y*." One suggestion is to preface feedback with an inquiry about whether or not the person wants feedback in a specific area.

From Sauer, J., O'Nell, S., Sedlezky, L., Scaletta, K., Taylor, M., & Silver, J. (1997). *An introduction to teamwork in community health and human services* (p. 44). Cambridge, MA: Human Services Research Institute; adapted by permission.

tion newsletter; or 5) simply saying, "Hooray, we did it!" No matter how accomplishments are celebrated, the team facilitator and team members should remember to always look for and recognize the team's accomplishments, big or small. The positive effect this can have on team spirit may be surprising.

Evaluate Team Effectiveness

It is important for team members to frequently evaluate the team's effectiveness as they work together to achieve desired outcomes or goals (Rees, 1997; Sauer, 1994). The team should evaluate itself by asking the following important questions:

- How effective is the team at defining its mission, vision, and goals?
- Does the team use agendas? If not, why not?
- Do team members come prepared and ready to contribute? If not, why not?
- What could make the team operate more effectively?
- Do team members think team meetings are productive? If not, why not?
- Do team members believe that the team sessions are effectively facilitated? If not, why not?
- How do team members feel about the outcomes of the team?
- How do team members feel about the process that was used to reach the outcomes?

• Does the team use effective communication strategies? If not, why not?

This evaluation process does not have to be complex or long. Sometimes the team facilitator can simply check in with team members during each meeting. The Team Performance Evaluation at the end of this chapter provides one quick and easy way to evaluate the process and the outcomes of a team.

In addition to evaluating the overall performance of the entire team (e.g., process, outcomes), it is often helpful to provide specific feedback to the team facilitator. Important elements to include in this feedback are the facilitator's ability 1) to keep the team focused and on task, 2) to involve the group in developing the agenda and make sure that it is followed, 3) to ensure that all members get to participate and that their ideas are expressed, 4) to work with the team to make a decision or reach consensus on an issue, and 5) to manage and facilitate the resolution to any conflict that arises. The Team Facilitator Evaluation at the end this chapter can be useful in evaluating the effectiveness of the team facilitator.

Manage Conflicts Among Team Members

Conflict is a natural part of any team's development. All teams experience conflict. What is important is that teams learn how to effectively manage their conflict. Table 10.6 identifies common ways in which groups or teams may respond to conflict (ineffectively or effectively). All group members need to be involved in determining how the group will handle conflict when it arises.

As mentioned previously, team members may have agreed on a conflict management approach as a part of group norms during the *getting together* stage of development. If that did occur, the group will want to use that conflict resolution process when a conflict emerges. Remember, if team members are involved in making this process decision, they will be more willing to participate in conflict resolution when it is needed.

Create and Support Self-Directed Work Teams

A self-directed work team is a type of work group that has the authority and responsibility, within certain parameters approved by organization administrators, to establish its mission, accomplish its goals, and be accountable for its outcomes. For example, a self-directed work team could be composed of DSPs who provide supports for four individuals living in a home and who require 24-hour supervision. This self-directed team does not have a supervisor but rather has a team leader who rotates periodically, and the team members work together, with the help of a manager, to complete the responsibilities usually assigned to a supervisor, including recruiting, selecting, and hiring DSPs (co-workers); establishing and monitoring work schedules; coordinating or ensuring orientation and training programs; completing peer performance evaluations; and, most important, developing, implementing, and evaluating support plans for the individuals served. Usually a manager who has responsibility to supervise several different work supervisors manages, coaches, and evaluates the work of the self-directed work team.

Self-directed work teams are uncommon within community human services. However, the In the Spotlight segment about Vinfen Corporation that appears later in this chapter provides insight into one organization's experience with using self-directed

Table 10.6. Team reactions to conflict and disagreements

Reaction type and description	Outcome
Denial or withdrawal The team attempts to get rid of the conflict by denying it even exists. For example, a team member may always come to meetings late and no one may mention it. If this topic is brought up, team members may say, "It's just a part of our team culture" or "We seem to get our work done."	The conflict rarely goes away when this reaction type is used. Often the conflict becomes unmanageable. Denial or withdrawal may occasionally be effective when the team is not facing a critical deadline related to the conflict. Sometimes with enough time things can get better.
Suppression or smoothing it over The team deals with the conflict by smoothing it over. Common phrases are "Let's be positive" and "We run a happy ship around here." Differences between team members are played down and are not openly discussed or appreciated. For example, some team members may say, "That's just the way she is" or people may comment after a meeting, "Why does he always say something contrary when an idea is shared?"	The conflict rarely goes away when this reaction type is used. Preserving a relationship between team members may sometimes be more important than dealing with a conflict that does not involve critical issues. In these situations, suppressing the conflict may be a viable way for team members to react.
Power or dominance The team deals with the conflict by letting a person with authority or a majority vote resolve the conflict.	This reaction type results in winners and losers and may affect the future performance of team members. This approach should rarely be used. If it is used, all team members need to openly discuss the approach and agree to its use.
Compromise or negotiation The team deals with the conflict by bargaining or attempting to reach a middle ground or a compromise. For example, when trying to reach a decision after a number of ideas have been heavily discussed, some team members sensing frustration might say, " Why don't we just combine ideas 1 and 2?" or "Let's just vote on each idea and use the one with the most votes."	The conflict can be resolved using this strategy, but often the resulting outcome is less effective and watered down. This strategy can result in people inflating or overstating their positions so that when a compromise is reached it is closer to their original favored position. Team members sometimes lack commitment to the compromised position. When time is limited or there are not enough resources to implement another desired solution to the conflict, compromise can be effective.
Integration and collaboration The team deals with the conflict by recognizing and understanding the strengths of all positions. Team members try to find a resolution that is win–win for everyone instead of trying to defend their positions and having a win–lose or a lose–lose outcome.	Team members recognize that in managing the conflict, they will likely have to modify their positions. The group process results in an outcome that every member agrees with or is comfortable with.

Source: Sauer et al., 1997.

work teams. As this industry moves toward more person-centered and -directed supports, self-directed teams may become more common because they offer solutions to many of the problems that occur during the provision of community supports.

Self-directed teams provide the infrastructure for DSPs and FLSs to identify and implement supports that meet the needs of people who have unique needs and expectations for services. Even though a manager may work closely with a self-directed work team in matters relating to meeting organizational quality outcomes, the power for shaping and enriching the quality of individual supports and services lies with the self-directed team members. This empowering process often results in more satisfying jobs for DSPs by providing greater challenge, variety, and opportunity for improved quality in the work they perform.

Members of self-directed work teams share the responsibility for achieving certain outcomes for a specific work site (e.g., residential program site, supported employment unit). Members share their talents and strengths to complete the tasks required of the overall team. Most important, these types of teams have the authority, resources, and support of management to design, implement, monitor, and control the work processes needed to complete the assigned tasks of the group (Bucholz & Roth, 1987; Torres & Spiegel, 1990). Members of these teams share responsibilities. Often they have to learn new skills to achieve all of the desired outcomes.

Self-directed teams have a number of common responsibilities including but not limited to the following (Bucholz & Roth, 1987; Sauer et al., 1997; Torres & Spiegel, 1990):

- Monitoring and reviewing overall processes and team performance
- Scheduling
- Assigning responsibilities to group members
- Problem solving
- Improving the performance and efficiency of the group
- Conducting performance reviews of all members
- Selecting new team members
- Preparing, implementing, and monitoring budgets
- Training and mentoring all team members
- Coordinating work with other teams and with the management of the organization

With self-directed work teams, the roles and responsibilities of supervisor and managers change (see Table 10.7). In traditional work situations, supervision comes from middle management outside the group. With self-directed teams, supervision comes from within the group. Top management in an organization delegates work responsibilities to the self-directed work team, many of which are typically borne by supervisors and managers in a traditional organization. In self-directed teams, supervisors become the initial team leaders for a given period (e.g., 6 months, 1 year, or longer). As other self-directed team members become more skilled, however, the leadership role often rotates.

The roles and responsibilities of program managers also change with the development of self-directed work teams. Fewer managers are usually required when an organization employs self-directed work teams. The roles of managers who are members of self-directed work teams change from directing and controlling work and team processes to leading, supporting, troubleshooting, and providing feedback and training.

Table 10.7.   The role of the manager in traditional and self-directed team environments

Responsibility	Role of manager in traditional work environment	Role of manager who works with a self-directed work team
Monitoring and reviewing overall work processes	Controls and delegates to supervisors	Works with self-directed teams and their leaders, provides orientation, and helps set the direction for teams
Scheduling work shifts	Delegates to supervisors	Delegates to self-directed work teams; listens to wants and needs of team and provides ideas and support related to scheduling
Assigning work responsibilities	Delegates to supervisors	Delegates to self-directed work teams within specific parameters
Identifying and resolving problems	Works with supervisors based on information they provide about work situations	Delegates to self-directed work teams and may act as facilitator in certain situations
Improving and enhancing the quality of work	Holds supervisors responsible through periodic quality checks	Works with self-directed work teams and their leaders within the framework developed by top management
Conducting performance reviews	Delegates to supervisors	Delegates to self-directed work team, provides resources for training, expects periodic reports, recognizes team successes, and works to correct weaknesses
Selecting new employees	Delegates to supervisors	Delegates to self-directed work team, provides resources for training, expects periodic reports, recognizes team successes, and works to correct weaknesses
Managing budgets	Maintains overall control and delegates small amount of responsibility to supervisors	Works with self-directed work teams and their leaders using specific parameters established by top management
Training and mentoring	Holds supervisor responsible for most training and mentoring Provides needed resources (e.g., money, equipment, training space) to supervisors	Delegates to self-directed work teams, provides resources and support, and expects periodic reports
Coordinating work with other teams and with management	Coordinates with other managers through meetings with top management	Works with self-directed work team representatives, acts as advocate for self-directed teams with top management, and supports self-directed team representatives to meet with top leadership

Responsibility	Role of manager in traditional work environment	Role of manager who works with a self-directed work team
Communicating organization's mission, vision, and values	Works with and delegates to supervisors	Shares with self-directed work team through dialogues and training
Setting overall direction of the organization	Works with supervisor to channel this information to direct support professionals (DSPs)	Works with self-directed work team and involves team members through dialogue and training
Designing and implementing organizational change projects (e.g., expansion of services, creating a system in which the organization is hired by a self-advocate or a family member who is in charge of meeting the supported individual's needs and operating a consumer-directed support services program)	Works through chain of command by carrying out top management plans and holding supervisor responsible for ensuring that DSPs execute any new plans	Works closely with self-directed team leaders and members by soliciting input; providing training; providing resources; acting as advocate for self-directed teams with top management; and providing active, constant, and persistent involvement throughout the change process

Certain aspects of work are not fully delegated or are not delegated at all to self-directed work teams. For example, top management may permit each work team to control the budget for its program services but not salaries. Self-directed teams may have input in redesigning the organization's mission, vision, and values, but top managers usually develop the overall direction, size, and scope of the organization.

In the Spotlight: Vinfen Corporation

In February 1997, the Co-op Network, a program of the Vinfen Corporation, shifted models from a traditional supervisory structure to a self-directed team. In 1996, a DSP from Switzerland came to work at the Co-op Network in Cambridge, Massachusetts, for 1 year as part of an international exchange fellowship program. She was impressed with depth of services provided but challenged the top-down hierarchical structure and successfully convinced some organization administrators to pilot a model that empowered DSPs; thus, the first self-directed team at Vinfen emerged.

The Co-op Network provides service coordination to individuals with mild to moderate intellectual disabilities who require intermittent supports and reside in independent community apartments throughout greater Boston. Before making the transition to a self-directed team model, the Co-op Network was composed of a program manager and four DSPs. DSPs worked in isolation under the direct supervision of the program manager.

The self-directed team enhanced the quality of supports by integrating the members of the Co-op Network and by increasing DSP autonomy. In this self-directed team, members meet biweekly to discuss issues that have arisen and to talk about the individuals who receive supports from the program. Team meetings are facilitated by a DSP who is elected by members of the team to serve as team leader for 6 months. In addition to facilitating meetings, the team leader attends organization manager meetings and training and is a liaison between the self-directed team and organization administration.

The change to the self-directed team format resulted in elimination of the program manager position and the addition of another DSP. Supervision was replaced with peer feedback as the self-directed team developed tools that are used each month to assess and observe the quality of required DSP work. The self-directed team members also share administrative responsibilities previously held by the program manager. Administrative and clinical staff members provide mentoring and support to team members based on needs identified by the team through training and roundtable discussions.

The success of this first self-directed team encouraged a similar program model in the Apartment Living Program at Vinfen. This program area made the transition from a traditional hierarchical management structure in January 1998. Vinfen recognized both self-directed teams for providing outstanding supports to individuals with intellectual disabilities, awarding the teams the Vinfen Mental Retardation Division's 1998 Outstanding Team Award. In February 1998, the Hewlett Street Apartments program of Vinfen, which serves individuals with mild to moderate intellectual disabilities who require 24-hour supervision, became a self-directed team. Currently, seven DSPs (two of whom are overnight employees) provide support to eight individuals living in a multifamily house. As with the Co-op Network staff, the DSPs at Hewlett Street share administrative responsibilities and rotate team leaders every 6 months. Challenges for this self-directed team have been different than for the other teams due to the needs associated with a 24-hour residential program. This self-directed team has quarterly retreats away from the program site to improve the quality of supports and the effectiveness of the program.

As a multiservice organization, Vinfen has met with success in its quest to implement and support self-directed teams. Vinfen started slowly and has been able to cross-pollinate the self-directed team concept throughout the organization.

OVERCOMING IMPLEMENTATION BARRIERS

Barriers to Implementing Self-Directed Work Teams

It sometimes is overwhelming to community human services managers and administrators to think about moving to self-directed teams. The most common reaction to the prospect of using self-directed teams is that turnover rates among staff are too high and that the DSPs do not have the skills needed for such significant responsibilities. Although these are valid concerns, perhaps one way to think about the possibility of developing self-directed teams is to consider some positive outcomes of using them. By becoming empowered to make a difference and to contribute value to the organization, perhaps more DSPs would be motivated to stay and develop the higher-level skills necessary to do DSP work. In addition, some organizations have realized that by investing in self-directed teams, they have been able to divert the salaries of middle managers back to DSPs, resulting in DSPs' earning higher wages and staying in their positions longer.

It is important that there be buy-in from all levels within the organization when considering the use of self-directed teams. An organizational change of this magnitude will not succeed without buy-in of all DSPs; the championing of the systems change by key managers and supervisors; and the visible, consistent, and constant support of the CEO, head administrator, or owner and the organization's board of directors. In other words, there must be a strong commitment at all levels of the organization for the principles of empowerment, respect, support, and celebration. In addition, there must be strong alignment between this specific organizational change process and the organization's mission, core values, and vision. (See Chapter 12 for more information on organizational change.)

If the organization decides to set up self-directed teams, sufficient preparation is critical. Starting slowly and building on successes that come easily are crucial. Being ready to ride out the rough spots and understanding the organization's tolerance for the rough ride is also important. The organization can look for one program component or site that has a great group of staff and build on its success.

Barriers to Implementing Other Types of Teams

Work groups and teams in community human services organizations can face unique challenges. As mentioned previously, because of the high turnover rates of DSPs, the membership of a team can be everchanging. It is common for half of the team members to leave in a year. It is then difficult for the work group or team to fully develop because so much time is spent on orienting new members. The team will not be able to move to the *performing together* stage of team development unless it has defined how it will negotiate and handle new membership. Team members need to quickly develop processes for group norms and role clarification. Otherwise, it is impossible for a team to accomplish its goals as new members join the group.

One result of changing team membership is that the group may become closed to new members. It is not uncommon to hear from newly hired DSPs that they have been ignored or excluded from group decision-making processes, that they feel unwelcome, or that their ideas are ignored or discounted. Often this occurs because the long-term group members identify themselves as a cohesive group and have learned how to work effectively together in achieving their goals. Over time they have come to realize that each time a new person enters the group, the group processes start all over again. They are likely protecting themselves from more orientation, which takes time away from their work tasks; from conflicts arising from new members; and from the loss of their current team cohesiveness. To avoid this, work teams need to have predetermined processes for how they will handle new group membership and need to restructure team roles to support the new group members.

Also, facilitators need to be aware of these dynamics so that the work team does not become closed. For example, a facilitator might ask for an existing team member to act as a mentor for a new team member to explain the group's norms; explain informal ways of operating; share the team mission, vision, and goals; provide past meeting minutes; and describe some of the team's strengths, challenges, and accomplishments. Another way the facilitator can help the team from closing off to new team members is to use part of a meeting to evaluate how well the team is functioning, what current challenges the team is facing, and how agreed-on deadlines are being met. In this way, the new member gets some orientation and the existing team members can do some routine checkups.

As mentioned earlier in this chapter, another issue that often arises for work teams within community human services is that daily job tasks change routinely even though the organization's broad goals and outcomes (e.g., supporting people to be included in the community and live better lives) do not change. For example, a person who receives supports might move away and a new person might begin receiving supports, a supported individual's health needs might change, an individual might decide he or she wants to attend a new place of worship, and so forth. Often negotiating and monitoring these new duties becomes difficult for team members. One way to address this issue is for the team to have a process of identifying and assigning new tasks to its members. If this process is predetermined, the work team will know what to expect and the likelihood of certain team members' becoming overburdened will be reduced. Involving all team members in developing this task assignment process is helpful.

Work teams in community human services also are isolated from each other. Communication among team members other than through a staff log is difficult to arrange and infrequent. Team members need time to network; get to know one another; determine group processes; and identify goals, roles, and responsibilities. Without this time, it is difficult for members to move beyond the initial stages of group development. Providing opportunities to meet is particularly challenging because of turnover. Team facilitators should ensure regular face-to-face meetings among team members who work different hours or days of the week. Here are some ways for facilitators to reduce isolation among team members:

- Provide flexibility in scheduling team meetings to ensure that different work schedules are recognized.
- Before a scheduled team meeting, gather input from individuals who are unable to attend the meeting.
- Disseminate meeting notes in a timely manner.
- Have team meetings frequently enough to allow sufficient time for development, yet not so frequently that team members become overwhelmed.
- Develop creativity in covering shifts (e.g., supervisor from another work site, temporary worker, off-duty DSP from another work site) and in scheduling meetings to encourage attendance at team meetings and to model the importance of teamwork in the work environment.

QUESTIONS TO PONDER

1. To what extent and in what ways do you feel that turnover rates in the organization in which you work are related to issues of teams and team building? In what ways?
2. Have you been a member of a healthy team? If so, what qualities made that team especially effective?
3. What roles do the various people on your work team take on as team members?
4. What types of conflicts have the DSPs with whom you work experienced? What was your role as a supervisor in intervening with these conflicts?
5. In what ways have you previously assessed how well your work group works as a team?
6. What activities have you used to facilitate team building among the DSPs you supervise? How successful were these activities? How might you modify these activities in the future?

7. How effective do you think a self-directed team might be within your organization?

8. What challenges would you face if you tried to create a self-directed team environment within your organization?

CONCLUSION

Given the pervasiveness of staff turnover in community human services, reducing turnover and enhancing employee retention are critical. DSPs report that conflicts with co-workers is a critical factor in their decision to stay with or leave an organization. One key strategy to help DSPs work more effectively and to deal creatively with conflict is to establish work teams. Knowing about, training others in, and using effective team processes is important in reducing turnover; teams can reduce misunderstandings and conflict and build cohesiveness.

For established work teams, providing targeted training and using needs-based teamwork learning activities can be energizing and help achieve new outcomes. In addition, understanding the stages of team development, recognizing common signs of trouble within teams, and evaluating the effectiveness of team functioning can help organizations find success. This chapter has provided ideas, tools, and reasons that supervisors and managers need to develop effective teams and evaluate their work.

RESOURCES

Rees, F. (1997). *Team work from start to finish*. San Francisco: Pfeiffer.

This book focuses on two factors essential for teams: getting work done and building and maintaining the spirit and momentum of the team. The book describes 10 steps teams can use to function more effectively: focusing the team, assigning roles, establishing guidelines, planning the work, doing the work, reviewing team performance, completing the work, publishing the results, rewarding the team, and moving on.

Sauer, J., O'Nell, S., Sedlezky, L., Scaletta, K., Taylor, M., & Silver, J. (1997). *An introduction to teamwork in community health and human services.* Cambridge, MA: Human Services Research Institute. (Available from the publisher, http://www.hsri.org)

This curriculum can be used to teach team members how to function efficiently together. It is based on the *Community Support Skill Standards* (CSSS; Taylor, Bradley, & Warren, 1996; see Chapter 6 for more information on the CSSS). Units include learning the basics of teams and teamwork, achieving success as a team, and tools and processes for enhancing team effectiveness. The curriculum also includes the handouts needed to teach the curriculum.

Team Performance Evaluation

On this evaluation form, *Task* refers to specific activities that the team is working on. *Process* refers to how well team members are or are not working together as a team.

1. Circle the numbers for *Task* and *Process* that best represent your level of performance as a team member during this work session. Discuss your responses with the team.

Personal performance

Task	1	2	3	4	5	6	7	8	9	10
	Needs improvement									Excellent
Process	1	2	3	4	5	6	7	8	9	10
	Needs improvement									Excellent

2. Circle the numbers for *Task* and *Process* that best represent your team's level of performance during this work session. Discuss your responses with the team.

Team performance

Task	1	2	3	4	5	6	7	8	9	10
	Needs improvement									Excellent
Process	1	2	3	4	5	6	7	8	9	10
	Needs improvement									Excellent

3. Jot down any insights you have gained as a result of the rating and discussion of your personal and team performance of *Task* and *Process*.

4. Identify any changes you would suggest for improving your own and the team's performance based on your discussion and insights. Be specific!

Personal	Team

From Sauer, J., O'Nell, S., Sedlezky, L., Scaletta, K., Taylor, M., & Silver, J. (1997). *An introduction to teamwork in community health and human services.* Cambridge, MA: Human Services Research Institute; reprinted by permission.

Team Facilitator Evaluation

Name of evaluator: _____

How long team has been working together: _____

Name of facilitator: _____

How long this person has served as facilitator: _____

Rate each item on a scale of 5 (*strength*) to 1 (*area to improve*), and list specific strengths and areas to improve.

Task	Strengths	Areas to improve
1. Bringing the group [members] back together if they begin to fragment into small discussion groups at inappropriate times 5 4 3 2 1		
2. Making sure members participate evenly so that some do not dominate while others never speak up 5 4 3 2 1		
3. Keeping [the] group focused on the topics on the agenda and moving the group along when discussion is no longer productive 5 4 3 2 1		
4. Helping the group to make a decision or reach consensus on a topic 5 4 3 2 1		
5. Informing the group when the time allotted for the agenda item has ended 5 4 3 2 1		
6. Working with the group to acknowledge that there is a conflict and to facilitate a resolution 5 4 3 2 1		

From Sauer, J., O'Nell, S., Sedlezky, L., Scaletta, K., Taylor, M., & Silver, J. (1997). *An introduction to teamwork in community health and human services.* Cambridge, MA: Human Services Research Institute; reprinted by permission.

11

SUPPORTING AND TRAINING SUPERVISORS

AMY S. HEWITT AND SHERYL A. LARSON

This chapter examines the role that front-line supervisors (FLSs) play in retaining direct support professionals (DSPs). It emphasizes the importance of supporting supervisors and ensuring that they have been adequately trained for their positions. The results of a comprehensive job analysis for FLSs who work in community services for people with disabilities are provided. This chapter identifies the competencies for which FLSs need training and suggests how organizations can develop effective job descriptions, training programs, and performance reviews using the information obtained in this job analysis. The strategies that one organization used to better support its FLSs are described. This chapter also includes sample FLS job descriptions, performance reviews, and a supervisor development self-assessment plan that organizations can use as a model as they develop these tools within their own organizations.

TARGETED FRONT-LINE SUPERVISOR COMPETENCIES

This chapter focuses on the need to train and develop supervisors to be effective in their roles. Consequently, all of the FLS competencies used throughout this book are related to this chapter.

UNDERSTANDING THE PROBLEM

FLSs have one of the most complex and difficult jobs in the field of community human services. They are responsible for the supervision of a workforce that is often undertrained and for which there is extremely high turnover and constant vacancies. In addition, supervisors often supervise people that they do not see on a regular basis who are working varied hours of the day and every day of the week. As a result, supervisors always have a group of new employees whom they are responsible to train. Supervisors also work direct support shifts when replacement employees cannot be found.

Many supervisors report that they were promoted to being a supervisor because they were good at doing direct care but also report that they were ill-prepared to be effective supervisors (Larson, Sauer, Hewitt, O'Nell, & Sedlezky, 1998). Organizations often do not have effective training programs for supervisors, which results in supervisors' feeling that they were thrown in with little training and support and that they learned through trial and error. However, perhaps the best offense and defense in battling the workforce challenges related to direct support is having excellent supervisors who know what they are supposed to do and who are supported in their jobs. This chapter provides suggestions and tools to assist organizations to better prepare, support, and value FLSs. It highlights the contributions FLSs make to improving turnover and vacancy rates in their organizations as well as improving the overall quality of the services provided by creating and developing employees who are effective and do a good job.

RESEARCH SUPPORT FOR SOLUTIONS

FLSs play a critical role in hiring, training, retaining, and supporting DSPs. They are essential to realizing the goals, purposes, and potential of community services (Barry Associates, 1999; Cohen, 2000; Hewitt, Larson, & Lakin, 2000; Lakin, Bruininks, Hill, & Hauber, 1982; Larson, Lakin, & Hewitt, 2002; Oklahoma Department of Human Services, Developmental Disabilities Services Division, 2000; Test, Solow, & Flowers, 1999). Few studies of DSP workforce challenges acknowledge this reality. Research, however, suggests that settings with relatively inexperienced FLSs have higher DSP turnover rates (Larson, Lakin, & Bruininks, 1998). Furthermore, two of the most frequently cited reasons by DSPs for leaving their positions relate to effective supervision: 1) difficulties in getting along with co-workers and 2) conflicts with supervisors (Larson, Lakin, & Bruininks, 1998).

Three focus groups with a total of 41 FLSs examined the question of what does and does not work in orientation, training, and supporting supervisors (Larson, Sauer, et al., 1998). Table 11.1 summarizes the orientation that these supervisors were given. Supervisors reported receiving various kinds of orientation and training. Many reported that they taught themselves because no orientation was provided. Others reported that a mentor helped them through their initial months on the job. A few attended formal training provided either by their organization or by an outside entity. In-service training opportunities tended to be based on self-study or on courses offered through colleges or provider groups. Some supervisors reported getting an allowance for their own training, whereas others reported a lack of money for training.

Supervisors and managers who had access to mentors and networking reported that these were the most helpful components of orientation. Supervisors who did not have mentors or networking opportunities frequently reported that they had little support in learning what they were supposed to do and that this lack of support was their biggest problem. Other issues for supervisors included a lack of training opportunities and an overwhelming amount of information to take in very quickly.

When asked what worked about in-service education and training, supervisors reported liking networking opportunities, opportunities to practice using the information learned, and training provided outside the organization (Larson, Sauer, et al., 1998; see also Table 11.2). A number of effective and useful training practices were identified by FLSs. These include being paired with experienced peers and having refresher courses on certain topics. Features of in-service education that supervisors

Table 11.1. Orientation for supervisors and managers

What worked?	What did not work?
Having access to mentors	Being thrown in to sink or swim
Having access to training resources	Administrator saying, "Here are your keys."
Using cross-peer support	Taught self
Having experience in the human services	Using organization-developed training with no outside guidelines
Receiving good support from direct support professionals	Receiving disciplinary action while still in training
Having support of immediate supervisor	Having training content that did not match the job
Knowing whom to call	Not having administrative support to accomplish tasks taught in training
Receiving help from mentors when needed	
Networking with people in same position	Being held to overly high expectations
Networking with supervisors in different organizations	Getting too much information at once
Using step system that identifies what to learn when	Not being told what the job tasks were (if they had told me, I would have done it)
Using trial and error	Just being given a set of keys and job description
Using interactive training	Not having training across all categories of job duties
Mentors who explained how to do things	Receiving supervisory training that was not specific enough to actual job tasks
Networking with other supervisors	
Purposeful on-the-job learning	Not receiving ongoing support for clarification
Training from person who previously held the position	Receiving training that did not accommodate individual learning styles
Work experience in human services	Not being given enough resources to do or get training
State-offered supervision and management courses	Being given policies to read
	Receiving only training required by regulations
	Not receiving training about new types of services
	Using interactive training

From Larson, S.A., Sauer, J., Hewitt, A., O'Nell, S., & Sedlezky, L. (1998). *SOS training and technical assistance project for direct support professionals, trainers and frontline supervisors* (pp. 39–40). Minneapolis: University of Minnesota, Institute on Community Integration, Research and Training Center on Community Living; adapted by permission.

did not like included poor trainers who did not gear training to adult learners, poor-quality materials, and training on topics that were not important.

STRATEGIES FOR RESPONDING TO THE PROBLEM

Organizations can use several important strategies to better support their FLSs to be effective at their job roles. The following sections provide an overview of many of these important considerations and interventions.

Define Supervisors' Roles and Responsibilities

One of the most important strategies that organizations can use to better support their FLSs is to clarify their roles and responsibilities. This can be done through using job analyses, creating purposeful job descriptions that clarify responsibilities, finding a balance between supervisory and direct support duties, limiting multisite responsibil-

Table 11.2. In-service training for supervisors and managers

What worked?	What did not work?
Combination of off- and on-site training	Patronizing or condescending trainers
Follow-up after training for implementation	Training consisting solely of participants talking to each other
Networking opportunities	Training with no practical application
Training selected based on own wants and needs	Poor or ineffective trainers
Opportunity to use what was learned in training and see it work	Training that is not geared toward adult learners
Incentive program for continuing education or college credit based on criteria	Training content that is read to participants
Peer-recommended training	Training that is only offered at one time
Time during training to practice and apply what was learned	Poor-quality printed materials
	Reading manuals, reports, and books
Training from outside agency	Role playing
Training outside of industry (e.g., human resources development and management training from college or private industry)	High costs for training
	Training sessions that are too far away or that are too short to travel so far
Funds (based on percentage of salary) devoted to training	Training sessions that are too long
Stipend for outside training	Repeated training with no variety
Training that offers concrete examples and strategies	Schedule driven by regulations and money
Videos for busy people	Training for one or two supervisors who then train the others
Permitting selection from opportunities listed in quarterly newsletter	
Ideal	
Pairing new with experienced supervisors for 2–4 weeks for training and rule review	
Resources and support staff to cover participant's job duties during training	
Refreshers on issues when needed	

From Larson, S.A., Sauer, J., Hewitt, A., O'Nell, S., & Sedlezky, L. (1998). *SOS training and technical assistance project for direct support professionals, trainers and frontline supervisors* (pp. 39–40). Minneapolis: University of Minnesota, Institute on Community Integration, Research and Training Center on Community Living; adapted by permission.

ities, and providing added incentives for FLSs who end up working nonscheduled direct support shifts.

Use Job Analysis

As described in Chapter 6, a job analysis is a careful exploration and rich description of the role that a specific group or category of people have in a given job. For FLSs, a job analysis describes what they actually do and what they should do on the job. This differentiation between what they do and what they should do is important because often FLSs are so busy managing crises and responding to other workforce problems (e.g., creating schedules, filling vacancies, providing direct support because of vacancies) that they never get time to do other more critical tasks (e.g., supporting and training new employees, observing employees and providing performance, communicating

SUPPORTING AND TRAINING SUPERVISORS • 243

in person with DSPs). A job analysis for FLSs also describes the specific knowledge, skills and attitudes that community human services supervisors need to be effective.

Researchers at the University of Minnesota created a comprehensive job analysis to identify the critical competencies and performance indicators for FLSs working in Minnesota (Hewitt, Larson, O'Nell, Sauer, & Sedlezky, 1998). This analysis was one of the first completed within community human services for the FLS position and is currently the subject of a national validation study (Doljanac, Larson, Hewitt, & Salmi, 2004). This FLS job analysis details the broad competency areas and specific skills required of FLSs (see Figure 1 in the Introduction; for information on how to obtain a copy of this job analysis, refer to the Resources section in this chapter). This job analysis provides insight into the vastly varied roles and responsibilities of FLSs. Although not every single supervisor has all of these job duties, most do.

Provide Clear Job Expectations and Descriptions

Organizations need to work hard to let FLSs know exactly what they are expected to do in their jobs. Most job descriptions do not provide sufficient detail for employees to understand everything they need to know or be able to do. Basing job descriptions on a comprehensive job analysis can be helpful in ensuring that employees know what is expected of them. A sample job description for FLSs in community human services appears at the end of this chapter. This sample may not accurately reflect the role and duties of all FLSs, but it can give organizations ideas on what to include in their FLS job descriptions.

In addition to describing exactly what the duties of a position are, organizations should let FLSs know exactly how their competence and skills will be evaluated. Using a job analysis to guide this assessment and evaluation ensures that the assessment and evaluation measure actual FLS job tasks. A sample Front-Line Supervisor Performance Assessment is also provided at the end of this chapter.

Create Balance Between Direct Support and Supervisory Roles

The job analysis results presented in *The Minnesota Frontline Supervisor Competencies and Performance Indicators* (Hewitt et al., 1998) indicate that supervisors have a complex and often difficult job. One of their broad areas of responsibility includes providing direct support to the people who are supported by the organization. Supervisors must demonstrate that they are willing and able to provide direct support. Modeling of excellent direct support skills is essential for FLSs during effective training of DSPs and is valuable in gaining the respect and trust of DSPs and the individuals supported and their family members. At the same time, being able to provide direct support is only 1 of the 14 competency areas mentioned in the job analysis. To expect that supervisors can complete all of their supervisory duties and still provide 20–30 hours per week of direct support across multiple sites is unrealistic. Unfortunately, that is the expectation for far too many FLSs and contributes substantially to their burnout and to turnover rates of 27% (Hewitt, Larson, & Lakin, 2000) in these positions. Organizations can employ several strategies to balance the number of supervisory and direct support hours an FLS works (see Table 11.3).

Table 11.3. Balancing supervisory work with direct support work for front-line supervisors (FLSs)

Be realistic in estimating the percentage of time FLSs need to spend on duties other than providing direct support. Limit the number of routinely required direct support hours to no more than 10–15 per week.

Have a pool of regular, full-time floater employees who can work across multiple sites and fill last-minute vacancies. These positions should be coveted positions within the organization, and, if possible, people who work in these roles should be given an hourly augmentation to their base pay for being willing to put in hours without a predetermined schedule.

Pay FLSs overtime or augment their salaries when they work unscheduled direct support shifts. This will provide an incentive to FLSs to complete their other supervisory duties in any given week so that they can dedicate any time left over to working direct support hours at a higher rate of pay.

Limit Multiple Site Responsibilities

As community human services settings have become more decentralized, the number of smaller community services organizations has dramatically increased. When services were provided in large congregate care settings, all of the employees for which supervisors were responsible worked in the same location during set shifts. Now, more often than not, supervisors guide and direct the work of DSPs working in many locations at many different times of day and days of the week. Obviously, when employees do not work in the same place as the supervisor, the challenges of overseeing these employees are greater. Some DSPs have indicated that they rarely if ever even see their supervisor (Larson, Lakin, & Bruininks, 1998). Many state that the reason they leave their positions is poor or limited supervision.

Certainly the costs associated with delivering effective services and the amount of funding an organization receives to a large extent dictate how organizations distribute supervision responsibilities. But, organizations need to consider certain important factors and can put supports in place to maximize supervisor efficiency and effectiveness, even when supervisors are responsible for multiple sites. Organizations should reduce or limit the number of locations or sites for which a supervisor is responsible. Although there is no magical maximum number of sites, some supervisors and managers have indicated to us in focus groups and training sessions that handling more than two or three sites becomes overwhelming. Capping the number of sites can reduce burnout among supervisors because they spend much less time traveling between sites and thus have more time to spend in person supporting the employees they supervise.

When an FLS is responsible for more than two or three sites, it is important for the organization to do a careful analysis of job duties and create a lead employee position in each site to take on many of the responsibilities that might otherwise be given to the FLS. Some of the job tasks that could be delegated to this lead staff person include

- Scheduling
- Filling open shifts when others are not available
- Arranging transportation
- Scheduling appointments
- Performing site-specific maintenance and upkeep

- Completing paperwork
- Doing specific liaison work and making routine contact with family members and support team members
- Scheduling training
- Reviewing and submitting time cards for payroll

These duties are not involved with direct supervision and can greatly relieve the burden on FLSs, freeing up precious time for them to guide and direct the work of DSPs and evaluate and provide feedback to DSPs on their effectiveness.

In addition to delegating responsibilities and relieving job stress caused by FLSs' having too many duties, organizations can assist FLSs in managing multiple sites or locations in other ways. Although in-person interaction between supervisors and employees is important, supervisors managing multiple sites need efficient ways to connect with all of their employees. Supervisors need technology that makes it convenient to interact several times a week with each employee they supervise so that they can keep in touch between times that they see each other face to face. Organizations need to support the use of internal computer networks and ensure that all employees have access to e-mail. E-mail can be a quick and effective way for supervisors to connect with their employees across locations. Supervisors could also greatly benefit from cellular telephones so that their employees can reach them on the first try. Often employees spend much time trying to track their supervisor down by calling different sites or by calling a pager and waiting for their supervisor to return their call. More immediate and available communication can go a long way in helping DSPs feel connected to and supported by their supervisor. Last, ensuring that supervisors have portable computers is important so that when supervisors move from location to location, they have access to all of their work-related computer files. Often supervisors are forced to be inefficient because they need to handwrite or type documents or need to use a centralized computer.

Offer Incentives for Extra and Unexpected Direct Support Work

Supervisors have to complete many essential tasks and duties, such as scheduling work shifts, providing guidance and support to DSPs, interacting with families, scheduling appointments, and ensuring that staff are trained. Yet, because of high DSP turnover and vacancy rates, supervisors often have to work direct support shifts so that enough staff are on duty providing supervision and support to the people receiving services. In fact, some supervisors report that they often work as many as 20–40 hours of direct support per week. In addition, they spend inordinate amounts of time trying to find staff to fill shifts. Without incentives to work these extra hours, many supervisors burn out.

Often supervisors are salaried employees. They quickly realize that if they were working as a DSP, they would be making much more money for the number of hours that they put in because they would be paid overtime. They also would have far fewer headaches in terms of regular supervisory duties and the hassles that accompany having to fill open shifts. This not only discourages supervisors and causes burnout, it also discourages DSPs from applying for open supervisory positions because they may be unwilling to work long hours without being able to earn overtime pay.

To address this problem, organizations should identify ways to provide incentives to supervisors for the many hours of extra direct support they work. Some organizations pay their supervisors an hourly rate for the hours they work in a direct care role beyond their 40 supervisory hours per week. Other organizations identify other forms of incentives such as offering gift certificates for shifts worked or points to redeem for a weeks' stay at a local inn. The type of incentive is not as important as the acknowledgment that the organization recognizes that the supervisor is working hard and expending extra energy for the betterment of the people supported. We caution organizations not to offer comp time as an incentive for supervisors unless organizations are committed to making it possible for supervisors to use the comp time within 30–60 days. Supervisors often do not have the opportunity to take the time off because of limited staff and numerous vacancies.

Proactively Cultivate a Cadre of New Supervisors

FLS turnover rates average around 27% (Hewitt, Larson, & Lakin, 2000; see Table 1.11 and Chapter 1 for more information on FLS turnover). This means that in any given calendar year more than one fourth of all FLSs who were at a site at the beginning of the year were no longer there at the end of the year. Organizations are constantly looking for new supervisors. The most important ways for organizations to proactively address this need are to find capable and competent people to bring into FLS positions; to support and train these individuals on how to be effective supervisors, preferably before they become supervisors; and to develop mentoring programs and support networks so that FLSs can interact with other FLSs both within and outside of the organization in which they are employed.

Find New Supervisors

Organizations can find new supervisors from within the organization or from outside the organization. Obviously promoting DSPs from within the organization provides opportunities for DSPs to see that they are not in dead-end jobs and that career paths exist for them. The risk with promoting from within is that DSPs may not get sufficient training regarding their roles and responsibilities as FLSs. Often because a DSP has worked for the organization, knows its practices, and has observed supervisors in action, the organization assumes that the DSP will be a good supervisor right away and fails to provide training to support the person's new role. Making the transition from DSP to FLS can also be a challenge for some DSPs because they may end up supervising people who used to be their peers.

To be successful, organizations must anticipate the need for new supervisors and provide leadership development and training opportunities for existing DSPs before an opening occurs. DSPs who are interested in moving into supervisory positions need to know how to be effective supervisors before they take on this role. The more skills training organizations can offer in FLS competency areas, the better prepared promoted DSPs will be in handling the challenges they will face as a new supervisor.

Recruiting new supervisors from outside the organization is sometimes necessary but is less preferable to developing internal candidates. Bringing in new supervisors from outside of the organization can cause existing DSPs to feel as if they have no opportunities and have been overlooked for such positions. Recruiting supervisors from outside requires the new supervisors not only to learn basic supervision skills and job duties but also to learn about the new organization and its policies, procedures, organizational norms, and culture. Sometimes when change is needed in the culture of a specific site or group of sites, however, an external candidate may be a better choice because the person will have less of a negative perception of the organization to overcome.

Whether a new supervisor is developed from within or hired from outside, it is critical to provide a realistic job preview (RJP) regarding that new position before the person makes a decision about the job (see Chapter 3 for more about RJPs). During an RJP for a potential FLS, it is useful to have the person review a very detailed job description or competency list. Some organizations have used *The Minnesota Frontline Supervisor Competencies and Performance Indicators* (Hewitt et al., 1998) for this purpose. Although other information should also be provided (see Chapter 3 for ideas) to a person who is seriously considering a move to an FLS position, *The Minnesota Frontline Supervisor Competencies and Performance Indicators* or a similar version tailored to the organization can be a real eye opener about the nature and extent of FLS responsibilities.

Support and Train New Supervisors

Developing effective supports for new FLSs involves both orientation and socialization activities (see Chapter 5) and skills training activities (see Chapters 6 and 7). Even if a supervisor has worked in another role in the organization, there are enough differences in the roles of DSPs and FLSs that a new orientation is usually helpful. The tasks and routines that are specific to FLS positions should be introduced during the socialization process.

Organizations have many options about how to socialize new supervisors. For example, some organizations put together an orientation checklist that is specific to each job. The checklist asks the new supervisor to review the forms and processes he or she will be expected to use, read specific materials that describe the organization's management culture, and review computer software and templates that are used for the FLS role (e.g., payroll, scheduling, and other management tools). The checklist also identifies the people the new supervisor should meet with to learn about their new role. The orientation checklist may also include such tasks as working with the office manager to order business cards; reading *The New Supervisor: A Guide for the Newly Promoted, Third Edition* (Chapman, 1992); completing an FLS self-assessment and/or self-development plan such as the ones that appear at the end of this chapter; reading the last two reports completed by the previous supervisor on certain topics; and meeting with a human resources staff member to review basic employment laws. The organization may also find it helpful to provide a list of abbreviations and acronyms used by supervisors and managers in the organization, a list of the major projects that the new supervisor is responsible for, and a list of the most important tasks that the person needs to complete each week for his or her first 4 weeks. The FLS orientation checklist that we have used also includes this pointer for each week: "Ask a lot of questions if you need more information."

Develop Mentoring Programs and Support Networks

Peer mentoring programs and other forms of peer support can be helpful to new FLSs. Supervisors have reported that mentoring was one of the strategies that worked best (Larson, Sauer, et al., 1998). Often it is important for new employees to learn from others who are actually doing the same job. Observing others who are already competent can assist in building confidence and support for FLSs. When hiring new FLSs, organizations should partner them with existing FLSs for mentoring and support. See Chapter 8 for more information about developing a mentoring program and important considerations in doing so.

Regardless of whether a supervisor is new to the organization or has been promoted from within, providing transition time and overlap with the current supervisor before the position changes hands can prevent many problems. If that is not possible, it will be critical for the organization to be realistic about the amount of time it will take for the person to learn and be comfortable with his or her new role. During the transition time, providing additional staff support is important. For a supervisor who is new to the sites he or she is responsible for supervising, it will be important to have the person spend several days getting to know the individuals supported and the staff in those sites before taking on the supervision role.

Provide Ongoing Support to Supervisors

Although orientation and training for new supervisors are important, it is also important to provide ongoing support to them while they remain in supervisory roles. Organizations have many options for providing such support; these options are described next.

Give Supervisors Time to Connect and Share

Supervisors need the opportunity to share and connect with one another. In fact, most employees in professional roles need opportunities to network, share stories, and learn from others in similar roles. There are numerous ways in which an organization can provide these types of opportunities to its supervisors (see Table 11.4).

Encourage Cultural Competence

FLSs are expected to provide supervision to people from every imaginable cultural, ethnic, religious, socioeconomic, linguistic, and religious background. As the population of the United States becomes more diverse and as more immigrants begin working in community human services, organizations will continually be broadening the diversity of their employee base. To effectively supervise a diverse group of employees, FLSs need to receive training and develop competencies related to working with diverse groups of people.

Hiring, training, and supporting employees who are new to the United States can provide new challenges to FLSs. Research has indicated that FLSs face certain challenges as they employ, train, and supervise these employees (Sedlezky et al., 2001):
* Differing communication styles
* Gender role differences

Table 11.4. Creating opportunities for front-line supervisors (FLS) to network

Provide at least 30–60 minutes before or after any organizational management meeting for FLSs to share information and network.

Develop and disseminate a list of internal experts on various topics. New supervisors can use this list to find out whom to call with questions on various aspects of their job.

Hold optional brown bag lunches for FLSs that are typically not attended by managers and administrators. Market these lunches as opportunities for FLSs to get together and celebrate their accomplishments and contributions with one another.

Create a chatroom or electronic message board on the organization's computer network or web site for FLSs to check in with one another and share ideas.

Send out a weekly e-mail with tips and strategies to support FLSs. This e-mail should be created by FLSs.

Seek input from FLSs or assign a group of them to develop a networking day to provide development and support specifically to FLSs in the organization.

Have managers establish routine lunch or dinner gatherings for the FLSs they supervise to provide networking and sharing opportunities.

Support an FLS networking group across all of the human services organizations in your community. This offers FLSs in your organization the opportunity to learn new strategies and ideas from other FLSs.

- Different experiences with and understanding of disabilities and disability service provision
- Differing cultural norms regarding work roles and expectations
- Different understandings of home making and other aspects of direct support

Although supervisors identified these differences as being difficult to deal with, these supervisors, over time and with the right support, were able to effectively supervise, support, and capitalize on the unique contributions of people from diverse backgrounds.

Hiring employees from diverse backgrounds brings a number of benefits to the organization. By expanding and effectively supporting this pool of potential DSPs, organizations can reap the rewards of a diversified workplace, such as the following:

- Attracting and retaining talented people, thus reducing the costs associated with recruitment and turnover
- Meeting the needs of diverse consumers
- Using creative and flexible problem solving that comes from different perspectives
- Providing a work environment that is welcoming to all employees

It is important for FLSs to develop an understanding of cultural competence and how to promote cultural competence in themselves, the DSPs they supervise, and their organization. It is impossible for FLSs to escape cultural differences and cultural conflict in their roles as supervisors. Culture can be defined as a "framework that guides and bounds life practices" (Hanson, 2004, p. 4). People acquire early in life their own cultural references and therefore tend to be unaware that many of their daily interactions and decisions are made within that framework. This lack of awareness of one's personal cultural practices becomes a problem when one experiences a difference with someone who does not share the same cultural practices. It is important for FLSs to also understand that there is wide variation of individual behavior within a given culture (Lynch & Hanson, 2004). For example, although European American culture is time conscious and values promptness, there are people within this culture who are not timely, who do not wear watches and are not concerned with the strict keeping of time.

Cross-cultural competence is sometimes viewed as a learning continuum of attitudes and beliefs through which a person progresses. People typically go through a variety of stages as they learn about new cultures. Very few people embrace all cultural differences readily and with complete understanding. But through increased awareness and information about different cultures, people are often able to begin developing cultural competence and embracing diversity. Learning about another culture, integrating this information, and then displaying competence through demonstrated beliefs, actions, and communications are part of an ongoing process. It is important for FLSs to develop an understanding of their own cultural practices and to become aware of the cultural practices of others to avoid misunderstandings and build more comfortable and effective workplaces. Table 11.5 includes some specific skills and competencies regarding cultural competence and working with diverse groups of people.

Set the Organizational Context

In addition to understanding how to influence and work with people from various cultural backgrounds, FLSs also need to understand how their organization does or does not use culturally affirming and responsive services and support, both with supported individuals and with employees. Just as individuals fall along a spectrum of cultural competence, so do organizations. Culturally competent organizations value diversity at all levels of the organization and demonstrate this through policies and practices (e.g., training, hiring, promotions, physical environment). Culturally competent organizations also support and reflect a commitment to understanding, valuing, and utilizing the full potential of each employee and his or her diverse perspectives. An organization bias assessment such as the one that appears at the end of this chapter, may help FLSs determine how culturally competent their organization is.

Table 11.5. Competencies for FLSs regarding cultural competence and diversity

FLSs understand culture and its impact on communication, interactions, and the broader context of the work environment.

FLSs use communication, team building, and conflict resolution strategies in a way that acknowledges and respects diversity.

FLSs implement training strategies that facilitate successful entry of employees who are recent immigrants into the organization and encourage competency building of these employees.

FLSs identify recruitment strategies that promote a diverse workforce and tap unique recruitment sources and opportunities within the community.

FLSs identify and implement strategies to make the interviewing process more culturally competent.

FLSs model culturally competent behavior and serve as change agents for increased cultural competence in the organization.

Adapted from Sedlezky, L., Anderson, L.L., Hewitt, A., O'Nell, S., Sauer, J., Larson, S.A., & Sjoberg, T. (2001). *The power of diversity: Supporting the immigrant workforce* (Facilitator guide and learner guide, pp. A1–A2). Minneapolis: University of Minnesota, Institute on Community Integration, Research and Training Center on Community Living.

Not only do supervisors need to be able to understand how culturally competent their organizations are, but they also need to learn effective strategies for getting an organization to become more culturally competent. FLSs can be instrumental in helping organizations move along the continuum of cultural competence. FLSs can help the whole organization become more culturally competent by observing and communicating how their organization's spoken and unspoken policies and procedures are understood and practiced by all DSPs; by listening to DSPs and gathering their suggestions for improving the organizational climate; and by sharing these ideas with other supervisors, managers, and administrators. A curriculum designed to assist organizations to do this is listed in the Resources section of this chapter.

In the Spotlight: REM-MN

Sherri A. Larson and Howard J. Miller

REM-MN is a for-profit, 35-year-old family-owned organization providing a wide variety of supports throughout Minnesota. REM-MN currently serves more than 30,000 individuals and employs 4,500 staff members. Training and supporting supervisors and managers has been on the front burner at REM-MN since the late 1990s.

REM-MN carries out its mission to create opportunities for people by adhering to its guiding beliefs and philosophy. Within these beliefs is the conviction that a well-trained, motivated, and engaged management and supervision team makes the difference between the provision of quality services and marginal services. In 1996, the organization began to introduce supervisors and managers to Covey's *The Seven Habits of Highly Effective People* (1989). Administrators supported the notion that supervisors and managers had to learn effective leadership skills for the organization to provide quality supports to individuals it served. REM-MN adopted the language of this training and incorporated it into their daily work lives. The training became increasingly focused on leadership skills and less focused on management skills.

In 2000, REM-MN developed a 3-day advanced leadership training that was supported by many of the concepts introduced in the book *First, Break All the Rules: What the World's Greatest Managers Do Differently* (Buckingham & Coffman, 1999). This advanced training emphasized performance-based skills, such as judging work performance, hiring and retaining quality staff, understanding basic employment law, and upholding professional integrity.

Due to restructuring in the organization, a number of additional managers joined the staff in 2001. The training no longer met the needs of the organization as newer and inexperienced managers were overwhelmed by the job tasks and information provided in the training and did not gain the leadership skills that REM-MN had hoped that the training would provide. The advanced leadership training was funneled into a 1-day training session on the intangibles of management and supervision, such as vision and leadership, and a separate orientation program was developed for supervisors and managers.

For the separate supervisor and manager program, training material was placed on CD-ROMs, to be used on laptop computers provided by the organization. The orientation covers becoming an effective leader, developing effective employees, developing effective teams, producing effective outcomes, controlling costs, and maintaining quality at homes. New supervisors and managers complete this program in conjunction with a mentoring program designed to support the further development of skills.

Since the implementation of this new approach to the training and orientation of supervisors and managers, REM-MN has seen a reduction in employment termination lawsuits thanks to the increased competency of supervisors and managers in understanding and applying employment law. There has also been a reduction in overall staff turnover. By offering a balance of soft and hard skills throughout orientation and training, supervisors and managers develop more effective teams, work more effectively with staff, and create better services for consumers.

From Larson, S.A., & Miller, H. (2002). *Supervisors of direct support professionals.* Paper presented at the 2002 Reinventing Quality conference, Chicago.

OVERCOMING IMPLEMENTATION BARRIERS

As with any organizational change, developing a new or improved system to support FLSs requires effort. It is important to involve current managers and supervisors as well as other stakeholders in defining the ideal system for the organization. Probably the biggest challenge is to create the system and actually implement it. It is very easy to get wrapped up in day-to-day crises and to lose track of the importance of making needed system improvements. An examination of the organization's current FLS turnover rate and satisfaction survey results from FLSs can provide some of the motivation for making the difficult changes.

It is also important for organizations to continually focus on what their supervisors need and how to fulfill these needs through improved practices. Often once FLSs are trained and oriented, they are forgotten about until it is time for them to be promoted. Organizations need to find and provide ways to recognize and support all employees, including their FLSs.

QUESTIONS TO PONDER

1. To what extent do supervisors in your organization have clear or unclear role expectations?
2. What competencies does your organization strive to develop in supervisors?
3. What strategies does your organization use to ensure that supervisors are not overburdened with direct support hours when they are unable to find DSPs to work these hours? How does your organization provide support and incentives for supervisors who are working additional hours?
4. How does your organization develop a cadre of effective new supervisors who are prepared to support, recruit, and retain DSPs? How does your organization develop leadership skills in DSPs who are preparing to become FLSs?
5. What opportunities exist within your organization for supervisors to mentor, network, and communicate with other supervisors within your organization? Outside of your organization?
6. Does your organization emphasize the importance of developing culturally competent supervisors?
7. What barriers exist within your organization regarding organizational cultural competence?

8. What other barriers to supporting and training effective supervisors exist within your organization?

CONCLUSION

Solving workforce challenges such as DSP turnover requires a careful examination of the processes used to develop, socialize, orient, train, and support supervisors. Many of the other chapters in this book outline techniques that work with both DSPs and FLSs. This chapter has detailed several additional processes that organizations can use to specifically support FLSs. When applied in a planful way with other techniques, the strategies in this chapter can help reduce supervisor turnover and improve working conditions for every member of the work team, which in turn can lead to improved supports and quality-of-life outcomes for the individuals served by the organization.

RESOURCES

Chapman, E.N. (1992). *The new supervisor: A guide for the newly promoted* (3rd ed.). Menlo Park, CA: Crisp Learning.

This short book introduces supervision to people who have just started or who are considering their first supervisory position. It includes two checklists to help individuals assess their attitudes about supervision roles. It also provides introductory information about the critical skills of discipline, delegation, coaching, and counseling. Designed to be read in 50 minutes, the book concludes with a 25-item true/false quiz that covers the content from the book.

College of Frontline Supervision (http://rtc.umn.edu/cfs)

The College of Frontline Supervision is an on-line training program designed to support FLSs in learning how to be most effective at what they do. New and experienced supervisors, managers, and human resources professionals in human services organizations can use this self-paced curriculum.

Haynes, M.E. (1991). *Stepping up to supervisor* (Rev ed.). Menlo Park, CA: Crisp Learning.

This book provides a bit more detail than *The New Supervisor* (Chapman, 1992) does about the process of becoming a new supervisor. Topics covered include being personally effective (e.g., communicating for understanding, managing your time, dealing with conflict), working with individuals (e.g., providing feedback, evaluating performance, handling discipline), and working with groups (e.g., using the talent in your group, conducting work-group meetings, building an effective team).

Hewitt, A., Larson, S.A., O'Nell, S., Sauer, J., & Sedlezky, L. (1998). *The Minnesota frontline supervisor competencies and performance indicators: A tool for agencies providing community services.* Minneapolis: University of Minnesota, Institute on Community Integration, Research and Training Center on Community Living. (Available from the publisher, 612-624-4512; http://www.rtc.umn.edu/pdf/flsupcom.pdf)

This booklet contains the results of a comprehensive job analysis for community FLSs. It describes the characteristics of a contemporary community support organization; describes the mission, vision, and values that underlie the competencies; and lists 14 broad FLS competency areas, competency statements within each area, and performance indicators for each of these statements.

O'Nell, S., Hewitt, A., Sauer, J., & Larson, S. (2001). *Removing the revolving door: Strategies to address recruitment and retention challenges* (Facilitator guide and learner guide). Minneapolis: University of Minnesota, Institute on Community Integration, Research and Training Center on Community Living. (Available from the publisher, 612-624-4512; http://rtc.umn.edu/wddsp/dol.html)

This curriculum is designed to train FLSs to become active and effective in the recruitment, retention, and training of DSPs. The curriculum covers much of the same content as this book but also provides lesson plans and exercise suggestions for each topic. The modules addresses organizational practices that influence recruitment, retention, and training; the FLS's role in recruitment, retention, training, orientation, and mentoring; recognition and motivation of employees; and selecting and implementing intervention strategies.

Sedlezky, L., Anderson, L.L., Hewitt, A., O'Nell, S., Sauer, J., Larson, S.A., & Sjoberg, T. (2001). *The power of diversity: Supporting the immigrant workforce* (Facilitator guide and learner guide). Minneapolis: University of Minnesota, Institute on Community Integration, Research and Training Center on Community Living. (Available from the publisher, 612-624-4512; http://rtc.umn.edu/wddsp/dol.html)

This curriculum assists FLSs in gaining cultural competency and other knowledge and skills necessary to manage and support a diverse workforce. The modules deal with such topics as understanding diversity; building a cohesive team; orienting and training workers who are recent immigrants; and using recruiting, hiring, and organizational practices that support these workers.

Job Description

Front-Line Supervisor Position, Community Human Services

MINIMAL QUALIFICATIONS
At least 1 year of experience in providing direct support to recipients of community human services. High school degree (or GED), valid driver's license, insurable.

DESIRED QUALIFICATIONS
A 2-year degree or certificate in a human services field. Five years of direct support experience in community human services and some supervisory training and experience.

GENERAL POSITION DESCRIPTION
The front-line supervisor (FLS) is responsible for guiding and directing the work of direct support professionals (DSPs) who work in community settings serving people with disabilities and other human services needs. In addition, the FLS is responsible for ensuring that organizational policies and procedures are implemented correctly and that the individuals who receive community supports live valued and high-quality lives in their communities.

BROAD AREAS OF RESPONSIBILITY
Participating in organizational activities, serving on committees, and communicating the organization's values and principles to others; assisting in recruiting, selecting, and supporting DSPs; providing training and mentoring to new and existing employees; guiding and directing the work of DSPs by setting clear expectations and monitoring progress; recognizing and valuing the skills and input of employees; and developing effective teams.

SPECIFIC JOB DUTIES
Area: Organizational Participation
The competent FLS knows and understands how recruitment and retention issues affect individuals receiving supports, the sites for which he or she is responsible, and the whole organization and effectively participates in organizationwide activities and communicates with others regarding these issues.

Skills and Duties
_____ Knows the actual annual turnover and vacancy rate at the sites for which he or she has direct responsibility and how these compare with rates for the organization as a whole

_____ Knows how to develop and implement a plan for reducing unwanted turnover and vacancies at the sites he or she supervises or across the organization as a whole

_____ Supports other FLSs in understanding and learning about recruitment and retention strategies and why they are important

_____ Monitors turnover, recruitment success, and employee satisfaction and uses the results to improve personnel practices

_____ Identifies necessary resources for individuals served and DSPs and advocates for these resources with managers

Area: Recruitment and Selection
The competent FLS is knowledgeable about a range of effective recruitment and selection strategies and has the skills necessary to find and hire new employees who are appropriate for the job, who can meet the needs of the people they support, and who are likely to stay.

Skills and Duties
_____ Recruits new DSPs by posting announcements about open positions both within the organization and externally in newspapers and on job boards; by encouraging existing staff to recruit potential new hires; and by networking with high schools, technical schools, job centers, welfare-to-work programs, and other sources of potential new hires

_____ Recruits and mentors community volunteers and interns

(continued)

Skills and duties from O'Nell, S., Hewitt, A., Sauer, J., & Larson, S. (2001). *Removing the revolving door: Strategies to address recruitment and retention challenges* (pp. 9–14 of learner guide). Minneapolis: University of Minnesota, Institute on Community Integration, Research and Training Center on Community Living; adapted by permission.

*Note: **This is only a sample of FLS job duties,** as they vary across organizations and sites. The Minnesota Frontline Supervisor Competencies and Performance Indicators* (Hewitt, Larson, O'Nell, Sauer, & Sedlezky, 1998) and other job analysis results can be used to develop a complete list.

_____ Assists in the development of promotional materials for the organization, including newsletters, newspaper articles, brochures, and videos, and maintains contacts with media

_____ Understands the importance and components of a realistic job preview (RJP) in the hiring process and uses RJPs effectively with potential new hires

_____ Schedules and completes interviews with potential new DSPs in collaboration with existing DSPs and individuals supported and their family members

_____ Understands, develops, and uses structured interviews and other methods for making decisions regarding an applicant's suitability to the job and organization

_____ Can articulate the difference between recruitment and selection and the importance of both

_____ Seeks input from other staff and from individuals receiving supports and family members in making hiring decisions

Area: Orientation, Training, and Mentoring

The competent FLS is knowledgeable about formal and informal training, orientation, and mentoring practices that respond to the needs, desires, and interests of new and existing employees.

Skills and Duties

_____ Takes a direct interest in the roles and responsibilities of the DSPs he or she supervises

_____ Coordinates, schedules, and documents DSPs' participation and performance in orientation, in-service training, and other self-directed learning and development

_____ Observes and solicits feedback from staff and supported individuals and their families regarding DSP training needs and desired opportunities for the individuals

_____ Provides orientation and answers questions from new DSPs through a variety of formal and informal instructional and learning activities

_____ Identifies potential trainers and provides resources, coaching, and opportunities for DSP training

_____ Provides mentorship opportunities to new and existing DSPs as needed or desired to promote retention

_____ Understands the purpose of orientation and implements strategies to welcome new DSPs and help them feel comfortable in their new positions

_____ Understands adult learning principles and uses them to effectively train DSPs

_____ Teaches and coaches DSPs in the most effective approaches to achieving direct support competencies

Area: Job Analysis and Performance Appraisal

The competent FLS is knowledgeable about the process of developing accurate job descriptions for DSPs and using them in performance appraisals.

Skills and Duties

_____ Is aware of the _Community Support Skill Standards_ (Taylor, Bradley, & Warren, 1996) and how they can be used in development of job descriptions and performance reviews

_____ Completes DSPs' performance reviews by gathering input from peers, individuals receiving supports and their family members, and organization personnel as required by policy and procedure

_____ Develops and modifies job descriptions as needed

_____ Understands the importance of accurate job descriptions and timely review processes

_____ Provides necessary coaching; constructive feedback, including demonstrating correct performance for DSPs; and, as needed, disciplinary action

Area: Participatory Management and Supervisory Skills

The competent FLS is knowledgeable about his or her management responsibilities and a range of participatory management techniques and is skilled in using strategies that collaboratively involve DSPs in management decisions and promote DSP job growth, promotion, and responsibility.

Skills and Duties

_____ Encourages or nominates DSPs to participate in organizationwide cross-functional teams, committees, or advisory boards

_____ Seeks input from other staff and from individuals supported and their family members in making hiring decisions

_____ Delegates tasks or duties to DSPs as needed (beyond those in their job descriptions) for special events and activities

_____ Seeks DSPs' opinions and input regarding various issues (e.g., program plans, budgets, procedures) and empowers DSPs to make decisions

_____ Attends and actively participates in organization management, planning, and cross-functional work groups

(continued)

Area: Recognition and Employee Motivation

The competent FLS understands the importance of recognition to job satisfaction and is able to match specific recognition techniques to the unique needs of individual DSPs.

Skills and Duties

_____ Effectively communicates with DSPs by listening to their concerns, supporting and encouraging their ideas and work, thanking them for their contributions, and providing positive feedback regarding performance

_____ Recognizes the need for and plans celebrations with DSPs

_____ Treats DSPs as professionals and acknowledges their unique skills and contributions

_____ Effectively uses organizationwide recognition plans, as well as personal ways of acknowledging others for work well done

Area: Team Building and Conflict Management

The competent FLS is proactive in developing and supporting work teams, identifies areas in which his or her work teams are having difficulty, and employs effective team building and conflict management strategies as needed.

Skills and Duties

_____ Facilitates teamwork and positive interactions and attitudes among staff

_____ Provides counseling and support to DSPs when conflicts arise

_____ Provides formal communication to DSPs by using communication log books or memos and by facilitating effective meetings and purposeful interactions

_____ Encourages staff to maintain appropriate boundaries regarding personal and professional issues

_____ Coordinates and facilitates annual, quarterly, and as-needed planning meetings for individuals receiving supports or assists DSP in this process

_____ Supports the coordination and facilitation of staff meetings

_____ Understands that factors such as culture, age, gender, and other life experiences or perspectives may affect communication and helps team members resolve conflicts based on miscommunication due to those and other factors

_____ Welcomes new employees and helps new and existing employees become a well-functioning team

Front-Line Supervisor Performance Assessment

Supervisor name: _____   Date completed: _____   Completed by: _____

Purpose of this tool: This assessment tool is designed to provide the front-line supervisor (FLS) with a clear understanding of his or her performance across a number of critical competence areas. As this FLS's designated supervisor, it is important for you to provide accurate, clear, and specific feedback to the FLS through this evaluation. **This is only a sample.** It includes only 2 of at least 14 needed competency areas; these areas are taken from *The Minnesota Frontline Supervisor Competencies and Performance Indicators* (see Hewitt, Larson, O'Nell, Sauer, & Sedlezky, 1998).

Instructions: Please rate the performance demonstrated by the FLS on each skill statement in each of the competency areas listed. Check the box to the right of the skill statement that most accurately reflects the supervisor's performance (*below expectations, meets expectations, above expectations, or substantially above expectations*, as defined below). If you have not had the opportunity to observe or evaluate a specific skill, check N/A. Then mark the actual performance indicator you used to assess the FLS's performance of the stated skill.

When you meet with the FLS, compare your assessment with the supervisor's self-assessment and discuss any areas in which there is significant difference. Together use the information gathered on each of the assessments to create a development plan for the FLS.

Performance level scale

Below expectations   The supervisor has little to no knowledge of this skill or strategies for implementing it. Improvement is needed.

Meets expectations   The supervisor has some knowledge of this skill and understands the importance of the skill but does not understand how to implement it.

Above expectations   The supervisor has good knowledge of this skill and is usually able to use the skill effectively one the job; however, he or she needs additional information and support in using this skill in new or unfamiliar situations.

Substantially above expectations   The supervisor has superior knowledge of this skill, always uses this skill well, and can deal with almost any related situation effectively.

N/A   There are no opportunities in this setting for the supervisor to practice or demonstrate competence in this skill.

(continued)

From O'Nell, S., Hewitt, A., Sauer, J., & Larson, S. (2001). *Removing the revolving door: Strategies to address recruitment and retention challenges* (pp. 9–14 of learner guide). Minneapolis: University of Minnesota, Institute on Community Integration, Research and Training Center on Community Living; adapted by permission.

Skill statements and performance indicators	Below expectations	Meets expectations	Above expectations	Substantially above	N/A
Competency Area: Participatory Management and Supervisory Skills					
The competent FLS is knowledgeable about his or her management responsibilities and a range of participatory management techniques and is skilled in using strategies that collaboratively involve DSPs input in management decisions and promote DSP job growth, promotion, and responsibility.					
Encourages or nominates DSPs to participate in organizationwide cross-functional teams, committees, or advisory boards ☐ DSPs supervised by this FLS are on cross-functional teams and committees within the organization (e.g., strategic planning, recruitment/retention). ☐ The FLS provides a summary of activities throughout the organization in which DSPs whom he or she supervises were involved (e.g., planning company picnic, human rights committee).					
Seeks input from other staff and from individuals receiving supports and their family members in making hiring decisions ☐ DSPs and individuals receiving supports and their family members report that the FLS has consulted them before making a hiring decision. ☐ Supervisors describe how they incorporate DSP, consumer, and family input into their hiring decision.					
Delegates tasks or duties to DSPs as needed (beyond those in their job descriptions) for special events and activities ☐ DSPs report that the FLS delegates various tasks to them and provides follow-up to ensure that the tasks have been completed. ☐ The FLS demonstrates for the manager his or her system for remembering what tasks have been assigned to various staff members and how he or she follows up to ensure completion.					
Seeks DSPs' opinions and input regarding various issues (e.g., program plans, budgets, procedures) and empowers DSPs to make decisions ☐ The staff meeting agenda and minutes clearly indicate that the FLS has sought DSP opinion, input, and ideas. ☐ DSPs report that the FLS has allowed them to make decisions. ☐ DSPs report that they have had direct involvement in the development of procedures and individual support plans.					

(continued)

Skill statements and performance indicators	Below expectations	Meets expectations	Above expectations	Substantially above	N/A
Attends and actively participates in organization management, planning, and cross-functional work groups					
☐ Manager observes the FLS participating in a cross-functional work group, planning meeting, or management meeting.					
☐ DSPs report that they are included in decision making regarding organization policy and procedures.					
☐ The FLS demonstrates active membership in management meetings, planning meetings, and cross-functional work groups by providing a summary of participation and issues important to the FLS that have evolved out of these meetings.					
Competency Area: Recognition and Employee Motivation					
The competent FLS understands the importance of recognition to job satisfaction and is able to match specific recognition techniques to the unique needs of individual DSPs.					
Effectively communicates with staff by listening to their concerns, supporting and encouraging their needs and work, thanking them for their contributions, and providing positive feedback regarding performance					
☐ DSPs report that the FLS listens to concerns, is approachable regarding issues, and supports their ideas and concerns.					
☐ The manager observes the FLS supporting staff members who have brought issues to the FLS's attention.					
☐ The FLSs provides a copy of written documents such as surveys used to solicit feedback and information from DSPs.					
Recognizes the need for and plans celebrations with DSPs					
☐ DSPs report various celebrations that the FLS has arranged.					
☐ The FLS describes his or her ideas regarding staff celebrations and illustrates several inexpensive examples to the manager.					
Treats DSPs as professionals and acknowledges their unique skills and contributions					
☐ DSPs report that the FLS challenges DSPs by capitalizing on their strengths.					
☐ The FLS reports to the manager the various ways in which he or she has acknowledged specific contributions.					
☐ Staff meeting minutes reflect that the FLS acknowledged individual contributions.					
Effectively uses organizationwide recognition plans, as well as personal ways of acknowledging others for work well done					
☐ Organization expenditure reports indicate that the FLS used an incentive plan					
☐ DSPs indicate to the manager how they have utilized their incentives (e.g., saw a movie with tickets received, purchased items with a gift certificate, went home early to spend time with family).					
☐ The FLS often contributes organization newsletter articles regarding DSP accomplishments.					

Front-Line Supervisor Self-Assessment

Your name: _____   Date completed: _____

Purpose of this tool: This assessment tool is designed to help you as a front-line supervisor (FLS) to identify your current level of skill in recruitment and retention of qualified direct support professionals (DSPs) and to serve as a basis for a self-development plan in these areas. You may also consider having others, such as some of the people you supervise or your supervisor, fill out copies of this form to give a more well-rounded review of your skills. By seeking others' input you will discover not only how well you apply the skill statements listed but also how important others feel these skill statements are to your role as an FLS.

Instructions: Please rate your performance on each skill statement in the tables on the following pages. Check the box to the right of the skill statement that most accurately reflects your performance (*introductory, practicing, proficient, advanced,* or *N/A,* as defined below). In the left-hand columns, please describe how important that skill is in your job duties, using the rating scale below. For example, if the skill is part of your job description and you use it frequently, check *high;* if a skill is not frequently required, check *low.*

Performance level scale

Introductory I have little or no knowledge of this skill or strategies for implementing it.

Practicing I have some knowledge of this skill. I understand the importance of the skill but do not have an understanding of how to implement it.

Proficient I have good knowledge of this skill and am usually able to use this skill effectively on the job; however, I need additional information and support in using this skill in new or unfamiliar situations.

Advanced I have superior knowledge of this skill, always use this skill well, and can deal with almost any related situation effectively.

N/A There is no opportunity in this setting for me to practice or demonstrate competence in this skill.

Job priority level scale

Low This skill is rarely required of me and is not necessary.

Medium This skill is required of me but is not used daily and/or I could get by with not knowing or practicing the skill.

High This skill is extremely necessary to my position. Either I use it almost daily, or it is critical that I have the skill when the job does require it.

(continued)

From O'Nell, S., Hewitt, A., Sauer, J., & Larson, S. (2001). *Removing the revolving door: Strategies to address recruitment and retention challenges* (pp. 9–14 of learner guide). Minneapolis: University of Minnesota, Institute on Community Integration, Research and Training Center on Community Living; adapted by permission.

Note: Many of these skill statements come from *The Minnesota Frontline Supervisor Competencies and Performance Indicators* (Hewitt, Larson, O'Nell, Sauer, & Sedlezky, 1998). See the resources section of this chapter for more information on this publication.

Priority level			Skill statements	Performance level				
High	Medium	Low		Introductory	Practicing	Proficient	Advanced	N/A
			Competency Area: Organizational Participation					
			The competent FLS knows and understands how recruitment and retention issues affect receiving supports, the sites for which he or she is responsible, and the whole organization and effectively participates in organizationwide activities and communicates with others regarding these issues.					
			Knows the actual annual turnover and vacancy rate at the sites for which he or she has direct responsibility and how these compare with rates for the organization as a whole					
			Knows how to develop and implement a plan for reducing unwanted turnover and vacancies at the sites he or she supervises or across the organization as a whole					
			Supports other FLSs in understanding and learning about recruitment and retention strategies and why they are important					
			Monitors turnover, recruitment success, and employee satisfaction and uses the results to improve personnel practices					
			Identifies necessary resources for individuals served and DSP and advocates for these resources with managers					
			Competency Area: Recruitment and Selection					
			The competent FLS is knowledgeable about a range of effective recruitment and selection strategies and has the skills necessary to find and hire new employees who are appropriate for the job, who can meet the needs of the people they support, and who are likely to stay.					
			Recruits new DSPs by posting open positions both within the organization and externally in newspapers and on job boards; by encouraging existing staff to recruit potential new hires; and by networking with high schools, technical schools, job centers, welfare-to-work programs, and other sources of potential new hires					
			Recruits and mentors community volunteers and intern students					

(continued)

Priority level			Skill statements	Performance level				
High	Medium	Low		Introductory	Practicing	Proficient	Advanced	N/A
			Assists in the development of promotional materials, including newsletters, newspaper articles, brochures, and videos, and contacts with media					
			Understands the importance and components of a realistic job preview (RJP) in the hiring process and uses RJPs effectively with potential new hires					
			Schedules and completes interviews with potential new DSPs in collaboration with existing DSPs and individuals supported and their family members					
			Understands, develops, and uses structured interviews and other methods for making decisions regarding an applicant's suitability to the job and organization					
			Can articulate the difference between recruitment and selection and importance of both					
			Seeks input from other staff and from individuals receiving supports and family members in making hiring decisions					
			Competency Area: Orientation, Training, and Mentoring					
			The competent FLS is knowledgeable about formal and informal training, orientation, and mentoring practices that respond to the needs, desires, and interests of new and existing employees.					
			Takes a direct interest in the roles and responsibilities of the DSPs he or she supervises					
			Coordinates, schedules, and documents DSPs' participation and performance in orientation, in-service training, and other alternative self-directed learning and development					
			Observes and solicits feedback from staff and supported individuals and their families regarding DSP training needs and desired opportunities					

(continued)

Priority level			Skill statements	Performance level				
High	Medium	Low		Introductory	Practicing	Proficient	Advanced	N/A
			Provides orientation and answers questions from new DSPs through a variety of formal and informal instructional and learning activities					
			Identifies potential trainers and provides resources, coaching, and opportunities for DSP training					
			Provides mentorship opportunities to new and existing DSPs as needed or desired to promote retention					
			Understands the purpose of orientation and implements strategies to welcome new DSPs and help them feel comfortable in their new positions					
			Understands adult learning principles and uses them to effectively train DSPs					
			Teaches and coaches DSPs in the most effective approaches to achieving direct support competencies					

Competency Area: Job Analysis and Performance Appraisal

The competent FLS is knowledgeable about the process of developing accurate job descriptions for DSPs and using them in performance appraisals.

Priority level			Skill statements	Performance level				
High	Medium	Low		Introductory	Practicing	Proficient	Advanced	N/A
			Is aware of the *Community Support Skill Standards* (Taylor, Bradley, & Warren, 1996) and how they can be used in development of job descriptions and performance reviews					
			Completes DSPs' performance reviews by gathering input from peers, individuals receiving supports and their family members, and organization personnel as required by policy and procedure					
			Develops and modifies job descriptions as needed					
			Understands the importance of accurate job descriptions and timely review processes					
			Provides necessary coaching; constructive feedback, including demonstrating correct performance for DSPs; and, as needed, disciplinary action					

(continued)

High	Medium	Low	Skill statements	Introductory	Practicing	Proficient	Advanced	N/A
			Competency Area: Participatory Management and Supervisory Skills					
			The competent FLS is knowledgeable about his or her management responsibilities and a range of participatory management techniques and is skilled in using strategies that collaboratively involve DSPs in management decisions and promote DSP job growth, promotion, and responsibility.					
			Encourages or nominates DSP to participate in organizationwide cross-functional teams, committees, or advisory boards					
			Seeks input from other staff and from individuals supported and their family members in making hiring decisions					
			Delegates tasks or duties to DSPs as needed (beyond those in their job descriptions) for special events and activities					
			Seeks DSPs' opinions and input regarding various issues (e.g., program plans, budgets, procedures) and empowers DSPs to make decisions					
			Attends and actively participates in organization management, planning, and cross-functional work groups					
			Competency Area: Recognition and Employee Motivation					
			The competent FLS understands the importance of recognition to job satisfaction and is able to match specific recognition techniques to the unique needs of individual DSPs.					
			Effectively communicates with DSPs by listening to their concerns, supporting and encouraging their ideas and work, thanking them for their contributions, and providing positive feedback regarding performance					
			Recognizes the need for and plans celebrations with DSPs					
			Treats DSP as professionals and acknowledges their unique skills and contributions					
			Effectively uses organizationwide recognition plans, as well as personal ways of acknowledging others for work well done					

(continued)

Priority level			Skill statements	Performance level				
High	Medium	Low		Introductory	Practicing	Proficient	Advanced	N/A
			Competency Area: Team Building and Conflict Management					
			The competent FLS is proactive in developing and supporting work teams, identifies areas in which his or her work teams are having difficulty, and employs effective team building and conflict management strategies as needed.					
			Facilitates teamwork and positive interactions and attitudes among staff					
			Provides counseling and support to DSPs when conflicts arise					
			Provides formal communication to DSPs through communication log books or memos and by facilitating effective meeting and purposeful interactions					
			Encourages staff to maintain appropriate boundaries regarding personal and professional issues					
			Coordinates and facilitates annual, quarterly, and as-needed planning meetings for individuals receiving supports or assists DSPs in this process					
			Supports the coordination and facilitation of staff meetings					
			Understands that factors such as culture, age, gender, and other life experiences or perspectives may affect communication and helps team members resolve conflicts based on miscommunication due to those and other factors					
			Welcomes new employees and helps new and existing employees become a well-functioning team					

Front-Line Supervisor Self-Development Plan
for Recruitment and Retention

Name: _____   Date: _____

1. List the two competency areas from your Front-Line Supervisor Self-Assessment which had the most skill statements listed as high priorities and low performance levels. These are your most critical and immediate needs.

   a.

   b.

2. Identify where these skills are taught (what training units or modules will be most helpful in learning about these skills).

3. Create goal statements (what you want to accomplish) regarding these critical need areas:

During training	In the next 3–6 months

4. List four specific steps that you can take to meet your goal statements:

During training	In the next 3–6 months

From O'Nell, S., Hewitt, A., Sauer, J., & Larson, S. (2001). *Removing the revolving door: Strategies to address recruitment and retention challenges* (p. 15 of learner guide). Minneapolis: University of Minnesota, Institute on Community Integration, Research and Training Center on Community Living; adapted by permission.

Organizational Bias Assessment

Does your organization . . .	Yes	No	Don't know
1. Welcome and accept all employees regardless of cultural, ethnic, socioeconomic, religious, or linguistic background?			
2. Ensure that all staff members are given equal opportunity to voice their concerns and comment about the workplace with no repercussions?			
3. Ensure that meetings are not dominated by one particular point of view?			
4. Respond to concerns and comments about the work environment in a respectful and timely manner?			
5. Openly disapprove of any ethnic, racial, religious, sexual, or other demeaning slur or joke in the workplace?			
6. Encourage and respect interaction between people of diverse backgrounds in meetings and/or in the everyday work environment?			
7. Allow variety in dress and grooming?			
8. Recognize and respect different religious and ethnic holidays in terms of release time for employees, program planning, and food for public and staff events?			
9. Demonstrate flexibility with and provide support to staff who have limited English language skills?			
10. Offer training on multicultural topics to all staff members?			
11. Seek to diversify its staff, administration, and board of directors, by actively recruiting people of diverse cultures, races, abilities, and gender?			
12. Have a written commitment to diversity in its mission statement, bylaws, and policies?			

From Texas Association of Museums. (n.d.) *A survey for management.* Retrieved from http://www.io.com/~tam/multicultural/management.html; adapted by permission.

IV

ASSESSING PROBLEMS AND DESIGNING SOLUTIONS

12

CREATING ORGANIZATIONAL CHANGE INITIATIVES

ELIZABETH LIGHTFOOT, AMY S. HEWITT, AND JOHN K. SAUER

Since the late 1970s, there has been a fundamental paradigm shift in service provision for people with intellectual disabilities. The shift from institution-based services to consumer-driven supports represents a great leap forward for inclusion and self-determination for people with intellectual disabilities and other supported individuals. It also represents a call to change for organizations that have traditionally provided services. Along with this change has come significant challenge in relation to personnel. Not only are organizations forced to reconsider service paradigms, but they are also faced with severe challenges in creating a workforce that understands, promotes, and has the necessary knowledge, skills, and attitudes (KSAs) to provide supports in this new paradigm. As community human services organizations strive to address workforce challenges, it is important for them to select and implement interventions that not only improve workforce outcomes but also advance inclusion and self-determination for the people they support. This chapter will provide an overview of the changing context of service provision, typical organizational responses to the changes, common types of resistance to organizational change and effective strategies for organizational change.

TARGETED FRONT-LINE SUPERVISOR COMPETENCIES

Primary Skills

Front-line supervisors (FLSs) understand and implement current state licensing rules and regulations and organization policies and practices and protect the rights of supported individuals.

FLSs write, review, and update policies and procedures in response to licensing reviews, changes in rules and regulations, and needs of individuals receiving supports.

FLSs solicit the input of individuals receiving supports and their families as well as follow federal and state rules and laws in the development of organization policies and procedures.

UNDERSTANDING THE PROBLEM

The changing environment in which organizations provide direct support requires organizations to fundamentally change and restructure the way they provide services. There have been enormous shifts in since the late 1960s in how people with intellectual disabilities live and receive services. And, until the 1980s, most people with intellectual disabilities had to reside in institutions in order to receive educational and habilitative services (Kiracofe, 1994). The passage of the Education for All Handicapped Children Act of 1975 (PL 94-142) changed this dynamic because it offered children with disabilities a free appropriate public education without requiring them to leave their parents' homes. During the 1980s, community-based services evolved as organizations developed group homes or large congregate care settings where people lived; day treatment sites or sheltered employment sites for people to spend their days; and special recreation opportunities for social activities. Since then, the field has been moving toward providing community supports that people with intellectual disabilities themselves choose and control. The advent of person-centered planning approaches has assisted in supporting individuals to make choices about how they want to live their lives. In unprecedented numbers, people with disabilities are now living in (and sometimes owning) their own homes in the community; working at real jobs for real wages; and participating in a wide range of community activities, from athletics to the arts.

Although this new approach to supporting people with intellectual disabilities signifies great opportunities for individuals and organizations, it requires enormous changes in both program design and the organizational culture of community human services organizations. It also requires new ideas about and approaches to personnel issues within these organizations. Studies on organizational change often describe the difficulties and barriers that organizations face when changing. Some of the most commonly documented sources of resistance to organizational change include 1) employees' perceptions of or past experience with change, 2) fear of the unknown, 3) an organizational climate of mistrust, 4) fear of failure, 5) concerns about job security, 6) peer pressure, and 7) fears about disruption of organizational culture. Studies of human services organizations shifting from institution- to community-based services have highlighted similar barriers.

Organizational development consultant William Bridges (1991) noted that resistance is sometimes mistaken as fear of change, when really the resistance reflects a fear of loss. As Bridges explained, the most common types of losses that employees fear are security (no longer being in control), competence (not knowing what to do and feeling embarrassed), relationships (losing contact with favorite team members or other people), sense of direction (clouded mission and confusion), and territory (uncertain feeling of work space and job assignments). In addition, Bridges described the stages that individual employees go through during an organizational change process: denial (e.g., saying "Things were good before," feeling stunned, rationalizing, refusing to hear information), resistance (e.g., expressing anger, feeling loss and hurt, blaming others, getting sick, doubting self), exploration (e.g., seeing possibilities, experiencing chaos, having unfocused work, clarifying goals, learning new skills), and commitment (e.g., having a clear vision, using teamwork and collaboration, finding balance). So, leaders and top management of community human services organizations must pay close attention to and provide the necessary supports for their employees to ease their transition through any organizational changes, such as moving from a service-based residential program to a person-centered, choice-based, program that supports self-determination for individuals receiving support. As workforce interventions are selected, their impact on the overall mission of the organization and on the provision of person-centered supports should be kept in mind.

RESEARCH SUPPORT FOR SOLUTIONS

Organizational Change Models

Consultants and academics have created numerous models to explain how organizational change works. Some of the most prominent approaches are described here.

Classic Three-Step Model

The classic three-step model of organizational change, developed by Lewin (1951), still makes sense today. The first step is *unfreezing*, or creating an organizational climate ready for change by developing a sense of urgency, providing organizational vision, and attending to possible resistance to change. The second step is *changing*, in which the organization undergoes this change. In this stage, the organization's employees learn new information and develop new operating models and/or new concepts and values. The third step is *refreezing*, or institutionalizing the change. In this stage employees try out this new change and make any necessary adaptations. Positive reinforcement for this change is crucial during this stage. Many models of organizational change are based on these three steps.

Strategic Planning

Strategic planning involves an organizationwide attempt to identify the strategic direction (mission and vision) of the organization and to devise plans and time lines for moving in this direction. Numerous consultants have used and advocated strategic planning, but John Bryson (1988) has designed the most well-known model. In general, strategic planning entails first articulating the vision and mission or the organization. Next comes analysis of the external environment, including the general economy, funding sources, trends in services, and demographic characteristics, and the internal environment, including the strengths, capacity, and limitations of the organization. The organization then sets specific goals, determines measurable objectives for each goal, and devises an action plan to reach each objective. At each step in the strategic planning process, the organization must stay focused and committed to its strategic direction, that is, its mission. For example, an organization that provides residential services could decide that its mission will be "to provide supports to individuals to allow them to live where they desire in the community." This mission would then be the basis for all future decisions about the organization's goals, objectives, and actions. Strategic planning is most effective when people throughout the entire organization participate in the process.

Reengineering

A relatively new approach to organizational change is reengineering, also known as business process reengineering. Reengineering is often equated with radically redesigning an organization, rather than letting existing processes dictate what the future looks like for the organization. Reengineering usually focuses on redesigning the structures and processes governing how work gets completed within the organization (Davenport, 1993). The organization pays close attention to reevaluating what the customer or client views as the end product or outcome of the organization and rethinks how it can achieve this end product. Reengineering calls for structural and cultural change across all aspects of an organization and typically is designed in a top-down manner in which the executive leaders of an organization initiate and take the lead role in designing, implementing, and evaluating a systems change effort. The leadership team then involves the top management and mid-level managers, who, in turn, engage the FLSs and direct support professionals (DSPs).

Total Quality Management

In contrast to reengineering, the total quality management (TQM) or quality improvement model to organizational change involves more gradual changes to an organization's processes. TQM starts from how an organization is currently functioning and makes incremental changes in the organization's processes and outcomes. TQM calls for participation among all levels of employees and other stakeholders but is usually implemented within smaller subsections of an organization, such as at the unit level. The focus in implementing TQM is for the organization to consistently meet or exceed the demands of the customers or clients. Typically, quality improvement initiatives use statistical controls or other evaluative measures to ensure that the organization is meeting the customer's or client's needs.

Large-Scale Systems Change

Another kind of organizational change is large-scale systems change. This model, advocated by Bunker and Alban (1997), contends that involving the entire system in which the organization functions, including people both internal and external to the organization, is an effective method for organizational change. At the broadest holistic level, for a human services organization the entire system could involve the organization's staff, including the executive director, other managers, FLSs, and DSPs; consumers of the services, including individuals receiving supports and their family members; and other external concerned parties, including service coordinators, advocates, and government agency personnel. Other, less holistic large-scale systems change processes may be limited to change within an organization. In this case the entire system might include representatives from all departments, staff members working in various positions, and individuals receiving supports and their families. In large-scale systems change, all of these individuals work closely together in creating organizational change. Echoing what research has documented, Bunker and Alban (1997) suggested that the large-scale approach is effective because it includes all of the stakeholders affected by the change and shares information with these relevant parties and because change occurs more rapidly when all are involved.

Summary of Organizational Change Models

In many community human services organizations, visions and strategies for change are developed in a top-down fashion. Often executives, leaders, and sometimes boards of directors create a new mission or vision or institute new processes for an organization and completely exclude supervisors, DSPs, individuals receiving supports and their families, and other key stakeholders from these changes. Thus, many of the key stakeholders often have little commitment to achieving the vision. Conversely, when all of the key stakeholders are invited and encouraged to participate in the process, a common understanding emerges of the organization's strengths and weaknesses. The organization can use this information to create a preferred future that includes individual, small-group, and large-group ideas and can begin to move toward this vision. The lack of motivation, disillusion, mistrust, and unaligned direction in the first scenario is replaced with excitement, synergy, hope, and community in the second.

There are many approaches to achieving organizational change other than the ones just discussed, and many successful organizational change efforts have entailed activities that fit so closely with an organization's context that they cannot be distilled into a general model. However, there are similarities in many of these models. For example, most of the change models are linear and seem like a broader expansion of Lewin's (1951) basic three-step model. Other commonalities include the focus on deliberate planning of the proposed change; the inclusion of many people within the change process; the strong focus on goals, missions, or organizational outcomes as important in the change; and some attempt to cement the change in the culture of the organization. The next section illustrates how these theoretical models have proved helpful for community organizations in moving from institution-based to person-centered services. In the following section, the lessons learned from those examples are applied to strategies to achieve change in the area of workforce development.

Organization Conversion

There is a growing body of research on the ingredients of successful organizational change in shifting from institution-based services to person-centered, consumer-directed community supports that promote choice, respect, and recommended practice. Most of this research is in the form of case studies or small surveys of organizations making transformations, including studies of organizations converting from running sheltered workshops to providing supported employment (Albin, Rhodes, & Mank, 1994; Butterworth & Fesko, 1999; Garner, 1998; Magis-Agosta, 1994; Marrone, Hoff, & Gold, 1999; Murphy & Rogan, 1995); studies of organizations making the conversion from facility-sponsored services to supported living (Hulgin, 1996); and larger systems change strategies (Moseley, 1999). From these studies, eight common themes emerge as keys for successful organization change within consumer support organizations:

- Planned change strategy
- Action orientation
- Clear vision
- Strong leadership
- Organizational culture

- Continual staff support
- Flexible organizational structure
- Strong coalitions

Planned Change Strategy

The first common theme that emerges as key for making the change from facility-based services to providing person-centered supports is having a *planned change strategy*. A planned change can be either an incremental change, in which an organization slowly changes the way it provides services (e.g., phasing out several components of a sheltered workshop over 10 years and allowing people to continue to work during that time), or a radical change, in which an organization completely changes the way it provides services in one fell swoop (e.g., literally closing the doors of a sheltered workshop on a selected date). Although the organizational change literature shows that there is a growing need for more radical change because of today's turbulent environment, research in developmental disabilities has not shown that one type of planned change strategy is clearly superior.

Several case studies have shown that a rapid change strategy can be successful in making the conversion. For example, Garner (1998) described how a rapid change at Buffalo River Services in Tennessee worked better than a gradual change would have. Garner noted that this rapid change would not have been successful if it had not been planned in detail. Marrone et al.'s (1999) study of two organizations converting to supported employment from facility-based services also suggest that rapid change is essential to organizational change. Dufresne and Laux (1994) also asserted that holistic change is superior to incremental change. And, Hulgin's (1996) case study of an organization that switched from running group homes to offering supported living services discussed one of the main benefits of rapid change: avoiding the problems inherent in managing dual systems. One of the most noted barriers in incremental change is the problems organizations face when they are providing both facility-based services and person-driven services (Albin et al., 1994; Moseley, 1999; Walker, 2000).

Other studies, however, have shown that incremental change can be a successful strategy for some organizations. For example, Butterworth and Fesko's (1999) study of 10 organizations shifting from facility-based employment to community employment reported that organizations can be successful using either an incremental approach or a rapid approach to conversion. Similarly, Moseley's (1999) survey of 14 project coordinators implementing self-determination projects found that a variety of different types of implementation strategies were successful, ranging from a one-person-at-a-time incremental approach (implementing self-determination practices with one supported individual at a time), to a pilot program incremental approach (selecting a small group of individuals to try new self-determination approaches), to a radical system-wide reorganization (implementing new self-determination approaches throughout the organization for all individuals supported at the same time). The unifying theme of all successful change strategies is that all of them were planned.

Action Orientation

Although developing a strategy for change is important, the literature also shows that too much planning can inhibit change (Dufresne & Laux, 1994; Marrone et al., 1999;

Murphy & Rogan, 1995). An organization must be *action oriented*, whether it is planning a rapid, radical change or a more incremental change. If too much time is spent on planning, an organization may lose the momentum for change (Murphy & Rogan, 1995). This sense of urgency present in an action orientation can be the catalyst for an organization to successfully change from a facility-based to person-centered framework (Dufresne & Laux, 1994). If an organization has an action orientation, it will also begin making changes before actually knowing the details of how the change will proceed. Experiencing the change gives staff, managers, and individuals receiving supports the opportunity to see how the change actually works in practice and thus provides a framework for them to understand the proposed changes and move toward systematic change (Magis-Agosta, 1994; Marrone et al., 1999).

Clear Vision

A *clear vision* has been a key factor in organizational change in almost every documented study of organization conversion (Albin et al., 1994; Butterworth & Fesko, 1999; Dufresne & Laux, 1994; Garner, 1998; Magis-Agosta, 1994; Marrone, et al., 1999; Murphy & Rogan, 1995; Racino, 1994). An organization in need of change must recognize that the services that it has been providing have not been the best for the individuals whom it supports (Garner, 1998; Magis-Agosta, 1994) and must craft a unifying vision that clearly defines how the organization will provide services that are person centered. Developing a new vision requires an organization to understand the philosophical base of person-centered services and community supports and probably also to continually reexamine organizational values and practices (Walker, 2000). Albin et al.'s (1994) study of eight organizations pursuing changing from facility-based services to community supported employment programs found that the main challenges to pursuing changeover were conflicts in vision, values, and assumptions about community services.

Strong Leadership and Powerful Champions

An organization needs *strong leadership* to gain the momentum for change and to consistently articulate the organization's vision. This leadership is often found in the executive director or other top organization staff. Studies of organization conversion, however, have found that organizations making successful change have multiple leaders at both top and middle-level positions (Butterworth & Fesko, 1999). Although some organizations are lucky enough to have natural leaders who are committed to the change process (Garner, 1998), all organizations can benefit from developing leaders who are well versed in the dynamics of organizational change (Racino, 1994).

Organizational Culture

One of the key roles of a leader is to facilitate an *organizational culture* that is not only mission driven but also supportive of organizational change. A primary component includes generating in the organization support for risk taking by staff members (Butterworth & Fesko, 1999; Dufresne & Laux, 1994; Garner, 1998; Magis-Agosta, 1994). Because person-centered supports are radically different from the way staff may be used to providing services, staff need the freedom to take risks even though their actions might not always be successful. This focus on risk-taking can be tied to a culture of a learning organization (Racino, 1994).

Continual Staff Support

Another key element to the change process is to provide *continual support* to staff members who will actually be implementing these changes. When an organization shifts its values, the staff within the organization may have to make difficult, internal changes to their own values and perceptions of people with disabilities (Garner, 1998; Racino, 1994). Organization leadership and managers need to support staff members in making these changes and, in particular, should emphasize that although the organization had been providing well-intentioned services to supported individuals were well intentioned, these services were not resulting in the best outcomes (Racino, 1994). Organizations that have been successful in making changes have invested heavily in staff training (Albin et al., 1994; Moseley, 1999; Murphy & Rogan, 1995), consistently marketed the vision to the staff (Marrone et al., 1999), celebrated staff success (Magis-Agosta, 1994; Murphy & Rogan, 1995), and placed a strong emphasis on valuing the contributions of staff (Racino, 1994). One organization found support groups to be successful in helping staff process the changes they were making (Albin et al., 1994).

Flexible Organizational Structure

Along with culture, an organization's structure must also be *flexible* and conducive to organizational change. Some studies have noted that the change to person-centered supports works best when an organization flattens its hierarchy, removing levels of middle management (Garner, 1998; Murphy & Rogan, 1995). Although this may be ideal, an organization should at least allow for the flexibility that is required in providing person-driven rather than facility-based supports (Dufresne & Laux, 1994). This flexibility is needed in all aspects of the organization, from the establishment of staff procedures to the development of creative funding sources (Walker, 2000). Finding funds for person-driven supports can be a major difficulty (Albin et al., 1994; Moseley, 1999). An organization must focus unwaveringly on the quality of the lives of people, rather than on policies, organizational structure, regulations, or funding (Racino, 1994). In summary, although an organization must be flexible in all its efforts to make successful broad organizational change (e.g., moving from facility-based services to community-based supports), maintaining a focus on the quality of supported individuals' lives always needs to be paramount.

Strong Coalitions

Although strong leadership and an organization that promotes change are clearly important, organizations act within a broader external environment. Organizations must build *strong coalitions* that include all the people who the organizational change will affect. These coalitions must include key stakeholders both internal and external to the organization. These stakeholders include self-advocates, family members, DSPs, organization management, state organization staff, other community organizations, and other people in the community. A sense of joint commitment to community inclusion by all people involved in the change allows for better collaboration. Walker's (2000) case study of an organization changing from facility-based services to providing supported employment and supported living services found that focusing on relationships among all members of the coalition was essential for successful organizational change. Moseley (1999) found that involving these key stakeholders from the beginning is essential.

STRATEGIES FOR RESPONDING TO THE PROBLEM

Just as organizations have had to undergo substantial change to move from promoting institutional or organization-focused services to providing person-centered and consumer-directed services, substantial change will also be needed to successfully revamp practices related to workforce development in organizations. Most community human services organizations have a hierarchical, top-down process for handling personnel policies and practices. People in direct support roles are not empowered and are rarely involved in determining effective strategies to improve retention and recruitment challenges. Organizations also tend to still use personnel practices that worked when they provided institutional or provider-focused services but that likely do not work as they offer person-centered, consumer-directed supports. As organizations consider changes specifically to address workforce development challenges, incorporating the characteristics of effective change processes into the plan is also helpful. Table 12.1 provides suggestions for how the key elements of the change process can be applied to workforce development issues faced by community human services organizations.

Use a Three-Step Model of Change

Lewin's (1951) three-step model of change can be applied to change related to personnel issues within organizations. To create a climate for change by stressing the urgency of the problem (*unfreezing*), organization leadership can provide quantitative data on turnover rates, vacancy rates, maltreatment reports, overtime usage, and increased costs related to staffing problems. These data are often a powerful tool (see Chapter 13 for strategies on gathering this critical data). Setting goals and establishing a vision, also parts of *unfreezing*, might be as simple as stating, "Turnover rates will be reduced to 20%, and there will be no more than a 5% vacancy rate across all DSP positions in the organization by year end." Or, the vision for change could connect consumer satisfaction and outcomes to direct support workforce issues (e.g., "Develop a competent, stable workforce to meet the expectations and desired outcomes of the people we support so that they live personally enriched and satisfying lives"). What is important is that there be a common vision that everyone is working toward. One of the best ways to ensure this and to anticipate resistance to change is to involve all key stakeholders affected by the change in determining the vision and the change process.

In Lewin's (1951) model, once the vision is set and key people know what needs to be done and are on board, the change has to occur. Often organizations get stuck during this *changing* phase. They are good at planning what should be done but not so good at doing it. Numerous steps can make up a process for change in workforce development. This book provides many examples of the interventions and actions that can be taken and that have been proven effective. During the changing phase it is criti-

Table 12.1.   Important elements of effective change processes and their application to workforce development change

Element	Application
Planned change strategy	Determine at the onset whether or not the change will be radical or incremental. Radical change addresses an entire organization and occurs at once. Incremental change occurs slowly over time. For example, changes in wage scales or benefits would typically involve radical change, whereas developing a mentoring program might be more effective if incremental.
Action orientation	Select specific interventions and strategies. Identify the key players, resources, action steps, benchmarks, and time lines up front. Identify a task master to ensure that time lines are met and that action occurs. Hold people accountable for progress in carrying forward the plan of action. For example, if an organization is going to decrease vacancy rates through the use of a recruitment bonus, specific steps and benchmarks should be determined; a deadline for implementation should be set; and the key players for this action should be identified, understand their roles, and commit to the time lines.
Clear vision	All stakeholders must understand the scope and nature of the problem being addressed and the need for change. Everyone has to have a clear vision of how the change process will improve the situation or address the problem in an effective way. For example, at one organization everyone involved agrees that staff turnover rates of 80% have a negative effect on people who receive services. Everyone at the organization also agrees that reducing turnover to 40% will improve the lives of the people supported. Without a common vision, change could be stymied.
Strong leadership and powerful champions	Every change process needs strong leaders and powerful champions for whom the need for the change permeates their focus. Usually leadership only is thought of as the top executives and managers of an organization, and most of the time that is true. However, FLSs and direct support professionals (DSPs) are often overlooked as leaders and champions of change. When changes are being made to better the work lives of DSPs, DSPs are often the best leaders. In addition, self-advocates or family members may be strong leaders on these topics. Often these people's lives have been affected by turnover, vacancies, and poorly trained employees.
Organizational culture	Creating an organizational climate that expects and supports change and risk taking is important. One effective retention strategy is to empower direct support professionals to have decision-making authority and control over program-based issues. Often this is difficult for organization leaders because they perceive a loss of control or increased risk. Creating supports for such a change throughout the organization are imperative to the successful implementation of the change.
Continual staff support	All staff involved in a change process need ongoing support. Provide opportunities for them to discuss their fears, frustrations, experiences, and ideas. For example, if a new on-line training program for DSPs is implemented at an organization, it is important to provide support to employees as they enter the learning environment and as they figure out how to use their new knowledge in a real work environment. Also, it is important to check in with employees to ensure that they are doing okay and have the needed resources. It is also important to support organization trainers who take on new roles, such as moving from providing classroom training to acting as on-site coach.
Flexible organizational structure	One strategy to address workforce challenges is to move to self-managed teams. In this case, it is essential for an organization to be willing to flatten out its structure and modify many practices.
Strong coalitions	Often, it is hard to think about change outside of the environment where the change needs to occur. One thing is certain; the overwhelming majority of community human services organizations have similar problems. Partnering and building coalitions are critical. For example, any wage or incentive initiative requires strong coalitions because usually legislative action is required. Other interventions require or benefit from coalitions as well. For example, developing new training programs for supervisors or DSPs would be enhanced and more cost-effective if done in collaboration with other organizations in a given community.

cal not to underestimate the need for information and training. Everyone in the organization will need to understand what is occurring and why. Supervisors clearly must learn new ways of supporting, coaching, and mentoring employees; boards of directors must learn how to reprioritize budgets and priorities; administrators and managers will have to learn strategies to effectively reach out and include the opinions, knowledge, and skills of DSPs in all aspects of the organization's operation; human resources personnel may need to learn new methods of gathering and using data; and DSPs may need to learn new ways of supporting and embracing new employees. A learning environment must be established in order for the change process to be effective.

Measure Effectiveness of the Changes Made

It is equally important to measure the effectiveness of changes related to workforce development. Chapter 13 provides an overview of how to measure whether specific interventions actually worked. Organizations periodically and systematically need to evaluate the extent to which their identified mission or vision has been achieved and, if it has not, to refine its policies or procedures. Change processes, when effective, never end. Organizations must be prepared to continually change.

Chapters 13 and 14 provide more specific information about how to make organizational change to address specific workforce development issues. The models mentioned in this chapter may be helpful for organizations that are implementing a new intervention based on the strategies suggested in this book.

In the Spotlight: Lutheran Social Service of Minnesota — Organizational Change

Sheryl A. Larson

Lutheran Social Service of Minnesota (LSS) participated in a multiyear incremental change process to create a set of values within its Home and Community Living Services (HCLS) division that would support the emerging LSS mission and vision and guide the work of DSPs as well as the policy, program, and human resources development work of supervisors, managers, and administrators. A secondary outcome of this change initiative was to include FLSs and DSPs in the development of the core values for HCLS as well as in the creation and implementation of other interventions related to specific workforce challenges such as recruitment, retention, orientation, and training. LSS hoped to achieve higher staff satisfaction and productivity and the alignment among employees, policies, and practices about the mission, vision, and values of the organization and the HCLS division.

LSS, the largest private, nonprofit social service organization in Minnesota, has central offices in St. Paul and more than 200 statewide program sites. The HCLS division provides residential services to 685 individuals with intellectual or developmental disabilities in 100 settings, including small group homes (about half of which are funded by Medicaid's Home and Community-Based Services Waiver program and half of which are funded by the intermediate care facility for persons with mental retardation program), parental homes, semi-independent living services settings, and small homes supporting individuals who are senior citizens. During the year 2000, the HCLS division employed 681 DSPs and 26 FLSs.

Beginning in January 2000, the HCLS leadership team decided to focus its attention on specific workforce development interventions to address challenges in recruitment, retention, and training. To guide their work in these areas, the team decided to

- Create a set of core HCLS values that would support the emerging LSS mission and vision as well as guide the work of direct support and managerial staff
- Include supervisors and DSPs in the development of these core values and any specific future interventions to address specific workforce challenges

Over the next several months, the team agreed to create a number of opportunities for all staff to help craft the set of core values:

- A values discussion at regularly scheduled meetings of supervisors and managers
- A process at each LSS residential site in the state to engage FLSs and DSPs in dialogues to provide input into the development of core HCLS values
- A values synthesis workshop (composed of four DSPs, five FLSs, three program managers, and three organization administrators) that reviewed the ideas from each site; created a first draft of core values; brainstormed strategies for incorporating the core values into the structures, practices, policies, and processes within HCLS; and explored how the core values could influence and shape individual supports and strengthen relationships among all key stakeholders.

The outcomes of these major events were exciting. Staff members were affirmed for their bright ideas and intensity of participation, and the leadership team was acknowledged for its planning, insight, and inclusive behavior.

Following these change events, the HCLS leadership team reviewed all the values material and developed five core values: *respect, personal development, individual support, safety,* and *sound management.* With the assistance of staff and administrators at different levels in the organization, the core values were incorporated into the fabric of HCLS structure and practice in the following ways: They were highlighted in realistic job previews and the process for hiring DSPs, inserted in orientation packets and discussed with new employees, described in the HCLS brochure of programs and services, infused into job descriptions and training curricula, and reviewed in the policy and procedures manual.

The development of core values and inclusion of staff in their creation was not always easy. The HCLS leadership team, DSPs, FLSs, and managers faced a number of struggles throughout this 18-month organizational process, including the following:

- The difficulty of maintaining employee motivation, focus, and momentum over a long period of time
- The barriers related to scheduling, costs, and time of DSPs and FLSs to participate in all change events
- The struggle of communicating the importance of staff input; deciding what feedback to use in changing products, practices, and policies; and informing all participants about the results of each change event

These and other struggles were acknowledged and dealt with by the leadership team, supervisors, and managers through meetings and discussions during the lengthy change process.

Creating a set of core values to guide HCLS and including DSPs and FLSs in more of HCLS's ongoing processes and operations was a success. The HCLS core values, in tandem with the LSS mission and vision, are now integrated in the organization's most important components. The HCLS core values do influence and guide employee actions. Also, HCLS continues to include DSPs and FLSs in operational teams, in planning groups, in workforce development activities and processes, and in external professional associations.

OVERCOMING IMPLEMENTATION BARRIERS

There are several potential barriers for an organization considering broad organizational change initiatives such as creating or revising the organization's mission, vision, and values. Some of the potential barriers include the following:

- The organization's leadership group and other employees may not believe that the initiative will have a direct and lasting impact on employee or organizational behavior or outcomes. This belief could become a self-fulfilling prophecy, meaning the change would never become a part of the culture of the organization or be used for direction-setting activities, for guiding problem solving or decision making, or for creating milestones for the organization's history and accomplishments.

    To deal with this type of barrier, the organization can 1) focus on consistent and continual communication between top leadership and managers and between managers, FLSs, and DSPs about the purpose, intended outcomes, support, and milestone accomplishments of the change initiative; 2) survey all employee groups about their thoughts, feelings, hopes, concerns, and suggestions related to the change effort's success and challenges and share the results with everyone; and 3) respond to employee's concerns, issues, and suggestions quickly, respectfully, and directly throughout the change process.

- There may be a lack of strong and ongoing support for developing and periodically renewing, improving, and revising the change initiative. This lack of change would lead to the certain and quiet death of the change initiative.

    To deal with this potential obstacle, top leadership as well as managers and supervisors must include discussions about the change initiative at every opportunity, from board of director's meetings, to work unit discussions, to policy and procedure development and revisions, to providing training sessions. Through these ongoing support activities, the organization's leadership and all employees will understand that the change effort is really going to take place.

- The organization may not have the time or money to creatively and openly develop and incorporate the change initiative.

    To respond to this potential barrier, the organization's leadership must make a strong commitment, both during initial discussions about the change effort and throughout the life of the change initiative, that the money and time to successfully implement a change process will be available.

- The organization may not incorporate the change initiative into all of its operations, practices, processes, and ongoing improvements. Or, the change may not be accepted and implemented by all the organization's units or sites.

    One key strategy to deal with this possible challenge is to design, implement, evaluate, and revise a pilot program with a few work units who embrace the change. Successful units should share the results of the change process with other units that initially were reluctant to become involved with the change process.

    The following list identifies how certain beliefs and actions of an organization's leadership group related to empowering employees to participate in a change initiative can have dire consequences within the organization:

- A leadership team that does not embrace employee empowerment, believe strongly in staff participation in decision making, or share information equally and quickly to all employees will not be successful in the long term. Employees will not support the change effort, will not volunteer to pilot test the change, and will only share the bad news about the change process and outcomes.

- The leadership team that attempts to provide employees with only a sense of involvement rather than encouraging and supporting their meaningful and authentic participation will fail to garner the powerful ideas and strong enthusiasm of the employees. Token involvement is easily detected and will hinder the true empowerment of employees. For example, an organization that uses a survey instrument to gather employee ideas about a change process and then does not use or share the survey results risks complaints from the employees and resistance to engaging in the change process.

- Organization leaders that do not inform employees about an upcoming change project, inform staff adequately about the goals and intended outcomes of the project; or update staff about the progress, accomplishments, and problems of the project isolate employees from the change initiative and prevent them from sharing their ideas, volunteering their time, and embracing the change process.

All of these barriers may seem daunting, but knowing about them and incorporating strategies into the change process to deal directly with them can reduce the likelihood that they will stymie the change effort.

QUESTIONS TO PONDER

1. What are some of the strategies that can be developed and nurtured for incorporating your organization's mission, vision, and core values into the fabric and culture of that organization? How can one evaluate whether they have been incorporated?

2. How would you plan a large-scale systems change intervention for your organization? What potential barriers could you foresee encountering?

3. How can the principles of organizational change described in this chapter be incorporated into a plan to address recruitment, retention, or training challenges in your organization?

4. What is the meaning of *empowerment* as it is applied within your organization, to managers and supervisors, to work teams, to DSPs, and to the individuals receiving supports and their families?

5. How can supported individuals and their families be meaningfully included in your organization's change processes?

6. In the private sector, organizational change can ultimately be measured through the bottom line, or profit. If your organization is a nonprofit or public organization, how can your organization evaluate whether an organizational change effort was successful?

CONCLUSION

Selecting, designing, and implementing strategies to address workforce challenges in community human services organizations require substantial organizational change.

This chapter provides an overview of the dynamics of organizational change and describes several processes that can be used during organizational change to increase the likelihood that the workforce interventions described in this book will be successfully implemented. It will be helpful to keep these processes in mind while reading Chapters 13 and 14, which provide much more detailed information about the form organizational change might take to address specific workforce challenges. These chapters focus specifically on how to assess current status and evaluate change and on how to design a plan to guide the change process, respectively. Readers may wish to return to this chapter as they are designing their interventions for reminders about factors to consider in the process.

RESOURCES

Bunker, B., & Alban, B. (1997). *Large group interventions: Engaging the whole system for rapid change.* San Francisco: Jossey-Bass.

This book provides detailed descriptions about 12 different types of large-scale organizational interventions to bring about change. These methodologies deliberately involve a critical mass of the people affected by the change, both internally and externally, to make organizational change happen.

Carter, L., Giber, D., & Goldsmith, M. (2002). *Best practices in organizational development and change.* Indianapolis: Pfeiffer.

This state-of-the-art resource presents the most important ideas and effective strategies from experts and top companies in the field. Comprehensive in scope, this book addresses the five most important organization and human resource development topics—organization development and change, leadership development, recruitment and retention, performance management, and coaching and mentoring—and offers a practical framework for design, implementation, and evaluation.

Cummings, T., & Worlsey, C. (2000). *Essentials of organization development and change.* Cincinnati, OH: South-Western Publishing. (Streamlined version of textbook)
Cummings, T., & Worlsey, C. (2001). *Organization development and change* (7th ed.). Cincinnati, OH: South-Western Publishing. (Textbook)

These texts are comprehensive overviews of organizational development and change. Although mostly geared for students, the texts provide a very detailed analysis. Either would be ideal as a desk reference for an organization that is contemplating organizational change.

Kotter, J. (1996). *Leading change.* Cambridge, MA: Harvard Business School Press.

This practical resource for change was written by an expert in business leadership. It describes an eight-step process for organizational change that can be applicable to most organizations and places a key emphasis on changing behavior.

13

ASSESSING AND EVALUATING WORKFORCE CHALLENGES

SHERYL A. LARSON, TRACI L. LALIBERTE, AND PATRICIA SALMI

This chapter offers practical suggestions for organizations about how to develop an internal system for monitoring interventions that address workforce challenges. Formulas for measuring turnover rates and tenure are provided. Strategies to assess recruitment success, staff satisfaction, organizational commitment, and other important outcomes are described. In addition, feedback processes such as surveys, focus groups, and exit interviews are discussed. Sample surveys are provided at the end of the chapter.

This chapter focuses on the assessment of the problem or challenge in an organization, the selection and use of measurement methods or tools, and the evaluation of progress and success. Other stages are briefly outlined to put the assessment information into context. Chapter 14 provides a more in-depth look at identifying a *specific* problem or challenge and choosing the appropriate intervention with which to address that problem.

TARGETED FRONT-LINE SUPERVISOR COMPETENCIES

The front-line supervisor (FLS) competencies addressed in this chapter focus on personnel management skills needed to assess turnover rates, vacancy rates, consumer satisfaction and other workforce outcomes. Effective FLSs and managers assess challenges and evaluate organizational outcomes on an ongoing basis using the following skills:

Primary Skills

FLSs know the annual turnover and vacancy rate at the sites for which they have direct responsibility and how these compare with those for the organization as a whole.

FLSs monitor turnover, recruitment success, and employee satisfaction and use the results to improve personnel practices.

Related Skills

FLSs maintain regular contacts with and follow up with supported individuals and their family members and support team members regarding complaints and issues.

FLSs design, implement, and develop strategies to address issues identified in satisfaction surveys completed by individuals receiving supports.

UNDERSTANDING THE PROBLEM

Throughout this book, a host of strategies for addressing recruitment, retention, and training challenges have been described. To devise effective solutions for those challenges, it is essential to have a clear idea of the size and nature of the problems in the organization. Organizations need a baseline of their current status so that they can measure whether a selected intervention actually makes a difference. A study examining more than 1,000 organizations found that those that conduct formal job analyses for all positions and administer attitude surveys on a regular basis have lower turnover, improved productivity, and improved corporate financial performance (Huselid, 1995). Up-to-date information about organizational outcomes such as turnover rates, employee satisfaction, and satisfaction of supported individuals is also important when an organization is deciding which problem is most important to address first. Furthermore, assessment and evaluation are important to identify strategies that work and those that do not so that changes can be made.

RESEARCH SUPPORT FOR SOLUTIONS

Many research textbooks describe how to use a scientific approach to identify challenge, create a hypothesis or idea about why the challenge exists, and test whether the hypothesis or idea is true (e.g., Cook & Campbell, 1990; Cozby, 2004). This chapter describes this approach in nontechnical terms to assist FLSs to use the scientific method to define a problem, select a solution, and test whether the solution has actually remedied workforce challenges. In this chapter, we describe tools that supervisors can use in this process, along with the scientific or research support for these tools.

STRATEGIES FOR RESPONDING TO THE PROBLEM

Jeremy's Story: A Template for Assessment and Evaluation

The following fictional example of Jeremy and his approach to his weight problem is a simplified version of an approach that organizations can use when assessing workforce issues.

Identify the Problem

Like many other Americans, on New Year's Day, Jeremy made several resolutions to improve his life. One of his challenges was to identify the problem he most wanted to overcome. This decision was complicated because he had several top priorities. He wanted to improve his health by stopping smoking, limiting his alcohol intake, and reducing his weight. He also wanted to spend more time with his children. He realized, however, that trying to make all of those changes at once could be a formula for failure. So he decided his top priority would be to lose some weight.

In this illustration, Jeremy first identified his concerns and then selected the issue most important to him. It is much the same in an organization. To make positive changes, an organization must first identify the most important problems or issues and then prioritize them, selecting the most pressing issue(s) first.

Assess the Problem

Once Jeremy has decided that the goal of weight loss was most important, several related questions remain. For example, how does Jeremy know that he should lose weight? His doctor once told him that losing some weight would help to reduce his risk of diabetes. Also, Jeremy struggles to walk up a flight of stairs at his current weight but remembers that he didn't have any trouble with that when he was thinner. In addition, Jeremy realizes that none of his clothes fit anymore. Weight problems, like workforce challenges, can present themselves in a variety of ways. It is important to use available information to assess whether a problem exists.

Once a problem has been identified, the next step is to determine the size of the problem, and, if possible, its cause. In this example, Jeremy needs to find out how much a person of his age and height should weigh so that he can compare that with his weight. After weighing himself, Jeremy learns that he is 20 pounds heavier than the recommended weight for a person of his age and height. This information provides Jeremy with a starting point, or a baseline measurement.

Another part of the assessment is to determine why Jeremy weighs too much. He needs to learn where the problem *really* lies. Is he eating too much at each meal? Is he skipping breakfast, then gulping down a huge lunch because he is too hungry to worry about how much he is eating? Is he eating the wrong types of food (e.g., too much fast food)? Does he need to add exercise to his life? It would be foolish to make an action plan without knowing the real cause of the problem. Jeremy needs to gather information about his behavior and then compare his information with some kind of standard. Keeping a food diary would help Jeremy compute his calorie intake for the day. Then he could use a reference book or his doctor's guidelines to see how many calories he should be eating for a person of his age and height. If his total calorie intake exceeds the recommendations for his age and height, he would know that reducing the amount he eats or changing the types of foods he is eating could help him come closer to the standard. If he learns that his calorie intake is about right compared with the standard, however, he would have to continue his assessment to identify another possible reason for his problem. Perhaps tracking how many minutes per week spent exercising would reveal that Jeremy is not getting the recommended amount of exercise.

Through these assessments, Jeremy learns that although his food intake is reasonable, he only gets 15 minutes of exercise per week. His doctor recommended at least 20 minutes per day, 4 or more days per week. Jeremy's assessment has helped him identify the likely source of the problem and also points to a possible solution. The lesson is the same when evaluating problems in the workplace. A thoughtful assessment helps in identifying the extent of the problem, and it can often highlight a problem's causes or related issues. If the goal is to make a plan and take action, a solid understanding of the nature of the problem is critical to the process. Without this understanding, an organization could end up spinning its wheels while going nowhere.

Select an Intervention Strategy

Having identified and assessed the problem, Jeremy's next step is to decide on a plan of action and to implement that plan. He has to choose one intervention from the many available (e.g., working out at a gym, buying a treadmill, swimming at the local pool). After considering the alternatives, he decides to start walking with his children for 20 minutes, 4 days per week. This plan meets his need to increase his exercise and his desire to spend more time with his children. Similarly, in addressing workforce challenges, an intervention that is appropriate for the problem should be identified and put into place. Chapter 14 describes how to select interventions based on assessment results and reviews available alternatives.

Set Goals and Measure Progress

Jeremy set a goal of losing 20 pounds in 6 months by increasing his level of exercise. In measuring his progress, Jeremy has several choices. As mentioned earlier, Jeremy took a baseline measurement by weighing himself at the beginning of his weight-loss plan. He could also have chosen to measure various points on his body or to assess his body fat percentage. Regardless of the method, Jeremy needs to use the same tool or assessment procedure again to accurately measure any change. By weighing himself, Jeremy would obtain accurate information on the impact of his weight loss program. If he were to use the same measurement tool in the beginning and at the end, he would accurately measure his progress. Likewise, when creating workforce interventions, accurate assessment of the impact of the intervention can best be made by obtaining a baseline measurement and then assessing progress by utilizing the same measurement tool used in the initial evaluation.

Establish a Time Frame for the Intervention

The next step for Jeremy is to decide how and when to evaluate his progress. His initial assessment of the problem (i.e., his baseline) revealed that he was 20 pounds heavier than his desired goal. To evaluate his progress, he needs to measure any change in weight as a result of implementing the intervention. He needs to decide the time frame in which the evaluation would occur.

Jeremy has several choices with regard to time frames. In the beginning, Jeremy chose walking for his exercise (intervention) because he was overweight (identified problem). He decided to walk four times per week for 6 months (duration). Finally, Jeremy decided to check his progress by using a scale to weigh himself (measurement tool). However, he has one last decision before implementing his weight-loss program: He has to decide the points in time that he wants to weigh himself to check his progress. He could weigh himself once at the beginning and once at the end of the 6 months. He also could weigh himself once per week. Sometimes people want to measure at the beginning, in the middle, and at the end, so he could weigh himself at the beginning, at the third month, and at the end of the 6 months. He could also track his progress in a journal or on a wall chart.

Jeremy realizes that weighing himself on a scale every day is not an efficient use of his time. Instead, he decided to weigh himself once each week. It is the same in the workplace. The measurement intervals should be an effective use of the time, money, and energy available for the project. For an evaluation that is shorter in duration, one baseline measurement and one final measurement are adequate. In a longer time frame, additional measurement times may be useful.

Evaluate Success

Jeremy began to exercise with his children. He soon found that they grew bored walking the same route each day, so to keep things interesting he had his children select the route two days a week and he selected the route twice a week. He and the children put a check on the calendar each day they walked and celebrated each week's progress by renting a video. After 3 months, Jeremy and his children averaged 3.5 walks per week and Jeremy had lost 10 pounds. He had developed plans to walk at an enclosed shopping mall on days when the weather was bad. By the end of 6 months, Jeremy had achieved his goal of losing 20 pounds and felt more energetic. Similarly, when organizations implement interventions to reduce turnover or improve training, evaluating whether those interventions were successful is critical. By checking success against the goal at least twice during the intervention, an organization can learn whether the intervention is working.

Summary of the Assessment and Evaluation Steps

Although workforce issues can often appear more complicated and involved than a weight problem, by following the six steps just outlined, dealing with such workforce issues should be no more intimidating or difficult than Jeremy's task. In the following sections, the six assessment and evaluation steps are discussed as they relate to creating change within a community human services organization.

Identify the Problem

Organizations often realize that problems exist in their workplace. Often, however, there are so many concerns or problems that knowing which problem to address first can be difficult. Or, the opposite might be true: The organization understands that problems exist but is not quite sure what those problems are. Often, the issues or concerns center on recruitment and retention of staff members. Although an organization might understand the overall issues, it may have difficulty pinpointing the exact nature of the problem. Common workforce challenges include the following:

- The organization has trouble finding new employees.
- The organization has difficulty recruiting individuals who are qualified to take open positions.
- New hires quit in the first 6 months.
- Supervisors are constantly hiring new employees to replace those who have left the organization.
- New employees are unsure of their job roles and functions.
- The organization has difficulty finding training that addresses the skills needed by employees.
- Training does not produce desired results. Employees display poor skills on the job.
- Co-workers do not get along.
- There is conflict between employees and supervisors or managers.
- Employees complain about the supervision they get.
- Supervisors report being overwhelmed or do not know how to do their job.

- Employees have morale problems.
- Long-term employees are dissatisfied with or quit their jobs.
- Employees have inadequate wages or benefits.

The first step in assessing challenges and evaluating outcomes is to select a specific challenge as the focus. The challenges just listed are common, but an organization may identify another problem that is not on this list at all.

Assess the Problem

Knowing that a challenge exists is often one of the easiest parts of developing an organizational change plan. Challenges are the things that make daily work life unpleasant. Once a specific challenge has been identified, the next step is to assess the nature and extent of challenge. Questions to answer include:

- What exactly is the challenge?
- How big is the challenge?
- How costly is the challenge?
- Whom does the challenge affect the most?

To accurately and efficiently assess the problem or challenge, an organization needs to select a measurement tool or method. This measurement tool will also be used to evaluate progress at the end of the determined time frame. (See Table 13.1 for a summary of common workforce challenges and ways of assessing them.) Both general and specific assessments may be needed. General assessments are those that all organizations should conduct at least annually.

Baselines are critical to defining the challenge. Baseline information can be from numerical data, such as turnover, vacancy, and tenure rates. Calculating these rates both at the organizational level and at the program or work-site level offers the most complete picture of the organization's experiences with staff transitions. It is also important to gather other types of baseline information. For example, if high turnover is one of the organization's biggest challenges, then turnover, tenure, and vacancy rates are of great importance, but so are exit interviews, which can provide a clearer picture of why people are leaving. Calculating the costs of turnover in terms of money and service outcomes is crucial. Depending on the challenge identified, the organization may benefit from consumer satisfaction surveys, which can identify training needs; job satisfaction surveys, which can identify challenges related to benefits, the work environment, or supervision; and/or an assessment of recruitment sources and strategies, which can identify challenges in finding qualified applicants. Baseline data can be compared with benchmarks in other organizations (see Chapter 1) and with future annual assessments for the organization itself.

The baseline assessment should allow the organization to determine if the challenge is systemwide or if it is isolated to particular work sites or programs. For example, if higher staff turnover or lower staff satisfaction exists only at some locations, a targeted intervention can be more effective than an intervention designed to blanket the entire organization. It may be that certain supervisors have not been adequately trained for their roles and responsibilities or that a new program has just begun at one location.

Although identifying the challenge is important, it is easy to fall into the trap of spending an inordinate amount of time and resources studying a challenge without

Table 13.1. Workforce challenges and ways to assess them

Challenge	Assessment measures or strategies
The organization has trouble finding new employees.	Recruitment source cost–benefit analysis Vacancy rate
The organization has difficulties recruiting qualified individuals.	Wage–benefit market analysis Recruitment and hiring bonuses effectiveness analysis
New hires quit in the first 6 months. Supervisors are constantly hiring new employees to replace those who have left the organization.	Turnover (crude separation rate) Tenure of current employees (stayers) Tenure of leavers Staff satisfaction survey (given to new hires) New staff survey Exit interview or survey
New employees are unsure of their job roles and functions.	Job description review Training needs assessment (given to new hires)
The organization has difficulty finding training that addresses the skills needed by employees.	Training needs assessment Inventory of current employee skills
Training does not produce desired results. Employees display poor skills on the job.	Competency assessments Performance review system
Co-workers do not get along.	Teamwork assessment Staff satisfaction survey Personality or style inventories
There is conflict between employees and supervisors or managers. Employees complain about the supervision they get. Supervisors report being overwhelmed or do not know how to do their job.	Teamwork assessment Supervisor training needs assessment Staff satisfaction survey
Employees have morale problems.	Staff satisfaction survey Organizational commitment survey
Long-term staff are dissatisfied with or quit their jobs.	Staff satisfaction survey (given to current and exiting long-term employees) Training needs assessment Exit interviews or survey

taking any action to address the challenge. To avoid that trap, an organization should determine ahead of time what information will be sought, develop an assessment strategy, and stick to the assessment plans and time lines.

Specific follow-up assessments should be used as needed to measure the nature, extent, and cause of specific problems. In many cases, instruments or strategies to conduct the suggested specific assessment are included in earlier chapters of this book. There are many types of specialized workforce assessment strategies, including standardized and nonstandardized instruments and other methods. The following sections describe general and specialized workforce development assessments and review factors that should be considered in selecting or constructing an assessment.

General Workforce Development Assessments

Several general workforce development assessments can help organizations understand the challenges they face and select the most important challenge for intervention. To establish a baseline, the organization must clearly define who is considered a direct support professional (DSP) and how employees performing job duties at multiple sites or only serving as on-call staff will be counted. It is most efficient if the same definitions and formulas are used for all sites and services within the organization. Retention outcomes for DSPs and FLSs that should be assessed at baseline and again at least annually include the following:

- Turnover (crude separation rate)
- Average tenure (months worked)
- Percentage of employees who leave the organization within 6 months of hire (tenure category of leavers)
- Vacancy rate (percentage of positions vacant on a specific day)

A worksheet with the formulas (Larson, 1998) used in these general computations appears at the end of this chapter.

It is also helpful to identify factors that may have contributed to the turnover rates in each site and differences in rates between sites. This includes gathering information about positive and negative job features and describing any changes or special incentives that may have influenced retention outcomes. Establishing benchmark rates and goals for each site and for the organization as a whole allows the organization to identify sites that are struggling and those that are doing well. This can help the organization to identify why recruitment outcomes differ across sites. It is also important to understand turnover differences in new programs, in programs located in areas of low unemployment, in programs in which wages compare unfavorably with prevailing wages, and so forth.

Turnover (Crude Separation Rate)

Turnover, or the crude separation rate, compares the number of people who left the organization with the number of positions in a site or organization. Turnover is a convenient measure to compare retention problems across sites within an organization or to compare an organization with similar organizations. To compute the turnover rate in a particular site, count the number of employees in a particular category (e.g., DSPs) who left the site within the last 12 months (leavers). Include all employees who left or were fired, even if they quit 1 day after hire or were hired but never showed up for work. Divide this number by the average number employees at the site during the last 12 months. Multiply the result by 100. The resulting percentage (which may be higher than 100%) reflects the annual crude separation rate for that category of employees. Turnover rates can be compared across sites and can be computed for the organization as a whole.

$$\text{turnover (crude separation rate)} = \frac{\text{number of leavers in 12 months at the site (or in the organization)}}{\text{number of positions at the site (or in the organization)}} \times 100$$

Tenure of Current Employees (Stayers)

Tenure is the length of time an employee has worked for a site or organization. Like turnover, the average tenure of current employees (stayers) is a convenient measure to use when comparing retention success for sites within an organization or to compare an organization's retention success with that of similar organizations. To compute the average tenure of employees at a particular site (or across the organization), list each employee and the number of months the employee has been at the site (or in the organization). Add the number of months for all employees at the site (or in the organization) and divide by the total number of employees. This calculation will yield the average number of months employees have been at the site (or in the organization). Be sure to consider the number of months the site has been open when evaluating the results. Separate computations for DSPs and FLSs can be helpful.

$$\text{average tenure of current employees (stayers)} = \frac{\substack{\text{total number of months' tenure} \\ \text{of current staff at the site} \\ \text{(or in the organization)}}}{\substack{\text{total number of staff at the site} \\ \text{(or in the organization)}}}$$

Tenure of Leavers

To compute the average tenure of people who have left a site or an organization (leavers), identify all those who have left in the past 12 months. For each leaver, note the total number of months worked before leaving the organization. Sum the number of months for all leavers and divide the total by the number of leavers. The result is the average number of months the employees stayed before leaving. Computing separate numbers for employees who were fired and for those who left voluntarily may be helpful. Be sure to include all employees who were paid for 1 or more hours of work, even those who quit after training or in their first few days.

$$\text{average tenure of leavers} = \frac{\text{total number of months worked by all leavers}}{\text{total number of leavers}}$$

Tenure Category (of Stayers or Leavers)

Examining tenure in more detail can assist organizations in targeting interventions for employees at a particular point in their career. For example, when many leavers have 6 or fewer months' tenure, intervention strategies that address the needs of recruits and new hires are likely to be helpful, such as using inside sources to refer potential new hires, providing realistic job previews (RJPs; see Chapter 3), providing mentoring for new hires, and conducting socialization interventions. Conversely, if most of the leavers have 2 or more years' tenure, a different set of interventions may be called for. To compute tenure category, divide stayers or leavers into groups according to the number of months they have worked. For example, to compute the proportion of leavers who stayed less than 6 months, count the number of employees who left in the last 12 months. Then count the number of employees in that group who stayed less than 6 months before leaving. Divide this number by the total number of employees who left, and multiply the result by 100.

$$\text{percentage of leavers with less than 6 months' tenure} = \frac{\substack{\text{total number of} \\ \text{leavers with less than} \\ \text{6 months' tenure}}}{\text{total number of leavers}} \times 100$$

This same formula can be used to compute the proportion of leavers who stayed 6–12 months, 12–24 months, and more than 2 years.

Vacancy Rates

One indicator of recruitment problems at a particular site or within the organization is the vacancy rate. Vacancies can occur either because a new position was created or because an existing employee left the position. The vacancy rate can be computed by counting the number of positions at the site (or in the organization) that are currently funded but that have no specific person assigned (the organization may be using overtime or substitutes to cover these open positions). Divide that number by the total number of positions at the site (or organization), and multiply the result by 100.

$$\text{vacancy rate} = \frac{\text{total number of funded positions currently vacant}}{\text{total number of funded positions}} \times 100$$

Table 13.2. Direct support professionals (DSPs) in Site A (11/1/03–10/31/04)

Staff member (ID or initials)	Status	Hire date	Compute date	Months at site	Tenure group
1. JB	Stayer	11/6/99	10/31/04	60	13+
2. MC	Stayer	8/12/00	11/31/04	45	13+
3. YX	Stayer	11/30/01	10/31/04	35	13+
4. JM	Stayer	10/3/02	10/31/04	25	13+
5. RJ	Stayer	7/5/03	10/31/04	20	13+
6. AA	Stayer	1/31/04	10/31/04	10	7–12
7. SM	Stayer	6/14/04	10/31/04	5	0–6
8. JW	Stayer	9/5/04	10/31/04	2	0–6
9. JC	Stayer	10/1/04	10/31/04	1	0–6
10.	Vacancy				
Stayer total	10			203	
11. MR	Quit	2/5/02	3/5/04	25	13+
12. PC	Quit	10/2/02	1/2/04	15	13+
13. JN	Fired	11/1/03	6/10/04	8	7–12
14. AP	Quit	4/30/04	9/25/04	5	0–6
15. OT	Quit	6/25/04	9/1/04	2	0–6
Leaver total	5			55	

From O'Nell, S., Hewitt, A., Sauer, J., & Larson, S. (2001). *Removing the revolving door: Strategies to address recruitment and retention challenges* (p. 41 of facilitator guide). Minneapolis: University of Minnesota, Institute on Community Integration, Research and Training Center on Community Living; adapted by permission.

Turnover (crude separation rate)

$$\frac{5 \text{ leavers in the last 12 months}}{10 \text{ funded positions}} \times 100 = 50\% \text{ turnover rate}$$

Average tenure of current employees (stayers)

$$\frac{203 \text{ months}}{9 \text{ stayers}} = 22.6 \text{ months per stayer}$$

Tenure category of stayers

0–6 months $\quad \dfrac{3 \text{ stayers have 0–6 months' tenure}}{9 \text{ total stayers}} \times 100 = 33\% \text{ have 0–6 months' tenure}$

7–12 months $\quad \dfrac{1 \text{ stayer has 7–12 months' tenure}}{9 \text{ total stayers}} \times 100 = 11\% \text{ have 7–12 months' tenure}$

13+ months $\quad \dfrac{5 \text{ stayers have 13+ months' tenure}}{9 \text{ total stayers}} \times 100 = 56\% \text{ have 13+ months' tenure}$

Average tenure of leavers

$$\frac{55 \text{ months}}{5 \text{ leavers}} = 11 \text{ months per leaver}$$

Tenure category of leavers

0–6 months $\quad \dfrac{2 \text{ left with 0–6 months' tenure}}{5 \text{ left during the last 12 months}} \times 100 = 40\% \text{ left in first 6 months}$

7–12 months $\quad \dfrac{1 \text{ left with 7–12 months' tenure}}{5 \text{ left during the last 12 months}} \times 100 = 20\% \text{ left after 7–12 months}$

13+ months $\quad \dfrac{2 \text{ left with more than 12 months' tenure}}{5 \text{ left during the last 12 months}} \times 100 = 40\% \text{ left after 12 months}$

Vacancy rate

$$\frac{1 \text{ funded position is vacant}}{10 \text{ funded positions}} \times 100 = 10\% \text{ vacancy rate}$$

Figure 13.1. Computation summary of turnover, tenure, and vacancy of direct support professionals (DSPs) in Site ABC (11/1/03–10/31/04). (From O'Nell, S., Hewitt, A., Sauer, J., & Larson, S. [2001]. *Removing the revolving door: Strategies to address recruitment and retention challenges* [p. 42 of facilitator guide]. Minneapolis: University of Minnesota, Institute on Community Integration, Research and Training Center on Community Living; adapted by permission. *Source of formulas used as basis for these calculations:* Larson, 1998.)

Examining Retention Outcomes: An Example

The following is an example of how these general retention measures were calculated for one particular site. Table 13.2 shows the information needed to compute the values for the baseline, and Figure 13.1 shows the computations. Included in Table 13.2 are all of the current employees at the site (stayers), positions that have been funded but are currently not filled (vacancies), the employees from this site who have left (leavers), and whether each person who left did so voluntarily or was fired. Data are included for every person who worked at this site in a 12-month period.

Tenure for stayers at the site, recorded in terms of months and rounded to the nearest month, was calculated by using each person's start date and the date the analysis was conducted as the reference points. At the time of the analysis, current employees had been at Site ABC for an average of 22.6 months. Among the stayers, 33% had been at the site for less than 6 months, 11% had been at the site 7–12 months, and 56% had been in the home for more than 1 year.

Employees who left Site ABC during the last 12 months had worked at the site an average of 11 months before quitting. The turnover rate was 50% for the last 12 months. Among the people who left, 40% left in the first 6 months after hire, 20% left 7–12 months after hire, and 40% had been with the home for more than a year before they left. Four of five of the leavers left voluntarily. The fifth was fired (20% of all leavers were fired). The vacancy rate in this home was 10%.

This site has two distinct groups of employees, long-term staff and new hires. Interventions such as RJPs (see Chapter 3) or improved orientation practices (see Chapter 5) designed to reduce the number of employees who leave early in their employment will be helpful. In addition, this organization needs to consider the needs of long-term employees. Perhaps interventions for this group might include enhanced training or career development opportunities (see Chapters 6 and 7). Using other specialized assessments could help the organization to understand these issues more fully and could point to particular intervention strategies.

Specific Workforce Development Assessments

Many different types of workforce assessments can be used to learn more about the specific types of challenges an organization is facing. These assessments can be used periodically to measure the general status or health of an organization or to assess a particular problem that has emerged. Specific assessments include measures of job satisfaction, organizational commitment, leadership, socialization, opinions of exiting employees, skills or competency assessments for employees, and so forth.

One specific assessment that should be used periodically (every 1–2 years) is a survey or assessment of employee job satisfaction. Regular assessments of job satisfaction show how employees feel about their job. Using such indexes over time allows the organization to identify areas of relative weakness within the organizational culture and to monitor changes that might be associated with positive initiatives (e.g., a training program for supervisors) or with changing contextual factors (e.g., decreasing real dollar wages). Another area for ongoing evaluation is the extent to which the expectations of new hires were met during their first few months on the job. The results of such evaluations can be used to improve the information provided to recruits before they are hired.

The Gallup Organization evaluated responses to hundreds of questions obtained from more than 1 million employees on different aspects of the workplace (Buckingham & Coffman, 1999). Buckingham and Coffman identified the top 12 questions that predicted productivity, profit, employee retention, and improved customer service:

- Do I know what is expected of me at work?
- Do I have the materials and equipment I need to do my work right?
- At work, do I have the opportunity to do what I do best every day?
- In the last 7 days, have I received recognition or praise for good work?
- Does my supervisor, or someone at work, seem to care about me as a person?
- Is there someone at work who encourages my development?
- At work, do my opinions seem to count?

- Do the mission and/or purpose of my company make me feel like my work is important?
- Are my co-employees committed to doing quality work?
- Do I have a best friend at work?
- In the last 6 months, have I talked with someone about my progress?
- At work, have I had opportunities to learn and grow? (1999, p. 28)

These questions can help an organization decide what questions to include in a staff satisfaction survey. For further guidance, an organization may want to consult the Minnesota Satisfaction Questionnaire (Griffin & Bateman, 1986; discussed later in this chapter) and the satisfaction survey that appears at the end of this chapter. It includes several of the items just listed, as well as other items that may be helpful.

The following sections describe some existing standardized and nonstandardized assessment instruments that can be used to examine a specific challenge that an organization is dealing with.

Standardized Specific Assessment Instruments

Careful consideration should be given to the type of instrument to be used based on what information the organization hopes to obtain. One type of measurement tool is a *standardized* instrument, which is a survey or a questionnaire that has been tested for validity and reliability.

Validity is the degree to which a measure accurately captures the concept it is intending to measure (Babbie, 1990; Price, 1997). In other words, does the question ask what it is supposed to ask, and how well does it do this? Validity plays an important role in the quality of a question (Price, 1997). *Reliability* looks at the quality of an instrument by examining the extent to which it produces the same results when used repeatedly (Price, 1997). For example, "Did you fill out a report in the last week?" would yield higher reliability than the question "How many times in the last year have you filled out a report?" Most respondents would remember whether they filled out a report for the last week but might struggle to recall the reporting events for the last year and may therefore give different answers on different days or at different times. Validity and reliability can be relatively difficult to establish, which is why many organizations use measurement instruments that are standardized rather than create their own and test them for validity and reliability.

Many standardized instruments have been constructed to measure the workforce challenges mentioned in Table 13.1. Only a few of the thousands of instruments measuring workforce issues and outcomes are profiled here.

Minnesota Satisfaction Questionnaire

The Minnesota Satisfaction Questionnaire (MSQ) is one of three widely accepted measures of job satisfaction (Griffin & Bateman, 1986). The MSQ measures satisfaction with several different aspects of the work environment (Weiss, Dawis, England, & Lofquist, 1967). The short form contains 20 items that measure satisfaction with the present job on a scale of 1 (*very dissatisfied*) to 5 (*very satisfied*). For example, one item asks, "On my present job, this is how I feel about the chance to do things for other people." The MSQ yields three scale scores: intrinsic satisfaction, extrinsic satisfaction, and general satisfaction. Intrinsic satisfaction includes items such as the chance to do things for other people and the chance for a person to do something that makes use of his or her abilities and that focuses on internal factors the person values. Extrinsic satisfaction focuses on items that describe things other people do to recognize a person's value and work, such as the pay for the amount of work the person does. Other standardized assessments of job satisfaction include the Job Description Index (Smith, Kendall, & Hulin, 1969) and the Michigan Measure of Facet Satisfaction (Quinn & Staines, 1979).

Organizational Commitment Questionnaire

Organizational commitment is "the relative strength of an individual's identification with and involvement in a particular organization" (Mowday, Porter, & Steers, 1982, p. 226) and is characterized by a strong belief in and acceptance of the organization's goals and values, a willingness to exert considerable effort for the organization, and a strong desire to maintain membership in the organization. Although several instruments measure organizational commitment, the most commonly used scale is the Organizational Commitment Questionnaire (OCQ; Mowday, Steers, & Porter, 1979). This 15-item scale has been normed on 2,563 employees in nine different occupations, including psychiatric technicians working with people with intellectual disabilities. The items ask employees to rate items on a scale of 1 (*strongly disagree*) to 7 (*strongly agree*). For example, one item states, "I am proud to tell others that I am part of this organization." Several studies document that the OCQ has adequate reliability and validity (e.g., Ferris & Aranya, 1983; Sullivan, 1982).

Leader Behavior Descriptive Questionnaire

The extent to which a supervisor is considerate of the people he or she supervises is a predictor of turnover identified by Michaels and Spector (1982). Perception by the DSPs of their supervisors can be assessed using the Leader Behavior Descriptive Questionnaire (College of Administrative Science, 1957). Respondents rate the frequency that their supervisors engage in specific behaviors on a 5-point Likert scale with 1 meaning *always* and 5 meaning *never*. This instrument rates supervisors on initiating structure and consideration. For example, one of the items is "makes his/her attitudes clear to the group."

Organizational Socialization Scale

A scale by Jones (1986) measures organizational socialization, the manner in which a person new to the job is taught the customary and desirable behavior and perspectives for a particular role within the work setting (Bachelder & Braddock, 1994). Items are rated on a scale of 1 (*strongly disagree*) to 7 (*strongly agree*). For example, one item is "This organization puts all newcomers through the same set of learning experiences."

Nonstandardized Specific Assessment Instruments

Although using a standardized instrument is beneficial for collecting valid and reliable data, it can also be potentially limiting. A standardized instrument may not ask questions or collect data on issues that are important to an organization. Furthermore, there is often a cost associated with using a standardized instrument.

Modifying an existing standardized instrument allows an organization to capture additional information specific to that organization. A modified instrument, however, may not be as valid or reliable as the original standardized version.

If no existing survey is found that fits the organization's needs, a tool may need to be designed. In creating an instrument, validity and reliability are important. Although an organization may choose to test an instrument prior to its actual use, numerous repeat trials will probably not occur. Therefore, it is vital to build an instrument based on carefully thought-out questions. Poorly written questions will yield poor data.

Before designing a survey, the organization should ask, "What do we want to measure?" The organization needs to prepare a clear, detailed statement of the purpose of the survey and the type of information to be obtained. Do one or two key issues such as recruitment and/or retention seem most important? The organization can limit the scope of the survey by addressing the most pressing concerns.

The next step is to construct specific questions. There are two types of questions: open-ended and closed. In open-ended questions respondents provide their own answers to the questions (Babbie, 2001). Responses to open-ended questions must be categorized for analysis. This involves transcribing all of the responses, grouping similar responses together, and naming each group. This is time-consuming and costly (Singleton, Straits, & Straits, 1993). In contrast, closed-ended questions require that respondents select an answer from a list. This type of question is popular in surveys because it can provide greater uniformity of responses and is more easily processed. A disadvantage of this type of question is that it forces the respondent to select an answer that may not be a good fit. In general, response choices should include all possible responses to be expected and should be mutually exclusive; respondents should not feel compelled to select more than one answer for each question (Singleton et al., 1993).

Both open-ended and closed-ended questions should have the following features:

- Questions should be clear and unambiguous. The organization should avoid questions that ask about two things. The use of the word *and* in a question can signal that the designer should take a second look at the question. For example, if respondents are asked to agree or disagree with the statement "DSPs are not paid enough, and the state government should do something about this," it will be difficult to know if they are responding to the statement that DSPs aren't paid enough, the suggestion that states should help increase DSP wages, or both. It might be clearer to ask respondents to disagree or agree with the statement "DSPs aren't paid enough" and then ask them to disagree or agree with the statement "State governments should help increase DSP wages." In addition, the organization should avoid using indefinite words such as *usually, seldom, many, few, here,* and *there,* which can have different meanings to different people (Singleton et al., 1993).
- Questions should be relevant to most respondents. If not, respondents might make up answers on the spot to questions they have never really thought about. Respondents should be able to understand the connection between the questions, the purpose of the survey, and their role as respondents.
- Questions should use vocabulary that is appropriate to the respondents. The words should be understandable and should be culturally relevant and sensitive.
- Questions should be short. Respondents should be able to read each question quickly, understand its intent, and select an answer without difficulty (Babbie, 2001).
- Negative items should be avoided. Negation in a questionnaire item can lead to misinterpretation. For example, asking respondents to agree or disagree with the

statement "FLSs should not have to provide direct support" could be confusing. Too often, readers misinterpret the question to mean the opposite of its intended meaning.

- Biased items and terms should be avoided. Biased questions or terms such as "Don't you agree that . . . " should instead be phrased as "Do you agree or disagree that. . . . " The first question is an example of a leading question. This type of question suggests a possible answer or makes some responses seem more acceptable than others (Babbie, 2001; Singleton et al., 1993).

- Include a complete listing of alternatives. For closed-ended questions, give a complete listing of alternatives to a question, representing both moderate attitudes and extreme attitudes in each direction (Singleton et al., 1993).

Several different types of questions can be used on a survey. Rating scales that convert respondents' reactions to a numerical rating can prove useful. For example, a Likert scale uses numbers representing degrees of liking something; such as 1 = *dislike very much*, 2 = *dislike somewhat*, 3 = *like somewhat*, 4 = *like very much*. It is the most commonly used question type in surveys (Babbie, 1990; Singleton et al., 1993).

Another type of scale is the behaviorally anchored rating scale. In this type of scale, skills needed to function in a job are anchored around a midpoint. For example, on a scale of 1–5, the midpoint would be described as the level of skill required to perform the job competently. A rating of five would be considered ideal; conversely, a score of one would represent a severe deficiency. To create a rating scale that can be used objectively and uniformly, it is helpful to attach a behavior to each score (Barnhart, 2002). This type of rating scale is often used in structured interviews (see Table 4.2 in Chapter 4 for an example).

Asking respondents to rank questions is also useful. Pretesting with open-ended questions, however, should be done to ensure that the items chosen are inclusive and meaningful to respondents (Singleton et al., 1993). For example, employees may be asked to select the top three reasons they want to leave their job. The first 50 to 100 respondents may be asked to answer an open-ended question. Those first responses would be used to establish a set of categories that reflect common responses to the question. The question can then be converted to a ranking question by listing all of the responses given by three or more people and leaving a space for people to enter responses that are not on the list.

Instructions at the beginning of any survey should inform the participant how many questions are included and should estimate the length of time it will take to complete the survey. Demographic questions at the beginning or the end of the survey can be used to learn whether certain groups of employees have better outcomes (e.g., lower turnover, greater job satisfaction) than others (e.g., FLSs versus DSPs). A set of sample demographic questions are included at the end of this chapter. As with any other type of question, only include demographic items that are directly related to the purpose of the survey. Each organization using a survey or other assessment technique should be careful to comply with legal requirements such as managing private information as mandated by the Health Insurance Accountability and Portability Act of 1996 (PL 104-191). In some organizations, a human subjects review board will also need to be consulted.

A cover letter should point out the purpose of the study. The cover letter should also explain how confidentiality will be handled. A coding system on each survey could be used to protect the identity of the participants yet allow those conducting the survey to distinguish between respondents. Some organizations hire an independent consultant to design, administer, and analyze survey results. This lends additional objectivity to the survey and has the added advantage of discreetness. Respondents feel more secure in giving an honest response when they know that a disinterested party is reviewing their written reactions. Other organizations have the human resources department handle the survey and present only aggregate responses to supervisors and managers. Maintaining confidentiality is critical to avoid retaliation against respondents who report a negative reaction to a question. Furthermore, respondents who do not trust that their responses will be treated confidentially are less likely to answer truthfully and are more likely to avoid responding at all. Such a problem can make it very difficult to accurately assess the extent and nature of concerns.

Once the questions for a survey have been drafted, it is helpful to have a small group of employees complete the survey to test the questions. This test group can be asked to report how long it took them to complete the survey and if any of the questions were confusing, difficult to understand, ambiguous, and/or unclear. The feedback can then be used to refine the survey before it is used with the rest of the employees (Babbie, 2001). This testing can help the organization to avoid irritating employees with instructions that are unclear, questions that are difficult to answer, or surveys that take too long to complete.

Sometimes surveys are given to all possible respondents (the whole population). Other times, only a sample of respondents is used. A sample is a subset of respondents that represents a larger group. An adequate sample can allow an organization to learn about the total population without having to ask everyone to participate (Babbie, 1990). With organizations of fewer than 100 employees, it is often advisable to survey all appropriate staff members. In larger organizations, however, it is often possible to select a sample of the target population to survey.

In selecting a sample, the objective is to obtain a representation of a particular group of employees, also known as the sample frame. For example, an organization interested in learning more about its 500 DSPs would select participants from this sample frame. To achieve this, the basic principle of probability sampling must be applied. That is, all members of a particular group should have an equal chance of being included in the sample (Babbie, 1990). One approach is to employ systematic sampling, in which every nth person is selected from a list. For example, in a list of 500 people, every fifth person is selected to be in the sample, for a total sample of 100 (20% of the total population).

The question of size of sample depends on how the answers will be used. For purposes of grouping the answers by division, unit, or manager, it is important to get surveys back from at least 10–20 people per division, unit, or manager. This number is usually large enough for a statistical test of differences to detect true differences that exist between groups. Another consideration is the extent of involvement or proportion of the organization to be involved in the survey. If at least 20% involvement is desired, and there are 600 people at the organization, the sample size should be at least 120 participants.

Another factor in deciding on how many people to survey is the proportion of people who actually return the survey. This proportion is called the response rate. The goal should be to get surveys back from at least 50%–80% of respondents. If 120 people receive surveys and 60 people return them, the response rate is 50% (60 divided by 120 times 100). If 96 people return surveys, the response rate is 80%. Response rates can be increased with encouragement from supervisors who emphasize the importance of the feedback that is obtained from the survey. Also, higher response rates can be obtained by preliminary notification of the survey and its importance (Singleton et al., 1993). Once staff members understand that the organization is interested in issues of concern to the staff and is looking to make necessary changes, the participation rate usually increases. Response rates are also often higher when responses are anonymous or when another trusted mechanism to ensure confidentiality is used.

Several assessment instruments (described next) are included at the end of this chapter. They were developed for research purposes by the University of Minnesota. Other examples can be found at the ends of other chapters in this book.

Staff Satisfaction Survey

The Staff Satisfaction Survey was created with the assistance of a large provider organization in Minnesota. The first part solicits information about satisfaction with various job components. The second part asks employees to provide suggestions about what they like and do not like about their jobs and what they wish would be changed. It was developed based on analysis of hundreds of responses to open-ended questions about these topics. The responses were grouped into themes that were then incorporated into the survey. This instrument has not undergone reliability testing. Its face validity has been assessed through reviews by managers, administrators, and human resources professionals. It has been used with hundreds of employees in several different organizations.

New Staff Survey

The New Staff Survey was developed to evaluate the extent to which the expectations of newly hired DSPs matched their experiences on the job. It has been used in conjunction with RJPs to assess the effectiveness of those interventions. In some organizations, it is used as a survey to be completed independently by a newly hired employee after 30 days on the job. In other organizations, the survey is completed and is discussed directly with the new employee's supervisor.

Training Experiences Satisfaction Survey

The Training Experiences Satisfaction Survey was developed to assess staff satisfaction with the training provided by the employer. An earlier eight-item version of the Training Experiences Satisfaction Survey was used in a series of research projects to evaluate employee opinions about the training they had received. Internal consistency (a measure of whether all of the items on the scale measure the same category of information) for the eight-item scale was .81 based on responses from more than 100 DSPs in community residential settings. The Training Experiences Satisfaction Survey that appears in this chapter is a later version of this instrument, refined based on research use of the original version.

Other Methods of Workforce Assessment

Exit Interview or Survey

Exit interviews or surveys can ask leavers the extent to which several factors made them want to stay or leave. A recent national study of human resources managers found that 87% of all organizations surveyed conducted exit interviews or surveys (Society for Human Resource Management, 2001b). Some organizations have found it useful to ask leavers questions similar to or the same as those asked on the Staff Satisfaction Survey. Qualitative exit interviews are also useful in drawing out information to assess and modify organization practices. Among the most productive qualitative interview items are questions such as the following:

- If your best friend were considering a job like yours at this site, what two or three things would you tell him or her? Give specific examples.
- Give an example of one or two specific incidents that made you want to stay on this job.
- Give an example of one or two specific incidents that made you want to leave this job.
- What could (your supervisor and/or this organization) do to make your job better?
- What type of position (if any) do you plan to work in after you leave this position (e.g., DSP, supervisor, job coach, bank teller, full-time student, stay-at-home parent)?

Asking leavers to respond to these questions can provide valuable information to assess and modify organization practices. Other information to review includes the employee's status at exit (e.g., whether leavers were fired or left for other reasons such as spousal transfer or to complete a college degree). Organizations may also want to include the job performance of the leavers, whether the leavers will continue to be on-call workers, and where the people went when they left the organization (e.g., to perform similar roles for another organization; to better position in the field; to make lateral move for higher pay, such as becoming a paraprofessional in the public schools).

Focus Groups

Focus groups are another common method to gather information from people about what they think and feel. Focus groups can help an organization discover underlying concerns and issues or to identify perceptions about a specific area. Focus groups are used not only to determine concerns but also to further refine questions, define challenges, or gather ideas about solutions to problems that exist in the work environment. Focus groups can be used alone or in conjunction with another strategy such as a survey.

A focus group is a specific group of people who have been brought together for the purpose of informing others about important issues. Focus groups have a specific structure and a strategic process designed to yield certain outcomes. When an organization uses focus groups on workforce practices and issues, it is important to identify the specific purpose for the focus group before it occurs. The purpose provides the reason for the focus group, is the driving force when the organization is formulating questions to ask participants, defines the scope of the focus group process, keeps the group focused during the meeting, and guides analysis of the information gathered.

Participants are selected for a focus group because they share characteristics that relate to the topic of the focus group. They can provide information about the topic. For example, all FLSs with 1 or more years of experience in that position may be selected to discuss how training for supervisors might be improved. A group of newly hired DSPs may provide greater insight into how well the organization does at welcoming new employees. When using focus groups, carefully consider who should be involved in the group. Asking the questions shown in Table 13.3 assists an organization in defining who should attend.

Once the characteristics of participants have been identified, the next step is to seek participants. When recruiting participants, the organization should be certain to inform them of the purpose of the focus group. The organization needs to ensure that potential participants know the extent of their commitment, including how long meetings will last, the number of meetings they will be asked to attend, and whether they will be paid or will receive other incentives for participation. Finally, the organization should be certain that people clearly understand the logistics of the focus group (e.g., location, date, time, directions, dress code).

Some potential participants may be intimidated by the words *focus group*. Thus, it may help to call them *discussion groups*. It is important for the organization to inform the participants as to why they were selected for participation. It is also important to let participants know what process will be used and that the information shared within the focus group will remain confidential (if this is the case).

Table 13.3. Questions to consider when planning whom to include in focus groups

---

Whose perspectives do we need to obtain? Possibilities include

    Direct support professional (DSP), front-line supervisor (FLS), manager, administrator, supported individual and his or her family, support staff (e.g., office assistants, maintenance workers), trainees, human resources professionals, board members, community members, professionals outside the organization

    New hires, long-term employees

    Employees from different racial, ethnic, cultural, linguistic, or religious groups

    Young employees, older employees

    Single, married, partnered employees

    Excellent performers, poor performers

Should participants know one another, or should they be unfamiliar with one another?

Who are topic, issue, or content area experts on the questions to be discussed?

    Within the organization

    Within the community

Is it important to get a blended perspective in one group or to get separate perspectives from different groups?

What resources are available regarding the following?

    Time

    Ability to pay participants

    Incentives for participation

    Analysis of gathered data and information

How can people be encouraged to participate?

Finding a skilled facilitator is as important as selecting the correct participants. The facilitator needs to be comfortable working with groups and should have experience facilitating focus groups. Facilitators must promote a nonjudgmental, permissive environment that encourages self-disclosure among participants. Participants should feel free to share their perceptions and points of view without feeling pressure to conform or reach consensus (Krueger & Casey, 2000). It is also important to note that the moderator is not in a position of power and should promote comments of all types, both positive and negative.

Facilitators also need to be familiar with and have the ability to use various types of group processes including brainstorming and the nominal group process, in which each group member independently generates answers to a question and then shares, or nominates, an idea one at a time until all ideas have been shared (Morrison, 1998). In some circumstances, especially when controversial issues will be discussed or when the participants are very mistrustful, it may help to use a facilitator from outside of the organization. The person selected should be someone the participants can easily trust.

The ideal size for a focus group is 5–10 people. In groups smaller than 5, there is more opportunity to share ideas, but the restricted size results in a smaller pool of total ideas. If the group size exceeds 10, there is a tendency for the group to fragment (Krueger & Casey, 2000). When selecting the focus group size, the organization can consider how many different groups will be used. It is often better to have more than one group than to have one group that is too large.

Whatever technique is used to assess the organization, it will be necessary to summarize the results so that they can be used to inform decision making about strategies to remediate identified challenges.

Select an Intervention Strategy

The previous sections of this chapter have described many ways to learn the nature, size, and scope of the challenge an organization has. Once the problem or challenge has been identified, the next step is to select an intervention strategy to address that problem. Detailed instructions and guidance on how to select and implement an intervention for a specific problem can be found in Chapter 14 of this book. In that chapter, intervention selection and implementation are broken down into several parts:

- Selecting a strategy
- Identifying the major components of the strategy
- Identifying the major barriers to implementation
- Identifying supporting arguments and supporting stakeholders for the strategy
- Setting goals, measuring progress, and establishing a time frame

In addition, most of the chapters in this book describe one or more intervention strategies that can be used to overcome various challenges. For example, Chapter 3 describes how to use RJPs to reduce turnover by new employees who would not otherwise really understand what the job would be like. Readers are referred to those chapters for more information about selecting an intervention.

Set Goals and Measure Progress

Once the baseline measurement is established and the intervention is selected and implemented, a plan is needed for how to measure and evaluate any changes in the problem since the baseline measurement. This measurement will likely include both annual updates of all general workforce development assessments (e.g., turnover calculations, staff satisfaction surveys), as well as periodic reassessments of specific indicators used to establish the nature and extent of the problem (e.g., organizational commitment measures). The plan should specify what will be assessed, when it will be assessed, and how the information will be shared with those involved in the intervention. The guidelines described in the section on assessing the problem also apply to the process of selecting a measurement method or tool to assess progress once an intervention has been implemented.

When an organizational plan is created to address workforce challenges, an important component of that plan is the establishment of goals that can easily be observed and can be measured. Goals should be *s*pecific, *m*easurable, *a*ttainable, *r*ealistic, and *t*ime bound (SMART; Sauer et al., 1997). Such goals help set the direction for the intervention and help to determine, organize, and measure accomplishments or desired outcomes (Sauer et al., 1997). For example, a turnover goal might be "The organizationwide crude separation rate will decline from 50% to 40% for DSPs for the 12-month period following full implementation of the mentoring intervention." A goal for retention of new hires might be "The proportion of newly hired DSPs who stay at least 6 months will increase from a baseline of 45% to 60% when measured 1 year after an RJP intervention has been implemented." A goal for training might be "Within 6 months after the new training program has been implemented, 90% of the DSPs who have completed the training program will demonstrate competence in 8 of the 10 skills listed in the training program's performance checklist." The goals should also be based on the baseline data. An organization that is concerned about a baseline turnover rate of 60% per year may aim for reducing organizationwide turnover to 45% by 1 year after beginning its chosen intervention.

Establish a Time Frame for the Intervention

Different organizations need differing amounts of time to set up and use an intervention. In addition, different interventions will take different amounts of time to develop, implement, and evaluate. For example, it may be possible to design and implement a recruitment bonus program within a few months and to measure its effects within a year. In contrast, an RJP video may take substantially longer to plan and implement. The effects of using an RJP video may not be obvious until it has been in place for 6 months or more (depending on how many people are hired in a typical month).

Another consideration is whether a pilot test of the intervention will be conducted. Often, especially in larger organizations, it is helpful to select a few sites with supervisors who are highly motivated to change to pilot test the intervention. The pilot test sites devise and implement the initial intervention. They would then spend time evaluating whether changes are needed to make the intervention work. Then, when the intervention is implemented organizationwide, most of the bugs will have been worked out. In one organization, a pilot study was used to figure out exactly how to implement an RJP. One of the supervisors in the pilot study was not sold on the idea that RJPs would actually work and did not implement the intervention. When the pilot study was evaluated, all of the other supervisors had noticed measurable improvement in turnover, but this person had not. The feedback that person got from the other supervisors helped to motivate him to implement the intervention.

The organization should consider how long the intervention will be in place. Often an intervention can last many months to several years. Different situations may dictate different time frames for evaluation of progress. There is no one correct answer, but a definite time frame for checking progress should be selected. The organization should not allow the intervention to continue indefinitely without an evaluation.

Evaluate Success

After the intervention is implemented, a final step is to evaluate the intervention, to identify whether it actually produced the results it was designed to produce. An organization can use the assessment strategies identified in this chapter to learn whether the intervention made a difference. For example, after initially having identified turnover as the problem, the organization may have decided to assess both the turnover rate and the proportion of new hires who left the organization during the first 6 months after hire. If those assessments showed that turnover was 50% and that 40% of all newly hired DSPs left the organization within 6 months after hire, the organization may have selected an RJP as its intervention. The intervention is not complete until an evaluation has been conducted to learn if it actually made a difference or not. In this example, the organization may choose to assess turnover and the tenure categories of leavers 1 year after the intervention started. If that evaluation shows no change in turnover or in the tenure of people who get an RJP, the organization will need to use some of the specialized assessment tools to learn more about why there was no change. For example, using the New Staff Survey may reveal that most new hires still have many unmet expectations when they are hired. In this case, the organization would need to refine the RJP to incorporate more of the information that new hires have unmet expectations about. In contrast, if the 1-year assessment shows that turnover has declined to 45% and that only 30% of all newly hired DSPs left within 6 months after hire, the organization can conclude that the intervention is working as designed and that it should be continued. What is important is that the organization have an evaluation plan and use it to learn if the intervention worked.

OVERCOMING IMPLEMENTATION BARRIERS

Just as some people resist going to the doctor for regular physical examinations, some organizations resist conducting regular assessments of their workforce. Without this assessment, however, it is impossible to accurately identify problems, assess potential causes, and monitor the effectiveness of strategies to address those challenges. Common barriers to evaluating progress on workforce development interventions and how they might be overcome are discussed next.

- *Not seeing the value of the assessment ("We don't have time because we already have too much paperwork to do"):* It is common for supervisors and human resources professionals who are struggling to find, hire, and train sufficient staff to not see the value of collecting assessment and evaluation information. An organization can overcome this barrier by involving supervisors and human resources staff in planning the interventions so that they have a stake in the outcome. The organization can explain that the information from supervisors and human resources staff is needed to assess whether interventions actually make a difference or not and by using the most succinct assessment strategies that will actually get the job done. Organizations should not collect more information than is needed. In addition, they should be certain to use existing data whenever possible. Many organizations already have a database that can be used to assess turnover rates, tenure of stayers and leavers, and vacancy rates. Using those databases rather than asking employees to provide new information reduces the burden on those employees. Organizations that do not have such databases may wish to invest in a human resources database system as part of their intervention.

- *Not being familiar with existing instruments or assessment procedures:* It is difficult to assess or evaluate workforce outcomes without the necessary tools. Often, organizations do not know where to obtain assessment tools including surveys, formulas, and comparison data. This chapter includes several instruments and instructions on how to compute common baseline data. The literature review in Chapter 1 provides some of the needed comparison data. The resources section in this chapter lists other sources of information about instruments and assessment procedures.

- *Lacking resources to pay for acquiring and using published instruments:* Published instruments can be expensive to use, but many have the advantage of being standardized. Some organizations find that investing in standardized instruments pays off because the information gathered is of high quality. Other organizations may wish to consult several published tools and, using the principles described in this chapter, modify them or create their own. A third option is to hire a consultant to create an instrument. Tools for conducting the most basic general workforce development assessments are included at the end of this chapter.

- *Forgetting to seek input from DSPs throughout the process:* A complete understanding of workforce issues and how to address them can only be obtained if all of the affected stakeholders are involved in the process. DSPs are key stakeholders for the issues discussed in this book, yet organizations often resist reaching out to DSPs to ask them about their problems and ideas for solutions. This resistance is sometimes the result of fear that if DSPs are brought together to discuss problems, they might organize a union. Other concerns include a reluctance to share information about what is learned with DSPs, having difficulty with work coverage so that DSPs participate in data collection and problem-solving meetings, and a reluctance to pay DSPs for work other than providing direct support. Although these fears are very real, organizations that reach out and include DSPs often find that the benefits of doing so far outweigh the negatives. Including DSPs can help DSPs feel empowered, important, and valued. It validates their opinions and input and fosters increased commitment to both the organization and to the field. Overcoming the barrier of excluding DSPs requires the organization to be open to change and to value the opinions of all its employees, including DSPs.

- *Spending too much time assessing the problem and never implementing an intervention:* Assessment and evaluation are very important parts of the intervention process, but they are not the end in themselves. The lead authors of this book have worked with organizations that have spent years getting baseline information without actually implementing interventions to produce change. The predictable results of such a strategy are that the organization obtains a better idea of how it measures up to other organizations but that there is no change in the important indicators. Organizations should establish a baseline but should not let the process of doing so overwhelm its effort. Organization should begin implementing at least one intervention within 3–6 months of the baseline assessment so that progress can be made toward better workforce outcomes.

- *Implementing an intervention without first conducting a baseline assessment:* When an organization neglects to establish a baseline, it has no way to know if the intervention has made a difference, aside from relying on a gut feeling that may or may not be accurate. Organizations should be sure to conduct at least general workforce development assessments before moving on to interventions and evaluation of progress.

- *Neglecting to create a plan to evaluate progress:* It is easy for an organization to get so wrapped up in conducting interventions that it totally forgets to check if any progress is being made. To avoid this, the intervention plan should incorporate a plan to evaluate progress that is specified before the intervention is ever implemented (see the end of Chapter 14 for a tool to organize intervention planning). The organization can consult the plan periodically to ensure that it is being implemented as intended. Then at the specified interval, the evaluation can be conducted to assess progress.

- *Forgetting to provide feedback to people involved in the intervention to monitor progress and identify when adjustments are needed:* The purpose of conducting an evaluation is to measure progress and to motivate others in the organization to continue to implement selected interventions. People who have completed surveys or who have participated in focus groups need to learn how the information they provided was used. Failing to give this feedback will cause people to wonder if they wasted their time. Furthermore, if the organization does nothing visible with the results, the people who gave their time to the process will be much more reluctant to participate the next time the organization needs information. Another important function of providing feedback is to help people understand how they are doing. Providing information to supervisors about their turnover rates and vacancy rates and how those rates compare with those for the organization as a whole helps them to understand how well they are doing or to understand the extent of the problem they have.

QUESTIONS TO PONDER

1. How big are the workforce challenges your organization is experiencing? How do you know? How does your organization learn whether interventions actually make a difference?

2. How often does your organization measure turnover, tenure of leavers, and vacancy rates? (Does it measure those factors at least annually?)

3. How is information about turnover and retention challenges shared with employees at your organization?

4. When was the last time your organization measured staff satisfaction? What did you do with the results? What is your next step now?

5. What procedures has your organization established to gather information from employees who are leaving the organization?

6. In what ways does your organization seek information from various employees and stakeholders about workforce problems and solutions?

7. Have the purpose and outcome of data collection efforts been made clear to those asked to provide information?

8. How has your organization used the assessment information to guide its next steps?

CONCLUSION

This chapter provides an overview of the assessment and planning process that organizations can use to learn about the nature and extent of their workforce challenges. It suggests that baseline and follow-up evaluations are essential to guide the process of identifying a problem, understanding the scope and nature of the problem, guiding the selection of an intervention, and assessing whether an intervention worked as intended. Chapter 14 provides more detailed information about how to use the assessment process to select a strategy for change and to develop comprehensive organizational change interventions.

RESOURCES

On-line Cost Calculators

iFigure (http://www.ifigure.com/business/employee/employee.htm)

This site has links to calculators to estimate the costs of hiring and training, wages and benefits, and scheduling. (*Note:* Some of the links on this page do not work.)

University of Wisconsin Extension Services (http://www.uwex.edu/ces/cced/publicat/turn.html #calc)

This on-line calculator of the cost of turnover was developed by W.H. Pinkovitz, J. Moskal, and G. Green.

Information on Workforce Development Surveys

Information about other standardized surveys useful for workforce assessments can be obtained from the following web sites:

Society for Human Resources Management
(http://www.shrm.org/ hrresources/surveys_published/AllSurveysTOC.asp#TopOfPage)

Workforce Management
(http://www.mediabrains.com/client/workforcema/bg1/shortlist.asp?ct_categoryID=
{9B3D366D-DBF2-11D4-A007-009027FC2163}&ct_categoryname=
Testing+and+Assessment)

Direct Support Professional Workforce Status and Outcomes

Please fill in the blanks for your organization, focusing only on direct support professional (DSP) positions. These formulas assume you are making computations based on a calendar year.

Turnover (crude separation rate) of DSPs

$$\frac{\text{total number of DSPs who left during the year}}{\text{total number of funded DSP positions as of December 31}} \times 100 = \text{turnover rate}$$

Fill in: $\dfrac{\underline{\hspace{1cm}}\ \text{total number of DSPs who left}}{\underline{\hspace{1cm}}\ \text{current staff} + \underline{\hspace{1cm}}\ \text{vacant positions}} \times 100 \qquad = \underline{\hspace{1cm}}\ \%$ turnover rate

Average tenure of current DSPs (stayers)

$$\frac{\begin{array}{c}\text{total number of months worked by all current}\\ \text{DSPs in the organization as of December 31}\end{array}}{\begin{array}{c}\text{total number of DSPs employed by the}\\ \text{organization as of December 31}\end{array}} = \text{average tenure of stayers}$$

Fill in: $\dfrac{\underline{\hspace{1cm}}\ \text{total number of months worked by current DSPs}}{\underline{\hspace{1cm}}\ \text{total number of DSP stayers}} = \underline{\hspace{1cm}}\ \text{months' average tenure}$

Average tenure of DSPs who left in the last 12 months (leavers)

$$\frac{\begin{array}{c}\text{total number of months worked during the year by}\\ \text{DSPs who left the organization by December 31}\end{array}}{\begin{array}{c}\text{total number of DSPs who worked during}\\ \text{the year and resigned by December 31}\end{array}} = \text{average tenure of leavers}$$

Fill in: $\dfrac{\underline{\hspace{1cm}}\ \text{total number of months worked by DSPs leavers}}{\underline{\hspace{1cm}}\ \text{total number of DSPs leavers}} = \underline{\hspace{1cm}}\ \text{months' average tenure}$

Percentage of DSP leavers with less than 6 months' tenure

$$\frac{\begin{array}{c}\text{total number of DSPs who}\\ \text{worked during the year and left}\\ \text{before working 6 months}\end{array}}{\begin{array}{c}\text{total number of DSPs who worked}\\ \text{during the year and resigned}\\ \text{by December 31}\end{array}} \times 100 = \%\text{ of leavers with less than 6 months' tenure}$$

Fill in: $\dfrac{\begin{array}{c}\underline{\hspace{1cm}}\ \text{total number of DSPs who}\\ \text{left before 6 months}\end{array}}{\underline{\hspace{1cm}}\ \text{total number of DSP leavers}} \times 100 \quad = \underline{\hspace{1cm}}\ \%\text{ of leavers with less than 6 months' tenure}$

Vacancy rate

$$\frac{\text{total number of vacant positions as of December 31}}{\text{total number of funded DSP positions as of December 31}} \times 100 = \%\text{ vacancy rate}$$

Fill in: $\dfrac{\underline{\hspace{1cm}}\ \text{total number of vacant positions}}{\begin{array}{c}\underline{\hspace{1cm}}\ \text{total number current staff} +\\ \underline{\hspace{1cm}}\ \text{total number of vacant positions}\end{array}} \times 100 \qquad = \underline{\hspace{1cm}}\ \%\text{ vacancy rate}$

From O'Nell, S., Hewitt, A., Sauer, J., & Larson, S. (2001). *Removing the revolving door: Strategies to address recruitment and retention challenges* (p. 13 of Appendix C in facilitator guide). Minneapolis: University of Minnesota, Institute on Community Integration, Research and Training Center on Community Living; adapted by permission. Also available on-line: http://rtc.umn.edu/pdf/turnover.pdf

Source of formulas: Larson, 1998.

Staff Satisfaction Survey

Name: _____   Supervisor name: _____

Job title: _____   Site name: _____

Date: _____   Site number: _____

This survey will be used to improve our workforce practices. Please answer each question as accurately as possible. If you do not understand a question, answer it as well as you can and note your question(s) in the margin. *Your answers will be kept confidential and will not affect your status as an employee at our organization.* When you have completed this survey, please return it in the envelope provided. If you have questions, you can contact _____ . Thank you.

Please rate your work at our organization in the following areas. For each numbered item, mark in the column that most closely describes your overall opinion of each item.

Topic	1 Poor	2 Fair	3 Good	4 Excellent	0 No opinion/ N/A
Orientation and Training					
1. Availability of a clear job description for your position					
2. Communication of expectations about your job performance					
3. Completeness and timeliness of orientation about our organization in general and your workplace in particular					
4. Sufficient training materials and training opportunities to allow you to perform your job well					
5. Availability of follow-up training					
Supervision					
6. Availability of a supervisor to answer your questions and to assist you to carry out your duties					
7. Feedback and evaluation regarding your performance					
8. Recognition by your supervisor for your accomplishments					
9. Fairness in supervision and employment opportunities					
10. Relationship with your supervisor					
Compensation and Benefits					
11. Your rate of pay for your work					
12. Paid time off you receive					
13. Our policy regarding eligibility for paid time off					
14. Benefits you receive (for example, health and dental insurance, retirement)					
15. Our policy regarding eligibility for benefits					

(continued)

From University of Minnesota, Institute on Community Integration, Research and Training Center on Community Living. (n.d.-b). *Staff satisfaction survey* (developed by Sheryl A. Larson in collaboration with Lutheran Social Service of Minnesota); adapted by permission. Retrieved from http://rtc.umn.edu/pdf/staffsatisfaction.pdf

Funding to develop this survey was provided by the Partnerships for Success Grant awarded by the U.S. Department of Labor (Grant No. N-7596-9-00-87-60).

Topic	1 Poor	2 Fair	3 Good	4 Excellent	0 No opinion/ N/A
Other Aspects of Your Experience					
16. Opportunities to share your ideas about improving the services provided. You feel that your opinions count.					
17. Your schedule/flexibility					
18. Access to internal job postings					
19. Opportunities for ongoing professional development					
20. Degree to which your skills are used					
21. Morale in your office or program					
22. Relationship with your co-workers					
23. Relationship with your supervisor's manager					
24. Attitude of consumers and families toward our organization					
25. You have the opportunity to do what you do best every day.					
26. Your supervisor or someone at work cares about you as a person.					
27. Someone at work encourages your development.					
28. Your co-workers are committed to doing quality work.					
29. You have opportunities to learn and grow.					

30. What do you like best about our organization? (Mark up to 3 choices.)
_____ a. Nothing
_____ b. Benefits
_____ c. Co-employees
_____ d. Supervisors and managers
_____ e. Individuals supported
_____ f. The mission and service goals
_____ g. The tasks I do for my job
_____ h. Opportunity for personal or professional growth
_____ i. Location
_____ j. Work atmosphere
_____ k. Training and development opportunities
l. Pay rate/salary
_____ m. Job variety
_____ n. Flexible hours/schedule
_____ o. Recognition for a job well done
_____ p. Rewarding work_____
_____ q. Other (specify):

31. What could our organization do differently to help you in your job? (Mark up to three choices.)
_____ a. Nothing
_____ b. My supervisor/manager could be more supportive.
_____ c. Improve training and support for supervisors.
_____ d. Increase wages.
_____ e. Improve access to paid time off.
_____ f. Improve access to benefits (health, dental, retirement).
_____ g. Clarify and communicate organization mission.
_____ h. Empower me to participate in decisions that affect my work.
_____ i. Provide more or better training.
_____ j. Reduce conflict between co-employees and/or improve team building.

(continued)

_____ k. Improve supervisor–employee relations.
_____ l. Address low morale of workforce.
_____ m. Improve scheduling policies and practices.
_____ n. Improve communication between main office and program sites.
_____ o. Improve communication between supervisors/managers and other staff.
_____ p. Increase number of staff members in my work site.
_____ q. Improve recognition and feedback.
_____ r. Improve orientation for new employees.
_____ s. Increase opportunities for advancement.
_____ t. Reduce vacancy rate and turnover.
_____ u. Other (specify): _____

32. What are the top factors that make you want to leave our organization? (Mark up to three choices.)
_____ a. Nothing
_____ b. Low wages or benefits
_____ c. Conflicts with co-workers
_____ d. Not enough hours or unsatisfactory schedule
_____ e. Job is too stressful, difficult, or demanding.
_____ f. Our organization's focus or mission has changed for the worse.
_____ g. Demands of my other job or primary employment
_____ h. Lack of opportunities for professional growth or advancement
_____ i. Personal reasons
_____ j. Relocating out of area
_____ k. Conflict with supervisor or manager
_____ l. Favoritism or lack of fairness
_____ m. Lack of staff
_____ n. Too much criticism or lack of support
_____ o. Challenges with clients/individuals served
_____ p. Poor training
_____ q. None of the above
_____ r. Other (specify): _____

33. What makes you want to stay at our organization? (Mark up to 3 choices.)
_____ a. Nothing
_____ b. Benefits
_____ c. Co-workers
_____ d. Supervisors and managers
_____ e. I like the clients/individuals supported.
_____ f. The individuals supported like and/or appreciate me.
_____ g. The mission and service goals
_____ h. The tasks or activities I do for my job
_____ i. Opportunity for personal or professional growth
_____ j. Location
_____ k. Work atmosphere
_____ l. Training and development opportunities
_____ m. Pay rate or salary
_____ n. Job variety
_____ o. Flexible hours or schedule
_____ p. Recognition for a job well done
_____ q. Rewarding work
_____ r. The staff members are team players.
_____ s. This is a good company to work for.
_____ t. Other (specify): _____

New Staff Survey

Name: _____   Supervisor name: _____

Job title: _____   Site name: _____

Date: _____   Site number: _____

1. Is this your first job working with people with disabilities? (Mark one.)
   _____ 0. No
   _____ 1. Yes

2. Have your job responsibilities and working conditions turned out to be what you expected when you took this job? (Mark one.)
   _____ 1. Definitely not
   _____ 2. Somewhat not
   _____ 3. Neither yes nor no
   _____ 4. Somewhat yes
   _____ 5. Definitely yes

3. Overall, does this job meet your original expectations? (Mark one.)
   _____ 1. Definitely not
   _____ 2. Somewhat not
   _____ 3. Neither yes nor no
   _____ 4. Somewhat yes
   _____ 5. Definitely yes

4. Have you seen a copy of your job description? (Mark one.)
   _____ 0. No
   _____ 1. Yes

How closely have your experiences during your first 30 days at this site matched the expectations you had before you were hired in the following areas?

Job feature	1 (Didn't match my expectations at all)				5 (Completely matched my expectations)
5. The organization's mission and service goals	1	2	3	4	5
6. Your pay and benefits	1	2	3	4	5
7. Your schedule	1	2	3	4	5
8. Working conditions	1	2	3	4	5
9. Types of tasks you do	1	2	3	4	5
10. Needs and characteristics of the people supported at this site	1	2	3	4	5
11. Training you received	1	2	3	4	5
12. Acceptance and welcome from other DSPs	1	2	3	4	5
13. Help and support from other DSPs	1	2	3	4	5
14. How well staff at this site work together as a team	1	2	3	4	5
15. Availability of support from your supervisor	1	2	3	4	5

16. What do you wish you had known about this job before you were hired?

From University of Minnesota, Institute on Community Integration, Research and Training Center on Community Living. (n.d.-a). *New staff survey* (developed by Sheryl A. Larson in collaboration with Lutheran Social Service of Minnesota); adapted by permission. Retrieved from http://rtc.umn.edu/pdf/newstaffsurvey.pdf

Funding to develop this survey was provided by the Partnerships for Success Grant awarded by the U.S. Department of Labor (Grant No. N-7596-9-00-87-60).

Training Experience Satisfaction Survey

Please answer these questions about the training you have received from the organization in which you now work. Mark in the column that most accurately reflects your opinion.

	1 Strongly disagree	2 Disagree	3 Neither agree nor disagree	4 Agree	5 Strongly agree
The training I have received so far . . .					
1. Prepared me to complete my specific job responsibilities					
2. Assisted me to develop skills in interacting with individuals with disabilities					
3. Helped me improve the quality of life of the people I support					
4. Provided information I need to perform my job					
5. Has been worthwhile					
6. Has sparked my interest					
7. Was offered at a time that made it easy for me to attend					
8. Was offered at a place that made it easy for me to attend					
9. Offered an opportunity for me to share my experiences					
10. Was tailored to meet my learning style (the way I learn best)					
11. Allowed me to test out of training on skills I already had					
12. Was delivered at a comfortable pace so that I could understand the content					
13. Inspired me to begin or continue my career as a DSP					
14. Gave me a chance to have my questions answered					
My recommendations					
15. This organization should keep its current training program.					
16. This organization should change its training program.					
17. I would recommend the training I have received so far to all new employees.					

University of Minnesota, Institute on Community Integration, Research and Training Center on Community Living. (n.d.-c). *Training experience satisfaction survey* (developed by Amy S. Hewitt & Sheryl A. Larson); adapted by permission. Retrieved from http://rtc.umn.edu/pdf/trainingsurvey.pdf

Funding to develop this survey was provided by Grant No. H133B031116 from the U.S. Department of Education, Office of Special Education and Rehabilitative Services, National Institute on Disability and Rehabilitation Research, to the University of Minnesota, Institute on Community Integration, Research and Training Center on Community Living.

Demographic Items for Surveys

1. Birth date: _____ _____
   　　　　　　Month　Year

2. Gender:
   _____ 0. Female
   _____ 1. Male

3. Is English your first language? (Mark one.)
   _____ 0. No
   _____ 1. Yes

4. Which of the following best describes your role? (Mark one)
   _____ 1. Direct support professional (DSP) (At least 50% of your time is spent in direct care.)
   _____ 2. Front-line supervisor (FLS) (You may provide direct support, but your primary role is to supervise direct support professionals.)
   _____ 3. Other supervisor/manager (You supervise FLSs or other staff.)
   _____ 4. Administrator (You provide overall direction and oversight for all workers.)
   _____ 5. Other (specify): _____

5. How many sites do you work at or are you responsible for? (Provide a number.)
   _____ Number of sites

6. How many years of paid employment experience do you having working with people with intellectual or developmental disabilities?

   _____ _____
   Years　Months

7. How many years of paid employment experience do you have supervising DSPs who support people with intellectual or developmental disabilities?

   _____ _____
   Years　Months

8. How long have you been working for your current employer?

   _____ _____
   Years　Months

9. How many years of formal education have you had? (Circle one.)
   10 11 12 (High school/GED)
   13　　　14 (Associate's or 2-year degree)
   15　　　16 (Four-year degree)
   17　　　18 (Master's degree)
   19 20 21 (Doctoral degree)

10. Are you currently enrolled in college or vocational or technical school? (Mark one.)
    _____ 0. No
    _____ 1. Yes

11. How many hours are you scheduled to work per week in your current position?
    _____ Hours per week

12. Are you considered by your employer to be a full-time employee? (Mark one.)
    _____ 0. No
    _____ 1. Yes

13. What is your race? (Mark the *one* that best represents your race)[a]
    _____ 1. Caucasian
    _____ 2. African American or Black
    _____ 3. American Indian
    _____ 4. Alaska Native, Eskimo, or Aleut
    _____ 5. Asian or Pacific Islander
    _____ 6. Middle Eastern
    _____ 7. Other (specify): _____

14. Are you of Hispanic ancestry? (Mark one.)
    _____ 0. No
    _____ 1. Yes

Developed by researchers at the University of Minnesota, Institute on Community Integration, Research and Training Center on Community Living; adapted by permission.

Note: These questions can be asked of current employees, but some of the questions should not be asked before hire unless they pertain to a candidate's ability to perform an essential job function as identified in a written job description.

[a]Organizations can let respondents mark more than one race, but this can make data analysis more complex.

14

SELECTING AND IMPLEMENTING STRATEGIES FOR CHANGE

SHERYL A. LARSON,
LYNDA ANDERSON, AND AMY S. HEWITT

Previous chapters have described methods to address recruitment, retention, and training challenges and ways to measure the extent to which these challenges affect an organization. Chapter 13 includes a detailed description of strategies for assessing challenges and evaluating the success of an intervention. This chapter answers the question, "Now what?" If by chance you have skipped ahead to this chapter hoping to find a quick answer, please review the previous chapters, paying special attention to Chapter 13. As that chapter also points out, having a baseline assessment helps an organization understand and define the challenge and can assist in selecting an intervention. The baseline also provides a point of comparison against which the results of the interventions can be compared.

This chapter focuses on a method to develop a comprehensive organizational plan to implement one or more interventions to address specific workforce challenges. It provides more detail about the organizational planning process introduced in Chapter 13 and introduces a process organizations can use to select an intervention to improve recruitment, retention, or training. The process helps an organization do the following:

1. Identify the challenge the organization wants to address (see the section of Chapter 13 called Identify the Problem).
2. Define the extent and nature of the challenge (see the section of Chapter 13 called Assess the Problem).
3. Select a strategy to address that challenge.
4. Detail what will be done, including strategies to involve stakeholders in planning and implementation.
5. Anticipate possible barriers impeding successful implementation.
6. Identify approaches to enlist support from stakeholders to overcome anticipated barriers.
7. Choose goals and monitor progress, then develop a time line for the intervention (see the sections in Chapter 13 called Select Goals and Measure Progress and Establish a Time Frame for the Intervention).
8. Evaluate whether the intervention succeeded (see the section in Chapter 13 called Evaluate Success).

These steps will assist organizations in addressing their workforce challenges by implementing a structured planning process and selecting the best intervention strategy for change. Although the process is designed to facilitate change, it emphasizes the need for stakeholder involvement and planning to increase the chance that the change process will be successful. This chapter assumes that the reader has completed a baseline assessment, as described in Chapter 13, that includes both general assessments and specific assessments needed to discern the size and the scope of the challenge.

TARGETED FRONT-LINE SUPERVISOR COMPETENCIES

Competent front-line supervisors (FLSs) and administrators assess and evaluate workforce development challenges and use those assessments to guide the development of an intervention plan. In developing that plan, they maintain regular contacts with individuals receiving supports and their family members, support team members and other stakeholders to ensure that these individuals' concerns are addressed and to facilitate the involvement of these people in the change process.

Primary Skills

FLSs monitor turnover, recruitment success, and employee job satisfaction and use the results to improve personnel practices by selecting appropriate interventions.

FLSs support other FLSs in understanding and learning about recruitment and retention strategies and why they are important.

FLSs know how to develop and implement a plan for reducing unwanted turnover and vacancies at their own site or across the organization as a whole.

Related Skills

FLSs maintain regular contacts and follow up with individuals receiving supports and their family members and with direct support professionals (DSPs) and other support team members regarding complaints and concerns.

FLSs design, implement, and develop strategies to address issues identified in consumer satisfaction surveys.

UNDERSTANDING THE PROBLEM

Choosing, implementing, and evaluating the effects of an intervention require change, which can be difficult for individuals and organizations. So, whether an intervention is meant for a particular segment of an organization (e.g., one work site) or for the whole organization, some challenges should be expected. Chapter 12 provides an overview of organizational change models and theories and describes general principles for effective organizational change efforts.

RESEARCH SUPPORT FOR SOLUTIONS

Aisha is an FLS who has struggled with high turnover at the home she supervises. The organization she works for used several of the assessment strategies presented in Chapter 13 (measuring turnover and using a staff satisfaction survey, a new hire survey, and exit interviews) to learn more about the challenges that Aisha and other supervisors were struggling with. The organization learned that a high proportion of staff left the organization left during the first 6 months after being hired, mainly because the job did not match their expectations. Aisha and her fellow supervisors reviewed the information they had read about the various interventions and decided that realistic job previews (RJPs; see Chapter 3) might help to solve their organization's problem of early turnover (see the In the Spotlight segment at the end of this chapter for further discussion). As the organization's leadership team considered how its supervisors and other stakeholders could work together on developing an RJP, they realized that one of their challenges would be to help those involved in the hiring process to change their behavior. Changing one's behavior or trying new behavior is a difficult thing for most people. This section looks at some of the theories about how to set the right conditions to motivate individual behavior change.

Fishbein and Ajzen's Theory of Reasoned Action holds that people intend to engage in a behavior and that this intention is based on two considerations (Bagozzi, 1992; Sheppard, Hartwick, & Warshaw, 1988). A person must believe that the benefits outweigh the costs and must sense some social pressure to engage in the behavior (DeBono, 1993; Hinkle, 1996; Madden, Ellen, & Ajzen, 1992). Consider Aisha, who was asked to create an RJP for the site she supervises. Aisha may be more inclined to develop an RJP if she sees that the benefits (having DSPs who make it past the first week of employment) outweigh the costs (the amount of time she must invest in creating the RJP) and if she sees that other FLSs and her supervisor are excited about creating and using RJPs.

Bandura's social cognitive theory (1977, 1989) also states that the benefits of taking an action must outweigh the costs. In this theory, however, the person taking action also must have self-efficacy. Self-efficacy is the belief that one has the skills and knowledge needed to take a particular action. So, not only must Aisha see that the benefits outweigh the costs, but she must also believe that she has the skills and knowledge needed to create an RJP (or that she can readily acquire the skills to do so). To help Aisha with this, the organization she works for will have Aisha learn about RJPs and will support her as she practices her new skills.

The Stages of Change model (Prochaska & DiClemente, 1982) holds that all people move through certain stages on their way to making change: pre-contemplation, contemplation, preparation, action, and maintenance. In the pre-contemplation stage, Aisha has not yet recognized that there is a problem with how rapidly newly hired DSPs have been leaving her site. In the contemplation stage, Aisha has started to think about making a change: She recognizes that a lot of newly hired people have been leaving and wonders what actions she could take to address the problem. The preparation stage is the planning stage: Aisha gathers information about the extent of the retention challenge; learns about the various intervention strategies that are available by reading various resources; identifies strategies to address that challenge, such as using RJPs; and creates an action plan. The action stage is the implementation stage. Aisha uses an RJP to address her site's retention problem. Finally, in the maintenance stage, Aisha continues to use RJPs, but based on information she has gathered, she may modify her site's RJPs. Still, she continues to take action to address retention challenges.

Understanding what motivates change can be useful when communicating about a proposed intervention. For example, when discussing a proposed intervention with the board of directors, a manager may need to talk about costs and benefits in terms of financial costs, but in presenting the same idea to FLSs, the manager may need to talk about costs and benefits in terms of the time that FLSs spend covering unfilled shifts because of vacant positions and recruiting and training new staff. Questions of self-efficacy need to be addressed on both an individual and an organization level. It is important to demonstrate that either the organization or the individual already has the skills and knowledge to implement the intervention or that these skills and knowledge are easy to come by. Organizations or people cannot be forced to move through the stages of change; however, knowing where people fall along the continuum can be very helpful to managers, organization leaders, or other change agents who need to offer appropriate support and information at each stage (people within an organization may be in different places at any one time). Table 14.1 shows Prochaska and DiClemente's (1982) stages of change model and how an organization might support a supervisor when an intervention is introduced and implemented. Understanding these stages of change can help organizations as they create and implement plans to address workforce challenges. This understanding can also help FLSs and managers as they begin to implement changes based within the units in which they work.

Efforts to improve workforce outcomes also involve change at an organizational level. See Chapter 12 for more information about how theories about organizational change can inform the process of selecting and implementing an intervention.

STRATEGIES FOR RESPONDING TO THE PROBLEM

As mentioned previously, there are eight components to crafting and implementing an effective organization recruitment and retention plan: 1) Identify the problem; 2) assess the problem; 3) select an intervention strategy; 4) identify components of the strategy (i.e., what will be done); 5) identify implementation barriers; 6) identify support for the strategy; 7) set goals, measure progress, and establish a time frame for the intervention; and 8) evaluate the intervention's success. Steps 1, 2, 7, and 8 are described in greater detail in Chapter 13. This chapter touches briefly on those components but focuses more on Steps 3–6. The strategies in Table 14.1 can be helpful in all

Table 14.1. Supporting a supervisor as he or she moves through the change process

Stage of change	Action
Precontemplation	Provide the individual with information about the problem. Discuss the costs and benefits of change with the individual.
Contemplation	Encourage the individual to take action.
Preparation	Provide the individual with the information and training that he or she needs to develop an action plan.
Action	Assist the individual with problem solving and data collection, and provide support.
Maintenance	Assist the individual in generating adaptations or alternatives to the action plan based on information gathered.

Source: The stages of change categories are from Prochaska and DiClemente (1982).

phases of the development of the plan but are particularly useful after the plan has been crafted and is ready to be implemented.

Identify and Assess the Problem

Before an intervention is selected, it is essential to understand the size and scope of the problem. Chapter 13 describes the processes of identifying and assessing the challenge in great detail. It is important for organizations to use the strategies described in that chapter to ensure that they have a comprehensive understanding of the nature and extent of the challenges they are facing. The information gathered using those techniques are essential to decisions about which interventions will best address the identified challenges. Having a summary of the information generated in identifying and defining the challenge are critical to selecting a strategy that matches the organization's needs most closely.

Select an Intervention Strategy

Once the challenge has been identified and an assessment of the size and scope of the challenge has been completed, the information gathered can be used to make an informed decision about which of the many possible interventions would be most appropriate. The organization should review the results of general and specific baseline assessments to pinpoint the challenges that are most troublesome or costly to the organization. Then, the organization can select an intervention strategy that directly addresses those specific challenges.

Many of the strategies described in this book can be useful in addressing more than one challenge. Some, however, are likely to have a more direct impact on certain challenges than others. Table 14.2 lists several of the most common workforce challenges reported by community human services organizations and intervention strategies that most directly affect these challenges. The table also lists the chapters in this book that provide more information about the listed strategies.

One challenge in reaching consensus about which intervention to select is that different people may have different information about the challenge. To overcome this challenge, the organization should make sure that all members of the planning team are involved from the beginning so that they have a complete summary of the baseline information. A chart or brief report that lists the major challenges and the data describing the size, scope, and impact of the challenge can be useful tools.

Once the baseline information has been summarized and reviewed, the planning team needs to prioritize the challenges to select one to address first. For example, one team's assessment revealed that turnover is 75% per year, that 60% of all new hires leave in the first 6 months, that 55% of new hires report that their expectations about the job did not match their actual experiences, and that 25% of the sites report significant interpersonal conflicts between staff members. (For further information and an intervention strategy for this organization, see the In the Spotlight segment at the end of this chapter). Each of these challenges by themselves are substantial, so trying to solve all of them at once could cause frustration and overload people who are already overwhelmed. The team may choose any one of those challenges as the first priority to address. That selection of the top priority should only be finalized after the baseline has

Table 14.2. Workforce challenges and strategies to address them

Challenge	Strategy (and chapter[s] that describe the strategy)
The organization has trouble finding new employees. The organization has difficulties recruiting qualified individuals.	(The following eight strategies are discussed in Chapter 2.) Expand recruitment sources. Use inside recruitment sources. Give recruitment bonuses. Advertise and give hiring bonuses. Devise long-term recruitment strategies. Draw on regional recruitment consortia. Market the organization. Implement internship programs for students.
New hires quit in the first 6 months. Supervisors are constantly hiring new employees to replace those who have left the organization.	Use inside recruitment sources. (2) Give recruitment bonuses. (2) Create realistic job previews. (3) Improve selection practices. (4) Develop structured interviewing. (4) Use effective orientation. (5) Improve socialization practices. (5) Establish peer mentoring programs. (8)
New employees are unsure of their job roles and functions	Use effective orientation. (5) Establish peer mentoring programs. (5) Improve co-worker support for new hires. (5)
Supervisors have difficulty finding time to coach and mentor new employees.	Establish peer mentoring programs. (8) Collaborate with other organizations to share training resources. (6, 7) Implement a strategy to reduce turnover so there are fewer new employees to coach and mentor. (13, 14)
The organization has difficulty finding training that addresses the skills needed by employees.	(The following four strategies are discussed in Chapters 6 and 7.) Offer web-based training or distance learning. Develop a training calendar. Collaborate with other organizations to share training resources. Create a staff development culture instead of offering only regulations-driven training opportunities.
Training does not produce desired results. Employees display poor skills on the job.	Establish competency-based training. (6) Have skills mentors to coach staff as they learn new skills. (8) Use performance evaluations and progressive discipline. (6)
Co-workers do not get along.	Use teams and team-building strategies. (10) Improve selection practices. (4) Train supervisors. (6, 7, 11) Offer training on conflict resolution. (10)
Supervisors report being overwhelmed or do not know how to do their job.	Support and train supervisors. (6, 7, 11) Provide mentoring for supervisors. (8, 11) Develop realistic job previews for supervisors. (3)

Challenge	Strategy (*and chapter[s] that describe the strategy*)
There is conflict between staff and supervisors or managers. Employees complain about the supervision they get.	Use teams and team-building strategies. (*10*) Provide networking opportunities. (*5*) Support and train supervisors. (*6, 7, 11*) Implement high-performance supervision practices. (*9, 11*)
Employees have morale problems.	(*The following four strategies are discussed in Chapter 9.*) Use participatory management. Set up employee recognition programs. Create mentoring opportunities for long-term staff to develop skills needed to advance in the organization. Reward long-term employees.
Long-term staff are dissatisfied with or quit their jobs.	Enhance career development opportunities. (*5, 6, 7, 11*) Establish peer mentoring programs. (*8*) Provide networking opportunities. (*5*) Treat DSPs as professionals. (*5*) Allow competent staff to test out of required training and take advanced training instead. (*6, 7*) Recognize tenure and reward long-term employees. (*9*) Implement equitable wage and benefit plans.
Individuals receiving supports/services are dissatisfied.	Conduct job analysis. (*6, 7*) Establish competency-based training. (*6*) Integrate code of ethics into socialization, orientation, and training practices. (*5*)
Employees have inadequate wages or benefits.	Investigate possible policy changes. (*15*) Tie competency-based training to salary increases. (*6*) Develop career paths. (*5, 6*) Professionalize direct support roles. (*5*)

been completed so that it is based on data rather than solely on the opinions or hunches of team members. It is better to prioritize and address the most important challenge first. Tackling several challenges at once can mean that the team wastes resources or gives unfocused, sloppy, and sporadic attention to each of the challenges. Once significant progress is made, the next challenge or intervention can become the focus.

Once the top-priority challenge has been identified, the next challenge is to select one of the several available interventions to try first. The first step in selecting an intervention is to identify the two or three interventions that seem most promising. Once two or three options have been identified, the planning team should make sure that everyone involved in the change process has a good understanding of each of the interventions and how they would be developed, implemented, and evaluated. A comparison of the costs and benefits of each intervention may be helpful in selecting which one to use. Discussing the relative strengths and weaknesses of each approach can also help the team in making an informed decision about which intervention to pursue. Keeping a record of why a particular intervention was selected can be useful in describing the decision process to those who were not involved in the initial planning effort.

The process of selecting interventions to address particular workforce challenges involves both art and science. Table 14.2 includes several interventions for each listed problem, and several problems in each category. That is because not all interventions will work in every organization. Sometimes the interventions an organization is interested in do not match the challenges revealed in the assessment process. In these situations, we recommend that additional information be collected to ensure that the underlying problem has been identified before the intervention is selected. For example, one organization began an intervention project after having decided that it wanted to implement a peer mentoring program to address turnover problems. As we gathered information from the DSPs and others in the organization, however, it became clear that other issues would also need to be addressed. One year after the peer mentoring program had been implemented, the organization had spent a considerable amount of time and energy refining the mentoring program to make it as good as possible, and they had indications that peer mentors were appreciated (staff who were not offered access to the peer mentoring program began asking for it). The program had improved the orientation, socialization, and training of DSPs. However, it had not reduced turnover among new hires to the desired level. The organization then realized that it needed to intervene more specifically in the hiring and selection practices. In the second year, the organization designed an RJP intervention paired with an improved structured interview to address unmet expectations of new employees. As a result, applicants did not accept positions if they were not a good match for the job (which is exactly what RJPs hope to accomplish) and the organization received unsolicited comments from applicants about how much they appreciated learning more about the organization during the hiring process.

This experience illustrates several important concepts. First, it is important to wait until the assessments have been completed before selecting an intervention. Second, it is important to carefully match the intervention to the highest priority problems identified in the assessment (in this case, early turnover of new hires). Finally, it is important to assess the results of the intervention so that if the first intervention selected does not solve the problem, another can be tried. Peer mentoring is not a bad intervention. It can be very helpful in improving skills and helping the person being mentored make connections with others in the organization. In this particular situation, those outcomes simply were not the most important to the organization.

Identify Components of the Strategy

Before an intervention is implemented, the planning team should identify crucial components of the intervention, such as the people who will be involved, possible collaborators, the role each person will play, the tasks involved, and the costs of implementing the intervention. The array of people involved in implementing a strategy is likely to be broader than most planning teams first imagine, although some people's involvement may be indirect or peripheral. To identify the key people, the team lists everyone who will be affected by the intervention or who may be asked to make decisions about the intervention. The list may include more obvious groups such as administrators, the board of directors, managers, and DSPs. Depending on the organization's size, other departments may be affected (e.g., accounting for paying bonuses, human resources for placing ads in community newspapers). The team needs to consider not only the people doing the work but also their supervisors. Individuals receiving supports and their family members are also likely to be affected by the intervention and should be involved either directly or indirectly in the planning and implementation process.

DSPs are one of the most important groups to involve in organizational change efforts. Several DSPs should be involved in planning and implementing the intervention. They should not be considered token participants but instead should be valued, integral members of the change process. Involving DSPs in change efforts is a change strategy in and of itself. Asking for input and valuing the opinions expressed by DSPs demonstrates increased respect for individuals in that role and is an important component of professionalizing the DSP role (see Chapter 5).

After listing the people who will be involved in the change process, the planning team should identify collaborators in the process. Each of the groups just mentioned may cooperate with the change initiative without being an active collaborator. For example, some people who are affected by the change (e.g., supported individuals) or who are interested in its outcome (e.g., service coordinators, taxpayers) may cooperate with the project without being collaborators in the change process. So, when thinking about possible partners for a collaborative effort, the planning team can think of those who have a common mission and who bring something new and diverse to the table. For example, the organization may wish to collaborate with disability advocacy organizations, other provider organizations, and local workforce development organizations to create a public awareness campaign about disabilities, direct support, and career opportunities.

Collaborators are people with a deep commitment to the change process. Collaboration requires shared mission, vision, and values and a joint planning process. It often means the redefinition of roles and requires trust among all of the involved partners (Reilly, 2001). Collaboration between and among similar organizations in the geographic region or between departments within the organization may be the result of an intervention, or may ultimately be the intervention.

Another step before the strategy is actually implemented is to define the roles and responsibilities of each person involved in the intervention. A person may simply present a plan to an administrator for approval and action or may be involved through every step of the process. Change is more likely to happen when there is a champion for the change—someone who is passionate about the idea and sees it through. Without a champion, the best plans can easily fail. Before assigning roles, the team should make an inventory the strengths, weaknesses, and interests of its members. If, for example, a team member loves to speak to groups but does not enjoy financial tasks, team members can define that person's role as one of sharing information and explaining the intervention, while assigning a partner with numerical strengths to work on cost–benefit analysis and budgeting.

Once the collaborators in the change effort have been identified, many different tasks will need to be assigned. The group will have to review relevant information about the chosen intervention, select the particular form the intervention will take, and develop a list of tasks to complete in implementing the intervention. Information about how to implement various intervention strategies can be found in the chapters describing those interventions. If the planning team opts to use an intervention not described in this book, the team may need to identify and acquire other resources to assist in conducting the intervention. The team may also decide that an internal or external consultant may be helpful in implementing certain parts of the change strategy.

Finally, it is important to consider the costs of implementing and evaluating the strategy. Some costs are direct, such as the financial costs of a hiring bonus program. But, there are also indirect or hidden costs, such as the salary of the employee who keeps the records and issues the checks for cash bonuses. Other indirect costs may include covering the shift of a DSP who is participating on a work group to design and implement an intervention. The intervention team would be wise to list as many direct and indirect costs as can be identified and then to develop a specific strategy for acquiring the needed resources before the intervention is implemented. This strategy will be helpful both in managing the cost of the intervention and in getting buy-in from stakeholders who need to assist in paying for the intervention.

Costs are not only financial; they also include time and personnel costs. There may, in fact, be an intervention that could be an answer to a lot of an organization's recruitment and retention challenges, but if there are not enough people to cover the daily business of the organization while others work on that special project, or if other projects are underway and people do not have the time to fully invest in yet another project, then that would not be an appropriate intervention to choose. Another cost to consider is the political cost, or goodwill. An intervention that is intensive or a multitude of smaller interventions can stretch the goodwill of colleagues. People will grow tired of frequent inundations of new methods or practices and will be less likely to cooperate. The intervention team is therefore wise to select one intervention that is likely to produce demonstrable results and carry it through; once that intervention has proved successful, the team can try another.

Identify Implementation Barriers

There can be barriers of many different types to implementing recruitment, retention, or training interventions. The intervention team should think of the "yeah, buts" that it will encounter in implementing the intervention—those statements made by stakeholders about why the intervention would not work. For example, a board member may say "*Yeah*, that sounds like a great idea, *but* how will we pay for it?" The goal is for the team to anticipate the "yeah, buts" in the planning process so that it can devise strategies to overcome these challenges. Each of the chapters describing interventions in Sections I–III includes a discussion of common barriers and suggestions for overcoming them. In this chapter, the sections called Identify Implementation Barriers and Identify Support for the Strategy are used instead of a section on overcoming implementation barriers.

Lack of adequate resources—time, money, and personnel—is another common barrier. This barrier can be overcome through a variety of means. A demonstration that the benefits of the intervention may outweigh the costs may convince administrators or boards of directors to reallocate resources for an intervention effort. Collaboration may also overcome some of these barriers because burdens may be shared across organizations. Grant writing and other fundraising activities may also provide additional resources.

The biggest barriers may not be due to inadequate resources but rather to attitude. Often people are resistant to change and prefer to do what is familiar and comfortable, to "do what they've always been doing," even if it continues to "get them what they always got." The planning team may encounter skeptical board members, cynical long-time DSPs who "have seen it all," and worried FLSs who wonder how they are going to fit one more thing into their busy schedules. This is where knowing and understanding change theories can be helpful. The team can look back at the organizational change theories described in Chapter 12 and the behavioral change theories discussed in this chapter for assistance in tailoring its message to address the arguments of those reluctant to change.

An important strategy for addressing the "yeah, but" barriers is to include from the beginning those stakeholders who are most likely to raise them in the planning process. That way these people will know the process that the team uses to conduct a baseline assessment, will understand the size and scope of the challenge, and will have good information about what the intervention is and why it was selected. It may also be helpful to solicit recommendations about alternatives from those who raise objections. Sometimes if a "yeah, but" is not adequately addressed in the planning process, it results in failure of the intervention to achieve the desired outcome.

Identify Support for the Strategy

Part of bolstering the argument for change and promoting change is gaining support for the intervention. Support can come from information and from stakeholders. One important source of information is research-based evidence. This evidence can come from a variety of places: web sites of reputable organizations such as university research centers, professional organizations, or on-line journals. Professional organizations, research centers, and even state organizations often publish reports and manuals that may provide the evidence needed to support a given intervention. Professional journals are also important sources of research-based evidence. In the case of the interventions described in this book, the literature review in Chapter 1 and the section called Research Support for Solutions in each intervention chapter are good sources of this information.

A second source of information that the planning team can use to support the intervention is internal data. This is one more reason that doing a baseline assessment is so critical. This baseline assessment provides the information needed to clearly define the challenge and how the intervention may help. It describes the current situation and can help define the direction of the intervention.

A third source of support comes from stakeholders. Stakeholders are those people who have some interest in the organization and its business. Some stakeholders are obvious: individuals who receive supports and their families, organization employees, administrators, and boards of directors. Other stakeholders may also be less obvious. Licensing organizations, funding organizations or purchasing agents, taxpayers, and the community are all potential stakeholders. The planning team can use support from stakeholders in a variety of ways. Some of that support might come in the form of information. For example, people who receive supports can share their experiences of how a particular staffing challenge affects their lives. Other stakeholder support might come in terms of material or instrumental support. Stakeholders may be willing to share skills or make financial contributions to support an intervention they see as beneficial to their interests in the organization. For example, a parent of an individual receiving supports may work in the human resources department of a Fortune 500 company and may be able to offer assistance with calculating the cost of turnover to the organization. State departments of disabilities, local units of government, and/or advocacy groups may be sources of grants or other funds for a pilot project to address recruitment and retention issues. Stakeholders may also put pressure on the organization's board or administration to provide the resources necessary to address recruitment, retention, and training challenges. The intervention team can think broadly and creatively about who the stakeholders are and what they may be able to contribute in terms of support.

Set Goals, Measure Progress, and Establish a Time Frame

Once the team has selected an intervention, time lines and steps in the actual implementation will have to be identified, along with strategies to measure the effectiveness of the intervention. As mentioned in Chapter 13, these goals should be SMART: *s*pecific, *m*easurable, *a*ttainable, *r*ealistic, and *t*ime bound (Sauer et al., 1997). The team can use goals that fit these guidelines to later demonstrate the effectiveness of a particular intervention, which will make the case stronger for the next change.

After identifying its goals, the team needs to decide how to implement the strategy. As Chapter 13 explains, implementation can either be done on a pilot test basis (in a few selected sites) or as a full-scale implementation (across the whole organization). Pilot trials are beneficial because they can be done with employees that are excited about implementing the project. Pilot tests generally use fewer resources than do full-scale implementations. Pilot tests also have the benefit of showing what works and what does not so that the bugs can be worked out of an intervention before it is applied to the whole organization.

Smaller organizations (e.g., those with five or fewer FLSs) may want to move straight to full-scale implementation. In some instances, full-scale implementation may be better than a pilot test, which can fade out or lose steam before the entire organization implements the intervention. An organization may also want to consider a full-scale implementation if the intervention is very focused or it only makes sense as a full-scale intervention (e.g., practices related to advertising open positions, wage increases, or benefits). Full-scale interventions are also a wise choice if the organization has other significant projects in the future that may require the organization's resources.

When planning an intervention, it is important for the team to lay out each of the steps necessary to implement the strategy, the person responsible for each step, and the date by which each step should be accomplished. Effective project management can keep the project on track within its planned scope, time lines, and budget and other resource allotments (Martin & Tate, 1997). The team can use a number of project management tools, from computer programs, to charts, to sticky notes. A simple Intervention Plan Questionnaire worksheet appears at the end of this chapter that could be used to track progress.

Implement and Evaluate the Success of the Intervention

Two final steps are to actually implement and evaluate whether the intervention succeeded. Chapter 13 describes the many tools and processes that can be used not only in baseline assessment but also in evaluations after an intervention has been put in place. The organization can use the lessons learned when planning future interventions.

QUESTIONS TO PONDER

1. Think about a workforce challenge that your organization is facing or has faced. What intervention is being planned or has been used? Which stakeholder groups must be included in planning, implementing, and evaluating the intervention?
2. To what extent has your organization assessed the nature and extent of the challenge before selecting an intervention? How can you be confident that the intervention you have selected will address your highest priority problem?
3. What process did/will the team use to select an intervention? What factors did/will the team use to select one intervention if team members were/are interested in several different interventions?
4. Given the baseline assessments your team has conducted, which intervention strategy should your team consider using to address your identified challenges?
5. What are the "yeah, buts" that could derail the selected intervention if they are not addressed?
6. How can the baseline information be used to bolster support for this intervention? What other support will be required?
7. At your organization, how are individuals receiving supports and their family members and DSPs involved in identifying challenges, selecting intervention strategies, implementing solutions, and measuring the results?
8. What process have you established to measure whether the intervention you selected has actually been implemented as it was designed? At what points in time will you reassess your decisions to see if the intervention should be modified, or if another intervention should be selected?

CONCLUSION

Planning an intervention to address a specific workforce development challenge can be daunting. This chapter provides guidelines to assist organizations to translate the ideas in this book into a plan that can be carried out. There is nothing magical about the steps in this task analysis. Some organizations may want to add additional steps or components, whereas others may wish to condense the number of steps. We have used the process described in Chapters 13 and 14, however, to assist many community human services organizations in dealing with workforce problems. We encourage organizations to at least discuss each of the steps during the planning process. Intervention teams may also find it useful to refer to Chapter 12 to be sure that their plans incorporate each of the eight elements of change mentioned there (i.e., planned change strategy, action orientation, clear vision, strong leadership, organizational culture, continual staff support, flexible organizational structure, and strong coalitions).

RESOURCES

Dykstra, A., & Gustafson, D. (1999). *The exemplar employee: Rewarding and recognizing outstanding direct contact employees.* Homewood, IL: High Tide Press.

This book tells the story of how one organization developed an intervention to improve professionalization and recognition, providing a useful example of how to implement a workforce development intervention.

In the Spotlight: Intervention Plan Questionnaire — An Example

This In the Spotlight segment shares a hypothetical intervention plan questionnaire for XYZ Homes, Inc., an organization that is struggling with turnover among new hires. It illustrates the various steps in developing and implementing an intervention.

XYZ Homes, Inc., is a multisite organization providing community residential supports to individuals with intellectual disabilities in a large metropolitan area. The organization has experienced turnover and vacancy problems for the past few years. This has caused considerable problems for the organization as a whole. Some DSPs have had to work at multiple sites in the same week to cover unfilled shifts and thus log many hours on the road. FLSs report that they are feeling burnt out from having to do so much direct support work and from not being able to find adequate candidates. FLSs and DSPs feel so overwhelmed by the workload that they have not been able to figure out how to reduce turnover and vacancy.

A team consisting of Aisha (the FLS mentioned earlier in this chapter), her colleagues at the home where she works, and staff in two other homes in the same community completed the following Intervention Plan Questionnaire to develop a plan to address turnover and vacancy problems at XYZ Homes, Inc. (A blank copy of this questionnaire appears at the end of the chapter.)

Intervention Plan Questionnaire[1]

1. **What problem/challenge will your organization address?**
   We are constantly hiring new people but never have enough to fill all the hours. The new people barely get started before they quit.

2. **How big is the challenge? What is the baseline level of performance at your site in regard to this challenge (e.g., crude separation rate, percentage of new hires recruited by current workers, organizational commitment level, job satisfaction rates, areas staff have identified as needing improvement, average tenure of workers who quit, reasons workers give for leaving your organization, vacancy rates)?**

   _____

   (continued)

---

[1]Questions from O'Nell, S., Hewitt, A., Sauer, J., & Larson, S. (2001). *Removing the revolving door: Strategies to address recruitment and retention challenges* (p. 44 of Module 1 in facilitator guide). Minneapolis: University of Minnesota, Institute on Community Integration, Research and Training Center on Community Living; adapted by permission.

A baseline analysis reveals that the annual turnover rate is 75% per year; 60% of all new hires leave in their first 6 months on the job; 55% of new hires report that their expectations about the job did not match their actual experiences; and 25% of sites report significant interpersonal conflict between staff members. Exit interviews show that many of those who left within 6 months of being hired did not know what the job was really going to be like.

3. **What strategy do you propose to address this challenge?**
    We will develop a realistic job preview (RJP) to increase the chance that newly hired staff members will have realistic expectations about their jobs and will stay in their jobs for at least 1 year.

4. **What are the major components of the intervention strategy? (What will be done?)**
    We will use an RJP intervention. The major components are outlined in 4a–4c.

4a. **Who will be involved in developing, implementing, and evaluating the intervention? What roles will each person play?**
    - A planning team consisting of an administrator, a manager, three FLSs (one from each of the three pilot sites), three DSPs, and an individual who receives supports will develop the intervention plan.
    - Each FLS on the planning team will work with a team of DSPs and individuals receiving supports and their families to develop an RJP for the site they supervise.
    - The planning team will reconvene quarterly to review progress and evaluate the RJPs.

4b. **What are the steps involved in the intervention?**
    - Meet with the planning team to establish a time line for the project.
    - Train team members about how to conduct an RJP intervention. Supplement that information with the lesson on RJPs offered by the College of Direct Support (http://www.collegeofdirectsupport.com).
    - Survey current and new staff, asking the following:
        - What specific incidents would make you want to leave this organization or job?
        - What is the best part of your job? What would make you want to stay at this organization or in this job?
        - What could your employer do to make your job better?
        - What has been the hardest part of starting this job? Give specific examples.
        - What would you tell a friend if he or she were applying for your job?
    - Use the results of the survey to review and revise the job description for DSPs to ensure that it is complete and accurate.
    - Use assessment results to identify what to include in the RJP. Summarize information that recruits are unlikely to know or that they may have unrealistic expectations about, including the following:
        - Basic information about the job (e.g., hours and scheduling, pay, paid leave time policies, job prerequisites)
        - A description of typical job duties, such as cooking, shopping, assisting with personal care, helping supported individuals develop and maintain friendships, helping supported individuals manage their own behavior, and keeping records of supported individuals' activities and progress toward their personal goals
        - General information about the interests and needs of the people supported
        - A description of the organization's mission and vision
        - Basic expectations about work behavior (e.g., the importance of showing up and being on time for every shift, expectations about respectful interactions)
        - Testimonials from current employees about why they love their jobs
        - Testimonials from current employees about the hard parts of their jobs
    - Develop a strategy to present the information to new recruits. (We can consider using photo albums or scrapbooks, structured observations at the sites, and interviews with current employees.)
    - Get consent from DSPs and supported individuals or their guardians for use of their images in photographs and for the structured observations.
    - Implement the RJP in pilot sites. (The RJP will be implemented with 10 new hires in each of the three sites.)
    - Measure the results, evaluate success, and modify the RJP based on feedback, using the following steps:
        - The team will assess the extent to which each pilot study participants' expectations were met (30 days after hire).
        - The new hires will be followed for 1 year. The percentage of new hires that stay 3 months, 6 months, and 1 year will be calculated.

(continued)

- The team will ask pilot study participants what they liked and did not like about the RJP, and should be added or removed.
- The RJP will be revised based on the feedback received.
- Develop a training session for supervisors who did not initially participate to describe RJPs and how they worked in the pilot sites:
  - Identify trainers from FLSs and DSPs of pilot sites.
  - Develop training materials describing RJPs and pilot process.
  - Train participants how to create and implement RJPs.
  - Support the learners as they craft and implement an RJP.
  - Assess the competence of those implementing the RJPs by measuring whether people hired after the RJP is implemented have fewer unmet expectations about the job than people hired before the RJP was implemented.
- Implement the intervention organizationwide.
  - Once the three pilot sites have established successful RJP interventions, plan an opportunity with those involved in the RJP to share what they did and what happened as a result with supervisors in other parts of the organization.
  - Identify supervisors and others throughout the organization who are interested in implementing RJPs. Provide training and support to those individuals on how to develop a successful RJP intervention.
  - FLSs hold meetings with DSPs to identify site-specific job duties.
  - FLSs identify DSPs to lead RJP development.
  - Get consents for use of photographs and participation in structured observations.
  - Each site creates an RJP and uses it for interviews.
  - The success of the interventions are measured for each site and for the organization as a whole to learn whether the intervention made the anticipated difference in reducing turnover of newly hired DSPs.

4c. What are the costs associated with this intervention?
- Time for planning group meetings
- Time for each person to complete surveys
- Time to analyze and revise job descriptions, analyze surveys, and develop a list of content for the photo albums or scrapbooks
- Paper and printing for surveys and reports
- Purchase of scrapbook (albums, special pens, and paper) and photo (film, developing) supplies
- Time to create and update the scrapbooks

5. What are the main barriers to using this intervention? Consider the board, administration, staff, individuals receiving supports and their family members, and other stakeholders.
- Investment of time by all stakeholders can be stressful because people are already overwhelmed.
- Getting buy-in to actually use the scrapbooks during hiring could be difficult.
- People who are unfamiliar with RJPs may not understand how they might be helpful.
- Some may be concerned about confidentiality issues for the people whose photos would be included.
- Getting staff to participate in the surveys and discussions could be difficult.
- Individuals receiving supports and their families may object to the RJPs, especially if they do not understand the purpose of the RJPs.

6. Identify the arguments the planning team will use to support using this intervention. How will it enlist the support of various stakeholders?
- Research findings [described in Chapter 3] suggest that RJPs are especially effective when turnover rates are particularly high, and our turnover rates are high.
- Sharing our organization's baseline data will help demonstrate that we have a problem and that it is substantial.
- Providing training for supervisors about why and how to use the RJP will be an important part of the implementation process.
- Involving individuals receiving supports and their family members (including getting consent to include their photos in the scrapbook) is a critical part of the project. We will explain that we think we can improve the quality of services we offer by reducing turnover. We will also explain that showing a picture is better than having a DSP start, learn the intimate details of a supported individual's life, and quit within a week.
- We will encourage staff to participate by presenting the surveys at a staff meeting where great snacks are available.

(continued)

- We will increase buy-in by inviting all staff at the site to share their ideas about which pictures should be included in the scrapbook and by recruiting a champion at each site who is creative and likes to do crafts such as scrapbooking.
- Funds for the project will come from the cost savings of running one less ad in the major newspaper per month for 2 months.

7. **What are the next steps? How will progress be monitored? What are the time lines?**
   - Month 1: Recruit planning committee members, train members about RJPs, and develop surveys to collect needed information.
   - Month 2: Collect survey information from staff.
   - Month 3: Analyze survey data, review and revise job descriptions as needed, plan how information about the project will be shared with all stakeholders, and get consent and buy-in from individuals receiving supports and their families.
   - Months 4–6: Train staff at pilot sites on using RJPs, create RJP scrapbooks in each pilot site, and test the RJPs with new hires to make sure the scrapbooks do what they are supposed to do.
   - Months 7–12: Use RJPs in pilot sites, maintain data about whether each applicant received an RJP, the percentage of applicants who were offered a position accepted, and tenure of new hires. Keep other sites informed of the progress of intervention at the pilot sites. Invite other sites that express interest to begin developing RJPs.
   - Month 13: Evaluate how the RJPs are working, make any needed changes, and share process and outcomes with other sites in the organization to build excitement about full-scale implementation.
   - Months 14–24: Implement RJPs organizationwide, train supervisors on how to develop and use RJPs effectively, and continue to collect and analyze evaluation data.

8. **How will the planning team assess whether the intervention worked?**
   We will assess the extent to which we meet the following project goals to decide whether the RJP intervention worked:
   - Project goal 1: Reduce the percent of new hires who have unmet expectations about the job from 55% to 20% within 6 months of implementation by presenting an RJP to each potential new hire before making a job offer.
   - Project goal 2: Reduce the percent of new hires who quit within the first 6 months from 60% to 40% by the end of the first year of implementing RJPs.

Intervention Plan Questionnaire

1. What problem/challenge will your organization address? _____

   _____

   _____

2. How big is the challenge? What is the baseline level of performance at your site in regard to this challenge (e.g., crude separation rate, percentage of new hires recruited by current workers, organizational commitment level, job satisfaction rates, areas staff have identified as needing improvement, average tenure of workers who quit, reasons workers give for leaving your organization, vacancy rates)? _____

   _____

   _____

3. What strategy do you propose to use to address this challenge? _____

   _____

   _____

4. What are the major components of the intervention strategy? (What will be done?)
   a. Who will be involved in developing, implementing, and evaluating the intervention? What roles will each person play?
   b. What are the steps involved in the intervention?
   c. What are the costs associated with this intervention?

   _____

   _____

   _____

5. What are the main barriers to using this intervention? Consider the board, administration, staff, individuals receiving supports and their family members, and other stakeholders.

   _____

   _____

   _____

6. Identify the arguments the planning team will use to support using this intervention. How will it enlist the support of various stakeholders? _____

   _____

   _____

7. What are the next steps? How will progress be monitored? What are the time lines?

   _____

   _____

8. How will the team assess whether the intervention worked? _____

   _____

   _____

From O'Nell, S., Hewitt, A., Sauer, J., & Larson, S. (2001). *Removing the revolving door: Strategies to address recruitment and retention challenges* (p. 44 of Module 1 in facilitator guide). Minneapolis: University of Minnesota, Institute on Community Integration, Research and Training Center on Community Living; adapted by permission.

Intervention Management Chart

Use this chart to track the major components of the intervention, including the tasks to be completed, the person responsible for making sure each task is completed, the target deadline for each task, and the date each task is completed.

Problem/challenge selected: _____

_____

Intervention selected: _____

_____

Goal(s): _____

_____

_____

Task	Person responsible	Target date	Date completed

V

THE BIGGER PICTURE

15

STRATEGIES FOR POLICY CHANGE

SHERYL A. LARSON AND AMY S. HEWITT

This chapter discusses the importance of addressing direct support workforce challenges through policy and legislative initiatives to enhance wages, improve training, create opportunities, and enhance the status and image of direct support professionals (DSPs). Suggestions are made as to how to influence local, state, and federal policy decisions and the importance of including DSPs in this process. Specific successful examples of policy and legislative efforts to address direct support workforce development are provided.

TARGETED FRONT-LINE SUPERVISOR COMPETENCIES

Primary Skills

Front-line supervisors (FLSs) identify necessary changes in the program planning and monitoring systems within the organization and at the local, state, and federal levels and advocate for these changes with their managers and government officials.

FLSs attend and actively participate in organization management, planning, and cross-functional work group meetings.

RESEARCH SUPPORT FOR SOLUTIONS

This book has focused on what administrators, managers, and supervisors can do to address recruitment, retention, and training challenges within their organizations. We hope that it is clear by now that organizations can do many things to make a difference. It is also true, however, that effective systemic improvements in workforce challenges will not happen without policy changes (through governmental policy shifts, legislation, and/or litigation). This chapter describes many policy interventions that have been used to make improvements in workforce outcomes in supports for people with disabilities.

Recruitment, retention, and training challenges threaten the sustainability, growth, and quality of community human services. The ability to create new services and to maintain those that already exist is made enormously more difficult by the direct support staffing crisis. Even as the U.S. Department of Health and Human Services issues requests for proposals for systems change grants that will provide greater access to community services (Thompson, 2001), community human services organizations, individuals receiving supports and their families, and advocates express concern about the sustainability of existing services and great reluctance on the part of federal, state, and local government agencies to expand to meet new demand (Hewitt, Larson, & Lakin, 2000). Pressure to reduce waiting lists; to increase the availability of community supports for individuals who want them; and to provide high-quality, individualized supports that deliver desired outcomes make this workforce crisis more severe and underscore the importance of finding solutions to these challenges.

Many states still have large numbers of people living in institutions and large congregate care settings. In fact, an estimated 42,835 people with developmental disabilities in the U.S. still live in state-operated institutions compared with 443,217 who now receive community Medicaid-funded long-term care supports (Prouty, Smith, & Lakin, 2004). With the pending lawsuits that have resulted from the *Olmstead v. L.C.* decision (Smith, 2003), there could not be a more pressing urgency for federal and state agencies to find solutions to the direct support workforce crisis. The New Freedom Initiative (http://www.cms.hhs.gov/newfreedom) and the related Executive Order 13217 were presented to the public in 2001 by the Bush administration. This initiative set forth a series of grants, programs, and new policies designed to increase access to community services for all people with disabilities and to ensure that adequate infrastructure supports exist in the community, including an adequate, well-trained DSP workforce. There is no foreseeable way that efforts to provide equal access to community services can succeed without finding resolutions to the problems of DSP recruitment, retention, and training. Systems change efforts to enhance community opportunities for people with developmental disabilities must include specific, planned, proactive, and comprehensive efforts to increase the public awareness of the direct support profession; efforts to increase the numbers of people who enter this line of work; and serious efforts to enhance DSP wages, benefits, and incentives to get DSPs to remain in their positions.

Local governments, community human services organizations, individuals receiving supports and their families, and advocates report that these issues are among the *most important* challenges to overcome today (Hewitt, Larson, & Lakin, 2000). Recruitment and retention concerns have been noted by individuals receiving supports (Jaskulski & Whiteman, 1996) and their families (Hewitt, Larson, & Lakin, 2000; Jaskulski & Whiteman, 1996; Larson & Lakin, 1992), provider organizations (ANCOR, 2001b; Rosen, 1996), and policy makers (Chao, 2002; National Association of State Directors of Developmental Disabilities Services, 2000a).

Congressional Direct Support Professional Recognition resolutions were passed in the U.S. House of Representatives (H. Con. Res. 94) and U.S. Senate (S. Con. Res. 21) in 2003,

> Expressing the sense of the Congress that community inclusion and enhanced lives for individuals with mental retardation and developmental disabilities is at serious risk because of the crisis in recruiting and retaining direct support professionals, which impedes the availability of a stable, quality, direct support workforce

Furthermore, the concurrent resolutions found that "this workforce shortage is the most significant barrier to implementing the Olmstead decision and undermines the expansion of community integration as called for by President Bush's New Freedom Initiative, placing the community support infrastructure at risk." The resolution ended by noting that

It is the sense of the Congress that the Federal Government and States should make it a priority to ensure a stable, quality direct support workforce for individuals with mental retardation or other developmental disabilities that advances our Nation's commitment to community integration for such individuals and to personal security for them and their families.

The resolutions were further reinforced by report language in the FY 2004 appropriations for the Departments of Labor, Health and Human Services, and Education and related agencies (part of the Consolidated Appropriations Act of 2004, PL 108-199) that recognized "the growing crisis in recruiting and retaining quality direct support professionals to serve people with mental retardation and other developmental disabilities living in the community" (Lakin, Gardner, Larson, & Wheeler, n.d.).

Perhaps the most detrimental workforce challenge is the high turnover of DSPs, which hinders 1) the development and maintenance of relationships, 2) the development of mutual respect between DSPs and individuals who receive support and their family members, and 3) the development of trust between supported individuals and every new DSP that enters their lives. High vacancy rates, an increased use of overtime, and DSP turnover rates averaging 50% or more have negative effects on the quality of supports provided (Larson, Hewitt, & Lakin, 2004). Without continuity, quality, commitment, and competence in direct supports, the opportunity for people with disabilities to become full citizens and active community members is greatly diminished. The nature of the current workforce crises makes it difficult for organizations to provide even basic support such as help with self-care and medical support.

In the Spotlight: Camphill Association of North America
by Camphill Association of North America

Camphill communities promote social renewal through community living with children, youth, and adults with developmental and other disabilities. The communities vary in scope and size, with more than 90 worldwide. The seven communities in the United States, most of which are in rural settings (a residential school, two training centers for youth, and four villages for adults), are member sites of the Camphill Association of North America. In each of these communities, people with and without disabilities live alongside each other.

The Camphill way of life developed out of the belief that every person, with or without a disability, is unique and is entitled to lead a full and purposeful life in freedom and dignity as a contributing citizen. Camphill communities work hard to remove the social barriers that limit opportunities for people with disabilities and are environments where all people can discover, develop, and realize their abilities, becoming partners and contributors rather than recipients of services. In Camphill communities, staff are referred to as co-workers. Farmers, gardeners, crafters, therapists, administrators, and other supporters come from around the globe as full-time volunteers. Some people come for a short-term experience (generally, 1 year); others make it a way of life. The volunteers do not receive a salary in the usual sense. Each person works for the well-being and benefit of the others in the community, and, in turn, his or her living needs are supported (e.g., room and board, health insurance, vacation time).

Because the Camphill movement was founded in Europe, it has historically attracted international volunteers, mainly from Europe. As it becomes increasingly difficult for these volunteers to obtain visas to enter the United States, a key strategic objective of the Camphill Association of North America is to increase the number of American volunteers in its communities. To do so, the association decided to participate in the AmeriCorps program.

The National and Community Service Trust Act of 1993 (PL 103-82) created the Corporation for National and Community Service and various AmeriCorps programs (see http://www.americorps.org for more information about AmeriCorps). The AmeriCorps Education Awards program provides grants to national, state, and local community service programs that can support most or all of the costs associated with managing the work of AmeriCorps volunteers. The Camphill Association of North America chose to participate in the Education Awards program because it identified difficulty repaying education loans as a significant barrier to recruiting volunteers.

In April 2001, the Camphill Association of North America became an AmeriCorps member program with spots available for 20 full-time volunteers. Participation in the AmeriCorps program meant that the association had to institute a number of changes. To identify which changes each of its communities needed to make, the association conducted a needs assessment through multiple training workshops for supervising personnel. Participants discussed the requirements and responsibilities of site supervisors and program sites and identified priorities for skill development, administrative duties, and program infrastructure.

During this assessment, it became apparent that the technical assistance required for each site varied depending upon multiple factors relating to existing infrastructure. The Camphill Association of North America regional office began providing technical assistance to all sites to exceed AmeriCorps participation criteria, to streamline efforts across multiple sites, and to meet the particular needs of each site.

The U.S. Camphill communities thus moved toward greater accountability for admitting, supporting, and training AmeriCorps members to achieve goals to directly benefit community members with developmental or other disabilities. The volunteer application process was made clearer, with in-depth reference requirements and stringent background checks. The Camphill Association of North America also instituted formal mentoring arrangements and feedback tools such as reviews, exit interviews, and surveys. In addition, the regional office worked with a number of sites to improve pre-arrival orientation, interviewing, orientation, and mentoring.

The Camphill Association of North America encountered a variety of challenges while making these changes. The changes needed to be adapted to Camphill culture. For example, the feedback tools had to be appropriate to Camphill culture and also collect data in a measurable form. In addition, the Camphill Association of North America began to provide a great deal of education for site supervisors and communities about concrete obligations regarding being a member program of AmeriCorps.

Another challenge for the Camphill Association of North America was for its communities to coalesce as a cohesive AmeriCorps member program across great distances. To address this issue, the communities created common orientations, evaluations, and social events for volunteers from multiple sites. The communities encouraged peer support during orientation by inviting volunteers to provide contact information to be shared among interested volunteers.

During the Camphill Association of North America's first year as an AmeriCorps member program, nine AmeriCorps volunteers enrolled, all of whom had committed to volunteering at Camphill before learning about the AmeriCorps program. The low enrollment of AmeriCorps volunteers was attributed to an initial lack of know-how within Camphill about effective recruiting strategies. With increased knowledge and skills during the second program year, recruitment efforts strengthened and enrollments of AmeriCorps volunteers at Camphill communities increased. By October 2002, the Camphill communities had enrolled 20 AmeriCorps members and had received approval for 6 additional AmeriCorps slots, with the expectation of a further increase in enrollments in the year ahead.

STRATEGIES FOR RESPONDING TO THE PROBLEM

Improve Recruitment Strategies

Given severe difficulties in finding qualified workers, the likelihood is small that organizations providing direct support will be able to overcome the challenges without policy initiatives.

Federal and State Jobs Programs

Several policy initiatives have tried to address recruitment challenges. As noted in the In the Spotlight segment on the Camphill Association of North America, AmeriCorps and Job Corps programs target underutilized pools of potential workers to improve recruitment success. Other efforts increase the number of recruits by maximizing linkages with recent immigrants, students in secondary schools (through school-to-work programs and community service requirements), and students in postsecondary educational institutions. For example, the Minnesota WorkForce Center in Rochester works with community human services organizations to give web-based multimedia English lessons to personal care attendants who have emigrated from East Africa and who speak little or no English. This initiative increased the skills of the immigrants while they were working. Other states have begun to connect organizations that hire DSPs with state workforce initiatives. For example, in one economically depressed area of New Jersey, people who are in welfare-to-work programs are being recruited and trained specifically to work in DSP roles in state-run residential service settings.

Recruitment and Marketing Campaigns

Policy initiatives to improve recruitment success also include efforts to broaden the visibility of careers in community services. Several states, including Colorado, Connecticut, Kansas, Louisiana, Maryland, Massachusetts, New York, Ohio, Pennsylvania, and Rhode Island, have developed sophisticated recruitment programs using a variety of professional marketing mechanisms, including public service announcements; web sites such as http://www.rewardingwork.org/, http://hspeople.com/, and http://www.omr.state.ny.us/rr/index.jsp; news conferences; and a statewide DSP recognition day. In some states (e.g., Colorado, Connecticut, Massachusetts, New York), these initiatives are funded and sponsored in conjunction with the state developmental disabilities entity, whereas in other states, the state Developmental Disabilities Councils (DD Councils) or coalitions of provider organizations have organized these recruitment initiatives (e.g., Arizona, Arkansas, Illinois, Kansas, Ohio, Rhode Island; ANCOR, 2001b).

A federal initiative has also improved the profile of community DSPs by establishing a DSP apprenticeship program within the U.S. Department of Labor. The program guidelines describe work experience competencies and related instruction guidelines for human services organizations that wish to certify their employees as apprentices through this program. Apprenticeship programs include training and mentoring components (some of which use the College of Direct Support for content; see Chapter 7) that require documentation of competence on areas defined by the Community Supports Skills Standards (CSSS; Taylor, Bradley, & Warren, 1996) as well as a required number of hours of employment as an apprentice to become credentialed. Successful participants are awarded some form of salary increase. States such as Kansas, Massachusetts, Ohio, and Wyoming have been working to implement this apprenticeship program and have improved the linkages between state departments of labor staff and providers of community services. This has not only helped to implement the apprenticeship program but has also improved networking between the industry and the U.S. Department of Labor. This initiative also enhances career development opportunities for DSPs.

Other Federal, State, and Local Initiatives

The Kansas Mobilizing for Change project (Hewitt & Larson, 2002) initially addressed recruitment challenges through efforts to change policy. One component of this multifaceted project was the creation of a statewide recruitment taskforce to identify and develop plans to implement recruitment interventions. The task force developed a realistic industry preview video (similar to a realistic job preview; see Chapter 3 for more on RJPs). The video shows the good and not so good features about DSP careers in Kansas. The video is being adapted so that individual organizations in Kansas can use it. It also can be edited to be useful in other states and specific organizations (for more information, see http://rtc.umn.edu/wddsp/rjp.html). In June 2004, the state of Kansas committed to funding copies of the RJP video and a marketing toolkit as well as to provide training based on the *Removing the Revolving Door* curriculum (O'Nell, Hewitt, Sauer, & Larson, 2001) for FLSs in all provider organizations in Kansas.

In 2003 and 2004 the federal government funded 10 initiatives aimed at helping recruit, train, and retain DSPs. Part of the President's New Freedom Initiative, the Demonstration to Improve the Direct Service Community Workforce, granted $1.4 million each to six entities to increase access to health insurance for DSPs during 3-year demonstration periods:

- Bridges, Inc., a nonprofit service organization in Indiana
- The Maine Governor's Office of Health Policy
- The New Mexico Department of Health
- Finance and Pathways for the Future, a service provider in North Carolina
- The Virginia Department of Medical Assistance Services
- The Home Care Quality Authority, a Washington State organization

Four entities received grants of more than $600,000 each to develop educational materials, training for DSPs, mentorship programs, and other recruitment and retention activities:

- Arkansas Department of Human Services
- The University of Delaware
- Seven Counties Services, Inc., a service provider in Kentucky
- Volunteers of America in Louisiana

(More information about this program and the New Freedom Initiative is available at http://www.cms.hhs.gov/newfreedom)

Some organizations have had success in connecting with local workforce initiative boards, which guide policy initiatives within local communities and often determine how federal and state resources will be spent on various industries. In New York and Maryland, consortia of programs and organizations have had success in using support dollars to improve access to training, increase wages, and make other enhancements to the status and image of DSPs (see, e.g., the In the Spotlight segment on the Mid-Hudson Coalition in Chapter 5). The establishment of personal connections is critical to pressure workforce initiative boards to acknowledge the professionalism of the direct support workforce by supporting DSP apprenticeship programs in their states. The community human services industry must let communities know how big the profession is and the contribution it makes to the communities.

Federal, state, and local governments can assist in recruiting DSPs by funding training and technical assistance to organizations on recruitment and selection. Although Chapter 4 identified many relevant strategies, organizations and supervisors are often unaware of these recruitment and selection techniques. Projects such as the U.S. Department of Labor's Partnerships for Success Project, which funded training for supervisors and organizations and technical assistance in implementing recruitment and other workforce interventions, are needed throughout the United States to bridge the gap between such research-based strategies and actual practice. The Partnerships for Success Project reduced turnover by one third in 13 participating organizations over a 3-year period (Hewitt, Larson, Sauer, Anderson, & O'Nell, 2001).

Consumer-Directed Community Support Services Programs

Consumer-directed community support services (CDSS), funded by Medicaid Home and Community-Based Services Waiver dollars, can also be used to address recruitment challenges. CDSS were primarily designed to support self-determination, control, and choice for people with disabilities. They use a very different approach to recruiting DSPs. In CDSS programs, individuals with disabilities and their family members are given control over how they will spend the public dollars available to them through the waiver. They can use those dollars to recruit and hire family members, friends, and other people they know to provide supports rather than rely on provider organizations to find DSPs. This expands the pool of potential DSPs by tapping the natural support networks of the individuals who receive supports.

Address Wage and Compensation Issues

Research has consistently shown that higher turnover is associated with low wages (e.g., Braddock & Mitchell, 1992; Lakin & Bruininks, 1981; Larson et al., 2004; Larson & Lakin, 1999; Larson, Lakin, & Bruininks, 1998; State of Minnesota Department of Employee Relations, 1989). Improving pay, paid leave time policies, benefits, and opportunities for advancement must become priorities among policy makers if community support services are to continue. Interventions must include restructuring local, state, or federal government funding to community human services organizations for the supports they provide to build in cost-of-living salary adjustments. Since the late 1990s, several state legislatures have financed cost-of-living adjustments for

DSPs in community residential settings (Polister, Lakin, & Prouty, 2003), but in most cases this was not a recurring increase but rather one that had to be fought for anew in each legislative session. Providing cost-of-living adjustments may be the only way to forestall the regression of already low wages and benefits behind other industries. Additional efforts are needed to develop initiatives to raise wages to a livable level, using competency-based wage incentives.

Efforts to provide competency-based wage incentives have been proposed in New York and Minnesota. Minnesota legislation that was proposed in 2001–2002 (Minnesota H.F. 1483 and S.F. 1426, 82nd Legislative Session), which had not passed as of 2004, creates a direct support incentive program. To participate in the incentive program, organizations that hire DSPs must develop and implement a workforce development plan; submit data on turnover, tenure, wages, vacancies, and number of staff annually; agree to develop an organizational workforce development plan to address workforce issues identified by the organization as priorities; use their portion of the incentive to address priorities listed on the organization's workforce development plan; and document eligibility of DSPs for the program. This strategic plan could be in the form of the Intervention Plan Questionnaire that is discussed at the end of Chapter 14.

To be eligible to get a bonus the first time, a DSP must document 12 months of continuous satisfactory employment at the same organization, complete 10 semester credits of job-related coursework from an accredited postsecondary educational institution, demonstrate basic competence in the CSSS (Taylor et al., 1996), agree to abide by the NADSP Code of Ethics (see Chapter 5 and Figure 5.4), provide a letter of support from an individual receiving supports and/or his or her family, provide a letter from an employer documenting satisfactory job performance, and demonstrate competence in a required number of skill standard areas.

The proposal has a three-tiered incentive available to DSPs. In Tier 1, full-time DSPs who demonstrate competence in four areas in the CSSS (Taylor et al., 1996) and who meet the other requirements earn a $1,000 annual bonus, and their provider organization earns $500 to support training and other project costs. In Tier 2, eligible full-time employees who demonstrate competence in eight areas can earn an annual bonus of $1,750, and the provider organization earns $600. In Tier 3, eligible full-time employees who demonstrate competence in all 12 areas of the CSSS earn an annual bonus of $2,500, and the provider organization earns $700. Eligible part-time employees who work 20–39 hours per week and demonstrate competence in the specified areas can earn half of the corresponding tiered bonus amount annually. Employers also receive a prorated amount for eligible employees.

To be eligible for subsequent bonuses, a DSP must document continuous employment in the same organization for an additional 12 months, earn 20 hours or 2 semester credits (10 hours or 1 semester credit for a part-time DSP) advanced training on approved community support topics for which a certificate is earned, and document continued satisfactory job performance and competence in the same areas as the initial award. To earn a higher tier bonus, the person has to document competence in the additional number of skill areas required.

The proposed program also includes a statewide stakeholder group to conduct program oversight, establish policies and procedures, and identify administrative functions for eligibility determination. A management entity would be awarded a contract to administer the financial components of the proposal. The proposed program would also provide technical assistance to organizations on assessing competence, developing and implementing workforce development plans, providing training, and completing forms. The proposed program would provide technical assistance to DSPs on the contents of the CSSS (Taylor et al., 1996) and on how to gain access to training and document competence. The benefits of this proposal are that it provides increased wages and delivers a more stable and highly skilled workforce.

In addition to policy initiatives that increase wages, initiatives that fund alternative employment compensation and benefit packages, such as tuition credits at public colleges, universities, and technical schools, may be a valuable recruitment tool among younger workers. These initiatives require either policy or legislative changes in most states. Alternatively, organizations could lobby for tax credits to be developed to allow retirees on Social Security to benefit from employment in the human services industry. Organizations could also lobby for funding to provide other types of compensation, such as room and board; access to state health care plans; child care (especially nighttime care and care for sick children); discounts for DSPs at local retailers; free entrance to state and national parks; transportation that is paid for, subsidized by, or provided by the employer; and tuition or loan forgiveness.

Enhance Professional Identity and Recognition

Unfortunately, society tends to disregard the direct support profession. A significant disincentive, this lack of role recognition impedes workforce recruitment and retention. Several policy initiatives address this problem and help organizations develop viable career paths for DSPs. For example, sponsoring and holding statewide conferences specifically for DSPs or supporting state and national associations increases the visibility of DSP careers. Coalitions in states such as Kansas, Louisiana, Massachusetts, Michigan, Minnesota, Missouri, New Mexico, New York, Ohio, and Tennessee have formed local chapters of the National Alliance for Direct Support Professionals (NADSP) to enhance professional identity and recognition for DSPs (see Chapter 5 for more about professionalization and the NADSP). Membership in state or national task forces and working groups offers individuals the opportunity to contribute to discussions about workforce issues and other components of human services work and increases recognition of DSPs as professionals. Creating state and national awards to recognize excellence in DSPs can move the direct support profession to a level now enjoyed by other workforce segments. State agencies could show support for state and national DSP associations by providing meeting space, hosting project web sites, and identifying potential participants (through registries of DSPs).

Provide Education and Training

Ensuring adequate training for DSPs and FLSs is a substantial workforce development challenge, especially because organizations must often deal with inadequate resources for training while maintaining operations. Although some training and development occurs at the organization level, success will also require concerted policy initiatives to make pre- and in-service training opportunities available. Policy initiatives that support developing, disseminating, and updating effective training materials to keep learning opportunities fresh and focused on best practices is essential. Using skill standards, such as the CSSS (Taylor et al., 1996) and *The Minnesota Frontline Supervisor Competencies and Performance Indicators* (Hewitt, Larson, O'Nell, Sauer, & Sedlezky, 1998) offers opportunities to link demonstrated skills to credit-bearing and competency-based training. When workers are provided with incentives to complete training, such as tuition vouchers or loan forgiveness programs, these initiatives spark renewed interest in training experiences. Likewise, programs which result in a portable credential that can be carried from one organization to another maximize learning and minimize duplicated training among organizations.

In New York, the Kennedy Fellows Mentoring Program provides scholarships and career mentoring to DSPs enrolled for at least 6 credits at one of two colleges (Hewitt, Larson, & Ebenstein, 1996). Developed by John F. Kennedy, Jr., this program encourages DSPs to complete a 2-year degree and enhances eligibility for promotion to positions with greater responsibility. Across the United States more career paths and focused pre-service training opportunities are being developed each year. Many of these programs were sparked by Training Initiative Project (TIP) funds through the Administration on Developmental Disabilities, which is part of the U.S. Department of Health and Human Services. Although TIP funding no longer exists, University Centers for Excellence in Developmental Disabilities Education, Research, and Service (formerly called University Affiliated Programs) have maintained vital roles in providing training and continuing education for educators and DSPs. These projects reflect the growing national interest in and concern for developing, respecting, and supporting DSPs. They are designed to increase the visibility of direct support careers and can thus assist in recruiting new workers to the industry. The College of Direct Support (see Chapter 7) and the College of Frontline Supervision (see the Resources section of Chapter 11) are potential vehicles for the provision of credit-bearing and competency-based training based on skill standards.

The South Central Technical College in Minnesota has a training program for DSPs called Community Supports for People with Disabilities, which recruits high school students and then places program graduates in DSP positions in local companies (see the following In the Spotlight segment on this program).

In the Spotlight: Community Supports for People with Disabilities

The Community Supports for People with Disabilities (CSP) program was developed and implemented at South Central Technical College in Minnesota in the fall of 1997. It is intended for students who want to pursue careers as DSPs in health, human services, and education working with individuals who have disabilities. The CSP program evolved from a community-based model rather than a more traditional medical model of providing services to people with disabilities. Rather than teach future DSPs how to take care of people, program instructors teach participants to support individuals to care for themselves and learn to manage their own lives.

Many students who enroll in the CSP work in residential, vocational, education or special education, recreation, social service, or health settings. Other students have no experience in those settings but desire to learn to work with people who have abilities and challenges in their everyday life experiences. Some students are family members or friends of people with disabilities or are advocates with a wide range of backgrounds.

CSP is a credit-based program and is accredited by North Central Accreditation. Seven CSP students graduated with a certificate, a diploma, or an associate of applied science (AAS) degree in 1997–1998. Since then, the program has grown, with on-line distance education added in 2002 to complement its already respected face-to-face component. CSP now serves approximately 45–75 students throughout Minnesota at any given time. The course content is based on the CSSS (Taylor et al., 1996), is competency driven, and emphasizes skill application.

To earn a CSP certificate, students must complete 16 credits of coursework, including the following courses: Direct Service Professional, Physical Developmental Supports I, Facilitating Positive Behavior I, Person Centered Planning, Introduction to Computers, and Employment Search Skills. The 44-credit CSP diploma requires completion of the 16-credit CSP certificate, a 4-credit internship, and 24 additional credits selected from the following courses: Physical Developmental Supports II, Facilitating Positive Behavior II, Challenging Behaviors, Supportive Interventions, Person Centered Planning, Medical Terminology, Trained Medication Aide, Basic Nursing 101 (Certified Nursing Assistant), CPR, or First Aid. To earn an AAS degree, students must complete the 44-credit diploma and earn 20 transferable general education credits. Additional courses in sign language and leadership in service provision are also available for more experienced DSPs and supervisors who want to be role leaders in the health, human services, and education occupations.

As the use of intermediate care facilities for persons with mental retardation (ICFs/MR) declined with deinstitutionalization and Home and Community-Based Services funded by Medicaid Waiver and other sources grew, Minnesota required organizations supporting people with intellectual or developmental disabilities to employ Designated Coordinators, staff who had specialized training in providing supports to people with disabilities and who had educational and experiential backgrounds similar to those of Qualified Mental Retardation Professionals (QMRPs). (QMRP is a federal designation for certain employees in ICFs/MR. To obtain the QMRP designation, a person usually has to have at least a 4-year degree and must meet other requirements.) However, in Minnesota, people who complete the CSP diploma or AAS degree and who have 2 years' direct support experience can be Designated Coordinators and do not need to have a 4-year degree. The Designated Coordinator status allows students to apply for supervisory management positions in most service settings.

The benefits of the CSP program are many. Students who have earned a CSP certificate have professional credentials to show that they have obtained education in providing services to people with disabilities. Students who have earned a CSP diploma or an AAS degree can apply these college credits toward a social service, humanity, psychology, or social science degree at most 4-year colleges. CSP graduates have learned to apply a professional, knowledgeable, and skillful philosophy and attitude to direct support work. These people have shown commitment in the time they have put into their education and can be expected to maintain the same commitment to the industry, thus workforce retention is increased.

The CSP program is cost-effective. It costs employers $2,500 or more per employee to hire and train new DSPs. For about the same amount, CSP students meet these and more requirements at a mastery level before graduating from the program and entering the workforce. A background check is conducted for each student before the end of his or her first semester to prevent any students who are ineligible for direct support work, the educational institution, and industry from wasting time and money on training.

By paying for employees to attend or by providing time for them to participate in the CSP program, an organization provides recognition, praise, and value for its DSPs and provides an incentive for high-performing DSPs to remain with the organization and move up the career ladder.

Individuals receiving supports and their family members, their friends, and other advocates benefit because CSP students understand rules and regulations that apply to direct support and are skilled in advocating, reinforcing, and promoting a healthy, safe, secure, and independent lifestyle. Students learn Minnesota's regulations on preventing abuse and neglect and promote a self-advocating, empowering life experience. CSP students learn to teach people who have abilities and make contributions to their communities to be as independent as possible.

To learn more about the CSP program, go to http://www.southcentral.edu/dept/csp/ or contact W.C. Sanders, CSP developer, coordinator, and lead faculty member (South Central Technical College, 1920 Lee Boulevard, North Mankato, MN 56003; 507-389-7299; e-mail: wcs@southcentral.edu).

It is increasingly important that training initiatives not be limited just to organizations that provide traditional community human services (e.g., group homes). With the growth of CDSS, it is important that local-, state-, or federally funded legislative or policy-driven training initiatives develop, identify, and distribute competency-based training materials and technical assistance to assist supported individuals and their families to find, train, and keep DSPs.

Local, state, and federal programs could also assist education and training efforts by supporting training and providing technical assistance on effective orientation strategies; supporting organizations who catalog resources available to organizations to develop high-quality orientations that welcome new employees (e.g., the American Society for Training and Development, http://www.astd.org); funding contracts to develop, disseminate, and update effective training materials; establishing tuition voucher or loan forgiveness programs for DSPs; increasing reimbursement for training costs incurred by organizations and individuals who employ DSPs; and supporting voluntary credentialing programs. For example, in a 2001 program funded by the Commonwealth of Massachusetts, a pilot project offered a 1-year certification program with free tuition and books for 67 DSPs (ANCOR, 2001b).

States that are interested in developing voluntary credentialing for DSPs should build in the following components, which were identified by the NADSP (Hewitt, O'Nell, Lei, & Jendro, 2000):

- Participation should be *voluntary*.
- The credential should be based on a set of standardized competencies that are measured.
- The credential should allow local or regional autonomy yet be transportable for DSPs who move from one organization to another or from one geographic location to another.
- The credential should consider the satisfaction of the supported individual and/or his or her family with the supports provided by applying DSPs.

- DSPs should be required to have worked for a single provider for a specified length of time to earn the initial credential.
- The credential should be accessible to DSPs (e.g., in terms of cost, location, and support).
- The credential should articulate to other educational awards.
- The credential should lead to higher value (e.g., wage increase, college credit, other opportunities).

In addition to supporting voluntary credentialing programs, local, state, and federal governmental agencies can improve training opportunities and outcomes by doing the following:

- Providing DSPs and FLSs with encouragement and financial incentives to complete training and skill development
- Funding or developing statewide training and trainers to support organizations
- Offering test-out options for all competencies mandated in regulation
- Maximizing the use of technology-supported learning
- Requiring organizations to measure whether participants actually apply learning to their jobs (competency-based training)
- Supporting the development of peer mentoring programs for DSPs and FLSs

In the Spotlight: The Ohio PATHS Project

Marianne Taylor, Human Services Research Institute

The Ohio PATHS Project, funded by the Ohio Developmental Disabilities Council and directed by the Ohio Providers Resource Association in collaboration with the Ohio Alliance for Direct Support Professionals and the Human Services Research Institute (HSRI), was developed to strengthen the state's direct support workforce. PATHS stands for *p*rofessional *a*dvancement through *t*raining and education in *h*uman *s*ervices. Ohio PATHS is an employer-based, multilevel skills training program aligned with U.S. Department of Labor guidelines for apprenticeship as a DSP. Candidates who pursue the PATHS credentialing program can earn several certificates.

The planning consortium for Ohio PATHS used lessons from successful efforts in technical preparation along with a deep understanding of the direct support role and the human services industry in Ohio to design a relevant, practical, and robust credentialing framework plan. Among the recommended practices incorporated in the plan are

- Customization to human services industry characteristics
- Involvement of key stakeholders in planning and subsequent administration of credential operations
- Criterion-referenced competency-based approaches
- Use of valid and legally defensible employment skill, knowledge, and ethical practice sets customized to direct support
- Emphasis on assessment practices that are embedded in job performance or that closely approximate job performance
- Multiple credential levels/award tiers to create a defined career path
- Alignment with recently approved federal apprenticeship guidelines for direct support
- Planning for needs and marketing analysis
- Provisions for credential renewal

The planning consortium's mission is to "create clear and desirable career paths within the direct support role and from direct support to other roles within human services." Implicit in this mission is that the program should help candidates adopt a career focus as a DSP and that the credential program should offer a means of attracting people to pursue careers in direct support. Moreover, the content of the credential must be meaningful and relevant to effective direct support work. Benchmarks for mastery must be within the scope of incumbent workers who do not desire postsecondary degrees but should also bring candidates through a manageable sequence of learning that connects explicitly with more advanced programs for those who seek this path.

Planners extended this vision by suggesting the possible and desirable outcomes of the credential program if the identified mission is fulfilled. These aspirations create a portrait of a much healthier human services workforce than currently exists in Ohio and elsewhere. By taking steps to move toward this vision, Ohio has moved into the leading edge of progressive leaders in workforce development.

As of 2004, the PATHS project is in its second phase, which is aimed at implementing the PATHs credentialing program on a pilot basis. Growing from a core group of about 15 people, the PATHS project now has Regional Councils who have piloted the Certificate of Initial Proficiency in Direct Support with 60 DSPs from 15 organizations in three separate regions: Cleveland, Cincinnati, and Toledo. The first cohort of DSPs completed the initial certificate in January 2004. An evaluation is currently underway and coalition members are preparing the training infrastructure to pilot the Certificate of Advanced Proficiency in Direct Support. Several consortium partners have recently been approved to offer national apprenticeship status through the PATHS program. The U.S. and Ohio Departments of Labor have committed $100,000 in grant resources to assist Ohio's human services employers in offering apprenticeship opportunities.

The next phase will expand pilot capability to prepare candidates who have received their initial certificate to obtain the advanced certificate. The requirements for the advanced certificate are equivalent to the challenging requirements of the federally recognized senior specialist status in direct support.

Support Front-Line Supervisors

Training and supporting FLSs to do their jobs well is critical. Policy initiatives that can help these efforts include supporting the development of systematic training for FLSs based on established competencies (e.g., *The Minnesota Frontline Supervisor Competencies and Performance Indicators;* Hewitt et al., 1998), building in routine cost-of-living adjustments for FLSs, developing and distributing competency-based FLS training materials to organizations, and providing competency-based wage incentives for FLSs. These are similar to the policy recommendations for DSPs. The importance of supporting a highly qualified cadre of FLSs should not be minimized as workforce initiatives are crafted. As with DSPs, there is a need for governmental support for technical assistance for organizations to build competent FLSs. Developing a credential for FLSs based on established competencies would also be helpful. Finally, policy initiatives should support ongoing research to identify recommended practices in recruiting, training, and retaining FLSs.

Supervisor training initiatives funded by state DD Councils have begun in Illinois and Kansas. Community human services organizations in New Jersey, New York,

Tennessee, West Virginia, and Wyoming are participating in a 3-year project (2003–2006) called the National Training Institute for Frontline Supervisors and Technical Assistance Project. This project is training trainers in each participating state to provide training using the *Removing the Revolving Door* curriculum (O'Nell, Hewitt, et al., 2001) and the College of Frontline Supervision (see Chapter 11) to improve the skills of FLSs in supporting DSPs to reduce turnover and vacancy rates and improve training practices. Funding for this project has been provided by the National Institute on Disability and Rehabilitation Research (in the U.S. Department of Education). For more information, see http://rtc.umn.edu/ntiffs/main/index.asp.

Encourage Systems Building

Two system-related policy initiatives hold promise for improving workforce outcomes. First, there should be improved collaboration among state and federal agencies that have some responsibility or expertise in workforce issues to target cross-industry needs and boost potential worker pools (e.g., workforce development systems; school-to-work initiatives; welfare-to-work initiatives; postsecondary educational institutions; and federal, state, and local disability agencies). The challenge is to gather and communicate information about the many different effective practices to the people who need it.

Second, there is a need to improve accountability of community human services organizations and state and local systems to document the impact of recruitment, retention, and worker competence on the satisfaction of the individuals receiving supports. Although the human services industry is highly regulated and there are many attempts to measure the quality of services people receive, few elements of the quality assurance system comprehensively assess quality indicators related to the direct support workforce, such as turnover and vacancy rates. One exception is a recruitment and retention initiative created by the Pennsylvania General Assembly in which counties received workforce initiatives allocations in exchange for providing data on workforce challenges and for implementing an intervention plan (ANCOR, 2001b). Unless federal, state, or local governmental agencies routinely collect and disseminate information about how organizations are doing in these areas, assessment of both organizational and systemwide progress will be very difficult.

Gather Workforce Data

Policy interventions should be based on accurate, current data on the number of DSPs, salaries, turnover rates, recruitment challenges, and training needs. Polister et al. (2002) summarized documentation from 37 state agencies and 32 state residential direct support organizations regarding starting or average wages for DSPs in 42 states. Although this represents a remarkable increase in available information, compared with earlier summaries (e.g., Larson, Lakin, & Bruininks 1998), adequate information about turnover, vacancy rates, unfilled hours of service for individuals who receive in-home supports, DSP and FLS competence, DSP and FLS training needs, and the characteristics of DSPs and FLSs are still very difficult to gather. This information should be routinely collected for both DSPs and FLSs, at least at a state level, if states are going to make a serious effort to address existing workforce challenges. It is not known how many people are in the roles of DSPs and FLSs in community settings, much less the number of people working with various individuals (e.g., individuals with developmental disabilities, older adults, individuals with mental health disorders) or in various types of community programs (e.g., residential, vocational, in-home). Furthermore, ongoing information about starting, average, and highest wages for various positions and various service types is also needed, as is information about access to paid time off and other benefits. States should also be routinely assessing the extent to which workforce challenges contribute to organizations' use of waiting lists of people who are underserved or unserved. Finally, research should be funded to assess the costs and outcomes of recruitment, retention, and training challenges. The Direct Support Professional Workforce Status and Outcomes worksheet at the end of Chapter 13 may be useful as part of an annual evaluation submitted to state or local governmental agencies.

Form Coalitions

This chapter has listed many different types of policy initiatives that might be helpful in addressing recruitment, retention, and training challenges. The implementation of those initiatives should be done in a way that mirrors the process recommended in the chapters in Section IV on organizational change and assessment and selection of strategies. Specifically, these efforts should be made by coalitions of relevant stakeholders. Relevant stakeholder groups in policy initiatives include representatives of key groups who are involved at the organization level, as well as some players who would not always be involved in organizational interventions. One group of stakeholders that should be involved is representatives in the many different state or federal agencies that implement relevant programs. That means that in addition to individuals representing state or federal disability agencies, representatives from other agencies should also be at the table, including representatives from the U.S. Department of Labor or state departments of labor; state workforce systems that assist job seekers and employers; school-to-work programs; welfare-to-work programs; postsecondary educational institutions (especially institutions that train DSPs or FLSs); and state, county, or local governmental agencies. In some cases, significant efforts will be necessary to make sure those agencies that ordinarily do not collaborate with one another work together on this topic. Nongovernmental stakeholders who should be at the table include the people who receive supports and their families, political activists, community human services organizations (e.g., public or private, for-profit or nonprofit), coalitions of community human services organizations, union officials, and advocates. Finally, and most important, DSPs and FLSs should be represented in large enough numbers so that they are not intimidated and so that they can actively participate in the coalition (e.g., at least 2–3 DSPs in a group of 15 stakeholders). These stakeholders should work together to articulate and implement broad, comprehensive solutions and strategies. It is increasingly important that these efforts not be confined to just one disability group (e.g., individuals with intellectual or developmental disabilities, people with Alzheimer's disease, individuals with mental illness, people with physical disabilities) but rather that they involve cross-disability group work. The challenges and the solutions are similar across these groups.

Seek Change Through Litigation

Systems change in community supports for people with disabilities is sometimes achieved through policy initiatives such as those described in this chapter. At other times, however, family members and advocates have found those changes occur far too slowly or not at all and that the desired outcomes can only be achieved through other channels. Several lawsuits have been filed since the late 1990s arguing that wages or rate-setting practices in various states are illegal violations of various federal or state statutes or policies (Smith, 2003). Lawsuits that seek relief in the form of rate increases include *Ball et al. v. Biedess et al.*, filed January 2000 in Arizona; *Sanchez et al. v. Johnson et al.*, filed May 2000 and dismissed in January 2004 in California; *Interhab, Inc. et al. v. Schalansky et al.*, filed October 2002 in Kansas; *Sandy L. et al. v. Martz et al.*, filed September 2002 in Montana; and *Network for Quality M.R. Services in Pennsylvania v. Department of Public Welfare*, filed March 2002 and dismissed in July 2003 in Pennsylvania. Among the allegations in these suits are that the huge differential in wages between institutional and community settings violates the law and that the rates paid to community providers are too low for organizations to recruit or retain DSPs, resulting in the provision of inadequate supports. Regular status updates on these and other lawsuits are available at the Quality Mall web site (http://www.qualitymall.org/products/prod1.asp?prodid=260).

OVERCOMING IMPLEMENTATION BARRIERS

Making systems change is a difficult and lengthy process because of the size and complexity of the federal, state, and local governmental agencies involved. Common barriers in systems change initiatives include 1) exclusion of people who have the power to make the needed change from the planning process; 2) difficulties getting stakeholders to reach a consensus about the nature of the problem and about the specific changes that are needed; 3) hidden agendas and widely divergent interests of the various players; 4) lack of understanding about the political realities of the situation; 5) impatience with the process or unwillingness to pursue options that have been tried unsuccessfully in the past but that may now be successful in the current political climate; and 6) inability to mobilize grass roots initiatives—in this case, among DSPs and supported individuals and their families—to advocate for the change. It is beyond the scope of this book to address all of these issues. Some basic principles, however, can be applied to systems change efforts to increase their chances of success:

- Make sure that the people with the power to make the needed changes are involved in the discussions.
- Make efforts to understand the boundaries around what specific governmental entities can and cannot do.
- Use active listening skills in meetings.
- Involve an experienced, skilled facilitator in the discussions.
- Ensure that the case for the needed change is clearly and adequately documented.
- Focus on solutions that have research support regarding their effectiveness.
- Provide opportunities for DSPs to network and meet other DSPs.

- Support connections and partnerships between DSPs and supported individuals and their family members in an organized way to encourage grass roots mobilization.

Organizations or individuals that advocate systems change through legislation should ensure that the lawmakers hear from the people with disabilities and their families about the nature of the problem and potential solutions. Policy makers listen to paid lobbyists all day long; thus, it becomes easy to tune those special interest groups out. People with disabilities and their family members are much more effective spokespeople in this context. Also, when the issue being discussed specifically affects DSPs, it is critical that DSPs are well represented among those offering public testimony. In Minnesota, one of the most effective cost-of-living adjustment campaigns for DSPs was successful in part because new stories about the need for the increase from the perspective of DSPs were distributed to legislators every day while the proposed bill was being considered.

QUESTIONS TO PONDER

1. Which of the workforce challenges that your organization faces can only be adequately addressed through policy change or new legislation?
2. Before attempting systems change, did your organization implement the strategies described in the other chapters of this book so that you can demonstrate you have done everything you can and still require systems change to effectively accomplish the desired outcomes?
3. How have you included representatives of all the important stakeholders in establishing coalitions to pursue systems change?
4. Who are your organizations' natural partners in pursuing systems change in your state?
5. How has your organization worked with those partners to reach consensus about the desired solution so that legislators are hearing the same message from all parties?
6. To what extent has your organization established good working relationships with representatives of relevant local, state, and federal governmental agencies whose policies directly affect your organization?
7. Does your state or region have a plan that describes how it will address workforce challenges? If not, what will you do to bring stakeholders together to create one?

CONCLUSION

This chapter describes a variety of policy initiatives that can be undertaken to change how services are organized and paid for so that direct support workforce needs can be better met. The initiatives listed here are only some of the many options that are available. We encourage readers to balance their work in the policy arena with organizational work to improve internal workforce practices. The reality is that policy-level changes are difficult and can take a long time to achieve. They will not occur without planned, concerted efforts on the parts of all interested stakeholders. Empowering DSPs and FLSs to participate in and/or lead these efforts can increase the professionalization of those positions and the effectiveness of the policy initiatives.

We hope that this book has provided many ideas about interventions that address workforce challenges. Clearly, workforce challenges are difficult to address and are growing. You can do something to improve your organization's success in addressing those challenges. Our challenge to you is to select one intervention today that you will work on with DSPs, individuals receiving supports and their families, FLSs, administrators, and others to develop, implement, and evaluate within your organization. Also, if one or more of the policy intervention strategies identified in this chapter would work for your situation, we encourage your organization to work with other stakeholders in your city or state to plan and implement those policy changes as well. We would love to hear about your successes. Contact us and the other authors who contributed to this book at the addresses shown in the biographical sketches at the front of the book. To get updated information about the work of the Research and Training Center on Community Living at the University of Minnesota, check the direct support section of the center's web site (http://rtc.umn.edu/wddsp) and the Quality Mall (http://www.qualitymall.org) regularly.

RESOURCES

Bureau of Labor Statistics (http://www.bls.gov)

The Bureau of Labor Statistics provides statistics on employment and unemployment rates nationally and for various states. It also provides wage information for broad classifications of employees and other workforce descriptors. The Summer 2000 issue of its *Occupational Outlook Quarterly* (http://www.bls.gov/opub/ooq/2000/summer/art04.htm) provides a comprehensive review of workforce trends.

Kansans Mobilizing for Workforce Change, Credentialing and Apprenticeship Training (http://rtc.umn.edu/kansas/groups/credentialing.asp)

This credentialing web site includes many different resources that can be used to support systems change initiatives. One such resource is a presentation titled Building a Career Structure for Direct Support Professionals. More information about the credentialing framework can be obtained from Marianne Taylor, Senior Project Director, Human Services Research Institute, 2336 Massachusetts Avenue, Cambridge, MA 02140; 617-876-0426 x 2330; e-mail: taylor@hsri.org.

National Alliance for Direct Support Professionals (NADSP; http://www.nadsp.org)

The NADSP web site contains information from local chapters across the United States with tips and resources for how to start a professional association for DSPs. The NADSP and its member organizations are active at the local, state, and national levels in articulating the need for policy changes that improve the status, image, and professionalization of DSPs.

National Clearinghouse on the Direct Care Workforce (http://www.directcareclearinghouse.org)

The National Clearinghouse on the Direct Care Workforce provides a vast listing of on-line resources on recruitment and retention challenges, with a focus on services for older adults in the United States in nursing homes and community-based settings.

Quality Mall (http://qualitymall.org/directory/store1.asp?storeid=11)

The Staffing Store of Quality Mall contains information about the people who provide direct support and other services to people with developmental disabilities. Departments cover staff recruitment and retention, staff supervision and management, and staff training.

Research and Training Center on Community Living (http://rtc.umn.edu/wddsp)

This site includes many different resources and tools on recruitment, retention, and training of DSPs. In the Research section, the Policy Research Brief on DSP wages is posted. The site also includes information about currently funded research projects on DSP and FLS issues.

Smith, G.A. (2003, June 29). *Status report: Litigation concerning home and community services for people with disabilities.* Tualatin, OR: Human Services Research Institute. (Also available from the publisher, 503-885-1436 x17, http://www.qualitymall.org/download/Litigation062903.pdf)

This publication, which is updated regularly, provides a summary of lawsuits regarding access to Medicaid Home and Community-Based Services, community placement for people living in institutions, and limitations on Medicaid Home and Community-Based Services benefits (lawsuits on wages and other staffing issues are discussed in this section).

REFERENCES

Albin, J., Rhodes, L., & Mank, D. (1994). Realigning organizational culture, resources and community roles: Changeover to community employment. *JASH, 19*(2), 105–115.

Americans with Disabilities Act (ADA) of 1990, PL 101-336, 42 U.S.C. §§ 12101 *et seq.*

ANCOR. (2001a). *ANCOR Staff Vacancy/Turnover Survey.* Alexandria, VA: Author.

ANCOR. (2001b). *State of the state report.* Alexandria, VA: Author.

Anderson, L., & Hewitt, A. (2002). *I should be the payroll.* Minneapolis: University of Minnesota, Institute on Community Integration, Research and Training Center on Community Living.

Askvig, B.A., & Vassiliou, D. (1991). *Factors related to staff longevity and turnover in a facility serving persons with developmental disabilities.* Minot: Minot State University, North Dakota Center for Disabilities.

Association of Residential Resources in Minnesota. (1998). *Workforce recruitment handbook.* St. Paul: Author.

Babbie, E. (1990). *Survey research methods* (2nd ed.). Belmont, CA: Wadsworth.

Babbie, E. (2001). *The practice of social research* (9th ed.). Belmont, CA: Wadsworth.

Bachelder, L., & Braddock, D. (1994). *Socialization practices and staff turnover in community homes for people with developmental disabilities.* Chicago: University of Illinois at Chicago, College of Applied Health Sciences, Institute on Disability and Human Development.

Bagozzi, R.P. (1992). The self-regulation of attitudes, intentions and behavior. *Social Psychology Quarterly, 55*(2), 178–204.

Balfour, D.L. & Neff, D.M. (1993). Predicting and managing turnover in human service agencies: A case study of an organization in crisis. *Public Personnel Management, 22,* 473–486.

Bandura, A. (1977). Self-efficacy: Toward a unifying theory of behavioral change. *Psychological Review, 84,* 191–215.

Bandura, A. (1989). Social cognitive theory. *Annals of Child Development, 6,* 1–60.

Barnhart, R. (2002). *Behaviorally anchored rating scales.* Retrieved September 28, 2004, from http://www.competinc.com/root.php?url=art3.htm

Barry Associates. (1999). *The Ohio Provider Resource Association 1999 Salary and Benefits Survey.* Kokomo, IN: Author.

Bartram, D., Lindley, P.A., Marshall, L., & Foster, J. (1995). The recruitment and selection of young people by small businesses. *Journal of Occupational and Organizational Psychology, 68,* 339–358.

Batten, J.D. (1989). *Tough-minded leadership.* New York: AMACOM.

Behling, O. (1998). Employee selection: Will intelligence and conscientiousness do the job? *Academy of Management Executive, 12,* 77–85.

Bell, C.R. (2002). *Managers as mentors: Building partnerships for learning* (2nd ed.). San Francisco: Berrett-Koehler Publishers.

Benson, G.S., & Cheney, S.L. (1996). Best practices in training delivery. *Technical and Skills Training, 7.*

Blank, W.E. (1982). *Competency-based training.* Upper Saddle River, NJ: Prentice-Hall.

Boo, K. (1999, March 14). Forest haven is gone, but the agony remains. *The Washington Post,* p. A1.

Bowsher, J.E. (1998). *Revolutionizing workforce performance: A systems approach to mastery.* San Francisco: Jossey-Bass/Pfeiffer.

Braddock, D., & Mitchell, D. (1992). *Residential services and developmental disabilities in the United States: A national survey of staff compensation, turnover and related issues.* Washington, DC: American Association on Mental Retardation.

Bridges, W. (1991). *Managing transitions: Making the most of change.* Reading, MA: Addison Wesley.

Brounstein, M. (2000). *Coaching and mentoring for dummies.* Foster City, CA: IDG Books Worldwide.

Brounstein, M., & Visconti, R. (1992). *Effective recruiting strategies: A practical guide for success.* Menlo Park, CA: Crisp Publications.

Bruce, C., & Moore, P. (1989). Successful telephone interviewing. *Recruitment Today, 2*(2), 38–43.

Bruininks, R.H., Kudla, M.J., Wieck, C.A., & Hauber, F.A. (1980). Management problems in community residential facilities. *Mental Retardation, 18,* 125–130.

Brull, H. (1996, May). Effective interviewing practices. Presentation given at the Association of Residential Resources in Minnesota annual conference, Bloomington.

Brumback, G.B. (1996). Getting the right people ethically. *Public Personnel Management, 25*(3), 267–276.

Bryson, J.M. (1988). *Strategic planning for public and nonprofit organizations: A guide to strengthening and sustaining organizational achievement.* San Francisco: Jossey-Bass.

Bucholz, S., & Roth, T. (1987). *Creating the high performance team.* New York: John Wiley & Sons.

Buckingham, M., & Coffman, C. (1999). *First, break all the rules: What the world's greatest managers do differently.* New York: Simon & Schuster.

Buckley, M.R., & Russell, C.J. (1999). Validity evidence. In R.W. Eder & M.M. Harris (Eds.), *The employment interview handbook* (pp. 35–48). Thousand Oaks, CA: Sage Publications.

Bunker, B., & Alban, B. (1997). *Large group interventions: Engaging the whole system for rapid change.* San Francisco: Jossey-Bass.

Bureau of Labor Statistics (BLS). (2001a). *BLS releases 2000-2010 employment projections* (USDL 01-443). Washington, DC: Author. Also available on-line: http://www.bls.gov/news.release/ecopro.nr0.htm

Bureau of Labor Statistics (BLS). (2001b). *Occupational employment and wages, 2000* (Bulletin 2549). Washington, DC: Author. Also available on-line: http://www.bls.gov/oes/2000/oes_pub2000.htm

Bureau of Labor Statistics (BLS). (2003–2004, Winter). *Occupational Outlook Quarterly: A Special Issue. Charting the Projections 2002–2012, 47*(4). Washington, DC: Author.

Bureau of Labor Statistics (BLS). (2004a). Health technologists, technicians, and healthcare support occupations. In *Occupational outlook handbook, 2004–05 edition.* Retrieved September 28, 2004, from http://www.bls.gov/oco/reprints/ocor009.pdf

Bureau of Labor Statistics (BLS). (2004b). *Labor force statistics from Current Population Survey.* Retrieved September 28, 2004, from http://www.bls.gov/cps/home.htm (In the Latest Numbers box, go to the Annual Averages section; click the dinosaur next to Unemployment Rate. In the Change Output Options section, change the "From" date to say 1975, then click Go.)

Bureau of Labor Statistics (BLS). (n.d.). *Standard occupational classification (SOC) system.* Retrieved September 28, 2004, from http://www.bls.gov/soc

Burton, S., & Warner, D. (2001, October). The future of hiring. *Workforce, 80*(10, Suppl.), 74–88.

Butterworth, J., & Fesko, S.L. (1999). The successes and struggles of closing a facility-based employment service. *Research to Practice, 5*(1). Boston: University of Massachusetts Boston, Institute on Community Inclusion; and Children's Hospital Boston. Retrieved September 28, 2004, from http://www.communityinclusion.org/publications/pdf/conversion.pdf

California State Auditor. (1999, October). *Department of Developmental Services: Without sufficient state funding, it cannot furnish optimal services to developmentally disabled adults.* Sacramento, CA: Bureau of State Audits.

Camp, R.R., Blanchard, N.P., & Huszczo, G.E. (1986). *Toward a more organizationally effective training strategy and practice.* Upper Saddle River, NJ: Prentice-Hall.

Carr, C. (1992). *Smart training: The manager's guide to training for improved performance.* New York: McGraw-Hill.

Carr, R. (2002). *The mentor hall of fame.* Retrieved September 28, 2004, from http://www.mentors.ca/mentorpairs.html

Cascio, W.F. (1987). *Applied psychology in personnel management* (3rd ed.). Upper Saddle River, NJ: Prentice-Hall.

Cascio, W.F. (1997). *Applied psychology in personnel management* (5th ed.). Upper Saddle, NJ: Prentice-Hall.

Caudron, S. (1999, November). Brand HR: Why and how to market your image. *Workforce, 78,* 30–33.

Caudron, S. (2000). Learning revives training. *Workforce, 79*(1), 34–37.

Chao, E. (2002, September 24). *The direct support workforce crisis.* Paper presented the annual government affairs conference of the American Network of Community Options and Resources, Washington, DC.

Chapman, E.N. (1992). *The new supervisor: A guide for the newly promoted* (3rd ed.). Menlo Park, CA: Crisp Learning.

Coelho, R.J. (1990). Job satisfaction of staff in unionized and non-unionized community residences for persons with developmental disabilities. *Journal of Rehabilitation, 56,* 57–62.

Cohen, A. (2000, March). *Focus on the front line: Perceptions of workforce issues among direct support workers and their supervisors. A staff report.* Boston: Governor's Commission on Mental Retardation. Also available on-line: http://www.state.ma.us/gcmr/pdf/Focus_on_Frontlines_032000.pdf

Colbert, J.A., & Wolff, D.E. (1992). Surviving in urban schools: A collaborative model for a beginning teacher support system. *Journal of Teacher Education, 43,* 193–199.

College of Administrative Science. (1957). *Leader Behavior Description Questionnaire.* Columbus: Ohio State University.

Collins, C. (2000, December). *Joining together to ensure a stable, well-qualified workforce: A cross stakeholder dialogue.* Presentation at the 2000 annual meeting of the National Association of State Directors of Developmental Disabilities Services, Alexandria, VA.

Colorado Department of Human Services, Office of Health and Rehabilitation Services, Developmental Disabilities Services. (2000, September 15). *Response to Footnote 106 of the FY 2001 appropriations bill: Capacity of the community service system for persons with developmental disabilities in Colorado. Submitted to the Joint Budget Committee.* Denver: Author.

Consolidated Appropriations Act of 2004, PL 108-199, 118 Stat. 3.

Cook, T.D., & Campbell, D.T. (1990). *Quasi-experimentation: Design and analysis issues for field settings.* Boston: Houghton Mifflin.

Corcoran, K., & Fahy, J. (2000, June 18). Painful lessons: Lives hung in the balance as firm moved mentally disabled into communities. As problems grew, the state failed to intervene. *Indianapolis Star.*

Cortina, J.M., Goldstein, N.B., Payne, S.C., Davison, H.K., & Gilliland, S.W. (2000). The incremental validity of interview scores over and above cognitive ability and conscientiousness scores. *Personnel Psychology, 53,* 324–351.

Covey, S. (1989). *The seven habits of highly effective people.* New York: Simon & Schuster.

Cozby, P.C. (2004). *Methods in behavioral research.* New York: McGraw-Hill.

Craven, K. (1999). *Recruitment and retention tool kit: Strategies for finding and keeping good employees.* Salem: Oregon Rehabilitation Association.

Cunningham, P.M. (1999). *Survey of Rural, Paraprofessional, Human Service Workers in Alaska.* Anchorage: University of Alaska, Anchorage.

Curzon, S.C. (1995). *Managing the interview: A how-to manual for hiring staff.* New York: Neal-Schuman Publishers.

Davenport, T.H. (1993). *Process innovation: Reengineering work through information technology.* Cambridge, MA: Harvard Business School Press.

DeBono, K.G. (1993). Individual differences in predicting behavioral intentions from attitude and subjective norm. *The Journal of Social Psychology, 133*(6), 825–832.

Deems, R.S. (1994). *Interviewing: More than a gut feeling* [Videotape and handbook]. West Des Moines, IA: American Media.

Deeprose, D. (1994). *How to recognize and reward employees.* New York: AMACOM.

Dipboye, R.L. (1997). Organizational barriers to implementing a rational model of training. In M. Quinones & A. Dutta (Eds.), *Training for 21st century technology: Applications of psychological research.* Washington, DC: American Psychological Association.

Dipboye, R.L., & Jackson, S.L. (1999). Interviewer experience and expertise effects. In R.W. Eder & M.M. Harris (Eds.), *The employment interview handbook* (pp. 259–278). Thousand Oaks, CA: Sage Publications.

Division of Developmental Disabilities. (2001). *Residential Staff Survey.* Olympia, WA: Author.

Doljanac, R., Larson, S.A., Hewitt, A.S., & Salmi, P. (2004). *National validation study of competencies and training for frontline supervisors and direct support professionals.* Unpublished manuscript, University of Minnesota, Institute on Community Integration, Research and Training Center on Community Living, Minneapolis.

Doljanac, R., Larson, S.A., & Salmi, P. (2003). *Market analysis: Characteristics of direct support professionals in Ohio residential support settings.* Minneapolis: University of Minnesota, Institute on Community Integration, Research and Training Center on Community Living.

Dufresne, D., & Laux, B. (1994). From facilities to supports: The changing organization. In V.J. Bradley, J.W. Ashbaugh, & B.C. Blaney (Eds.), *Creating individual supports for people with developmental disabilities: A mandate for change at many levels* (pp. 271–280). Baltimore: Paul H. Brookes Publishing Co.

Dykstra, A., Jr. (1999). Quality performance and human resources. In J.F. Gardner & S. Nudler (Eds.), *Quality performance in human services: Leadership, values, and vision* (pp. 123–140). Baltimore: Paul H. Brookes Publishing Co.

Dykstra, A., & Gustafson, D. (1999). *The exemplar employee: Rewarding and recognizing outstanding direct contact employees.* Homewood, IL: High Tide Press.

Ebenstein, W., & Gooler, L. (1993). *Cultural diversity and developmental disabilities workforce issues: A report on the developmental disabilities workforce in New York City.* New York: The City University of New York, Consortium for the Study of Disabilities.

Education for All Handicapped Children Act of 1975, PL 94-142, 20 U.S.C. §§ 1400 *et seq.*

Effective Compensation, Inc. (2001). *Staffing Stability Survey.* (Report prepared for the Colorado Department of Human Services, Developmental Disabilities Services.) Lakewood, CO: Author.

Employment Management Association. (2001). *Summary of findings: Staffing 2001 Performance Survey.* Plymouth Meeting, PA: Author, a professional emphasis group of the Society for Human Resource Management (SHRM), with Staffing.org.

Ernst & Young. (1991). *State of Connecticut Blue Ribbon Commission on Fair Wages: Final report.* Hartford, CT: Author.

Ferris, K.R., & Aranya, N. (1983). A comparison of two organizational commitment scales. *Personnel Psychology, 36,* 87–98.

Fiorelli, J.S., Margolis, H., Heverly, M.A., Rothchild, E., & Krasting, D.J., III. (1982). Training resident advisors to provide community residential services: A university-based program. *Journal of the Association for Persons with Severe Handicaps, 7,* 13–19.

Fullagar, C., Smalley, K., Flanagan, J., Walker, L., Downey, R., Bloomquist, L., Bratsberg, B., Shanteau, J., & Pickett, L. (1998). *Community service provider direct care staff turnover study.* Manhattan, KS: Institute for Social and Behavioral Research.

Fullerton, H.N., Jr. (1997, November). Labor force 2006: Slowing down and changing composition. *Monthly Labor Review,* 23–38.

Gardner, D.P., et al. (1983). *A nation at risk: The imperative for educational reform* (Report of the National Commission on Excellence in Education). Washington, DC: U.S. Government Printing Office.

Garner, P. (1998). Reflections on agency change at Buffalo River Services. *Mental Retardation 36*(4), 314–316.

George, M.J., & Baumeister, A.A. (1981). Employee withdrawal and job satisfaction in community residential facilities for mentally retarded persons. *American Journal of Mental Deficiency, 85*, 639–647.

Gilliland, S.W., & Steiner, D.D. (1999). Applicant reactions. In R.W. Eder & M.M. Harris (Eds.), *The employment interview handbook* (pp. 69–82). Thousand Oaks, CA: Sage Publications.

Goldstein, I.L. (1993). *Training in organizations: Needs assessment, development, and education* (3rd ed.). Pacific Grove, CA: Brooks/Cole.

Grant, R.H. (n.d.). Quotation retrieved from http://www.quotationspage.com/quotes/R._H._Grant/

Graves, L.M., & Karren, R.J. (1999). Are some interviewers better than others? In R.W. Eder & M.M. Harris (Eds.), *The employment interview handbook* (pp. 243–258). Thousand Oaks, CA: Sage Publications.

Greene, A. (2000). Barriers to self-determination—what's next?: A service coordinator and point of entry perspective. In *Measure for measure: Person-centered quality assurance*. Wingspread conference proceedings, Racine, WI.

Greengard, S. (1995, December). Are you well armed to screen applicants? *Personnel Journal, 74*(12), 84–95.

Griffeth, R.W., Hom, P.W., & Gaertner, S. (2000). A meta-analysis of antecedents and correlates of employee turnover: Update, moderator tests, and research implications for the next millennium. *Journal of Management, 26*(3), 463–488.

Griffin, R.W., & Bateman, T.S. (1986). Job satisfaction and organizational commitment. In C.L. Cooper & I. Robertson (Eds.), *International review of industrial and organizational psychology* (pp. 157–188). New York: John Wiley & Sons.

Guilford, J.P., & Zimmerman, W.S. (n.d.). *Guilford-Zimmerman Temperament Survey*. Minneapolis, MN: NCS Assessments.

H. Con. Res. 94, 108th Cong., 150 Cong. Rec. 10301 (2003) (enacted).

Hall, B. (1995). Is multimedia worth the investment? *Training and Development, 50*, 77–78.

Hanson, M.J. (2004). Ethnic, cultural, and language diversity in service settings. In E.W. Lynch & M.J. Hanson (Eds.), *Developing cross-cultural competence: A guide for working with children and their families* (3rd ed., pp. 3–18). Baltimore: Paul H. Brookes Publishing Co.

Harris, M.M., & Eder, R.W. (1999). The state of employment interview practice: Commentary and extension. In R.W. Eder & M.M. Harris (Eds.), *The employment interview handbook* (pp. 369–398). Thousand Oaks, CA: Sage Publications.

Harvey, E. (2000). *180 ways to walk the recognition talk: The "how to" handbook for everyone*. Dallas, TX: The WALK THE TALK Co.

Health Insurance Accountability and Portability Act of 1996, PL 104-191, 42 U.S.C. §§ 201 *et seq.*

Heinlein, K. (2001). *Report to the Joint Appropriations Committee on study of nonprofessional direct care staff recruitment, retention and wages*. Cheyenne: Wyoming Department of Health, Developmental Disabilities Division.

Heneman, R., & Schutt, W. (2001). *Ohio Association of County Boards of Mental Retardation and Developmental Disabilities/Ohio Provider Resource Association Direct Care and Paraprofessional Wage and Benefit Study*. Dublin, OH: Scioto Group.

Henry, S., Williamschen, O., & Smith, D. (1998, Winter). A new perspective on training at Dungarvin. *IMPACT: Feature Issue on Direct Support Workforce Development, 10*(4), 16.

Hermelin, E., & Robertson, I.T. (2001). A critique and standardization of meta-analytic validity coefficients in personnel selection. *Journal of Occupational and Organizational Psychology, 74*, 253–277.

Hewitt, A.S. (1998a). *Identification of competencies and effective training practices for direct support staff working in community residential services for persons with developmental disabilities*. Unpublished doctoral dissertation, University of Minnesota, Minneapolis.

Hewitt, A. (1998b). *Community residential core competencies: Necessary competencies for direct support staff working in community residential services for people with developmental disabilities*. Minneapolis: University of Minnesota, Institute on Community Integration, Research and Training Center on Community Living. Also available on-line: http://www.rtc.umn.edu/pdf/analysis.pdf

Hewitt, A., & Lakin, K.C. (2001). *Issues in the direct support workplace and their connection to the greater sustainability and quality of workers.* Durham: University of New Hampshire, Institute on Disability.

Hewitt, A., & Larson, S.A. (1994). Training issues for direct service personnel working in community residential programs for persons with developmental disabilities. *Policy Research Brief, 6*(2).

Hewitt, A.S., & Larson, S.A. (2002). *Kansans Mobilizing for Change: A comprehensive workforce development initiative. October 1, 2002–September 20, 2004: $300,000 per year.* Wichita: Kansas Council on Developmental Disabilities.

Hewitt, A., Larson, S.A., & Ebenstein, W. (1996). State initiatives to address direct support worker issues. In T. Jaskulski & W. Ebenstein (Eds.), *Opportunities for excellence: Supporting the frontline workforce* (pp. 19–39). Washington, DC: President's Committee on Mental Retardation.

Hewitt, A., Larson, S.A., & Lakin, K.C. (2000). *An independent evaluation of the quality of services and system performance of Minnesota's Medicaid Home and Community Based Services for persons with mental retardation and related conditions: Technical report.* Minneapolis: University of Minnesota, Institute on Community Integration, Research and Training Center on Community Living.

Hewitt, A., Larson, S.A., & O'Nell, S. (1996). Considerations for national voluntary credentialing for direct service workers. *Policy Research Brief, 8*(2).

Hewitt, A., Larson, S.A., O'Nell, S., Sauer, J., & Sedlezky, L. (1998). *The Minnesota frontline supervisor competencies and performance indicators: A tool for agencies providing community services.* Minneapolis: University of Minnesota, Institute on Community Integration, Research and Training Center on Community Living.

Hewitt, A., Larson, S., Sauer, J., Anderson, L., & O'Nell, S. (2001). *Partnerships for success: Retaining incumbent community support human service workers by upgrading their skills and strengthening partnerships among workforce centers, educational programs, and private businesses. University of Minnesota subcontract final report.* Minneapolis: University of Minnesota, Institute on Community Integration, Research and Training Center on Community Living.

Hewitt, A.S., O'Nell, S., Lei, N., & Jendro, J. (Eds.). (2000). Alliance update: NADSP on national credentialing for DSPs. *Frontline Initiative, 4*(2).

Hinkle, S. (1996). Grassroots political action as an inter-group phenomenon. *Journal of Social Issues, 52*(1), 39–52.

Holland, J.E., & George, B.W. (1986). Orientation of new employees. In J.J. Famularo (Ed.), *Handbook of human resources administration* (2nd ed., pp. 1–24, 35). New York: McGraw-Hill.

Hom, P.W., Griffeth, R.W., Palich, L.E., & Bracker, J.S. (1998). An exploratory investigation into theoretical mechanisms underlying realistic job previews. *Personnel Psychology, 51,* 421–451.

Homberger, R. (1990). The 20-minute interview. *Recruitment Today, 3*(1), 20–26.

How to increase retention. (1998, December 21). *Workforce Management.* Retrieved September 28, 2004, from http://www.workforce.com/archive/article/21/97/93.php

Hulgin, K.M. (1996). *Jay Nolan Community Services: The challenges and dilemmas of quick conversion from group homes to supported living services.* Syracuse, NY: Syracuse University, Center on Human Policy.

Huselid, M.A. (1995). The impact of human resource management practices on turnover, productivity, and corporate financial performance. *Academy of Management Journal, 38,* 635–672.

Hutchins, J. (2000a). Getting to know you. *Workforce, 79*(11), 36–40.

Hutchins, J. (2000b). Steps to effective orientation. *Workforce, 79*(11), 40.

IBM Multimedia Consulting Center. (1994). Multimedia cooks up mainframe training. *Training, 31*(7), 64–65.

Irwin Siegel Agency. (2001). *Staff recruitment and retention strategies: Results and analysis of the Staff Recruitment and Retention Survey.* Rock Hill, NY: Author.

Janz, T., Hellervik, L., & Gilmore, D.C. (1986). *Behavior description interviewing: New, accurate, cost effective.* Boston: Allyn & Bacon.

Jaskulski, T., & Ebenstein, W. (Eds.). (1996). *Opportunities for excellence: Supporting the frontline workforce.* Washington, DC: President's Committee on Mental Retardation.

Jaskulski, T., & Whiteman, M. (1996). Family member perspectives on direct support workers. In T. Jaskulski & W. Ebenstein (Eds.), *Opportunities for excellence: Supporting the frontline workforce* (pp. 56–75). Washington, DC: President's Committee on Mental Retardation.

Johnston, K. (1998). *Developmental disabilities provider direct service worker study: Results and findings.* Anchorage, AK: Governor's Council on Disabilities and Special Education.

Jones, G.R. (1986). Socialization tactics, self-efficacy, and newcomers' adjustments to organizations. *Academy of Management Journal, 29,* 262–279.

Kanfer, R. (1990). Motivation theory and industrial and organizational psychology. In M.D. Dunnette & L.M. Hough (Eds.), *Handbook of industrial and organizational psychology: Vol. 1. Theory in industrial and organizational psychology* (2nd ed., pp. 75–170). Palo Alto, CA: Consulting Psychologists Press.

Kanfer, R., & Ackerman, P.L. (1989). Motivation and cognitive abilities: An integrative/aptitude-treatment interaction approach to skill acquisition [Monograph]. *Journal of Applied Psychology, 74,* 657–690.

Kansans Mobilizing for Workforce Change Stakeholder Advisory Group. (2004). *Kansans Mobilizing for Change: A statewide workforce development plan to resolve the direct support workforce crisis.* Topeka: Kansas Council on Developmental Disabilities.

Kaye, B.L., & Jordan-Evans, S. (1999). *Love 'em or lose 'em: Getting good people to stay.* San Francisco: Berrett-Koehler Publishers.

Kiracofe, J. (1994). Strategies to help agencies shift from services to supports. in V.J. Bradley, J.W. Ashbaugh, & B.C. Blaney (Eds.) *Creating individual supports for people with developmental disabilities: A mandate for change at many levels* (pp. 281–298). Baltimore: Paul H. Brookes Publishing Co.

Kram, K.E. (1983). Phases of the mentor relationship. *Academy of Management Journal, 26,* 608–625.

Krueger, R.A., & Casey, M.A. (2000). *Focus groups: A practical guide for applied research* (3rd ed.). Thousand Oaks, CA: Sage Publications, Inc.

Laabs, J.K. (1998). Pick the right people. *Workforce, 77*(11), 50–52.

Lakin, K.C. (1981). Occupational stability of direct-care staff of residential facilities for mentally retarded people. *Dissertation Abstracts International–A, 42*(01). (Publication No. AAT 8115007)

Lakin, K.C., & Bruininks, R.H. (1981). *Occupational stability of direct-care staff of residential facilities for mentally retarded people.* Minneapolis: University of Minnesota, Center on Residential and Community Services.

Lakin, K.C., Bruininks, R.H., Hill, B.K., & Hauber, F.A. (1982). Turnover of direct care staff in a national sample of residential facilities for mentally retarded people. *American Journal of Mental Deficiency, 87,* 64–72.

Lakin, K.C., Gardner, J., Larson, S.A., & Wheeler, B.Y. (n.d.). Access and support for community lives, homes and social roles. In K.C. Lakin (Ed.), [Manuscript describing the proceedings of National Goals, the State-of-Knowledge and a National Agenda for Research on Intellectual and Developmental Disabilities: A National Invitational Conference. January 2003]. Unpublished manuscript.

Lankau, M.J., & Scandura, T.A. (2002). An investigation of personal learning in mentoring relationships: Content, antecedents, and consequences. *Academy of Management Journal, 45,* 779–790.

Larson, S.A. (1996). *Influencing staff recruitment and retention: Personnel practices and facility characteristics.* Paper presented at the 1996 annual meeting of the American Association on Mental Retardation, San Antonio, TX.

Larson, S.A. (1997). *Recruitment issues for Minnesota agencies serving people with developmental disabilities or severe and persistent mental illness: Final report.* Minneapolis: University of Minnesota, Institute on Community Integration.

Larson, S.A. (1998). Assessing workplace recruitment and retention: The first steps. *IMPACT: Feature Issue on Direct Support Workforce Development, 10*(4).

Larson, S.A., Coucouvanis, K., & Prouty, R.W. (2003). Staffing patterns, characteristics and outcomes in large state residential facilities in 2002. In R.W. Prouty, G. Smith, & K.C. Lakin (Eds.), *Residential services for persons with developmental disabilities: Status and trends through 2002* (pp. 47–59). Minneapolis, MN: University of Minnesota, Institute on Community Integration, Research and Training Center on Community Living.

Larson, S.A., Hewitt, A., & Anderson, L. (1999). Staff recruitment challenges and interventions in agencies supporting people with developmental disabilities. *Mental Retardation, 37,* 36–46.

Larson, S.A., Hewitt, A.S., & Lakin, K.C. (2004). Multiperspective analysis of workforce challenges and their effects on consumer and family quality of life. *American Journal on Mental Retardation, 109,* 481–500.

Larson, S.A., & Lakin, K.C. (1992). Direct-care staff stability in a national sample of small group homes. *Mental Retardation, 30,* 13–22.

Larson, S.A., & Lakin, K.C. (1999). Longitudinal study of recruitment and retention in small community homes supporting persons with developmental disabilities. *Mental Retardation, 37,* 267–280.

Larson, S.A., Lakin, K.C., & Bruininks, R.H. (1998). *Staff recruitment and retention: Study results and intervention strategies.* Washington, DC: American Association on Mental Retardation.

Larson, S.A., Lakin, K.C., & Hewitt, A.S. (2002). Direct-service professionals: 1975–2000. In R.L. Schalock, P.C. Baker, & M.D. Crosser (Eds.), *Embarking on a new century: Mental retardation at the end of the 20th century.* Washington, DC: American Association on Mental Retardation.

Larson, S.A., & Miller, H. (2002). *Supervisors of direct support professionals.* Paper presented at the 2002 Reinventing Quality conference, Chicago.

Larson, S.A., Sauer, J., Hewitt, A., O'Nell, S., & Sedlezky, L. (1998). *SOS training and technical assistance project for direct support professionals, trainers and frontline supervisors.* Minneapolis: University of Minnesota, Institute on Community Integration, Research and Training Center on Community Living.

Legislative Budget and Finance Committee. (1999). *Salary levels and their impact on the quality of care for client contact employees in community-based MH/MR programs: A report in response to House Resolution 450.* Harrisburg, PA: Author.

Levy, P.H., Levy, J.M., Freeman, S., Feiman, J., & Samowitz, P. (1988). Training and managing residences for persons with developmental disabilities. In M.P. Janicki, M.W. Krauss, & M.M. Seltzer (Eds.), *Community residences for persons with developmental disabilities* (pp. 239–249). Baltimore: Paul H. Brookes Publishing Co.

Lewin, K. (1951). *Field theory in social science.* New York: HarperCollins.

Lieb, S. (1991, Fall). Principles of adult learning. *Vision,* 11–13. Retrieved September 28, 2004, from the *Honolulu Community College Faculty Development Faculty Guidebook,* http://www.hcc.hawaii.edu/intranet/committees/FacDevCom/guidebk/teachtip/adults-2.htm

Locke, E.A., & Latham, G.P. (1990). Core findings. In E.A. Lock & G.P. Latham (Eds.), *A theory of goal setting and task performance* (pp. 27–62). Upper Saddle River, NJ: Prentice Hall.

Louis, M.R., Posner, B.Z., & Powell, G.N. (1983). The availability and helpfulness of socialization practices. *Personnel Psychology, 36,* 857–866.

Lubin, J.S. (1997, June 2). Now butchers, engineers get signing bonuses. *The Wall Street Journal,* B1, B8.

Luthans, F., & Kreitner, R. (1985). *Organizational behavior modification and beyond: An operant and social learning approach.* Glenview, IL: Scott Foresman.

Lynch, E.W., & Hanson, M.J. (Eds.). (2004). *Developing cross-cultural competence: A guide for working with children and their families* (3rd ed.). Baltimore: Paul H. Brookes Publishing Co.

M. Mulliken Consulting. (2003). *Wages and benefits for Wisconsin direct support workers.* Madison: Wisconsin Council on Developmental Disabilities, Bureau of Developmental Disabilities Services.

Madden, M.J., Ellen, P.S., & Ajzen, I. (1992). A comparison of the theory of planned behavior and the Theory of Reasoned Action. *Personality and Social Psychology Bulletin, 18*(1), 3–9.

Maddux, R.B. (1994). *Quality interviewing: A step-by-step action plan for success.* Menlo Park, CA: Crisp Learning.

Magis-Agosta, K. (1994). Organizational transformations: Moving from facilities to community inclusive employment. In V.J. Bradley, J.W. Ashbaugh, & B.C. Blaney (Eds.), *Creating individual supports for people with developmental disabilities: A mandate for change at many levels* (pp. 255–269). Baltimore: Paul H. Brookes Publishing Co.

The Marketing Solutions Co. (2001). *Michigan Assisted Living Association Mental Health Provider 2001 Wage & Benefit Survey.* Livonia, MI: Author.

Marrone, J., Hoff, D., & Gold, M. (1999). Organizational change for community employment. *Journal of Rehabilitation, 65*(2), 10–19.

Martin, P., & Tate, K. (1997). *Project management memory jogger.* Methuen, MA: GOAL/PC.

Martinez, M.N. (2001, August). The headhunter within: Turn your employees into recruiters with a high-impact referral program. *HR Magazine, 46*(8), 48–55.

Maurer, S.D., Sue-Chan, C., & Latham, G.P. (1999). The situational interview. In R.W. Eder & M.M. Harris (Eds.), *The employment interview handbook* (pp. 159–178). Thousand Oaks, CA: Sage Publications.

McEvoy, G.M., & Cascio, W.F. (1985). Strategies for reducing employee turnover: A meta-analysis. *Journal of Applied Psychology, 70,* 342–353.

Mercer, W.M. (1999). Employee turnover: A strategic point of view. In *Mercer Evalue Framework: The science and art of attracting and retaining employees.* New York: William M. Mercer Companies.

Michaels, C.E., & Spector, P.E. (1982). Causes of employee turnover: A test of the Mobley, Griffeth, Hand, and Meglino model. *Journal of Applied Psychology, 67,* 53–59.

Miller, H. (1998). Training grown-ups: Not for the faint of heart. In *Training Trainers Towards Excellence: A day of interaction and dialogue for people who train, or are interested in training, direct support professionals.* Conference proceedings from a statewide training conference cosponsored by the Minnesota Department of Human Services State Operated Services and the University of Minnesota, Institute on Community Living, Research and Training Center on Community Living, St. Cloud.

Minnesota Department of Human Services. (1993). *Continuous quality improvement.* Unpublished manuscript.

Minnesota H.F. 1483, 82nd leg. sess. (2001–2002). Also available on-line: http://www.revisor .leg.state.mn.us/cgi-bin/bldbill.pl?bill=H1483.1&session=ls82

Minnesota S.F. 1426, 82nd leg. sess. (2001–2002). Also available on-line: http://www.revisor .leg.state.mn.us/cgi-bin/getbill.pl?number=SF1426&session=ls82&version=latest

Mornell, P. (1998). *45 effective ways for hiring smart: How to predict winners and losers in the incredibly expensive people reading game.* Berkeley, CA: Ten Speed Press.

Morrison, J.L. (1998, June). The nominal group process as an instructional tool. *The Technology Source.* Retrieved September 28, 2004, from http://ts.mivu.org/default.asp?show=article&id =466

Moseley, C. (1999). *Making self-determination work.* Durham, NH: National Program Office on Self-Determination.

Motowidlo, S.J. (1999). Asking about past behavior versus hypothetical behavior. In R.W. Eder & M.M. Harris (Eds.), *The employment interview handbook* (pp. 179–190). Thousand Oaks, CA: Sage Publications.

Mowday, R.T., Porter, L.W., & Steers, R.M. (1982). *Employee-organization linkages: The psychology of commitment, absenteeism, and turnover.* San Diego: Academic Press.

Mowday, R.T., Steers, R.M., & Porter, L.W. (1979). The measurement of organizational commitment. *Journal of Vocational Behavior, 14,* 224–247.

Mulcahy, D., & James, P. (2000). Evaluating the contribution of competency-based training: An enterprise perspective. *International Journal of Training and Development, 4*(3), 160–175.

Murphy, S.T., & Rogan, P.M. (1995). *Closing the shop: Conversion from sheltered to integrated work.* Baltimore: Paul H. Brookes Publishing Co.

Myers, I.B., & Briggs, K.C. (n.d.). *Myers-Briggs Type Indicator (MBTI).* Palo Alto, CA: CPP. Available from the publisher, http://www.cpp.com/products/mbti/index.asp

National and Community Service Trust Act of 1993, PL 103-82, 42 U.S.C. §§ 12501 *et seq.*

National Association of State Directors of Developmental Disabilities Services. (2000a). *Annual meeting conference brochure.* Alexandria, VA: Author.

National Association of State Directors of Developmental Disabilities Services. (2000b). *Person-centered supports—they're for everyone!: Consensus statement.* Alexandria, VA: Author.

National Association of State Directors of Developmental Disabilities Services & Human Services Research Institute. (2002). *Provider Survey: Summary report of staff stability and board representation data reported in CIP Phases II, III, and IV.* Alexandria, VA, & Cambridge, MA: Authors.

National Governors Association Center for Best Practice & Mid-Atlantic Workforce Brokerage. (1999). *Lessons from state demonstration projects: A guide to incumbent worker training.* Washington, DC: National Governors Association.

Nelson, B. (1994). *1001 ways to reward employees.* New York: Workman Publishing.

Nelson, B., & Economy, P. (2003). *Managing for dummies* (2nd ed.). New York: Wiley.

Ness, J. (1994). *What is teaming all about: Working with paraprofessionals to improve services to students with developmental disabilities.* Paper presented at the MAASFEP spring workshop.

Ness, J., & Krawetz, N. (1999). *Strategies for paraprofessionals who support individuals with disabilities series. The paraprofessional: An introduction* (Facilitator guide and learner guide). Minneapolis: University of Minnesota, Institute on Community Integration.

NYSARC. (2000). *Staff recruitment and retention: Report on turnover and vacancies. Study and analysis.* Delmar, NY: Author.

O'Brien, J., & Lovett, H. (1992). *Finding a way toward everyday lives: The contribution of person centered planning.* Harrisburg: Pennsylvania Office of Mental Retardation.

Oklahoma Department of Human Services, Developmental Disabilities Services Division. (2000). *Direct support staff turnover reduction plan: Annual report to residential providers.* Oklahoma City: Author.

Olmstead v. L.C., 527 U.S. 581 (1999).

O'Neill, M. (1998). Do's and don'ts for the new trainer. In American Society for Training and Development (Ed.), *The new basic training for trainers: An info-line collection for training and development professionals* (Vol. 1; pp. 3–16). Alexandria, VA: Editor.

O'Nell, S., Hewitt, A., Sauer, J., & Larson, S. (2001). *Removing the revolving door: Strategies to address recruitment and retention challenges* (Facilitator guide and learner guide). Minneapolis: University of Minnesota, Institute on Community Integration, Research and Training Center on Community Living.

O'Nell, S., Larson, S.A., Hewitt, A., & Sauer, J. (2001). *RJP overview.* Minneapolis: University of Minnesota, Institute on Community Integration, Research and Training Center on Community Living. Also available on-line: http://rtc.umn.edu/pdf/rjp.pdf

O'Nell, S., & Westerman, J. (1998). Collaborative training: The MATC program. *IMPACT: Feature Issue on Direct Support Workforce Development, 10*(4).

Oregon Rehabilitation Association. (1999). *Executive director competencies.* Salem: Author.

Ostroff, C., & Kozlowski, S.W.J. (1992). Organizational socialization as a learning process: The role of information acquisition. *Personnel Psychology, 45,* 849–874.

Ostroff, C., & Kozlowski, S.W.J. (1993). The role of mentoring in the information gathering processes of newcomers during early organizational socialization. *Journal of Vocational Behavior, 42,* 170–183.

Ouelette, T. (1995). CD-ROM training wins audience. *Cosmopolitan, 29*(16), 60.

Personnel Decisions, Inc. (n.d.-a). *The Personnel Decisions Inc. Employment Inventory.* San Antonio, TX: Author.

Personnel Decisions, Inc. (n.d.-b). *The Personnel Decisions Inc. Job Preferences Inventory.* San Antonio, TX: Author.

Phillips, J.M. (1998). Effects of realistic job previews on multiple organizational outcomes: A meta-analysis. *Academy of Management Journal, 41,* 673–690.

Polister, B., Lakin, K.C., & Prouty, R. (2002). Wages of direct support professionals serving persons with intellectual and developmental disabilities. *Policy Research Brief, 14*(2).

Porter, L.W., & Steers, R.M. (1973). Organizational, work, and personal factors in employee turnover and absenteeism. *Psychological Bulletin, 80,* 151–176.

Premack, S.L., & Wanous, J.P. (1985). A meta-analysis of realistic job preview experiments. *Journal of Applied Psychology, 70,* 706–719.

Price, J.L. (1997). Handbook of organizational measurement. *International Journal of Manpower, 18,* 305–558.

Prochaska, J.O., & DiClemente, C.C. (1982). Transtheoretical therapy toward a more integrative model of change. *Psychotherapy: Theory, Research and Practice, 19*(3), 276–287.

Prouty, R.W., Smith, G., & Lakin, K.C. (Eds.). (2004). *Residential services for persons with developmental disabilities: Status and trends through 2003.* Minneapolis: University of Minnesota, Institute on Community Integration, Research and Training Center on Community Living. (Also available online [click under RISP 2003]: http://www.rtc.umn.edu/risp/index .html)

Quinn, R.P., & Staines, G.L. (1979). *The 1977 Quality of Employment Survey.* Ann Arbor: University of Michigan, Institute for Social Research.

Racino, J.A. (1994). Creating change in states, agencies, and communities. In V.J. Bradley, J.W. Ashbaugh, & B.C. Blaney (Eds.), *Creating individual supports for people with developmental disabilities: A mandate for change at many levels* (pp. 171–196). Baltimore: Paul H. Brookes Publishing Co.

Ragins, B.R., Cotton, J.L., & Miller, J.S. (2000). Marginal mentoring: The effects of type of mentor, quality of relationship, and program design on work and career attitudes. *Academy of Management Journal, 43,* 1177–1194.

Rees, F. (1997). *Team work from start to finish.* San Francisco: Pfeiffer. (Available from the publisher, 350 Sansome Street, 5th Floor, San Francisco, CA 94104; 800-274-4434; fax: 800-569-0443; http://www.pfeiffer.com)

Reid, D.H., & Parsons, M.B. (1995). *Motivating human service staff: Supervisory strategies for maximizing work effort and work enjoyment.* Morganton, NC: Habilitative Management Consultants.

Reilly, T. (2001). Collaboration in action: An uncertain process. *Administration in Social Work, 25*(1), 53–74.

Roche, G.R. (1979). Much ado about mentors. *Harvard Business Review, 57,* 14–28.

Roehling, M.V., Campion, J.E., & Arvey, R.D. (1999). Unfair discrimination issues. In R.W. Eder & M.M. Harris (Eds.), *The employment interview handbook* (pp. 49–68). Thousand Oaks, CA: Sage Publications.

Rosen, D. (1996). Agency perspectives on the direct support workforce. In T. Jaskulski & W. Ebenstein (Eds.), *Opportunities for excellence: Supporting the frontline workforce* (pp. 76–82). Washington, DC: President's Committee on Mental Retardation.

Rosen, L.S. (2001, November). Safe hiring audit. *Workforce.* Retrieved September 28, 2004, from http://www.workforce.com/archive/feature/22/16/22/223961.php

Rottier, A. (2001, October). The skill crisis grows. *Workforce,* 22.

Rubin, S., Park, H.J., & Braddock, D. (1998). *Wages, benefits and turnover of residential direct care staff serving individuals with developmental disabilities in Illinois.* Chicago: University of Illinois, Department of Disability and Human Development.

Russell, S. (1999). *Management development.* Alexandria, VA: American Society for Training and Development.

S. Con. Res. 21, 108th Cong., 150 Cong. Rec. 3751 (2003) (enacted).

Saks, A.M. (1994). A psychological process investigation for the effects of recruitment source and organization information on job survival. *Journal of Organizational Behavior, 15,* 225–244.

Sauer, J. (1994). *Formation and development of action teams.* Unpublished manuscript, University of Minnesota, Research and Training Center on Community Living, Minneapolis.

Sauer, J., O'Nell, S., Sedlezky, L., Scaletta, K., Taylor, M., & Silver, J. (1997). *An introduction to teamwork in community health and human services.* Cambridge, MA: Human Services Research Institute. (Available from the publisher, 2336 Massachusetts Avenue, Cambridge, MA 02140; 617-876-0426; fax: 617-492-7401; http://www.hsri.org)

Scholtes, P. (1988). *The team handbook.* Madison, WI: Joiner Associates.

Scioto Group. (2001). *Ohio Association for County Boards of Mental Retardation and Developmental Disabilities/Ohio Provider Resources Association Direct Care and Paraprofessional Wage and Benefits Study.* Columbus, OH: Author.

Sedlezky, L., Anderson, L.L., Hewitt, A., O'Nell, S., Sauer, J., Larson, S.A., & Sjoberg, T. (2001). *The power of diversity: Supporting the immigrant workforce* (Facilitator guide and learner guide). Minneapolis: University of Minnesota, Institute on Community Integration.

Senge, P., Roberts, C., Ross, R., Smith, B., & Kleiner, A. (1994). *The fifth discipline fieldbook.* New York: Doubleday.

Sheppard, B.H., Hartwick, J., & Warshaw, P.R. (1988). The theory of reasoned action: A meta-analysis of past research with recommendations for modifications and future research. *The Journal of Consumer Research, 15*(3), 325–343.

Singleton, R.A., Jr., Straits, B.C., & Straits, M.M. (1993). *Approaches to social research* (2nd ed.). New York: Oxford University Press.

Smith, G.A. (2003, June 29). *Status report: Litigation concerning home and community services for people with disabilities.* Cambridge, MA: Human Services Research Institute. Also available online: http://www.qualitymall.org/download/Litigation062903.pdf

Smith, P.C., Kendall, L.M., & Hulin, C.L. (1969). *The measurement of satisfaction in work and retirement.* Chicago: Rand-McNally.

Society for Human Resource Management. (2001a). *Employee referral programs.* Alexandria, VA: Author.

Society for Human Resource Management. (2001b). *Retention Practices Survey.* Alexandria, VA: Author.

Solomon, C.M. (1998). Stellar recruiting for a tight labor market. *Workforce, 77*(8), 66–71.

Spruell, G. (1987). *Off to a good start: Successful orientation programs.* Alexandria, VA: American Society for Training and Development.

State of Minnesota Department of Employee Relations. (1989). *Study of employee wages, benefits, and turnover in Minnesota direct care facilities serving persons with developmental disabilities.* St. Paul: State of Minnesota Department of Employee Relations and Minnesota Department of Human Services.

Stremmel, A.J. (1991). Predictors of intentions to leave child care work. *Early Childhood Research Quarterly, 6,* 285–298.

Sullivan, T.G. (1982). Organizational commitment, job satisfaction, and leadership behaviors within residential facilities for the mentally retarded (Doctoral dissertation, University of Pittsburgh). *Dissertations Abstracts International* (UMI No. 8303641).

Taylor, G.S. (1994). The relationship between sources of new employees and attitudes toward the job. *Journal of Social Psychology, 134*(1), 99–110.

Taylor, M., Bradley, V., & Warren, R., Jr. (1996). *Community support skill standards: Tools for managing change and achieving outcomes.* Cambridge, MA: Human Services Research Institute. (Available from the publisher, 2336 Massachusetts Avenue, Cambridge, MA, 02140; 617-876-0426; fax: 617-492-7401; http://www.hsri.org)

Taylor, M., Sauer J., Hewitt, A., O'Nell, S., & Larson, S. (2001). *The peer empowerment program (PEP): A complete toolkit for planning and implementing mentoring programs within community-based human service organizations* (Program coordinator, facilitator, and learner guides). Minneapolis: University of Minnesota, Institute on Community Integration, Research and Training Center on Community Living.

Taylor, M., Silver, J., Hewitt, A., VanGelder, M., & Hoff, D. (1997). *Career pathmaker: A toolkit for entering careers in human services and health care.* Cambridge, MA: Human Services Research Institute. (Available from the publisher, 2336 Massachusetts Avenue, Cambridge, MA 02140; 617-876-0426; fax: 617-492-7401; http://www.hsri.org)

Terpstra, D.E., & Rozell, E.J. (1993). The relationship of staffing practices to organizational measures of performance. *Personnel Psychology, 46,* 27–48.

Test, D.W., Flowers, C., Hewitt, A., & Solow, J. (2004). Training needs of direct support staff. *Mental Retardation, 42,* 327–337.

Test, D., Solow, J., & Flowers, C. (1999). *North Carolina Direct Support Professionals Study: Final report.* Charlotte: University of North Carolina at Charlotte.

Texas Association of Museums. (n.d.). *A survey for management.* Retrieved from http://www.io.com/~tam/multicultural/management.html

Thayer, P.T. (1997). A rapidly changing world: Some implications for training systems in the year 2001 and beyond. In M.A. Quinones & A. Dutta (Eds.), *Training for 21st century technology: Applications of psychological research.* Washington, DC: American Psychological Press.

Thomas, M., & Brull, H. (1993). Tests improve hiring decisions at Franciscan Health System. *Personnel Journal, 72*(11), 89–92.

Thomas, T. (1999). *Careers in caring* [Videotape]. Cleveland, OH: Residential Provider Consortium. (Available from the author, Welcome House, Inc., 23569 Center Ridge Road, Westlake, OH 44145)

Thompson, T. (2001, May 22). *HHS to give money to states to help states build disability programs* (Press release). Baltimore: Health Care Financing Administration Press Office.

Torres, C., & Spiegel, J. (1990). *Self-directed work teams: A primer.* San Francisco: Pfeiffer.

Tuckman, B.W. (1965). Development sequence in small groups. *Psychological Bulletin, 63,* 384–399.

Tullar, W.L., & Kaiser, P.R. (1999). Using new technology: The group support system. In R.W. Eder & M.M. Harris (Eds.), *The employment interview handbook* (pp. 279–296). Thousand Oaks, CA: Sage Publications.

University of Minnesota, Institute on Community Integration, Research and Training Center on Community Living. (n.d.-a). *New staff survey* (developed by Sheryl A. Larson in collaboration with Lutheran Social Service of Minnesota). Retrieved September 28, 2004, from http://rtc.umn.edu/pdf/newstaffsurvey.pdf

University of Minnesota, Institute on Community Integration, Research and Training Center on Community Living. (n.d.-b). *Staff satisfaction survey* (developed by Sheryl A. Larson in collaboration with Lutheran Social Service of Minnesota). Retrieved September 28, 2004, from http://rtc.umn.edu/pdf/staffsatisfaction.pdf

University of Minnesota, Institute on Community Integration, Research and Training Center on Community Living. (n.d.-c). *Training experience satisfaction survey* (developed by Amy S. Hewitt & Sheryl A. Larson). Retrieved September 28, 2004, from http://rtc.umn.edu/pdf/trainingsurvey.pdf

U.S. Census Bureau. (1990). *Statistical abstract of the United States: 1990* (110th ed.). Washington, DC: Author.

U.S. Census Bureau. (2000a, January 13). *Projections of the total resident population by 5-year age groups, and sex with special age categories: Middle series, 1998–2000.* Retrieved September 28, 2004, from http://www.census.gov/population/projections/nation/summary/np-t3-a.pdf

U.S. Census Bureau. (2000b, January 13). *Projections of the total resident population by 5-year age groups, and sex with special age categories: Middle series, 2001–2005.* Retrieved September 28, 2004, from http://www.census.gov/population/projections/nation/summary/np-t3-b.pdf

U.S. Census Bureau. (2000c, January 13). *Projections of the total resident population by 5-year age groups, and sex with special age categories: Middle series, 2006–2010.* Retrieved September 28, 2004, from http://www.census.gov/population/projections/nation/summary/np-t3-c.pdf

U.S. Census Bureau. (2001a, September 20). Historical poverty tables: Poverty by definition of income (R&D). In *Current Population Survey.* Retrieved September 28, 2004, from http://www.census.gov/hhes/poverty/histpov/rdp01a.html

U.S. Census Bureau. (2001b). *Statistical abstract of the United States: 2001* (121st ed.). Washington, DC: Author.

U.S. Department of Health and Human Services. (2004). *Prior HHS poverty guidelines and federal register references.* Retrieved November 8, 2004, from http://aspe.hhs.gov/poverty/figures-fed-reg.shtml

U.S. Department of Labor. (1999). *Future work: Trends and challenges for work in the 21st century.* Washington, DC: Author.

Utah Association of Community Services. (2001). *Staff Vacancy and Turnover Survey.* Salt Lake City: Author.

Varney, G. (1989). *Building productive teams.* San Francisco: Jossey-Bass.

Walker, P. (2000). *Acting on a vision: Agency conversion at KFI, Millinocket, Maine.* Syracuse, NY: Syracuse University, Center on Human Policy. Retrieved September 28, 2004, from http://soeweb.syr.edu/thechp/KFI.html

Wanous, J.P. (1992). *Organizational entry: Recruitment, selection, orientation and socialization of newcomers* (2nd ed.). Boston: Addison Wesley.

Wanous, J.P., & Reichers, A.E. (2000). New employee orientation programs. *Human Resource Management Review, 10,* 435–451.

Wehman, P., Revell, W.G., & Kregel, J. (1998). Supported employment: A decade of rapid growth and impact. *American Rehabilitation, 24*(1), 31–43.

Weiss, D.J., Dawis, R.B., England, G.W., & Lofquist, L.J. (1967). *Manual for the Minnesota Satisfaction Questionnaire.* Minneapolis: University of Minnesota, Vocational Psychology Research.

Wheeler, B. (2001). *Year One summary: A 3-year evaluation of the impact of WIC Section 4681.4 (rate increase) on direct support staff turnover in California's community care facilities for people with developmental disabilities Year 1 results: 1999-2000.* Oakland: University of Southern California University Affiliated Program.

Wiant, A. (1993). *DACUM practitioner's manual.* Cambridge, MA: DACUM Services.

Williams, C.R., Labig, C.E., & Stone, T.H. (1993). Recruitment sources and posthire outcomes for job applicants and new hires: A test of two hypotheses. *Journal of Applied Psychology, 78,* 163–172.

Williamson, M. (1994). High-tech training. *BYTE, 19*(12), 74–88.

Yate, M. (1994). *Hiring the best: A manager's guide to effective interviewing.* Holbrook, MA: Adams Media Corporation.

Young, A.M., & Perrewe, P.L. (2000). What did you expect? An examination of career-related support and social support among mentors and mentees. *Journal of Management, 26,* 611–632.

Zaharia, E.S., & Baumeister, A.A. (1978). Estimated position replacement costs for technician personnel at a state's public facilities. *Mental Retardation, 16,* 131–134.

Zottoli, M.A., & Wanous, J.P. (2000). Recruitment source research: Current status and future directions. *Human Resource Management Review, 10,* 353–382.

INDEX

Page references followed by *f* and *t* indicate figures and tables, respectively.